CW00959470

AN
ANGLICAN
PRAYER BOOK
1989

AN ANGLICAN PRAYER BOOK 1989

CHURCH OF THE PROVINCE
OF SOUTHERN AFRICA

COLLINS

Collins Liturgical Publications
distributed in Southern Africa by
David Philip, Publisher (Pty) Ltd
PO Box 23317, Claremont 7735

Collins Liturgical Publications
77–85 Fulham Palace Road, London W6 8JB

ISBN 0 00 599180 3
First published 1989
Sixth Printing 1993

Authorized by the Synod of Bishops for use in the Church of the
Province of Southern Africa from the date of publication.

Typographical design by Colin Reed
Typesetting by Morton Word Processing, England
Printed and bound by HarperCollins Manufacturing, Glasgow
BK2230

CONTENTS

GENERAL PREFACE 9

GENERAL NOTES 13

THE CALENDAR
The Church's Year 17
Great Festivals 18
Festivals 19
Days of Special Devotion 21
Commemorations and Other Special Days 22
Days of Fasting and Self-Denial 26
Rules for the Observance of the Calendar 27
Key Dates 1988–2025 30

THE OFFICES OF MORNING AND EVENING PRAYER
Preface 37
General Rubrics 41
Morning Prayer 42
Evening Prayer 54
Sentences 64
Advent Anthems 68

THE LITANY 71

PRAYERS AND THANKSGIVINGS FOR
VARIOUS OCCASIONS 79

THE HOLY EUCHARIST
Preface 101
General Rubrics 103
The Eucharist 104
An Alternative Order for the Eucharist 131
Proper Prefaces 134
The Ten Commandments 140
Sentences 141

COLLECTS AND READINGS
WITH SPECIAL SERVICES FOR LENT AND EASTER

General Rubrics   147
Sundays and Other Great Festivals
  Advent to Epiphany   149
  Ash Wednesday to Easter   161
  Easter to Corpus Christi   231
  Sundays of the Year   247
Festivals and Commemorations   290
Common Collects   319
Various Occasions   324

THE CANTICLES   337

BAPTISM AND CONFIRMATION

Preface   361
General Rubrics   364
Baptism and Confirmation   367
Baptism   378
Confirmation   388
Associated Services
  Conditional Baptism   395
  Emergency Baptism
    and Reception into the Congregation   396
  The Admission of Baptized Communicants
    from Other Churches   399
  Renewal of Baptismal Promises   402
  Thanksgiving for the Birth of a Child   405
  Thanksgiving after Adoption   412
  The Admission of Catechumens   417

A CATECHISM   421

CONFESSION AND ABSOLUTION   445

MARRIAGE

Preface   457
General Rubrics   460
The Marriage Service   461
Thanksgiving for a Marriage
  or the Reaffirmation of Vows   469
The Blessing of a Civil Marriage
  or Customary Union   476
Introduction for the Remarriage of Divorced Persons   484

MINISTRY TO THE SICK AND DYING

Preface	489
General Rubrics	491
Ministry to the Sick	
Suitable Passages of Scripture	492
Considerations for the Sick	494
Prayers	496
The Laying on of Hands	500
The Anointing of the Sick	502
The Eucharist of the Sick	508
Ministry to the Dying	
The Eucharist	517
Prayers for the Dying	517

FUNERAL SERVICES

Preface	525
General Rubrics	528
A Service for Use before a Funeral	531
The Funeral of an Adult	533
The Committal	541
The Funeral of a Child	545
The Committal of a Child	550
A Memorial Service	553
The Interment of Ashes	558
The Dedication and Unveiling of a Tombstone	560
Prayers for Use at any of the Services	563

ORDINATION

Preface	571
General Rubrics	573
The Ordination of Deacons and Priests	574
The Ordination and Consecration of a Bishop	594

THE PSALMS

A Note on Chanting	606
The Psalms	607

Acknowledgements	794

General Preface

The creation of this Prayer Book has been a joyful and inspiring task during a period of over twenty years of liturgical experiment and renewal. The same period has been a crucial one for human relations in our subcontinent, with the Church, in spite of its own inadequacy and sinfulness, lifted into a prophetic and pastoral witness to both the perpetrators and the victims of ideology, conflict and violence.

Is liturgical revision an offensive luxury at such a time as this? The answer is an emphatic 'no', because the Church's worship of God in prayer and sacrament is a priority in every circumstance, and very particularly in times of crisis and change. The steadfast love of the Lord endures for ever, and his children have no alternative, in good times and in bad, but to sing his praises, to take his word to heart, to acknowledge his rule, to repent, to intercede both for the Church and for the world, and to offer themselves in the daily rhythm of the Church's worship as well as in their witness and service in society. This worship should, moreover, express itself in a language and form which meets the needs of contemporary people.

This book stands alongside the South African Book of Common Prayer (1954), which in its turn is grounded upon the 1662 Book of Common Prayer, itself the heir to the three Prayer Books of 1549, 1552, and 1559. Behind these products of the sixteenth century lay the liturgical tradition, strongly influenced by the monastic movement with its sevenfold office of prayer, which reached back into the early centuries of the Church's life and ultimately to our Lord Jesus Christ himself, and through him to the worship of Israel.

Liturgy is the public worship of the Church of God, a living tradition, a treasure which is both old and new. It is hoped that the present book will be used and understood, and come to be loved, as a further contribution to this unfolding tradition. In its essential features it is true to the long history of our liturgical heritage. In its particular traits it aims to be true to contemporary language and insights.

The Church of the Province of Southern Africa uses many different languages, and it is our policy to make the liturgy available in as many of them as possible. The work of the Liturgical Committee in English has therefore been accompanied by the equally exacting labour of the Translation Committees. English texts have needed to be capable of translation, and translators have had to decide between dynamic and literal translation. Liturgy in Africa should be African. We hope that this Prayer Book will serve as a stimulus to the continuing development of indigenous liturgy; it contains in Form C of the prayers of intercession in the Eucharist one piece of vernacular liturgy which was translated into English.

Suggestions for the new book were invited from any member of the church, and many were received. All were carefully considered, and a good number were adopted. This means that, though the Synod of Bishops has given the final approval, there has been participation in the process by many people, lay and ordained. An attempt has been made to accommodate, wherever possible, different theological emphases or preferences which exist in our Church. *Lex orandi, lex credendi*: there has been a constant awareness of the link between belief and worship. At the same time, there has been a constant desire to express both in memorable language.

A prayer book provides a shape and structure for the worship of the Church. It does not work automatically or magically. Liturgy becomes true worship when the people of God, clergy and laity, clothe it with the devotion of heart and mind. Then it becomes a flame, kindled and re-kindled by the Holy Spirit, for our benefit and for God's glory. What is more, worship releases into the world, with its need and its pain, its sorrow and its hope, an influence for healing and wholeness which we shall never fully comprehend. 'For their sake I consecrate myself, that they also may be consecrated in truth' (John 17:19).

It is in this spirit that this Prayer Book is offered for use in these times, which, though daunting, yet quicken our faith in the living God.

General Notes

Bold Type denotes those parts of the service to be said by the congregation. The Minister participates at his discretion.

Marginal Numbers are given for ease of reference. A marginal number in brackets indicates that the section is optional.

Italics indicate a possible change of pronoun in respect of person or gender, or a choice of alternatives.

At the Penitence, section 11 in Morning Prayer and section 52 in Evening Prayer, the Minister, if he is a priest, may change the pronouns to the second person plural.

At the Penitence, section 14 in the Eucharist, the Priest may change the pronouns to the first person plural.

Musical settings. Other versions of liturgical texts may be substituted when a musical setting composed for them is being used.

Lessons and Readings. The lessons and readings are announced in this order: book, chapter, verse.

If the sense seems to require it, the Minister may extend the reading of any appointed passage.

Silences may be kept where appropriate in the services, particularly after the lessons and readings, and before receiving Communion.

Hymns and Acts of Praise may be introduced where appropriate in the services.

Collections may be taken when appropriate.

Posture. Local customs may be established and followed.

Saying and Singing. Where the rubrics direct a section to be 'said' it may be sung; and vice versa.

The Lord's Prayer may be used in its traditional form, given below.

The Lord's Prayer
(Traditional Version)

Our Father
who art in heaven
hallowed be thy Name
thy kingdom come
thy will be done
   on earth as it is in heaven.
Give us this day our daily bread.
And forgive us our trespasses
as we forgive those
   who trespass against us.
And lead us not into temptation
   but deliver us from evil.
For thine is the kingdom, the power
   and the glory
for ever and ever.   Amen

THE CALENDAR

THE CHURCH'S YEAR

1 The Church's Year both commemorates and proclaims how God came down from heaven to earth in Jesus Christ, who still lives among us by the Holy Spirit until he comes again at the end of time. The yearly observance of the holy days of the Calendar is a celebration of what God has done and is doing for our salvation.

Easter Day is the centre of the Church's Year, as the death and resurrection of our Saviour was the unique cause of our salvation. Easter Day is always the first Sunday following the full moon falling on or next after 21 March.

The Church's Year begins with the four Sundays of Advent, a preparation for celebrating the birth of our Saviour at Christmas.

Either one or two Sundays follow Christmas, and the season of Christmas ends with the festival of the Epiphany on 6 January.

After the Epiphany at least four Sundays follow before Lent begins, but according to the date of Easter, there may be as many as nine; the Table of Key Dates on pages 30-33 gives the number for each year.

Six Sundays in Lent follow; Lent begins with Ash Wednesday and ends on Holy Saturday.

There are six Sundays after Easter; Ascension Day is the Thursday following the fifth Sunday.

The Day of Pentecost is the seventh Sunday after Easter, and concludes Eastertide.

Sundays of the Year

The Sundays, not being those of Advent, Christmas, Lent or Eastertide, are called Sundays of the Year.

There are thirty four of them, and they are used for the periods between the Epiphany and Ash Wednesday, and between Pentecost and Advent.

The Table of Key Dates indicates for each year how many of these Sundays follow the Epiphany, and the number of the Sunday of the Year which coincides with the Day of Pentecost.

It will be noted
i that the fifth to the ninth of these Sundays may be used either before Lent or after Pentecost;

ii that in some years, one Sunday between the fifth and the ninth is not used at all.

The Thirty Fourth Sunday of the Year is the Sunday before Advent, and is the Festival of Christ the King.

In addition, the Church observes certain fixed days when it thankfully recalls the work and witness of men and women through whom Christ's saving victory has been manifested from the time of the apostles to the present day.

GREAT FESTIVALS

2 These are observed with the collect and readings provided.

The First Sunday in Advent
The Second Sunday in Advent
The Third Sunday in Advent
The Fourth Sunday in Advent
Christmas Day (25 December)
The First Sunday after Christmas
The Second Sunday after Christmas *(in some years)*
The Epiphany of our Lord (6 January)
The First Sunday of the Year: The Baptism of Christ
The Second Sunday of the Year
The Third Sunday of the Year
The Fourth Sunday of the Year

According to the date of Easter the Fifth to the Ninth Sundays of the Year *may occur before Lent*

The First Sunday in Lent
The Second Sunday in Lent
The Third Sunday in Lent
The Fourth Sunday in Lent
The Fifth Sunday in Lent
Palm Sunday: The Sunday of the Passion
Easter Day
The First Sunday after Easter
The Second Sunday after Easter
The Third Sunday after Easter
The Fourth Sunday after Easter
The Fifth Sunday after Easter
Ascension Day
The Sixth Sunday after Easter
The Day of Pentecost
Trinity Sunday: The Sunday after Pentecost
Corpus Christi: The Commemoration of the Holy
    Communion (the Thursday after Trinity Sunday)
The Sundays of the Year which follow Pentecost
    *(These vary in number according to the date of Easter. See Table of
    Key Dates, pages 30-33.)*
All Saints (1 November)   *(Collect and readings are found under
    Festivals and Commemorations.)*
The Thirty Fourth Sunday of the Year: Christ the King

FESTIVALS

3   These are observed with the collect and readings pro-
    vided on the appointed days, except where the rules in
    section 7 direct otherwise.

January
  1 The Holy Name of Jesus: The Circumcision of Christ
 11 *The Holy Innocents may be kept on this day instead of 28
     December.*
 18 The Confession of St Peter
 25 The Conversion of St Paul

February
2 The Presentation of our Lord in the Temple

March
25 The Annunciation of our Lord to the Blessed Virgin Mary

April
25 St Mark

May
1 St Joseph
3 St Philip and St James
6 *St John may be kept on this day instead of 27 December.*
14 St Matthias
31 The Visitation of the Blessed Virgin Mary

June
11 St Barnabas
24 The Birth of St John the Baptist
29 St Peter and St Paul

July
3 St Thomas
22 St Mary Magdalene
25 St James

August
3 *St Stephen may be kept on this day instead of 26 December.*
6 The Transfiguration of our Lord
15 St Mary the Virgin, Mother of our Lord
24 St Bartholomew

September
21 St Matthew
29 St Michael and All Angels

October
18 St Luke
23 St James the Brother of the Lord
28 St Simon and St Jude

November
30 St Andrew

December
26 St Stephen   *This Festival may be transferred to 3 August.*
27 St John   *This Festival may be transferred to 6 May.*
28 The Holy Innocents   *This Festival may be transferred to 11 January.*

The Festival of the Patron Saint or the Title of a church

The Dedication Festival of a church (*being the anniversary of its dedication, or else the first Sunday in October*).

DAYS OF SPECIAL DEVOTION

4   These are observed with the collect and readings provided.

Ash Wednesday
Monday in Holy Week
Tuesday in Holy Week
Wednesday in Holy Week
Maundy Thursday
Good Friday
Holy Saturday
The Easter Vigil
Monday in Easter Week
Tuesday in Easter Week
Wednesday in Easter Week
Thursday in Easter Week
Friday in Easter Week
Saturday in Easter Week

COMMEMORATIONS AND OTHER SPECIAL DAYS

5 These are observances in the Calendar, other than the above-mentioned Great Festivals, Festivals and Days of Special Devotion, which may be observed with the collect and readings provided, subject to the rules in section 7.

(a) The Commemorations of the Calendar

JANUARY

10 William Laud, Archbishop of Canterbury and Martyr, 1645
13 Hilary, Bishop of Poitiers and Teacher of the Faith, 368
14 Richard Benson of Cowley, Religious, 1915
17 Antony of Egypt, Founder of the Religious Life, 356
21 Agnes, Virgin and Martyr at Rome, c.304
23 Yona Kanamuzeyi, Deacon and Martyr in Africa, 1964
24 Francis de Sales, Bishop of Geneva, 1622
26 Timothy and Titus
27 John Chrysostom, Bishop of Constantinople and Teacher of the Faith, 407
28 Thomas Aquinas, Teacher of the Faith, 1274
29 Charles Frederick Mackenzie, Bishop in Central Africa, 1862

FEBRUARY

3 Anskar, Bishop and Missionary in Denmark and Sweden, 864
4 Manche Masemola of Sekhukhuneland, Virgin and Martyr, 1928
5 The Martyrs of Japan, 1597
9 James Mata Dwane, Priest, 1916
14 Cyril and Methodius, Missionaries to the Slavs, 9th century
15 Thomas Bray, Priest, 1730
20 Mother Cecile of Grahamstown, Religious, 1906
21 Missionaries and Martyrs of Africa
23 Polycarp, Bishop of Smyrna and Martyr, 156
27 George Herbert, Priest, 1632

MARCH

1 David, Bishop and Missionary in Wales, 6th century
2 Chad, Bishop of Lichfield, 672
3 John and Charles Wesley, Priests, 18th century
7 Perpetua and her Companions, Martyrs, 202
9 Maqhamusela Khanyile of Zululand, Martyr, 1877
12 Gregory the Great, Bishop of Rome and Teacher of the Faith, 604
17 Patrick, Bishop and Missionary in Ireland, 461
18 Cyril of Jerusalem, Bishop and Teacher of the Faith, c.386
19 Thomas Ken, Bishop of Bath and Wells, 1711
20 Cuthbert, Bishop of Lindisfarne, 687
21 Thomas Cranmer, Archbishop of Canterbury and Martyr, 1556
29 John Keble, Priest, 1866

APRIL

1 Frederick Denison Maurice, Priest, 1872
6 William Law, Priest, 1761
11 George Augustus Selwyn, Bishop and Missionary in New Zealand, 1878
21 Anselm, Archbishop of Canterbury and Teacher of the Faith, 1109
23 George, Martyr, 4th century
29 Catherine of Siena, 1380

MAY

2 Athanasius, Bishop of Alexandria and Teacher of the Faith, 373
4 Monica, Mother of Augustine of Hippo, 387
12 Simon of Cyrene
19 Dunstan, Archbishop of Canterbury, 988
21 Helena, Mother of the Emperor Constantine, 4th century
25 The Venerable Bede, Teacher of the Faith, 735
26 Augustine, First Archbishop of Canterbury and Missionary, 605

JUNE

1 Justin Martyr, c.165
2 The Martyrs of Lyons, 177
3 The Martyrs of Uganda, 1886
5 Boniface, Bishop and Martyr in Germany, c.755
9 Columba of Iona, Missionary in Scotland, 597
13 Antony of Lisbon, Religious, 1231
14 Basil and his Companions, Teachers of the Faith, 4th century
18 Bernard Mizeki, Martyr in Mashonaland, 1896
22 Alban, First Martyr in Britain, c.304
28 Irenaeus, Bishop of Lyons and Teacher of the Faith, c.202

JULY

6 Thomas More, Martyr, 1535
11 Benedict of Monte Cassino, Religious, c.540
13 Silas
29 William Wilberforce, Philanthropist, 1833
30 Mary and Martha of Bethany

AUGUST

7 Dominic, Religious, 1221
10 Laurence, Deacon and Martyr at Rome, 258
20 Bernard of Clairvaux, Religious, 1153
28 Augustine, Bishop of Hippo in Africa, 430
29 The Beheading of St John the Baptist

SEPTEMBER

1 Robert Gray, First Bishop of Cape Town, 1872
2 The Martyrs of New Guinea, 1942
8 The Birth of the Blessed Virgin Mary
13 Cyprian, Bishop of Carthage and Martyr, 258
14 Holy Cross Day
16 Ninian, Bishop and Missionary in Scotland, c.432
19 Theodore of Tarsus, Archbishop of Canterbury, 690
20 John Coleridge Patteson, Bishop of Melanesia and Martyr, 1871

26 Lancelot Andrewes, Bishop of Winchester, 1626
30 Jerome, Priest and Teacher of the Faith, 420

OCTOBER

 1 Remigius, Bishop and Missionary to the Franks, 530
 2 Anthony, Earl of Shaftesbury, Philanthropist, 1885
 4 Francis of Assisi, Religious, 1226
 7 William Tyndale, Priest and Martyr, 1536
11 Philip the Deacon
15 Teresa of Avila, Religious, 1582
16 Hugh Latimer and Nicholas Ridley, Bishops and
   Martyrs, 1555
17 Ignatius of Antioch, Bishop and Martyr, c.110
19 Henry Martyn, Missionary to the East, 1812

NOVEMBER

 2 The Commemoration of the Faithful Departed
 3 The Martyrs of Mbokotwana, 1880
 4 Martin de Porres, Religious, 1639
 7 Willibrord, Bishop and Missionary in Holland, 739
 8 Martyrs and Confessors of our Time
10 Leo the Great, Bishop of Rome and Teacher of the Faith,
   461
11 Martin, Bishop of Tours, 397
12 Charles Simeon, Priest, 1836
14 Samuel Seabury, Bishop in America, 1784
16 Margaret, Queen of Scotland, 1093
18 Hilda of Whitby, Religious, 680
22 Cecilia, Virgin and Martyr at Rome, c.230
23 Clement, Bishop of Rome and Martyr, c.100

DECEMBER

 1 Nicholas Ferrar, Deacon and Religious, 1637
 3 Francis Xavier, Priest and Missionary to the East, 1552
 4 John of Damascus, Teacher of the Faith, c.760
 5 Peter Masiza, Priest, 1907
 7 Ambrose, Bishop of Milan and Teacher of the Faith, 397
24 Christmas Eve
29 Thomas Becket, Archbishop of Canterbury and
   Martyr, 1170

(b) The Ember Seasons

The Ember Days are the Third Sunday in Advent, the Second Sunday in Lent, Trinity Sunday, the Twenty Sixth Sunday of the Year, together with the preceding Wednesdays and Fridays.

On these days prayer is offered for those about to be ordained, for vocations to the ordained ministry, for theological colleges and those preparing for ordination, and for all serving in the ordained ministry.

(c) Rogation Days

The Rogation Days may be kept on the Monday, Tuesday and Wednesday following the Twenty Eighth Sunday of the Year, or transferred to other days according to local needs.

On these days prayer is offered for God's blessing on the fruits of the earth and the sea, and on the labours of people on the land, at sea, in industry, mining and commerce.

(d) The Harvest Thanksgiving

(e) The Eve of Christmas

(f) The Eve of Ascension

(g) The Eve of Pentecost

DAYS OF FASTING AND SELF-DENIAL

Fast Days

6   Ash Wednesday and Good Friday are Fast Days, when the amount of food eaten is reduced.

Days of Self-Denial

The weekdays of Lent.

Other Fridays of the year (except Christmas Day, the Fridays following Christmas, Easter and Ascension Day, and also public holidays falling on a Friday.)

On these days remembrance is made of the suffering and death of our Lord.

They may be observed in one or more of these ways:
a By giving more time to prayer, Bible study, or spiritual reading;
b By eating less or simpler food;
c By giving up some pleasure or luxury, and using the money saved to help other people.

RULES FOR THE OBSERVANCE OF THE CALENDAR

7 a The Great Festivals of Christmas, the Epiphany and All Saints take precedence over a Sunday.

b The Dedication Festival and the Festival of the Patron Saint or Title of a church may take precedence over a Sunday, except during the seasons of Advent and Lent.

c The Epiphany may be observed on any Sunday between 2 and 8 January. Ascension Day, Corpus Christi, All Saints and the Dedication or Patronal Festival may be observed on the Sunday following (unless it is Easter Day, the Day of Pentecost or Trinity Sunday). This is in addition to the observance of these Festivals on the day appointed.

d Festivals occurring on a Sunday in Advent or Lent, on Ash Wednesday, Ascension Day, the Day of Pentecost, Trinity Sunday or Corpus Christi, or falling within Holy Week or Easter Week, are observed on the next day following not being a Festival. A Festival occurring on any other Sunday may be observed either on the Sunday, with precedence over the collect and readings of that Sunday, or else on the next day following not being a Festival.

27

For good cause, a Festival may be observed on another suitable weekday.

When the Festivals of St Stephen, St John and the Holy Innocents fall on the first Sunday after Christmas, they may be commemorated by the use of their collect after the Sunday collect, or else be transferred to the alternative dates appointed in the Calendar.

e With the permission of the Bishop and for sufficient reason some other occasion may be observed on a Sunday.

f A commemoration or other special day falling on any of the days listed in (d) above is not observed for that year. Its collect may be used after the Collect of the Day on a Sunday of the Year. Nevertheless, the Commemoration of the Faithful Departed occurring on a Sunday is observed on Monday 3 November, except in the diocese of St John's, where it is observed on 4 November.

g If a commemoration is the Patronal Festival, suitable Scripture readings may be chosen in place of those provided for the day.

h Where the title of dedication of a church is not in this Calendar, the Patronal Festival is kept on the day traditionally fixed for its celebration, subject to the above rules for a Patronal Festival. A suitable collect and readings may be chosen.

i A collect is provided for the morning services of Christmas Eve, the Eve of the Ascension and the Eve of Pentecost.

j The Sunday collect may be used at Evening Prayer on the day before, except that the Collect for Easter Day is not used at Evening Prayer on Holy Saturday.

A first Evening Prayer is provided for Christmas, the Epiphany, Ascension Day, Pentecost, Corpus Christi and All Saints.

All other observances are confined to the twenty four hours of the day to which they are assigned.

k The Sunday collect is used at the Eucharist and Offices of the weekdays following, unless other provision is made.

On the weekdays following Christmas Day, the Epiphany, Ash Wednesday and Ascension Day, the collect of these days replaces that of the previous Sunday, unless other provision is made.

Normally one collect only is used, unless otherwise allowed in this book.

l The liturgical colour is that of the season or other observance to which the Collect of the Day refers. A letter indicating the colour is found in the right margin of the title line in the table of Collects and Readings, thus: W, white; R, red; G, green; P, purple; B, black.

KEY DATES 1988–2006

A TABLE OF MOVEABLE FESTIVALS AND OTHER DAYS

	SUNDAY EUCHARIST CYCLE YEAR	OFFICE AND WEEKDAY EUCHARIST CYCLE★ YEAR	NUMBER OF SUNDAYS OF THE YEAR BETWEEN EPIPHANY AND LENT	ASH WEDNESDAY	EASTER
1988	B	2	6	17 Feb	3 Apr
1989	C	1	5	8 Feb	26 Mar
1990	A	2	8	28 Feb	15 Apr
1991	B	1	5	13 Feb	31 Mar
1992	C	2	8	4 Mar	19 Apr
1993	A	1	7	24 Feb	11 Apr
1994	B	2	6	16 Feb	3 Apr
1995	C	1	8	1 Mar	16 Apr
1996	A	2	7	21 Feb	7 Apr
1997	B	1	5	12 Feb	30 Mar
1998	C	2	7	25 Feb	12 Apr
1999	A	1	6	17 Feb	4 Apr
2000	B	2	9	8 Mar	23 Apr
2001	C	1	8	28 Feb	15 Apr
2002	A	2	5	13 Feb	31 Mar
2003	B	1	8	5 Mar	20 Apr
2004	C	2	7	25 Feb	11 Apr
2005	A	1	5	9 Feb	27 Mar
2006	B	2	8	1 Mar	16 Apr

★ Note: The readings for the Offices and for the weekday Eucharists are not in this book, but will be found in the annual lectionary.

KEY DATES 1988–2006

A TABLE OF MOVEABLE FESTIVALS AND OTHER DAYS

ASCENSION	PENTECOST	SUNDAY OF † THE YEAR COINCIDING WITH PENTECOST	ADVENT SUNDAY	
12 May	22 May	8th	27 Nov	1988
4 May	14 May	6th	3 Dec	1989
24 May	3 Jun	9th	2 Dec	1990
9 May	19 May	7th	1 Dec	1991
28 May	7 Jun	10th	29 Nov	1992
20 May	30 May	9th	28 Nov	1993
12 May	22 May	8th	27 Nov	1994
25 May	4 Jun	9th	3 Dec	1995
16 May	26 May	8th	1 Dec	1996
8 May	18 May	7th	30 Nov	1997
21 May	31 May	9th	29 Nov	1998
13 May	23 May	8th	28 Nov	1999
1 Jun	11 Jun	10th	3 Dec	2000
24 May	3 Jun	9th	2 Dec	2001
9 May	19 May	7th	1 Dec	2002
29 May	8 Jun	10th	30 Nov	2003
20 May	30 May	9th	28 Nov	2004
5 May	15 May	7th	27 Nov	2005
25 May	4 Jun	9th	3 Dec	2006

† Note: The Collect for this Sunday is used on the weekdays following the Day of Pentecost.

KEY DATES 2007–2025

A TABLE OF MOVEABLE FESTIVALS AND OTHER DAYS

	SUNDAY EUCHARIST CYCLE YEAR	OFFICE AND WEEKDAY EUCHARIST CYCLE★ YEAR	NUMBER OF SUNDAYS OF THE YEAR BETWEEN EPIPHANY AND LENT	ASH WEDNESDAY	EASTER
2007	C	1	7	21 Feb	8 Apr
2008	A	2	4	6 Feb	23 Mar
2009	B	1	7	25 Feb	12 Apr
2010	C	2	6	17 Feb	4 Apr
2011	A	1	9	9 Mar	24 Apr
2012	B	2	7	22 Feb	8 Apr
2013	C	1	5	13 Feb	31 Mar
2014	A	2	8	5 Mar	20 Apr
2015	B	1	6	18 Feb	5 Apr
2016	C	2	5	10 Feb	27 Mar
2017	A	1	8	1 Mar	16 Apr
2018	B	2	6	14 Feb	1 Apr
2019	C	1	8	6 Mar	21 Apr
2020	A	2	7	26 Feb	12 Apr
2021	B	1	6	17 Feb	4 Apr
2022	C	2	8	2 Mar	17 Apr
2023	A	1	7	22 Feb	9 Apr
2024	B	2	6	14 Feb	31 Mar
2025	C	1	8	5 Mar	20 Apr

★ Note: The readings for the Offices and for the weekday Eucharists are not in this book, but will be found in the annual lectionary.

KEY DATES 2007–2025

A TABLE OF MOVEABLE FESTIVALS AND OTHER DAYS

ASCENSION	PENTECOST	SUNDAY OF † THE YEAR COINCIDING WITH PENTECOST	ADVENT SUNDAY	
17 May	27 May	8th	2 Dec	2007
1 May	11 May	6th	30 Nov	2008
21 May	31 May	9th	29 Nov	2009
13 May	23 May	8th	28 Nov	2010
2 Jun	12 Jun	11th	27 Nov	2011
17 May	27 May	8th	2 Dec	2012
9 May	19 May	7th	1 Dec	2013
29 May	8 Jun	10th	30 Nov	2014
14 May	24 May	8th	29 Nov	2015
5 May	15 May	7th	27 Nov	2016
25 May	4 Jun	9th	3 Dec	2017
10 May	20 May	7th	2 Dec	2018
30 May	9 Jun	10th	1 Dec	2019
21 May	31 May	9th	29 Nov	2020
13 May	23 May	8th	28 Nov	2021
26 May	5 Jun	10th	27 Nov	2022
18 May	28 May	8th	3 Dec	2023
9 May	19 May	7th	1 Dec	2024
29 May	8 Jun	10th	30 Nov	2025

† Note: The Collect for this Sunday is used on the weekdays following the Day of Pentecost.

THE OFFICES OF
MORNING
AND
EVENING PRAYER

Preface

The two Offices[1] of Morning and Evening Prayer in their present form evolved from Cranmer's forms in the sixteenth century Book of Common Prayer, and behind that from the Offices used in monasteries from as early as the fourth century A.D. But from the very beginning the Church had its times of prayer, whether for groups of Christians or for individual disciples. In this it followed the example of our Lord, who himself grew up within the Jewish tradition of prayer. We read in the Acts of the Apostles that the disciples came together at the third hour (2:1-15); Peter went up on the housetop to pray at the sixth hour (10:9); Peter and John went to the temple at the ninth hour (3:1); and late at night Paul and Silas were praying and singing God's praises (16:25). Behind their practice lies what our Lord did (Lk 3:21-22; 6:12; 11:1; Mt 14:19 and 23; Mk 1:35; etc.). His times of prayer to his Father gave his life a foundation of prayer, so that it may be said that his whole life was one of prayer.

When we use these Offices we share in a form of prayer which is similar to that used by Christians throughout the world, and in very varied situations. They are used for large, corporate gatherings, often for a Sunday service when the Eucharist is not celebrated. They are used by religious communities, by small groups of Christians meeting together and by individuals on their own. Among these are the clergy, whose joyful obligation it is to pray with these Offices twice a day; for some of them the Eucharist takes the place of one of the Offices. There are also many lay Christians for whom the Offices are a means of bringing order to their prayer and to their life. By praying with these Offices, the individual Christian shares in the prayer of the whole Church, and so in the prayer of Christ.

[1]'Office' is from a Latin word which means 'duty'.

When we use these Offices of Morning and Evening Prayer, we are, first of all, offering worship, praise and thanksgiving to God the Holy Trinity, and at many points in these services we come back to this expression of our love for God.

In the holy Scriptures we receive the word of God, meditating on it in all its variety, as it challenges, nourishes, and always reminds us of our Lord Jesus Christ, the Word made flesh.

One of the principal parts of the Offices is the saying of the Psalms, the songs of God's people which tell of his action in the history of salvation. Even though they belong to the Old Testament and contain some difficult sections, they bring us back again and again to the infinite variety of God's relationship with his creatures. Christ himself knew the Psalms well and made them his own. As we use them we identify with him in his life of prayer.

Throughout these Offices we seek God's face. We acknowledge our need for his grace and guidance on our earthly pilgrimage. The Offices feed our personal prayers, and they strengthen our participation in the holy Eucharist.

Morning and Evening Prayer should be seen as the prayer of the Church for the whole world, both when we are praying specifically for others and in all the activities which make up the Offices. In this way the Church is sharing in the eternal prayer of Christ to his Father in the Spirit on behalf of this disordered and needy world.

When the Church prays it is united with Christ who is the Way to the Father, and it is the Holy Spirit who prays in us, by helping us in our weakness (Rom 8:26) and enabling us to cry 'Abba, Father' (Rom 8:15). So when we pray, corporately or individually, we share in the life of God the Holy Trinity, and we express our very nature as the community of the Church, and as human beings created in God's image. When God created the world, he brought order out of chaos, and the ordered prayer life of the Christian community should be a small reflection of the order which is God's purpose for the world.

General Rubrics

1   Unless prevented by sickness or some other grave cause, all ordained ministers are to pray daily, privately or publicly, Morning and Evening Prayer, according to the Book of Common Prayer or the South African Prayer Book, or the following Offices. Those present at the Eucharist may omit the Office belonging to that part of the day.

2   A bell should be rung, where possible, to invite the people to join in these services.

3   At the request of, or in the absence of, an ordained minister, a lay minister or any other lay person may conduct these Offices.

4   In the separately published Lectionary, psalms are provided for both Morning and Evening Prayer. Three readings are provided for each day; two of these are used at one Office (the first of them being taken from the Old Testament or Apocrypha) and the remaining reading is used at the other Office. If two readings are desired at both Offices, the Old Testament (or Apocrypha) reading from the alternate year is added.

5   Two canticles are provided for each Office, but one may be omitted. Suggestions as to seasonal choice of canticles are found on page 339.

6   Hymns and acts of praise may be introduced where appropriate.

7   A collection may be taken at some convenient point.

Morning Prayer

INTRODUCTION

1　In the name of God, Father, Son and Holy Spirit
Amen

2　The Minister may say

We have come together as the family of God
　　in our Father's presence
to offer him praise and thanksgiving
to hear and receive his holy word
to bring before him the needs of the world
to ask his forgiveness of our sins
and to seek his grace
that through his Son Jesus Christ
we may give ourselves to his service.

PRAISE

3　The Minister may read the appropriate Sentence (section 86), and the people respond

Let us worship and praise him (Alleluia during Eastertide)

4　Lord, open our lips
That we may glorify and praise your Name

Glory to the Father, and to the Son and to the Holy Spirit
**As it was in the beginning, is now, and will be for ever.　Amen
Praise the Lord.　Alleluia**

(In Lent 'Alleluia' is omitted.)

5 Here follows **O Come let us Sing** or **O Shout to the Lord in Triumph** or **The Easter Anthems** (Canticle 9, always used on Easter Day).

O Come let us Sing
(Psalms 95:1-8; 96:13)

6   1 O come let us sing | out · to the | Lord: let us shout in triumph to the | rock of | our sal|vation.

  2 Let us come before his | face with | thanks-giving: and cry | out to · him | joyfully · in | psalms.

  3 For the Lord is a | great | God: and a great | king a · bove | all | gods.

  4 In his hand are the | depths · of the | earth: and the peaks of the | mountains · are | his | also.

  5 The sea is his and | he | made it: his hands | moulded | dry | land.

  6 Come let us worship and | bow | down: and kneel be|fore the | Lord our | maker.

  7 For he is the | Lord our | God: we are his | people · and the | sheep of · his | pasture.

  8 If only you would hear his | voice to|day: for he comes he | comes to | judge the | earth.

†9 He shall judge the | world with | righteousness: and the | peoples | with his | truth.

Glory to the Father and | to the | Son: and | to the | Holy | Spirit.

As it was | in the · be|ginning: is now and | will be · for | ever · A|men

or

O Shout to the Lord in Triumph
(Psalm 100)

7 1 O shout to the Lord in triumph | all the | earth: serve the Lord with gladness and come before his | face with | songs of | joy.

    2 Know that the Lord | he is | God: it is he who has made us and we are his * we are his | people · and the | sheep of · his | pasture.

    3 Come into his gates with thanksgiving and into his | courts with | praise: give thanks to him and | bless his | holy | name.

    4 For the Lord is good * his loving mercy | is for | ever: his faithfulness through|out all | gener|ations.

      Glory to the Father and | to the | Son: and | to the | Holy | Spirit.

      As it was | in the · be|ginning: is now and | will be · for | ever · A|men

PENITENCE

8 This act of penitence (sections 9-11) may be omitted if an act of penitence is made at the Eucharist or at another Office during the day.

9 Let us call to mind and confess our sins

Silence may be kept.   Then is said

10 **Almighty God, our heavenly Father**
in penitence we confess
   that we have sinned against you
   through our own fault
in thought, word, and deed
and in what we have left undone.
For the sake of your Son, Christ our Lord
forgive us all that is past
and grant that we may serve you
   in newness of life
to the glory of your Name.

11 Almighty God have mercy on *us*, forgive *us our* sins and keep *us* in eternal life; through Jesus Christ our Lord.
Amen

THE WORD OF GOD

12 When this is the main Sunday service, all three readings set for the Eucharist are used, in which case the first reading comes before the psalm(s), the second reading at 14, and the third at 18.

The Psalm(s)

13 Here follow(s) the appointed psalm(s). After each psalm is said

Glory to the Father and I to the I Son: and I to the I Holy I Spirit.

As it was I in the · belginning: is now and I will be · for I ever · Almen

The First Scripture Reading

14 The first lesson is written in ...

After the reading

Here ends the first lesson

15 Silence may be kept.

16 Here follows **The Song of Zechariah** or another Canticle.

The Song of Zechariah
(Luke 1:68-79)

17 1 Blessed be the Lord the | God of | Israel: for he has come to his | people · and | set them | free.

2 He has raised up for us a | mighty | saviour: born of the | house · of his | servant | David.

3 Through his holy prophets he | promised · of | old: that he would save us from our enemies * from the | hands of | all that | hate us.

4 He promised to show | mercy · to our | forebears: and to re|member · his | holy | covenant.

5 This was the oath he swore to our | father | Abraham: to set us | free · from the | hands of · our | enemies.

6 Free to worship | him with·out | fear: holy and right-eous in his sight | all the | days of · our | life.

7 You my child shall be called the prophet of the | Most | High: for you will go before the | Lord · to pre|pare his | way.

8 To give his people knowledge | of sal|vation: by the for|giveness | of their | sins.

9 In the tender compassion | of our | God: the dawn from on | high shall | break up|on us.

10 To shine upon those who dwell in darkness and
the | shadow · of | death: and to guide our feet |
into · the | way of | peace.

Glory to the Father and | to the | Son: and | to the |
Holy | Spirit.

As it was | in the · be|ginning: is now and | will be · for |
ever · A|men

The Second Scripture Reading

18 The second lesson is written in ...

After the reading

Here ends the second lesson

19 Silence may be kept.

20 Here follows **The Song of the Church** or another Canticle, or a
hymn may be sung.

The Song of the Church
(Te Deum)

21 1 We praise | you O | God: we ac|claim | you as | Lord.

2 All creation | worships | you: the | Father |
ever|lasting.

3 To you all angels * all the | powers of | heaven:
cherubim and seraphim | sing in | endless | praise.

4 Holy holy holy Lord * God of | power · and | might:
heaven and | earth are | full of · your | glory.

5 The glorious company of ap|ostles | praise you: the
noble fellowship of prophets praise you * the white-
robed | army · of | martyrs | praise you.

6 Throughout the world the holy | Church ac|claims
you: Father of | majes|ty un|bounded.

†7 Your true and only Son | worthy · of | worship: and
the Holy | Spirit | advocate · and | guide.

8 You Christ are the | King of | glory: the e|ternal |
Son · of the | Father.

9 When you became man to | set us | free: you
humbly | chose the | Virgin's | womb.

10 You overcame the | sting of | death: and opened the
kingdom of | heaven · to | all be|lievers.

11 You are seated at God's right | hand in | glory: we
believe that you will | come to | be our | judge.

12 Come then Lord and | help your | people: bought
with the | price of | your own | blood.

13 And bring us | with your | saints: to | glory |
ever|lasting.

The following verses may be added

14 Save   your   people   Lord   and | bless · your
in|heritance: govern and up|hold them | now and |
always.

15 Day by | day we | bless you: we | praise your |
Name for | ever.

16 Keep us today Lord from | all | sin: have mercy | on
us | Lord have | mercy.

17 Lord show us your | love and | mercy: for we | put
our | trust in | you.

†18 In you Lord | is our | hope: let us | never · be | put to |
shame.

THE APOSTLES' CREED

22 **I believe in God, the Father almighty**
creator of heaven and earth.

I believe in Jesus Christ, his only Son, our Lord.
He was conceived by the Holy Spirit
and born of the Virgin Mary.
He suffered under Pontius Pilate
was crucified, died, and was buried.
He descended to the dead.
On the third day he rose again.
He ascended into heaven
and is seated at the right hand of the Father.
He will come to judge the living and the dead.

I believe in the Holy Spirit
the holy catholic Church
the communion of saints
the forgiveness of sins
the resurrection of the body
and the life everlasting.   **Amen**

23   The Minister says

Let us pray

Lord, have mercy upon us
Christ, have mercy upon us
Lord, have mercy upon us

24   **Our Father in heaven**
hallowed be your Name
your kingdom come
your will be done
on earth as in heaven.
Give us today our daily bread.
Forgive us our sins
   as we forgive those who sin against us.
Save us from the time of trial
and deliver us from evil.
For the kingdom, the power, and the glory are yours
now and for ever.   Amen

THE PRAYERS (first part)

25 The Versicles and Responses at 26 or the Prayer at 27 may be used, or both may be omitted. If desired, sections 36-39 from The Prayers (second part) may be substituted, or biddings or other prayers may be introduced before 27. The Office is always concluded with sections 28-32.

26 Show us your mercy, O Lord
And grant us your salvation

O Lord, be gracious to our land
And mercifully hear us when we call upon you

Let your priests be clothed with righteousness
And let your servants shout for joy

O Lord, make your ways known upon the earth
Let all nations acknowledge your saving power

Give your people the blessing of peace
And let your glory be over all the world

Make our hearts clean, O God
And renew a right spirit within us

or

27 Lord God
we ask you to give us your blessing
to your Church, holiness
to the world, peace
to this nation, justice
and to all people knowledge of your law.
Keep safe our families
protect the weak
heal the sick
comfort the dying
and bring us all to a joyful resurrection.
We ask these things through Jesus Christ our Lord.
Amen

The Collect of the Day

28 This may be omitted if Morning Prayer immediately precedes or follows the Eucharist.

29 Then may be said **The Collect for Peace.**

O God, the author of peace and lover of concord
to know you is eternal life
to serve you is perfect freedom:
defend us your servants from all assaults of our enemies
that we may trust in your defence
and not fear the power of any adversaries;
through Jesus Christ our Lord.
Amen

30 Then is said **The Morning Collect.**

Eternal God and Father
by whose power we are created
and by whose love we are redeemed:
guide and strengthen us by your Spirit
that we may give ourselves to your service
and live this day in love for you and one another;
through Jesus Christ our Lord.
Amen

or

31 Almighty and everlasting Father
you have safely brought us to the beginning
    of another day:
defend us by your mighty power
that we may be kept free from all sin
    and safe from every danger
and enable us this day to do
    only what is right in your eyes;
through Jesus Christ our Lord.
Amen

32 **The grace of our Lord Jesus Christ, and the love of God, and the fellowship of the Holy Spirit, be with us all for ever.   Amen**

33 Morning Prayer may end here.

The Sermon

34 When there is a sermon it follows here.

THE PRAYERS (second part)

35 After the Sermon these prayers may be used, or others may be substituted at the Minister's discretion. Further prayers are available in Prayers and Thanksgivings for Various Occasions and also in the Eucharist, sections 30-41.

36 The Minister leads the thanksgiving in which the congregation may be invited to join; after which they say together one or both of the following

37 **Blessing and honour and thanksgiving and praise**
more than we can utter
more than we can understand
be to you, O holy and glorious Trinity
Father, Son and Holy Spirit
from all angels
all people
all creatures
for ever and ever.

38 **God of all power, we acclaim you**
Lord of all grace, we worship you
we are not worthy of you
yet your goodness makes us praise you
and give you thanks.

We praise you for the life you have given us
and for all the blessings we have received
at your hands.

Above all, we give you thanks
   for your Son Jesus Christ
for the grace and hope which his death
   and resurrection have brought to us.
We ask this of you, our Father
that we may never forget your goodness to us
and that we may show our thankfulness
   not only in words
but by the service of our lives
both now and in all eternity.

39 The Minister leads the intercession and petition, in which the
    congregation may be invited to join; after which they say together

Heavenly Father
your Son has promised
that whenever we pray in his name
   you will hear us:
answer our prayers as may be best for us
granting us in this world the knowledge
   of your truth
and in the world to come the fulness
   of eternal life;
through Jesus Christ our Lord.

40 May the Lord bless us and watch over us.
    May the Lord make his face shine on us
       and be gracious to us.
    May the Lord look kindly on us
    and give us peace.

41 The Service may end with a blessing given by a priest.

Evening Prayer

INTRODUCTION

42 In the name of God, Father, Son and Holy Spirit
Amen

43 The Minister may say

We have come together as the family of God
   in our Father's presence
to offer him praise and thanksgiving
to hear and receive his holy word
to bring before him the needs of the world
to ask his forgiveness of our sins
and to seek his grace
that through his Son Jesus Christ
we may give ourselves to his service.

PRAISE

44 The Minister may read the appropriate Sentence (section 86),
and the people respond

Let us worship and praise him (Alleluia during Eastertide).

45 Lord, open our lips
That we may glorify and praise your Name

Glory to the Father, and to the Son and to the Holy Spirit
**As it was in the beginning, is now, and will be for
ever.   Amen
Praise the Lord.   Alleluia**

(In Lent 'Alleluia' is omitted.)

46 Here may follow **Come Bless the Lord** or **Hail Gladdening Light**.

Come Bless the Lord

(Psalm 134)

47 1 Come bless the Lord all you | servants · of the | Lord:
you who by night | stand · in the | house of · our | God.

2 Lift up your hands towards the holy place and | bless
the | Lord: may the Lord bless you from Zion
the | Lord who · made | heaven and | earth.

Glory to the Father and | to the | Son: and | to the |
Holy | Spirit.

As it was | in the · be|ginning: is now and | will be · for |
ever · A|men

or

Hail Gladdening Light

48 1 Hail, gladdening Light, of his pure glory poured
Who is the immortal Father, heavenly, blest,
Holiest of Holies, Jesus Christ our Lord!

2 Now we are come to the sun's hour of rest,
The lights of evening round us shine,
We hymn the Father, Son, and Holy Spirit divine.

3 Worthiest art thou at all times to be sung
With undefilèd tongue,
Son of our God, giver of life, alone:
Therefore in all the world thy glories, Lord, they own.

PENITENCE

49 This act of penitence (sections 50-52) may be omitted if an act of penitence is made at the Eucharist or at another Office during the day.

50 **Let us call to mind and confess our sins**

51 Silence may be kept. Then is said

**Almighty God, our heavenly Father
in penitence we confess
    that we have sinned against you
    through our own fault
in thought, word, and deed
and in what we have left undone.
For the sake of your Son, Christ our Lord
forgive us all that is past
and grant that we may serve you
    in newness of life
to the glory of your Name.**

52 Almighty God have mercy on *us*, forgive *us our* sins and keep *us* in eternal life; through Jesus Christ our Lord.
Amen

THE WORD OF GOD

53 When this is the main Sunday service, all three readings set for the Eucharist are used, in which case the first reading comes before the psalm(s), the second reading at 55, and the third at 59.

The Psalm(s)

54 Here follow(s) the appointed psalm(s). After each psalm is said

Glory to the Father and I to the I Son: and I to the I Holy I Spirit.

As it was I in the · be|ginning: is now and I will be · for I ever · A|men

The First Scripture Reading

55 The first lesson is written in ...

After the reading

Here ends the first lesson

56 Silence may be kept.

57 Here follows **The Song of Mary** or another Canticle.

The Song of Mary
(Luke 1:46-55)

58 1 My soul proclaims the | greatness · of the | Lord: my spirit re|joices in | God my | Saviour.

   2 For he has looked with favour on his | lowly | servant: from this day all gener|ations · will | call me | blessed.

   3 The Almighty has done | great things | for me: and| holy | is his | Name.

   4 He has mercy on | those who | fear him: in | every | gener|ation.

   5 He has shown the | strength · of his | arm: he has scattered the | proud in | their con|ceit.

   6 He has cast down the mighty | from their | thrones: and has | lifted | up the | lowly.

   7 He has filled the hungry with | good | things: and the rich | he has | sent a·way | empty.

   8 He has come to the help of his | servant | Israel: for he has re|membered · his | promise · of | mercy.

  †9 The promise he | made · to our | forebears: to Abraham | and his | children · for | ever.

   Glory to the Father and | to the | Son: and | to the | Holy | Spirit.

   As it was | in the · be|ginning: is now and | will be · for | ever · A|men

The Second Scripture Reading

59 The second lesson is written in ...

After the reading

Here ends the second lesson

60 Silence may be kept.

61 Here follows **The Song of Simeon** or another Canticle, or a hymn may be sung.

The Song of Simeon
(Luke 2:29-32)

62 1 Lord now you let your servant | go in | peace: your |
   word has | been ful|filled.

   2 My own eyes have | seen the · sal|vation: which you
   have prepared in the | sight of | every | people.

   3 A light to re|veal you · to the | nations: and the |
   glory · of your | people | Israel.

   Glory to the Father and | to the | Son: and | to the |
   Holy | Spirit.

   As it was | in the · be|ginning: is now and | will be · for |
   ever · A|men

63 If the Creed has been used at the Eucharist or Morning Prayer, the Baptismal Creed at 65 may replace the Apostles' Creed here.

THE APOSTLES' CREED

64 **I believe in God, the Father almighty
creator of heaven and earth.**

   **I believe in Jesus Christ, his only Son, our Lord.
   He was conceived by the Holy Spirit
   and born of the Virgin Mary.**

He suffered under Pontius Pilate
was crucified, died, and was buried.
He descended to the dead.
On the third day he rose again.
He ascended into heaven
and is seated at the right hand of the Father.
He will come to judge the living and the dead.

I believe in the Holy Spirit
the holy catholic Church
the communion of saints
the forgiveness of sins
the resurrection of the body
and the life everlasting.   Amen

THE BAPTISMAL CREED

65   **I believe and trust in God the Father**
      who made the world.
      I believe and trust in his Son Jesus Christ
      who redeemed humankind.
      I believe and trust in his Holy Spirit
      who gives life to the people of God.
      I believe and trust in one God
      Father, Son and Holy Spirit.   Amen

66   The Minister says

      Let us pray

      Lord, have mercy upon us
      Christ, have mercy upon us
      Lord, have mercy upon us

67   **Our Father in heaven
     hallowed be your Name
     your kingdom come
     your will be done
     on earth as in heaven.
     Give us today our daily bread.
     Forgive us our sins
         as we forgive those who sin against us.
     Save us from the time of trial
     and deliver us from evil.
     For the kingdom, the power, and the glory are yours
     now and for ever.   Amen**

THE PRAYERS (first part)

68   The Versicles and Responses at 69 or the Prayer at 70 may be used, or
     both may be omitted. If desired, sections 79-82 from The Prayers
     (second part) may be substituted, or biddings or other prayers may be
     introduced before 70. The Office is always concluded with sections
     71-75.

69   Show us your mercy, O Lord
     And grant us your salvation

     O Lord, be gracious to our land
     And mercifully hear us when we call upon you

     Let your priests be clothed with righteousness
     And let your servants shout for joy

     O Lord, make your ways known upon the earth
     Let all nations acknowledge your saving power

     Give your people the blessing of peace
     And let your glory be over all the world

     Make our hearts clean, O God
     And renew a right spirit within us

or

10 Lord God
we ask you to give us your blessing
to your Church, holiness
to the world, peace
to this nation, justice
and to all people knowledge of your law.
Keep safe our families
protect the weak
heal the sick
comfort the dying
and bring us all to a joyful resurrection.
We ask these things through Jesus Christ our Lord.
Amen

The Collect of the Day

1 This may be omitted if Evening Prayer immediately precedes or follows
the Eucharist.

2 Then may be said **The Collect for Peace.**

Eternal God, from whom all holy desires, all good
   counsels and all just works proceed:
give your servants that peace
   which the world cannot give
that our hearts may be set to obey your commandments
and that, free from the fear of our enemies
we may pass our time in rest and quietness;
through the merits of Jesus Christ our Saviour.
Amen

3 Then is said **The Evening Collect.**

Lighten our darkness, Lord
and by your great mercy defend us
   in all perils and dangers of the night;
for the love of your only Son
   our Saviour Jesus Christ.
Amen

74 **The grace of our Lord Jesus Christ, and the love of God, and the fellowship of the Holy Spirit, be with us all for ever.   Amen**

75 Sections 83-85 may be substituted for 74.

76 Evening Prayer may end here.

The Sermon

77 When there is a sermon it follows here.

THE PRAYERS (second part)

78 After the Sermon these prayers may be used, or others may be substituted at the Minister's discretion. Further prayers are available in Prayers and Thanksgivings for Various Occasions and also in the Eucharist, sections 30-41.

79 The Minister leads the thanksgiving in which the congregation may be invited to join; after which they say together one or both of the following

80 **Blessing and honour and thanksgiving and praise**
   more than we can utter
   more than we can understand
   be to you, O holy and glorious Trinity
   Father, Son and Holy Spirit
   from all angels
   all people
   all creatures
   for ever and ever.

81 **God of all power, we acclaim you**
   Lord of all grace, we worship you
   we are not worthy of you
   yet your goodness makes us praise you
       and give you thanks.

   We praise you for the life you have given us
   and for all the blessings we have received
       at your hands.

Above all, we give you thanks
    for your Son Jesus Christ
for the grace and hope which his death
    and resurrection have brought to us.
We ask this of you, our Father
that we may never forget your goodness to us
and that we may show our thankfulness
    not only in words
but by the service of our lives
both now and in all eternity.

2 The Minister leads the intercession and petition, in which the congregation may be invited to join; after which they say together

Almighty God, the fountain of all wisdom
you know our needs before we ask
and our ignorance in asking:
have compassion on our weakness
and those things which for
    our unworthiness we dare not
and for our blindness we cannot ask
grant us through your Son Jesus Christ our Saviour.

3 Preserve us, Lord, while waking
and guard us while sleeping
that awake we may watch with Christ
and asleep we may rest in peace.
Amen

4 May the Lord bless us and watch over us.
May the Lord make his face shine on us
    and be gracious to us.
May the Lord look kindly on us
and give us peace.

5 The Service may end with a blessing given by a priest.

SENTENCES

86 These Sentences are used at 3 of Morning Prayer and 44 of Evening Prayer. They may also be used before 1 in the Eucharist. The response in each case is

Let us worship and praise him. (Alleluia during Eastertide).

Advent Sunday until Christmas Day

He who reigns shall come in glory:

or

Our King and Saviour draws near:

Christmas Day until the Epiphany

Our Saviour is born:

or

The Word was made flesh:

The Epiphany and the Transfiguration of our Lord

The glory of the Lord is declared to the world:

or

The love of our God and Saviour is revealed:

Ash Wednesday until Palm Sunday

The goodness of God leads to repentance:

or

God will not judge by appearances; he will rule with justice:

Palm Sunday until Easter Day

Christ our Lord became obedient even to death:

or

Christ our Redeemer draws all nations to himself:

Easter Day until Ascension Day

Alleluia, Christ is risen; we are risen.   Alleluia:

or

Victory is ours through him who loved us.   Alleluia:

Ascension Day until the Day of Pentecost

God raised our Saviour from the dead and enthroned him at his right hand.   Alleluia:

or

Jesus, when he had offered one sacrifice for ever, sat down on the right hand of God.   Alleluia:

or

God has given us the Spirit of his Son.   Alleluia:

The Day of Pentecost

God has shed abroad his love in our hearts through the Holy Spirit he has given us.   Alleluia:

Trinity Sunday

Holy, holy, holy, is the one God of love, Father, Son and Holy Spirit:

Sundays and Weekdays after Epiphany
and after Pentecost

Sunday   This Sentence or any of the following may be used
This is the day which the Lord has made:

Monday   The Lord is King, let the earth rejoice:

Tuesday   The heavens declare the glory of God:

Wednesday Grace and truth came through Jesus Christ:

Thursday   God feeds his people with the bread of life:

Friday   Christ died for our sins once and for all:

Saturday   The Lord lifts up the humble and meek:

General

The earth is the Lord's:

or

Seek the Lord, and he will give life to your soul:

or

The Lord will free us from the hand of our enemies:

or

The Lord has visited his people:

or

God is the Lord, who gives us light:

or

God is the Lord, by whom we escape death:

or

Christ is our peace, who has made us one:

Festivals of the Blessed Virgin Mary

A virgin shall conceive and bear a son; his name shall be called Emmanuel:

or

God blessed Mary above all women:

Saints' Days

The Lord is glorious in his saints:

or

Blessed are the pure in heart for they shall see God:

The Dedication Festival

The heaven of heavens cannot contain him, yet the Lord God is here:

or

This is the gate of heaven, this is the house of God:

St Michael and All Angels

God commands his angels to guard us:

or

He makes his angels spirits and his ministers a flame of fire:

THE ADVENT ANTHEMS

87 On the appointed days these Anthems may be said before and after the Song of Mary.

December 17   O Sapientia

O Wisdom, you came from the lips of God most high
and you reach from one end of the universe to the other
powerfully and gently ordering all things:
come to teach us the way of prudence.

December 18   O Adonai

O Lord of Lords and leader of the house of Israel
you appeared to Moses in the flame of a burning bush
and at Sinai you gave him the law:
come with outstretched arm to save us.

December 19   O Radix Jesse

O Root of Jesse, you stand as a sign to the peoples
before you kings are silent
and the Gentiles pray with longing:
come now and set us free.

December 20   O Clavis David

O Key of David and ruler of the house of Israel
you open and none can shut
you shut and none can open:
come and lead out of the prison house
the captives who sit there in darkness and the shadow of
    death.

December 21   O Oriens

O Morning Star, you are the splendour of eternal light
you are the dawning sun, Sun of justice:
come and enlighten those who sit in darkness
    and the shadow of death.

December 22   O Rex Gentium

O King of the nations and the fulfilment of their longing
you are the corner stone and you make all one
you formed us from primeval clay:
come and save us.

December 23   O Emmanuel

O Emmanuel, our King and giver of the law
the people await you, their Saviour:
come and save us, Lord our God.

THE LITANY

THE TITAN

The Litany

1 The Litany may be said in whole or in part.

Sections 2, 9 and 11 are always used, together with a selection of suffrages.

Prayer of approach to God

2 O God the Father, creator of heaven and earth
Have mercy upon us

O God the Son, redeemer of the world
Have mercy upon us

O God the Holy Spirit, advocate and guide
Have mercy upon us

O holy, blessed, and glorious Trinity
three Persons in one God
Have mercy upon us

Prayers for deliverance

3 Lord, remember not our offences, nor the offences of our forebears; spare us, good Lord, spare your people whom you have redeemed with your precious blood
Spare us, good Lord

From all evil and wickedness; from sin; from the cunning assaults of the devil; from your wrath, and from everlasting condemnation
Good Lord, deliver us

From all spiritual blindness; from pride, vanity, and hypocrisy; from envy, hatred, malice, and all uncharitableness
Good Lord, deliver us

From disordered and sinful affections; from the deceits of the world and the snares of the devil
Good Lord, deliver us

From all false doctrine, heresy, and schism; from hardness of heart, and from contempt of your word and commandment
Good Lord, deliver us

From lightning, fire, and tempest; from earthquake, drought, and flood; from famine, plague, and pestilence
Good Lord, deliver us

From all oppression, conspiracy, and rebellion; from violence, battle, and murder; and from dying suddenly and unprepared
Good Lord, deliver us

Prayer recalling Christ's saving work

4　By the mystery of your holy incarnation; by your birth, childhood, and obedience; by your baptism, fasting, and temptation
Good Lord, deliver us

By your ministry in word and work; by your mighty acts of power; by your proclamation of the kingdom
Good Lord, deliver us

By your agony and sweat of blood; by your cross and passion; by your precious death and burial
Good Lord, deliver us

By your mighty resurrection; by your glorious ascension; and by the coming of the Holy Spirit
Good Lord, deliver us

In all times of trial and sorrow; in all times of joy and prosperity; in the hour of death and at the day of judgement
Good Lord, deliver us

Prayers of Intercession

5 Hear our prayers, O Lord our God
Hear us, good Lord

For the Church

6 Govern and direct your holy Church; fill it with love and truth; and grant it that unity which is your will
Hear us, good Lord

Give us boldness to preach the gospel in all the world, and to make disciples of all nations
Hear us, good Lord

Enlighten all bishops, priests, and deacons with true knowledge and understanding, that by their life and teaching they may proclaim your word
Hear us, good Lord

Give your people grace to hear and receive your word, to find and follow their true vocation, and to bring forth the fruit of the Spirit
Hear us, good Lord

Bring into the way of truth all who have erred and are deceived
Hear us, good Lord

Strengthen those who stand; comfort and help the faint-hearted; raise up the fallen; and finally beat down Satan under our feet
Hear us, good Lord

For the nations

7 Guide the leaders of the nations into the way of peace and justice
Hear us, good Lord

Enlighten and direct our rulers; grant that they may put their trust in you, and seek only your honour and glory
Hear us, good Lord

Grant wisdom and insight to all in authority, and to judges and magistrates the grace to administer justice with mercy
Hear us, good Lord

Give to all nations peace, unity, and concord; and grant to all people freedom and dignity, food and shelter
Hear us, good Lord

For all people according to their needs

8 Teach us to use the resources of the earth to your glory, that all may share in your goodness and praise you for your loving kindness
Hear us, good Lord

Enlighten with your Spirit all who teach and all who learn
Hear us, good Lord

Help and comfort the lonely and aged, the bereaved, the overworked, the exploited and the oppressed
Hear us, good Lord

Support and encourage all who are in poverty, unemployment or distress; protect those whose work is dangerous, and keep in safety all who travel
Hear us, good Lord

Keep fathers, mothers and children united in their family life, and give them wisdom and strength in times of stress
Hear us, good Lord

Heal the sick in mind and body; strengthen and preserve all women in childbirth and all young children
Hear us, good Lord

Defend and provide for the widowed and the orphaned, all migrant workers and refugees, the homeless and victims of strife; have pity on prisoners and all who live in fear
Hear us, good Lord

Forgive our enemies, persecutors, and slanderers, and turn their hearts
Hear us, good Lord

Concluding prayers

9 Saviour of the world
forgive our sins, known and unknown
things done and left undone;
grant us the grace of your Holy Spirit
that we may amend our lives
   according to your holy word.

**Holy God
holy and strong
holy and immortal
have mercy upon us.**

(10) **Our Father in heaven
hallowed be your Name
your kingdom come
your will be done
on earth as in heaven.
Give us today our daily bread.
Forgive us our sins
   as we forgive those who sin against us.
Save us from the time of trial
and deliver us from evil.
For the kingdom, the power, and the glory are yours
now and for ever.   Amen**

11 Almighty God
you have given us grace
to bring before you with one accord
   our common supplications
and you promise
that when two or three are gathered together
   in your name
you will grant their requests:
fulfil now, O Lord
the desires and petitions of your servants
as may be most expedient for them
granting us in this world knowledge of your truth
and in the world to come the fulness of eternal life.
Amen

PRAYERS AND THANKSGIVINGS FOR VARIOUS OCCASIONS

Contents

THE CHURCH

1, 2	For the Unity of the Church
3	For the Mission of the Church
4	For a Diocese or Pastoral Charge
5	During a Vacancy in a *Diocese/Pastoral Charge*
6	For Candidates for Confirmation
7	For the Children of the Church
8	For Religious Communities
9	For Theological Colleges
10	For Ordination Candidates

THE WORLD

11	For the Peace of the World
12	For our Country
13	For Responsible Citizenship
14	In Times of Conflict
15	For our Enemies
16	For Those who suffer for the Sake of Conscience
17	For the Oppressed
18	For the Unemployed
19	For Those who Influence Public Opinion
20	For the Preservation of the Environment

GENERAL

21	For Educational Institutions
22	For Young People
23	For Those suffering from Addiction
24	For the Aged
25	For our Homes
26	For Favourable Weather
27	A Prayer attributed to St Francis
28	A Prayer for Africa
29	For Guidance
30	For Family and Friends
31, 32	Evening Prayers
33-37	Concluding Prayers

THANKSGIVINGS

38	A General Thanksgiving
39	For the Church
40	For Favourable Weather
41	For Peace
42	For Deliverance from Sickness and Disease
43-47	Acts of Praise

Prayers and Thanksgivings for Various Occasions

Prayers for the sick and dying are to be found in Ministry to the Sick and Dying, sections 4 to 21 and 94 to 98.

Prayers for the departed and bereaved are to be found in Funeral Services, sections 109 to 124.

Further suitable prayers are to be found among the Collects for Various Occasions.

THE CHURCH

For the Unity of the Church

1 Almighty God, the Father of us all
hear our prayer
and grant to the whole Christian people
   unity, peace and true concord
both visible and invisible;
through Jesus Christ our Lord.

2 God, the Father of our Lord Jesus Christ
our only Saviour, the Prince of peace:
give us grace seriously to lay to heart
   the great dangers we are in
   by our unhappy divisions.
Take away all hatred and prejudice
and whatever else may hinder us
   from godly union and concord;
that, as there is but one Body, and one Spirit
and one hope of our calling
one Lord, one faith, one baptism
one God and Father of us all
so we may be united
   in one holy bond of truth and peace
   of faith and love

and may with one mind and one mouth
  glorify you;
through Jesus Christ our Lord.

For the Mission of the Church

3 Almighty Father
you have made of one blood
all the peoples of the earth
and sent your blessed Son to preach peace
    to those who are far off
    and to those who are near:
grant that people everywhere
    may seek after you and find you;
bring the nations into your fold;
pour out your Spirit upon all flesh
and hasten the coming of your kingdom;
through Jesus Christ our Lord.

For a Diocese or Pastoral Charge

4 Lord of heaven and earth
we ask you to provide this *Diocese*
    with everything necessary for its spiritual growth:
schools to educate children in your love and service
ministers to do your work in this area
churches in which to worship and glorify you.
Strengthen and confirm the faithful
protect and guide the children
comfort and heal the sick and afflicted
turn the wicked to repentance
rouse the careless
restore the penitent
remove every hindrance to the advancement of your
    truth
and bring us all to be of one heart and mind
    within the body of your holy Church
to the honour and glory of your Name;
through Jesus Christ our Lord.

During a Vacancy in a *Diocese/Pastoral Charge*

5   God our Father
    the giver of every good gift
    graciously regard the needs of your Church
    and guide with your heavenly wisdom
    the minds of those responsible for choosing
    a bishop for this Diocese:

or

a rector for this parish:

or other appropriate words:

send us a faithful pastor to feed your flock
and to lead us in the way of holiness;
through Jesus Christ your only Son our Lord.

For Candidates for Confirmation

6   Lord of all wisdom
    your Son Jesus Christ
    prepared his disciples for the coming of the Holy Spirit:
    make ready those who are seeking his strengthening gift;
    through Jesus Christ our Lord.

For the Children of the Church

7   Father of the beloved Son
    you have committed to your holy Church
        the care and nurture of children:
    enlighten with your wisdom
        those who teach and those who learn
    that rejoicing in the knowledge of your truth
    they may worship and serve you throughout their lives;
    through Jesus Christ our Lord.

For Religious Communities

8 Heavenly Father
your Son showed forth his love
   in a life of poverty, chastity and obedience:
strengthen the religious communities of your Church
   to follow the pattern of his life
that by their prayer and service
   the Church may be enriched;
through Jesus Christ our Lord.

For Theological Colleges

9 Heavenly Father
the riches of your glory are infinite
and your love endures for ever:
bless and guide those who teach and those who learn;
deepen their love
strengthen their faith
that Christ may dwell in their hearts;
to the glory of your Name.

For Ordination Candidates

10 God our Father, the Shepherd of Israel
you entrust to your Church the care of your people:
watch over your servants now preparing
   for the ministry of word and sacrament.
Fill them with faith, hope and love
and make them steadfast in prayer;
through Jesus Christ our Lord.

THE WORLD

For the Peace of the World

11 God our Father
you are the source of all truth and peace:
look with mercy on your children
purify our hearts from all hatred
    falsehood and prejudice
and so guide us by your loving wisdom
that peace and righteousness may be established
    among all people;
through Jesus Christ our Lord.

For our Country

12 Almighty God, the Father of us all
we ask you to inspire the people of this land
    with the spirit of justice, truth and love
so that in all our dealings with one another
we may show that together we are one in you;
for the sake of Jesus Christ our Lord.

For Responsible Citizenship

13 Lord Jesus Christ
the length, breadth, depth and height of your love
    is beyond our understanding:
grant that this love may so transform us
    through your suffering
as to make us reach out to the despairing
    and the desperate
and work for justice, reconciliation and peace
    among all people;
for your Name's sake.

In Times of Conflict

14 God our refuge and strength
you have bound us together in a common life:
help us, in the midst of our conflicts
to confront one another without hatred or bitterness
to listen for your voice amid competing claims
and to work together with mutual forbearance and
    respect;
through Jesus Christ our Lord.

For Our Enemies

15 O God, the Lord of all
your Son commanded us to love our enemies
    and to pray for them.
Lead us from prejudice to truth;
deliver us from hatred, cruelty, and the spirit of revenge;
and enable us to stand before you
reconciled through your Son Jesus Christ our Lord.

For Those who Suffer for the Sake of Conscience

16 God of love and strength
your Son forgave his enemies
    even while suffering shame and death:
strengthen those who suffer for the sake of conscience;
when they are accused
    save them from speaking in hatred or in anger;
when they are rejected
    save them from bitterness;
when they are imprisoned
    save them from despair;
give us grace to discern your truth
    that our society may be cleansed and made new;
in the name of our merciful and righteous judge
Jesus Christ our Lord.

For the Oppressed

17 Look with pity, heavenly Father
on those who are threatened by
    hunger, injustice, terror, or death:
help us to banish cruelty from our midst
strengthen those who seek equality for all
and grant that every one of us
    may receive a due share in the riches of this land;
through Jesus Christ our Lord.

For the Unemployed

18 Heavenly Father, creator and giver of all good things
your Son learned a carpenter's trade:
protect and defend all who suffer poverty
    and deprivation from being without work;
guide the people of this land
    so to use its wealth and resources
that all may find employment
and receive just payment for their labour;
through Jesus Christ our Lord.

For Those who Influence Public Opinion

19 Almighty God
you proclaim your truth in every age
    by many voices:
direct those who speak where many listen
those who write what many read
those who influence what many see
that they may do their part
    in making the heart of this people wise
its mind sound
and its will righteous;
to the honour of Jesus Christ our Lord.

For the Preservation of the Environment

20 Sovereign Lord
you are the creator and sustainer of the earth
and you have given us dominion
   over its resources:
forgive us for squandering your gifts
inspire us to conserve them and use them aright
   in the service of your people
and to the glory of your Name;
through Jesus Christ our Lord.

GENERAL

For Educational Institutions

21 Eternal God
worthy of all worship
your Son sat among scholars, asking them questions:
bless all schools, colleges and universities
(especially …)
that they may be lively centres
   for sound learning, new discovery
and the pursuit of wisdom;
and grant that those who teach and those who learn
may praise you as the source of all truth;
through Jesus Christ our Lord.

For Young People

22 Father of everlasting compassion
you see your children growing up
   in an uncertain and confusing world:
show them the path of life
enable them to triumph over failure and frustration
to hold fast their faith in you
and to keep alive their joy in your creation;
through Jesus Christ our Lord.

For those Suffering from Addiction

23 God our Father
   look with compassion upon those
      who through addiction to drugs or alcohol
   have lost their health and freedom:
   remove the fears that bind them
   strengthen them in their recovery
   assure them of your love
   and give them friends to support them;
   through Jesus Christ our Lord.

For the Aged

24 Lord God
   the giver of eternal life
   look with mercy on all whose increasing years
      bring loneliness, distress, or weakness:
   give them understanding helpers
   and the willingness to accept help
   and, as their strength diminishes
   increase their faith and their assurance of your love;
   through Jesus Christ our Lord.

For our Homes

25 Visit, Lord, our homes
   and drive far from them all the snares
      of the evil one:
   let your holy angels dwell in them
      to preserve us in peace
   and may your blessing rest upon us evermore;
   through Jesus Christ our Lord.

For Favourable Weather

26   God our heavenly Father
through your Son you promised
    to those seeking first your kingdom
    and your righteousness
all things necessary for bodily welfare:
send us such favourable weather
that we may receive the earth's produce
    to strengthen and sustain us
and always praise you for your bounty;
through Jesus Christ our Lord.

A Prayer attributed to St Francis

27   Lord, make us instruments of your peace
where there is hatred, let us sow love
where there is injury, pardon
where there is discord, union
where there is doubt, faith
where there is despair, hope
where there is darkness, light
where there is sadness, joy:
grant that we may not so much seek
    to be consoled as to console
to be understood as to understand
to be loved as to love;
for it is in giving that we receive
it is in pardoning that we are pardoned
and it is in dying that we are born to eternal life.

A Prayer for Africa

28   God, bless Africa
guard her children
guide her leaders
and give her peace;
for Jesus Christ's sake.

For Guidance

29 Go before us, Lord, in all our doings
with your most gracious favour
and encourage us with your continual help
that in all our works
    begun, continued, and ended in you
we may glorify your holy Name
and finally, by your mercy
    obtain the fulness of eternal life;
through Jesus Christ our Lord.

For Family and Friends

30 Almighty God, Father of everlasting mercy
we entrust all who are dear to us
    to your never-failing care and love
both for this life and for the life to come
knowing that you are doing for them
    things beyond all that we can ask or think;
through Jesus Christ our Lord.

Evening Prayers

31 Be with us, merciful God
and protect us through the silent hours of this night
so that we, who are wearied
    by the changes and chances of this fleeting world
may rest upon your eternal changelessness;
through Jesus Christ our Lord.

32 Look down, Lord, from your heavenly throne
lighten the darkness of the night
    with your celestial brightness
and from the children of light
    banish the deeds of darkness;
through Jesus Christ our Lord.

Concluding Prayers

33 Almighty and eternal God
    direct, sanctify and govern our hearts and bodies
    in the ways of your laws
        and the works of your commandments
    that under your protection, now and ever
    we may be preserved in body and soul;
    through Jesus Christ our Lord.

34 Almighty God
    you have promised to hear the prayers
        of those who ask in your Son's name:
    we pray that what we have asked faithfully
    we may obtain effectually;
    through Jesus Christ our Lord.

35 Remember, O Lord, what you have wrought in us
    and not what we deserve;
    as you have called us to your service
    make us worthy of our calling;
    through Jesus Christ our Lord.

36 Eternal God
    the light of the minds that know you
    the joy of the hearts that love you
    the strength of the wills that serve you:
    grant us
        so to know you that we may truly love you
    so to love you that we may freely serve you
    to the glory of your holy Name.

37 Almighty God
    you have given us grace
    to bring before you with one accord
        our common supplications
    and you promise
    that when two or three are gathered together
        in your name
    you will grant their requests:
    fulfil now, O Lord
    the desires and petitions of your servants
    as may be most expedient for them
    granting us in this world knowledge of your truth
    and in the world to come the fulness of eternal life.

THANKSGIVINGS

A General Thanksgiving

38 Almighty God and merciful Father
    we give you hearty thanks
        for all your goodness and loving kindness to us
        and to all people.
    We bless you for our creation and preservation
    and for all the blessings of this life;
    but above all for your love
        in redeeming the world by our Lord Jesus Christ;
    for the means of grace and for the hope of glory.
    Give us a due sense of your mercy
    that our hearts may be thankful
    and that we may praise you
        not only with our lips but in our lives
    by giving up ourselves to your service
    and by walking before you
        in holiness and righteousness all our days;
    through Jesus Christ our Lord.

For the Church

39 Almighty God
    we praise you for the blessings
        brought to humankind through your Church.
    We bless you for the grace of the sacraments
    for our fellowship in Christ
        with you and one another
    for the teaching of the Scriptures
    and for the preaching of your word.
    We thank you for the holy example of your saints
    for your faithful servants departed this life
    and for the memory and example
        of all that has been true and good in their lives.
    Number us with them
        in the company of the redeemed in heaven;
    through Jesus Christ our Lord.

For Favourable Weather

40 God our Father
    you have brought us relief and comfort
        by your gift of favourable weather:
    we thank you for this answer to our prayer;
    help us to use all your mercies
        to your glory and for the good of your people;
    through Jesus Christ our Lord.

For Peace

41 Almighty Father
    your will is that all people
        should live in unity:
    we bless you
        for the ending of this *war/civil strife*
    and for your gift of peace.
    Give your grace to all nations
        to walk in the way of your commandments
    and to live together
        in peace, justice and freedom;
    through Jesus Christ our Lord.

For Deliverance from Sickness and Disease

42 Heavenly Father
you are the source of life and health:
we give you thanks and praise
for recovery from ...

or

for deliverance from ...
disease/the recent epidemic/the outbreak of plague.
Keep us in health of body and spirit
ever rejoicing in your loving care;
through Jesus Christ our Lord.

Acts of Praise

43 To God the Father, who loved us, and made us
accepted in the Beloved:
to God the Son, who loved us, and loosed us from
our sins by his own blood:
to God the Holy Spirit, who pours the love of God
into our hearts:
to the one true God, be all love and all glory
for time and for eternity.

44 Now to him, who by the power at work within us
is able to do far more abundantly
than all that we ask or think
to him be glory in the Church and in Christ Jesus
to all generations, for ever and ever.   Amen

45 Now to him, who is able to keep us from falling
and to present us without blemish
before the presence of his glory with rejoicing
to the only God, our Saviour
through Jesus Christ our Lord
be glory, majesty, dominion, and authority
before all time and now and for ever.   Amen

46 To the King of ages, immortal, invisible, the only God
    be honour and glory for ever and ever.   Amen

47 To him who loves us
    and has freed us from our sins by his blood
    and made us a kingdom
    priests to his God and Father
    to him be glory and dominion for ever and ever.   Amen

THE HOLY EUCHARIST

Preface

At the Last Supper on the eve of his death, Jesus took, blessed, broke and gave. In the giving he used words which have awed and inspired his followers ever since: 'this is my body', 'this is my blood'. This great sacrament of the Church was brought into being in a drama of word and action. Each celebration is a fulfilment of our Lord's command to do this in remembrance of him; his presence is made real among us, and we lift up our hearts as we are caught up into the worship of heaven.

The Church has gathered around the mystery of the words and actions of Christ those other features which have become familiar to us: the praise; the penitence; the prayer which collects our thoughts around a particular theme or focus; the reading of the Scriptures; the sermon; the creed; the prayers of intercession; the giving of the Peace; the hymns and spiritual songs. Here we have the central act of the Church's worship. In Christ it is our eucharist, that is, our thanksgiving to God for his inexpressible love in giving his only Son for us: Lamb of God, bearer of our sins, redeemer of the world. It is our proclamation of the Lord's death until he comes.

It is also our communion as we receive, in and through the consecrated bread and wine, the benefits of his sacrifice made once for all, and as we in our turn offer ourselves as a living sacrifice to God. Now our Lord takes us and blesses us; he breaks us in renewed surrender and gives us as food for others.

It is because of this understanding that we need to approach each celebration of the Eucharist with joy and awe. Whether in the simplicity of a house Communion where 'two or three are gathered together', or in the grandeur of the great occasion in a cathedral, the essential truths are always the same.

In the Eucharist there is a twofold movement: the call to come, 'draw near and receive'; the summons to move out into a needy world, 'go in peace to love and serve the Lord'. These are the hallmarks of the eucharistic community.

General Rubrics

1   The Priest presides in the absence of the Bishop. He may ask lay persons to take sections 4-13, 17-20 and 27-42. It is the privilege of a deacon to read the Gospel. A deacon or lay minister who is so licensed may preach.

2   Silence may be kept after the readings and elsewhere.

3   Sentences from Scripture may be introduced at appropriate places, such as before 1 and 11, after 14, and at 44. Suitable sentences are suggested in sections 105-106 and in the Offices, section 86.

4   Hymns and acts of praise may be introduced at appropriate places.

5   Before the Introduction, the Priest may greet the people informally and welcome visitors and newcomers. Notices may be given out here, before the Prayers (sections 27-43), before or after the Peace, or before the Dismissal at 90. The service should not otherwise be interrupted by the giving of notices.

INTRODUCTION

1 The Lord be with you
And also with you

2 From Easter Day to the Day of Pentecost the following replaces 1

Alleluia! Christ is risen
He is risen indeed.   Alleluia

The Lord be with you
And also with you

3 Sections 4 and 5 may be omitted in Lent and Advent and on weekdays
which are not Festivals or Great Festivals. Another canticle or hymn may
replace 5.

4 Praise the Lord
Praise him you servants of the Lord

Blessed be God, Father, Son and Holy Spirit
Blessed be his Name, now and for ever

5 **Glory to God in the highest**
and peace to his people on earth.

Lord God, heavenly King
almighty God and Father
we worship you, we give you thanks
we praise you for your glory.

Lord Jesus Christ, only Son of the Father
Lord God, Lamb of God
you take away the sin of the world:
have mercy on us;
you are seated at the right hand of the Father:
receive our prayer.

For you alone are the Holy One
you alone are the Lord
you alone are the Most High
Jesus Christ
with the Holy Spirit
in the glory of God the Father.   Amen

6   The Minister may introduce **The Collect for Purity** by saying

Let us pray

7   **Almighty God**
to whom all hearts are open
all desires known
and from whom no secrets are hid:
cleanse the thoughts of our hearts
    by the inspiration of your Holy Spirit
that we may perfectly love you
and worthily magnify your holy Name;
through Christ our Lord.

(8) Lord, have mercy
   Lord, have mercy

    Christ, have mercy
    Christ, have mercy

    Lord, have mercy
    Lord, have mercy

PENITENCE

9   Sections 10-14 are used here or after the Sermon, or before the Peace at section 43.

10 At least on Ash Wednesday and the five Sundays following, the Ten Commandments (section 104) are said.

At other times the following may be said

Jesus said, 'You shall love the Lord your God with all your heart, and with all your soul and with all your mind.' This is the first and great commandment. And the second is like it, 'You shall love your neighbour as yourself.' On these two commandments depend all the law and the prophets.

The Holy Eucharist

11   The Minister exhorts the congregation to penitence in these or similar
     words

Let us confess our sins (firmly resolved to keep God's
commandments and to live in love and peace with our
neighbour).

12   Silence may be kept.

13   **Almighty God, our heavenly Father**
     in penitence we confess
     that we have sinned against you
     through our own fault
     in thought, word, and deed
     and in what we have left undone.
     For the sake of your Son, Christ our Lord
     forgive us all that is past
     and grant that we may serve you
     in newness of life
     to the glory of your Name.

14   The Priest stands and says

Almighty God, who forgives all who truly repent, have
mercy on *you*; pardon *your* sins and set *you* free from
them; confirm and strengthen *you* in all goodness and
keep *you* in eternal life; through Jesus Christ our Lord.

Amen

THE COLLECT OF THE DAY

15   Let us pray

The Priest says the Collect and the people respond

Amen

THE WORD OF GOD

16 The Gospel is always read.

On weekdays other than Festivals or Great Festivals one reading and the canticle may be omitted.

On Sundays, other Great Festivals and Festivals there are two readings and the Gospel. For good cause, one reading and the psalm may be omitted on a Sunday.

A hymn may replace the canticle.

The First Reading

17 A reading from …

After the reading

Hear the word of the Lord
Thanks be to God

18 The appointed psalm follows.

The Second Reading

19 A reading from …

After the reading

Hear the word of the Lord
Thanks be to God

20 A canticle or hymn follows.

The Gospel

21 Listen to the Good News proclaimed in …
Glory to Christ our Saviour

After the reading

This is the Gospel of Christ
Praise to Christ our Lord

The Sermon

22   A sermon is preached on Sundays and other Great Festivals, but may be omitted at other times. It may precede or follow the Creed. The Penitence (sections 10-14) may follow the Sermon in either position.

THE NICENE CREED

23   The Creed is said at least on Sundays, other Great Festivals and Festivals.

24   **We believe in one God**
the Father, the Almighty
maker of heaven and earth
of all that is, seen and unseen.

We believe in one Lord, Jesus Christ
the only Son of God
eternally begotten of the Father
God from God, Light from Light
true God from true God
begotten, not made, of one Being with the Father;
through him all things were made.
For us and for our salvation
  he came down from heaven
was incarnate of the Holy Spirit
  and the Virgin Mary
and was made man.
For our sake he was crucified under Pontius Pilate;
he suffered death and was buried.
On the third day he rose again
  in accordance with the Scriptures;
he ascended into heaven
  and is seated at the right hand of the Father.
He will come again in glory
  to judge the living and the dead
and his kingdom will have no end.

We believe in the Holy Spirit, the Lord
   the giver of life
who proceeds from the Father and the Son
who with the Father and the Son is worshipped
   and glorified
who has spoken through the prophets.
We believe in one holy catholic and apostolic Church.
We acknowledge one baptism for the forgiveness of
   sins.
We look for the resurrection of the dead
   and the life of the world to come.   Amen

The Apostles' Creed (section 22 of the Offices) may be used instead of
the Nicene Creed.

The Sermon (and Penitence) may follow.

THE PRAYERS

The Prayers of the Church are offered in one of the four forms following

A

Particular petitions and thanksgivings may be made by individuals
during the silences. One or more sections, other than 29 and 37, may
be omitted.

As we celebrate the holy Eucharist to the glory of God
and in thanksgiving for his mercies, let us pray for his
Church in Christ Jesus and for all people according to
their needs.

Almighty God, our heavenly Father, who promised
through your Son Jesus Christ to hear us when we pray
in his name;

We pray for your Church throughout the world and especially for this diocese, and for *N* our bishop, together with
N our metropolitan (particular thanksgivings or petitions may
follow)

Silence may be kept.

Give your Church power to proclaim the gospel of Christ;
and grant that we and all Christian people may be united
in truth, live together in your love, and reveal your glory
in the world.

Lord, in your mercy
Hear our prayer

31   We thank you, Father, for the resources of the world and
its beauty (particular thanksgivings or petitions may follow)

Silence may be kept.

Give to all a reverence for your creation and make us
worthy stewards of your gifts.

Lord, in your mercy
Hear our prayer

32   We pray for the nations of the world, ... and especially for
this country and its leaders (particular thanksgivings or petitions
may follow)

Silence may be kept.

Give wisdom to those in authority; direct this and every
nation in the way of justice and peace; that all may
honour one another and seek the common good.

Lord, in your mercy
Hear our prayer

33   We pray for our families and friends and those with
special claims upon us (especially ...)

Silence may be kept.

Give grace to all whose lives are closely linked with ours,
that we may serve Christ in them and love one another as
he loves us.

Lord, in your mercy
Hear our prayer

4 We pray for those in trouble, sorrow, need, sickness or any other adversity (especially …)

Silence may be kept.

To all who suffer give courage, healing and a steadfast trust in your love.

Lord, in your mercy
Hear our prayer

5 We remember with thanksgiving your servants who have gone before us (especially …)

Silence may be kept.

According to your promises, grant us with them a share in your eternal kingdom.

Lord, in your mercy
Hear our prayer

6 We bless and praise you for all your saints; for the blessed Virgin Mary, mother of our Lord, for the patriarchs, prophets, apostles and martyrs (especially … whom we remember today). And we commend ourselves and all Christian people to your unfailing love.

Lord, in your mercy
Hear our prayer

7 Merciful Father, accept these our prayers for the sake of your Son, our Saviour Jesus Christ.
Amen

The service continues at 43.

B

38 Particular intentions may be mentioned before this prayer but it is said without interpolation.

39 Almighty God, our heavenly Father, you have taught us to pray and to give thanks for all people:

Receive our prayers for the universal Church, that it may know the power of your Spirit, and that all your children may agree in the truth of your holy word and live in unity and godly love.

We pray for your servant *N* our bishop, together with *N* our metropolitan, and for all other ministers of your word and sacraments, that by their life and teaching your glory may be revealed and all nations drawn to you.

Guide and prosper, we pray, those who strive for the spread of your gospel, and enlighten with your Spirit all places of work, learning and healing.

We pray for those who have authority and responsibility among the nations (especially ...), that, ruling with wisdom and justice, they may promote peace and well-being in the world.

To this congregation and to all your people in their different callings give your heavenly grace, that we may hear your holy word with reverent and obedient hearts, and serve you truly all the days of our life.

In your compassion, Father, comfort and heal those who are in trouble, sorrow, need or sickness.

We praise and thank you for all your saints; for the blessed Virgin Mary, the mother of Jesus Christ our Lord, (for ... whom we remember at this time), and for the heroes of the faith in every generation; and we remember before you your servants who have died, praying that we may enter with them into the fulness of your unending joy.

Grant this, holy Father, for Jesus Christ's sake.

Amen

The service continues at 43.

C

0 Particular intentions may be mentioned before this prayer but it is said without interpolation.

One or more petitions, other than the first or last, may be omitted.

1 Father, we are your children, your Spirit lives in us and we are in your Spirit: hear us, for it is your Spirit who speaks through us as we pray
Lord hear us

Father, you created the heavens and the earth: bless the produce of our land and the works of our hands
Lord hear us

Father, you created us in your own image: teach us to honour you in all your children
Lord hear us

Father, in your steadfast love you provide for your creation: grant good rains for our crops
Lord hear us

Father, you inspired the prophets of old: grant that your Church may faithfully proclaim your truth to the world
Lord hear us

Father, you sent your Son into the world: reveal him to others through his life in us
Lord hear us

Lord Jesus, you sent your apostles to make disciples of all nations: bless the bishops of this province, especially *N* our bishop, together with *N* our metropolitan, and all other ministers of your Church
Christ hear us

Lord Jesus, for your sake men and women forsook all and followed you: call many to serve you in religious communities and in the ordained ministry of your Church
Christ hear us

Lord Jesus, you called your disciples to take up the cross: deepen in each of us a sense of vocation
Christ hear us

You prayed for your Church to be one: unite all Christians that the world may believe
Christ hear us

You forgave the thief on the cross: bring us all to penitence and reconciliation
Christ hear us

You broke down the walls that divide us: bring the people of this world to live in peace and concord
Christ hear us

You taught us through Paul, your apostle, to pray for kings and rulers: bless and guide all who are in authority
Christ hear us

You were rich yet for our sake you became poor: move those who have wealth to share generously with those who are poor
Christ hear us

You sat among the learned, listening and asking them questions: inspire all who teach and all who learn
Christ hear us

You cured by your healing touch and word: heal the sick and bless those who minister to them
Christ hear us

You were unjustly condemned by Pontius Pilate: strengthen our brothers and sisters who are suffering injustice and persecution
Christ hear us

You lived as an exile in Egypt: protect and comfort all refugees
Christ hear us

You knew the love and care of an earthly home: be with migrant workers and protect their families
Christ hear us

You open and none can shut: open the gates of your kingdom to those who have died without hearing your gospel
Christ hear us

You have been glorified in the lives of innumerable saints: give us strength through their prayers to follow in their footsteps
Christ hear us

Father, we know that you are good and that you hear those who call upon you: give to us and to all people what is best for us, that we may glorify you through your Son, Jesus Christ our Lord, who is alive and reigns with you and the Holy Spirit, one God, now and for ever.
Amen

The service continues at 43.

D

2 The Priest or another minister leads intercessions and thanksgivings in which the congregation may be invited to join.

3 The Penitence (sections 10-14) follows if it has not already been used.

THE PEACE

4 A sentence taken from one of the readings or the Gospel, or another appropriate verse of Scripture, may be said (see section 106).

5 **The peace of the Lord be with you always**
Peace be with you

6 The Peace is given according to local custom.

THE PRESENTATION OF GIFTS

47 Alms, and other gifts for the church and the poor, may be presented here
    or after sections 49-50. One of the following prayers may be said

48 Yours, Lord, is the greatness, the power, the glory, the
    splendour, and the majesty; for everything in heaven and
    on earth is yours. All things come from you, and of your
    own do we give you.
    Amen

    or

    Source of all life, the heaven and earth are yours, yet you
    have given us dominion over all things. Receive the fruits
    of our labour offered in love; in the name of Jesus Christ
    our Lord.
    Amen

THE TAKING OF THE BREAD AND WINE

49 The bread and wine are placed on the holy table. The following prayers
    may be said

50 At the taking of the bread

    Blessed are you, Lord, God of all creation. Through your
    goodness we have this bread to offer, which earth has
    given and human hands have made. For us it becomes
    the bread of life.
    Blessed be God for ever

    At the taking of the wine

    Blessed are you, Lord, God of all creation. Through your
    goodness we have this wine to offer, fruit of the vine
    and work of human hands. For us it becomes the cup of
    salvation.
    Blessed be God for ever

THE GREAT THANKSGIVING

1 A choice of four Eucharistic Prayers follows. A fifth Eucharistic Prayer is provided for optional use in **An Alternative Order** (sections 92-102).

THE FIRST EUCHARISTIC PRAYER

2 The Lord be with you
And also with you

Lift up your hearts
We lift them to the Lord

Let us give thanks to the Lord our God
It is right to give him thanks and praise

It is right and indeed our duty and joy, Lord and heavenly Father, God almighty and eternal, always and everywhere to give thanks through Jesus Christ, your only Son our Lord;

3 Section 54 may be omitted when a Proper Preface is used, except when Proper Preface 27 is used.

4 Because through him you have created everything from the beginning and formed us in your own image;

Through him you delivered us from the slavery of sin, when you gave him to be born as man, to die on the cross and to rise again for us;

Through him you claimed us as your own people when you enthroned him with you in heaven, and through him sent out your Holy Spirit, the giver of life;

5 The Proper Preface follows here (see section 103).

6 Therefore with angels and archangels, and with all the company of heaven, we acclaim you and declare the greatness of your glory; we praise you now and for ever saying:

Holy, holy, holy Lord
God of power and might
heaven and earth are full of your glory.
Hosanna in the highest.
Blessed is he who comes in the name of the Lord.
Hosanna in the highest.

Hear us, Father, through your Son Christ our Lord; through him accept our offering of thanks and praise, and send your Holy Spirit upon us and upon these gifts of bread and wine so that they may be to us his body and his blood.

For on the night that he was betrayed he took bread, and when he had given you thanks, he broke it, and gave it to his disciples saying, 'Take this and eat; this is my body which is given for you; do this in remembrance of me.'

So too after supper he took the cup, and when he had given you thanks, he gave it to them saying, 'Drink of it all of you; for this is my blood of the new covenant, which is shed for you and for many for the forgiveness of sins; whenever you drink it, do this in remembrance of me.'

57 Here may be said

So we proclaim the mystery of faith

Christ has died
Christ is risen
Christ will come again.

or

So we acclaim the victory of Christ

Dying you destroyed our death
rising you restored our life.
Lord Jesus, come in glory.

8 Holy Father, with these your gifts, we your people celebrate before you the one perfect sacrifice of Christ our
Lord, his rising from the dead and his ascending to the
glory of heaven.

Gracious Lord, accept us in him, unworthy though we
are, so that we who share in the body and blood of your
Son may be made one with all your people of this and
every age.

Grant that as we await the coming of Christ our Saviour
in the glory and triumph of his kingdom, we may daily
grow into his likeness; with whom, and in whom, and
through whom, by the power of the Holy Spirit, all glory
and honour be given to you, almighty Father, by the
whole company of earth and heaven, throughout all
ages, now and for ever.
Amen

The service continues with the Lord's Prayer at 77.

THE SECOND EUCHARISTIC PRAYER

9 The Lord be with you   or   The Lord is here
And also with you   **His Spirit is with us**

Lift up your hearts
We lift them to the Lord

Let us give thanks to the Lord our God
It is right to give him thanks and praise

It is indeed right, it is our duty and our joy, at all times
and in all places, to give you thanks and praise, holy
Father, heavenly King, almighty and eternal God,
through Jesus Christ your only Son our Lord;

60 Section 61 may be omitted when a Proper Preface is used, except when Proper Preface 27 is used.

61 For he is your living Word; through him you have created all things from the beginning, and formed us in your own image.

   Through him you have freed us from the slavery of sin, giving him to be born as man and to die upon the cross; you raised him from the dead and exalted him to your right hand on high.

   Through him you have sent upon us your holy and life-giving Spirit, and made us a people for your own possession.

62 The Proper Preface follows here (see section 103).

63 Therefore with angels and archangels, and with all the company of heaven, we proclaim your great and glorious Name, for ever praising you and saying:

Holy, holy, holy Lord
God of power and might
heaven and earth are full of your glory.
Hosanna in the highest.

This Anthem may also be used

Blessed is he who comes in the name of the Lord.
Hosanna in the highest.

64 Accept our praises, heavenly Father, through your Son our Saviour Jesus Christ; and as we follow his example and obey his command, grant that by the power of your Holy Spirit these gifts of bread and wine may be to us his body and his blood;

Who in the same night that he was betrayed took bread and gave you thanks; he broke it and gave it to his disciples, saying, 'Take, eat; this is my body which is given for you. Do this in remembrance of me.' In the same way, after supper he took the cup and gave you thanks; he gave it to them, saying, 'Drink this, all of you; this is my blood of the new covenant, which is shed for you and for many, for the forgiveness of sins. Do this, as often as you drink it, in remembrance of me.'

65   Here may be said

Christ has died
Christ is risen
Christ will come again.

66   Therefore, heavenly Father, we remember his offering of himself made once for all upon the cross, and proclaim his mighty resurrection and glorious ascension. As we look for his coming in glory, we celebrate with this bread and this cup his one perfect sacrifice.

Accept through him, our great high priest, this our sacrifice of thanks and praise; and as we eat and drink these holy gifts in the presence of your divine majesty, renew us by your Spirit, inspire us with your love, and unite us in the body of your Son, Jesus Christ our Lord.

Through him, and with him, and in him, by the power of the Holy Spirit, with all who stand before you in earth and heaven, we worship you, Father almighty, in songs of everlasting praise:

Blessing and honour and glory and power
be yours for ever and ever.   Amen

The service continues with the Lord's Prayer at 77.

THE THIRD EUCHARISTIC PRAYER

67 The Lord be with you
   And also with you

   Lift up your hearts
   We lift them to the Lord

   Let us give thanks to the Lord our God
   It is right to give him thanks and praise

   Father, it is our duty and our salvation, always and every-where to give you thanks through your beloved Son, Jesus Christ.

68 Section 69 may be omitted when a Proper Preface is used, except when Proper Preface 27 is used.

69 He is the Word through whom you made the universe, the Saviour you sent to redeem us.

   By the power of the Holy Spirit he took flesh and was born of the Virgin Mary.

   For our sake he opened his arms on the cross; he put an end to death and revealed the resurrection.

   In this he fulfilled your will and won for you a holy people.

70 The Proper Preface follows here (see section 103).

71 And so we join the angels and the saints in proclaiming your glory as we say:

   Holy, holy, holy Lord
   God of power and might
   heaven and earth are full of your glory.
   Hosanna in the highest.
   Blessed is he who comes in the name of the Lord.
   Hosanna in the highest.

Lord, you are holy indeed, the fountain of all holiness. Let your Spirit come upon these gifts to make them holy, so that they may become for us the body and blood of our Lord, Jesus Christ.

Before he was given up to death, a death he freely accepted, he took bread and gave you thanks. He broke the bread, gave it to his disciples, and said: 'Take this, all of you, and eat it: this is my body which will be given up for you.'

When supper was ended, he took the cup. Again he gave you thanks and praise, gave the cup to his disciples, and said: 'Take this, all of you, and drink from it: this is the cup of my blood, the blood of the new and everlasting covenant. It will be shed for you and for all so that sins may be forgiven. Do this in memory of me.'

72 Here may be said

So we proclaim the mystery of faith

**Christ has died
Christ is risen
Christ will come again.**

or

**Dying you destroyed our death
rising you restored our life.
Lord Jesus, come in glory.**

or

**When we eat this bread and drink this cup
we proclaim your death, Lord Jesus
until you come in glory.**

or

**Lord, by your cross and resurrection
 you have set us free.
You are the Saviour of the world.**

73   In memory of his death and resurrection, we offer you, Father, this life-giving bread, this saving cup.

We thank you for counting us worthy to stand in your presence and serve you. May all of us who share in the body and blood of Christ be brought together in unity by the Holy Spirit.

Lord, remember your Church throughout the world; make us grow in love, together with *N* our bishop, and all the clergy.

Remember our brothers and sisters who have gone to their rest in the hope of rising again; bring them and all the departed into the light of your presence.

Have mercy on us all; make us worthy to share eternal life with Mary, the virgin mother of God, with the apostles, and with all the saints who have done your will throughout the ages.

May we praise you in union with them, and give you glory through your Son, Jesus Christ.

Through him, with him, in him, in the unity of the Holy Spirit, all glory and honour is yours, almighty Father, for ever and ever.
Amen

The service continues with the Lord's Prayer at 77.

THE FOURTH EUCHARISTIC PRAYER

74   The Lord be with you
And also with you

Lift up your hearts
We lift them to the Lord

Let us give thanks to the Lord our God
It is right to give him thanks and praise

We give you thanks and praise, almighty God, through your beloved Son, Jesus Christ, our Saviour and Redeemer. He is your living Word, through whom you have created all things.

By the power of the Holy Spirit he took flesh of the Virgin Mary and shared our human nature. He lived and died as one of us, to reconcile us to you, the God and Father of all.

In fulfilment of your will he stretched out his hands in suffering, to bring release to those who place their hope in you; and so he won for you a holy people.

He chose to bear our griefs and sorrows, and to give up his life on the cross, that he might shatter the chains of the evil one, and banish the darkness of sin and death. By his resurrection he brings us into the light of your presence.

Now with all creation we raise our voices to proclaim the glory of your name:

Holy, holy, holy Lord
God of power and might
heaven and earth are full of your glory.
Hosanna in the highest.
Blessed is he who comes in the name of the Lord.
Hosanna in the highest.

Holy and gracious God, accept our praise, through your Son our Saviour Jesus Christ; who on the night he was handed over to suffering and death, took bread and gave you thanks, saying, 'Take, and eat: this is my body which is broken for you.' In the same way he took the cup, saying, 'This is my blood which is shed for you. When you do this, you do it in memory of me.'

75 Here may be said

So we proclaim the mystery of faith

**Christ has died
Christ is risen
Christ will come again.**

76 Remembering, therefore, his death and resurrection, we *offer/bring before* you this bread and this cup, giving thanks that you have made us worthy to stand in your presence and serve you.

We ask you to send your Holy Spirit upon the offering of your holy Church. Gather into one all who share in these sacred mysteries, filling them with the Holy Spirit and confirming their faith in the truth, that together we may praise you and give you glory through your Servant, Jesus Christ.

All glory and honour are yours, Father and Son, with the Holy Spirit in the holy Church, now and for ever.
Amen

THE LORD'S PRAYER

77 As Christ has taught us we are bold to say

**Our Father in heaven
hallowed be your Name
your kingdom come
your will be done
on earth as in heaven.
Give us today our daily bread.
Forgive us our sins
    as we forgive those who sin against us.
Save us from the time of trial
and deliver us from evil.
For the kingdom, the power, and the glory are yours
now and for ever.   Amen**

78   The traditional form of the Lord's Prayer may be used instead of 77 (see p. 14).

(see p. 14).

THE BREAKING OF THE BREAD

79   The Priest breaks the consecrated bread, saying

The bread which we break
is it not a sharing of the body of Christ?

**We, who are many, are one body
for we all partake of the one bread.**

(80)   **Jesus, Lamb of God: have mercy on us.
Jesus, bearer of our sins: have mercy on us.
Jesus, redeemer of the world: give us your peace.**

or

**Lamb of God, you take away the sin of the world:
have mercy on us.
Lamb of God, you take away the sin of the world:
have mercy on us.
Lamb of God, you take away the sin of the world:
grant us peace.**

This may be said after 82 during the distribution of the elements.

THE COMMUNION

(81)   **We do not presume
to come to this your table, merciful Lord
trusting in our own righteousness
but in your manifold and great mercies.
We are not worthy so much as to gather up
the crumbs under your table
but you are the same Lord
whose nature is always to have mercy.**

**Grant us therefore, gracious Lord
so to eat the flesh of your dear Son Jesus Christ
and to drink his blood
that we may evermore dwell in him and he in us.**

82 Draw near and receive the body of our Lord Jesus Christ which he gave for you, and his blood which he shed for you. Feed on him in your hearts by faith with thanksgiving.

83 The Priest and people receive the sacrament.

84 *Minister* The body of Christ (given for you)
   Amen

   Minister The blood of Christ (shed for you)
   Amen

   or

   Minister The body of our Lord Jesus Christ keep you in eternal life.
   Amen

   Minister The blood of our Lord Jesus Christ keep you in eternal life.
   Amen

85 After the people have received, a period of silence may be kept.

What remains of the consecrated bread and wine which is not required for the purposes of communion is consumed either here or at the end of the service.

CONCLUSION

86 Give thanks to the Lord for he is gracious
His mercy endures for ever

(87) Almighty and eternal God, we thank you for feeding us in these holy mysteries with the body and blood of your Son our Saviour Jesus Christ; and for keeping us by your grace in the Body of your Son, the company of all faithful people. Help us to persevere as living members of that holy fellowship, and to grow in love and obedience according to your will; through Jesus Christ our Lord, who lives and reigns with you and the Holy Spirit, one God, now and for ever.
Amen

88 **Father almighty**
we offer ourselves to you
as a living sacrifice
    in Jesus Christ our Lord.
Send us out into the world
    in the power of the Holy Spirit
to live and work
    to your praise and glory.

(89) The peace of God which passes all understanding, keep your hearts and minds in the knowledge and love of God, and of his Son Jesus Christ our Lord; and the blessing of God almighty, the Father, the Son, and the Holy Spirit, be among you, and remain with you always.
Amen

90 Go in peace to love and serve the Lord
In the name of Christ.   Amen

From Easter Day to the Day of Pentecost

Go in peace to love and serve the Lord, Alleluia, Alleluia
In the name of Christ.   Amen.   Alleluia, Alleluia

129

THE CONSECRATION
OF ADDITIONAL ELEMENTS

91 If the consecrated bread and wine do not suffice, the Priest consecrates
more of either or both by saying

Hear us, heavenly Father, and with your Word and
Holy Spirit bless and sanctify this *bread/wine* that it,
also, may be the sacrament of the precious *body/blood* of
your Son Jesus Christ our Lord, who took *bread/the cup*
and said, 'This is my *body/blood*'.
Amen

Or else he may consecrate more of both kinds, saying again the
words of one of the Eucharistic Prayers, from after the Sanctus up
to but not including the Acclamation.

AN ALTERNATIVE ORDER FOR CELEBRATING THE EUCHARIST

92 On informal occasions when a freer form of service is desired, the following rite is used. The permission of the Bishop is required. The rite is not for use at the principal Sunday service.

It requires careful preparation by the Priest and participants.

93 The service includes the following

Gathering in the Lord's name

Offering of praise and penitence

Proclamation of the word of God and response to it

These sections may include readings, music, dance and other art forms, comment, discussion and silence. A reading from a Gospel is always included.

Prayers for the world and the Church

The Peace

The preparation of the table, and the bread and wine

THE GREAT THANKSGIVING

94 The Great Thanksgiving is made in the following form. One of the four Eucharistic Prayers in sections 52-76 may be substituted for it. The form below may also be used at other celebrations of the Eucharist when desired.

95 The Lord be with you   or   The Lord is here
And also with you   **His Spirit is with us**

Lift up your hearts
We lift them to the Lord

Let us give thanks to the Lord our God
It is right to give him thanks and praise

It is indeed right, it is our duty and our joy, to give you thanks, holy Father, through Jesus Christ our Lord.

Through him you have created us in your image; through him you have freed us from sin and death; through him you have made us your own people by the gift of the Holy Spirit.

96 Here may be said

Holy, holy, holy Lord
God of power and might
heaven and earth are full of your glory.
Hosanna in the highest.
Blessed is he who comes in the name of the Lord.
Hosanna in the highest.

97 Hear us, Father, through Christ your Son our Lord, and grant that by the power of your Holy Spirit these gifts of bread and wine may be to us his body and his blood.

Who in the same night that he was betrayed, took bread and gave you thanks; he broke it and gave it to his disciples, saying, 'Take, eat; this is my body which is given for you; do this in remembrance of me.' In the same way, after supper he took the cup and gave you thanks; he gave it to them, saying, 'Drink this, all of you; this is my blood of the new covenant which is shed for you and for many for the forgiveness of sins. Do this as often as you drink it, in remembrance of me.'

98 Here may be said

So we proclaim the mystery of faith

Christ has died
Christ is risen
Christ will come again.

99 Therefore, Father, proclaiming his saving death and resurrection and looking for his coming in glory, we celebrate with this bread and this cup his one perfect sacrifice.

Accept through him, our great high priest, this our sacrifice of thanks and praise, and grant that we who eat this bread and drink this cup may be renewed by your Spirit and grow into his likeness.

Through Jesus Christ our Lord, by whom, and with whom and in whom, all honour and glory be yours, Father, now and for ever.
Amen

100 Then follow

The Lord's Prayer

The Breaking of the Bread

The Sharing of the Gifts of God

The bread and wine of the Eucharist are shared reverently. When all have received, any of the sacrament remaining is consumed.

101 The service concludes with

The Giving of Thanks

102 When a common meal is part of the celebration, it follows here.

PROPER PREFACES

103 **1 Advent**

And now we give you thanks because the day of our deliverance has dawned, and through him you will make all things new, as he comes in power and triumph to judge the world.

2 Christmas Day until the Epiphany; also the Presentation and the Annunciation

And now we give you thanks because by the power of the Holy Spirit he took our nature upon him and was born of the Virgin Mary his mother, that being himself without sin he might make us clean from all sin.

3 The Epiphany

And now we give you thanks because in coming to dwell among us as the Word made flesh, he revealed the radiance of your glory, and brought us out of darkness into your own marvellous light.

4 Ash Wednesday, the First Sunday in Lent, and any weekday until Palm Sunday

And now we give you thanks because through him you have given us the spirit of discipline, that we may triumph over evil and grow in grace.

The Proper Prefaces for the remaining Sundays in Lent may also be used on the weekdays following them.

5 The Second Sunday in Lent; also the Transfiguration

And now we give you thanks because his glory shone forth upon the holy mountain before eyewitnesses of his majesty, and manifested the power and coming of his kingdom.

6 The Third Sunday in Lent

And now we give you thanks because you have promised that whoever drinks the water that he gives, will never thirst again.

7 The Fourth Sunday in Lent

And now we give you thanks because through him you have rescued us from the power of darkness and have brought us into the kingdom of light.

8 The Fifth Sunday in Lent

And now we give you thanks because he has promised that those who believe in him, though they die, shall live.

9 Palm Sunday until Easter Day, excluding Maundy Thursday

And now we give you thanks because for our salvation he was obedient even to death, death on a cross. The tree of defeat became the tree of glory; and where life was lost, there life has been restored.

10(a) Maundy Thursday (at the Renewal of Priestly Vows)

And now we give you thanks because within the royal priesthood of your Church you ordain ministers to proclaim the word of God, to care for your people, to equip them for the work of ministry, and to celebrate the sacraments of the new covenant.

10(b) Maundy Thursday (at the Blessing of Oils, if there is no Renewal of Vows)

And now we give you thanks because having created us in your own image, you recreated us in him, and through anointing with oil, you strengthen and heal us for your service.

10(c) Maundy Thursday (at the Evening Eucharist) and Corpus Christi

And now we give you thanks because he is the true and everliving priest

*who established this eternal sacrifice, and

who offered himself as victim for our deliverance and taught us to do this in remembrance of him, so that by eating the bread of life in a holy meal, we might proclaim his death until he comes.

*This line may be omitted.

11 The Easter Vigil

And now on this Easter night we give you thanks for him, who is our paschal sacrifice, and praise you with a joy too great for words. He is the true Lamb who took away the sin of the world. By his death he conquered death, by rising he restored life to us.

12 Easter Day until Ascension Day

And now we give you thanks for his glorious resurrection from the dead. By his death he has destroyed death, and by his rising again he has restored to us eternal life.

13 Ascension Day until the Day of Pentecost

And now we give you thanks because in his risen body he appeared to his disciples, told them to wait for the promised Holy Spirit who would clothe them with power, and in their sight was taken into heaven to reign with you in glory.

14 The Day of Pentecost

And now we give you thanks because by the Holy Spirit we are led into all truth, and are given power to proclaim your gospel to the nations and to serve you as a royal priesthood.

15 Trinity Sunday

And now we give you thanks because you have revealed your glory as the glory of your Son and of the Holy Spirit: three persons equal in majesty, undivided in splendour, yet one Lord, one God, ever to be worshipped and adored.

16 The Blessed Virgin Mary

And now we give you thanks because through the power of the Holy Spirit the Blessed Virgin Mary, in obedience to your will, became the mother of your Son, who is for ever the Saviour of the world.

17 St Michael and All Angels

And now we give you thanks because you have appointed the angels for your service so that, by them in heaven as by us on earth, the message of your majesty and glory may be ceaselessly proclaimed.

18 All Saints; also Festivals of Saints other than apostles or evangelists

And now we give you thanks for the glorious pledge of the hope of our calling which you have given us in your saints; that, following their example and strengthened by their fellowship, we may run with perseverance the race that is set before us, and with them receive the unfading crown of glory.

19 Apostles and Evangelists

And now we give you thanks because you sent him to be the great shepherd of your flock; who after his resurrection sent forth his apostles to preach the gospel and to teach all nations; and promised to be with them always to the end of time.

20 Commemorations of Martyrs and Other Christian Heroes

And now we give you thanks because you have called us to follow in the footsteps of your saints on earth until we share with them in the fulness of life with you.

21 The Commemoration of the Departed

And now we give you thanks because by his resurrection he has conquered evil and death and banished sorrow and despair. By his victory he has given us eternal life, and delivered us from bondage to sin and the fear of death into the glorious liberty of the children of God.

22 The Dedication Festival

And now we give you thanks because although the heavens which you have created cannot contain your glory, you accept places built by human hands and dedicated to your Name, so that your children, gathering in their Father's house, may there receive your gracious gifts.

23 Baptism and Confirmation (or Proper Preface 14, for the Day of Pentecost, may be used)

And now we give you thanks because in him you have received us as your children, made us citizens of your kingdom, and given us the Holy Spirit to guide us into all truth.

24 Marriage

And now we give you thanks because you have ordained marriage to be a solemn covenant of love between husband and wife in the likeness of Christ's union with his Church.

25 Ordination

And now we give you thanks because within the royal priesthood of your Church you ordain ministers to proclaim the word of God, to care for your people, to equip them for the work of ministry, and to celebrate the sacraments of the new covenant.

26 Healing

And now we give you thanks because you sent him to share our sufferings and bear our sorrows, and revealed through him your power to make us whole.

27 Sundays (when no other Preface is provided)

(a) And now we give you thanks because in love you created us, in justice you condemned us, but in mercy you redeemed us.

(b) And now we give you thanks because today is the first day of the week, when you bid us give you thanks for the resurrection of your Son, whereby sin is overcome and hope restored.

(c) And now we give you thanks because today you have gathered us together at this eucharistic feast, so that we may be renewed in love, joy and peace.

THE TEN COMMANDMENTS

104 Hear the commandments which God has given to his people, and take them to heart.

I am the Lord your God; you shall have no other gods but me.
Amen.   Lord, have mercy

You shall not make an idol of anything and worship it.
Amen.   Lord, have mercy

You shall not make wrong use of the name of the Lord your God.
Amen.   Lord, have mercy

Remember the Lord's day and keep it holy.
Amen.   Lord, have mercy

Honour your father and mother.
Amen.   Lord, have mercy

You shall not commit murder.
Amen.   Lord, have mercy

You shall not commit adultery.
Amen.   Lord, have mercy

You shall not steal.
Amen.   Lord, have mercy

You shall not give false evidence.
Amen.   Lord, have mercy

You shall not covet the possessions of others.
Amen.   Lord, have mercy

SENTENCES

PENITENCE

105 One or more of these Sentences may be used in the Eucharist before 11 or after 14.

Jesus said, 'Come to me, all who labour and are heavy laden, and I will give you rest.'

God so loved the world that he gave his only Son, that whoever believes in him should not perish but have eternal life.

The saying is sure and worthy of full acceptance, that Christ Jesus came into the world to save sinners.

If anyone sins, we have an advocate with the Father, Jesus Christ the righteous; and he is the expiation for our sins.

If we say we have no sin, we deceive ourselves, and the truth is not in us. If we confess our sins, he is faithful and just, and will forgive our sins and cleanse us from all unrighteousness.

When a wicked man turns away from the wickedness he has committed and does what is lawful and right, he shall save his life.

Rend your hearts, and not your garments, and return to the Lord your God: for he is gracious and merciful, slow to anger, and abounding in steadfast love.

THE PEACE

106 One of more of these Sentences may be used in the Eucharist after 44.

GENERAL

Listen to the words of our Saviour Jesus Christ, 'I give you a new commandment: love one another. As I have loved you, so are you to love one another. If there is this love among you, then all will know that you are my disciples.'

If, when you are bringing your gift to the altar, you remember that someone has a grievance against you, leave your gift where it is before the altar. Go, make peace, and only then come and offer your gift.

We for our part have crossed over from death to life; this we know, because we love our brothers and sisters. Anyone who does not love remains in the realm of death.

Listen to the words of our Saviour Jesus Christ, 'Peace I leave with you; my peace I give to you; not as the world gives do I give to you.'

Christ is our peace.
He has reconciled us to God
  in one Body by the cross.
We meet in his name and share his peace.

We are the Body of Christ.
In the one Spirit we were all baptized into one Body.
Let us then pursue all that makes for peace
and builds up our common life.

SEASONAL

Advent and Epiphany

Our Saviour Christ is the Prince of Peace; of the increase of his government and of peace there shall be no end.

Christmas

Our Saviour Christ is the Prince of Peace; of the increase of his government and of peace there shall be no end.

or

The angels praised God and said, 'Glory to God in the highest, and on earth peace among people with whom he is pleased.'

Lent

Being justified by faith, we have peace with God through our Lord Jesus Christ.

Easter

The risen Christ came and stood among his disciples and said, 'Peace be with you.' Then they were glad when they saw the Lord.

Ascension

The risen Christ came and stood among his disciples and said, 'Peace be with you.' Then they were glad when they saw the Lord.

or

He who descended is he who also ascended far above all the heavens, that he might fill all things.

Pentecost

The fruit of the Spirit is love, joy, peace, patience, kindness, goodness, faithfulness, gentleness, self-control. If we live by the Spirit, let us also walk by the Spirit.

or

Be eager to maintain the unity of the Spirit in the bond of peace.

Saints' Days

We are fellow-citizens with the saints, and of the household of God, through Christ our Lord who came and preached peace to those who were far off and those who were near.

Baptism

Let the peace of Christ rule in your hearts; to this peace you were called as members of one Body.

Confirmation

God's love has been poured into our hearts through the Holy Spirit he has given us.

Marriage

God himself dwells in us if we love one another; his love is brought to perfection within us.

or

We love, because he first loved us.

Ordination

The Son of Man came not to be served but to serve, and to give his life as a ransom for many.

COLLECTS
AND READINGS
WITH
SPECIAL SERVICES
FOR LENT AND
EASTER

General Rubrics

1 Collects, and psalms and readings for the Eucharist, are provided for Sundays and other Great Festivals and for Festivals. Suitable canticles are suggested. The appropriate liturgical colour is indicated by an initial beside the title of the day.

2 The Sundays and Great Festivals are grouped as follows:

   1 Those from Advent to Epiphany.

   2 Those from Ash Wednesday to Easter. Special services for this season of the Church's year are included here.

   3 Those from Easter to Corpus Christi.

   4 The remaining Sundays of the Year, which are those which do not fall within the special seasons of Advent, Christmas, Lent and Easter. The Collects and Readings provided for these Sundays are used in the periods after Epiphany and after Pentecost. The dates given under each Sunday indicate when it is used. (See the explanatory note at the beginning of Sundays of the Year.)

3 The references for the readings are to the Revised Standard Version. If another translation is used the passage may need to be extended or reduced slightly.

4 The psalm verses refer to the translation of the Psalms printed in this book and vary in some other translations.

5 One collect only is used, with the following exceptions:

   The Collect for Advent 1 may be used daily throughout Advent after the Collect of the Day.

   The Collect for Ash Wednesday may be said daily in Lent after the Collect of the Day.

   An extra collect is permitted on a Rogation Day, on an Ember Day and Harvest Thanksgiving; also on the Festivals of St Stephen, St John and the Holy Innocents when they occur on the Sunday after Christmas. (Note: the three Festivals last named may be observed on dates out of Christmastide: see Calendar.)

6 The following endings, 'who is alive, and reigns with you and the Holy Spirit, one God, now and for ever', or 'who lives and reigns with you and the Holy Spirit, one God, now and for ever', may be added to those collects which conclude in any of these ways:

'through Jesus Christ our Lord ...'

'through our Lord and Saviour Jesus Christ ...'

'for Jesus Christ's sake ...'

7 Rules for transferring Festivals are in the rubrics with the Calendar.

Sundays and other Great Festivals
Advent to Epiphany

THE FIRST SUNDAY IN ADVENT   P
between 27 November and 3 December

The Collect

Almighty Father
your Son came to us in humility as our saviour
and at the last day he will come again
　in glory as our judge:
give us grace to turn away from darkness
　to the light of Christ
that we may be ready to welcome him
and to enter into his kingdom;
where he lives and reigns with you and the Holy Spirit
one God, for ever and ever.

or

Almighty God, give us grace to cast away the works of
darkness, and to put on the armour of light, now in the
time of this mortal life, in which your Son Jesus Christ
came to visit us in great humility; that in the last day
when he shall come again in his glorious majesty to judge
the living and the dead, we may rise to the life immortal;
through him who lives and reigns with you and the Holy
Spirit, now and for ever.

One of these collects may be used daily in Advent after the Collect of the
Day.

The Readings

YEAR A

Isaiah 2:1-5	God's kingdom of peace
Psalm 122	
Romans 13:11-14	Put on the armour of light
Matthew 24:36-44	Be ready for the coming of the Lord

YEAR B

Isaiah 63:16–64:8	You are our Father; come to us
Psalm 80:1-7	
1 Corinthians 1:3-9	God's grace and faithfulness
Mark 13:32-37	Watch, therefore

YEAR C

Jeremiah 33:14-16	The Lord is our righteousness
Psalm 25:1-10	
1 Thessalonians 3:9-13	Abounding in love to one another
Luke 21:25-36	Your liberation is near
Proper Preface 1	Canticle 2, 16, 18

THE SECOND SUNDAY IN ADVENT   P
between 4 and 10 December

The Collect

Blessed Lord
you gave us the Scriptures
   to point the way to salvation:
teach us to hear them, read them
   and study them with love and prayer
and strengthen us by their inspiration
to hold firm the hope of eternal life;
through Jesus Christ our Lord.

or

Blessed Lord, you caused all holy Scriptures to be written for our learning: teach us so to hear them, read, mark, learn and inwardly digest them, that strengthened by your holy word we may embrace and ever hold fast the hope of everlasting life, which you have given us in our Saviour Jesus Christ; who is alive and reigns with you and the Holy Spirit, one God, now and for ever.

The Readings

YEAR A

Isaiah 11:1-10	The character of the awaited Messiah
Psalm 72:1-8	
Romans 15:4-13	Joy, peace, and hope
Matthew 3:1-12	John proclaims the coming kingdom

YEAR B

Isaiah 40:1-11	Preparing the way of the Lord
Psalm 85:8-13	
2 Peter 3:8-15a	The day of the Lord will come, unexpected
Mark 1:1-8	John prepares the way of the Lord

YEAR C

Baruch 5:1-9	Put on the beauty of the glory from the Lord
or	
Malachi 3:1-4	The Lord sends a messenger to prepare his way
Psalm 126	
Philippians 1:3-11	Prepare yourselves for the day of Christ
Luke 3:1-6	The message of John the Baptist
Proper Preface 1	Canticle 2, 16, 18

THE THIRD SUNDAY IN ADVENT   P
between 11 and 17 December

The Collect

Merciful Father
you sent John the Baptist
　to announce the coming of your Son:
inspire all who minister in your Church
　to prepare for his coming again
　by turning us from disobedience
　to your loving service;
through Jesus Christ our Lord.

or

Almighty God, you sent John the Baptist to proclaim the
coming of your Son: inspire the ministers and stewards of
your word and sacraments to prepare for his coming
again by turning the hearts of the disobedient to the
wisdom of your law; through Jesus Christ our Lord, who
is alive and reigns with you in the unity of the Holy
Spirit, now and for ever.

The Readings

YEAR A

Isaiah 35:1-10	God is coming to save
Psalm 146:5-12	
James 5:7-10	Be patient until the coming of the Lord
Matthew 11:2-11	Christ bears witness to John and to himself

YEAR B

Isaiah 61:1-4, 8-11	Sent by the Spirit of the Lord
Psalm 45:1-7	
1 Thessalonians 5:16-24	May you be ready for the Lord's coming
John 1:6-8, 19-28	The one who is to come, stands among you

YEAR C

Zephaniah 3:14-20   Rejoicing at God's restoration of
                     his people

For the psalm:
  Canticle 2   Jerusalem, City of Peace
Philippians 4:4-9   Rejoice, the Lord is near
Luke 3:7-18   The preaching of John the
                     Baptist

Proper Preface 1   Canticle 16, 18

THE FOURTH SUNDAY IN ADVENT   P
between 18 and 24 December

The Collect

Heavenly Father
you chose the Virgin Mary
   to be the mother of our Lord and Saviour:
fill us with your grace
that in all things we may, like her, accept your holy will
and with her rejoice in your salvation;
through Jesus Christ our Lord.

or

Almighty and eternal God, purify our hearts and minds,
that when your Son Jesus Christ comes again in glory, he
may find in us a home prepared for himself; who is alive
and reigns with you in the unity of the Holy Spirit, now
and for ever.

The Readings

YEAR A

Isaiah 7:10-16   The promise of a Son
Psalm 24
Romans 1:1-7   Jesus, Son of David, Son of God
Matthew 1:18-25   Jesus is born of Mary, betrothed
                     to Joseph

YEAR B

2 Samuel 7:8-16	God's promise to the House of David
Psalm 89:19-30	
Romans 16:25-27	God's mystery revealed in his Son
Luke 1:26-38	God calls Mary, and she obeys

YEAR C

Micah 5:2-4	A shepherd will come from Bethlehem
Psalm 80:1-7	
Hebrews 10:5-10	I am come to do your will
Luke 1:39-55	Mary visits Elizabeth to their great joy

Proper Preface 1	Canticle The Song of Mary
	(Evening Prayer section 58)

CHRISTMAS EVE   P

The Collect

God our Father
we rejoice to remember the birth of your Son:
help us by faith to receive him as our redeemer
that we may face him with confidence
    when he comes to be our judge;
who is alive and reigns with you and the Holy Spirit
one God, for ever and ever.

or

O God, you make us glad with the yearly remembrance
of the birth of your only Son, Jesus Christ: grant that we
may joyfully receive him as our redeemer and with sure
confidence stand before him when he comes to be our
judge; who lives and reigns with you and the Holy Spirit,
one God, world without end.

CHRISTMAS   W
Midnight, or very early

The Collect

Heavenly Father
you made this holy night radiant
   with the brightness of your Son Jesus Christ:
help us to welcome him as the world's true Light
and bring us to eternal joy in his kingdom;
where he lives and reigns with you and the Holy Spirit
one God, for ever and ever.

or

Eternal God, you have caused this most holy night to
shine with the brightness of the Light of life; grant that
we who have known the revelation of that Light on earth,
may also enjoy him perfectly in heaven; where with you
and the Holy Spirit he lives and reigns, one God, in glory
everlasting.

The Readings

YEARS A, B, C

Isaiah 9:2-7   Unto us a Son is given

or

Isaiah 62:6-7, 10-12   Salvation comes
Psalm 96 or 97
Titus 2:11-14   The grace of God has appeared

or

Titus 3:4-7   We are saved by his love for us
Luke 2:1-20   The Saviour is born

Proper Preface 2   Canticle 5, 10, 11

CHRISTMAS DAY W
25 December

The Collect

God most high
you sent your Son into the world
   to take our nature upon him
   and to be born of a pure Virgin:
grant that he may continually live in us
   and reign on earth as he reigns in heaven;
where he lives with you and the Holy Spirit
one God, for ever and ever.

or

Almighty God, you have given us your only begotten Son
to take our nature upon him and to be born of a pure
Virgin: grant that we, who have been born again and
made your children by adoption and grace, may daily
be renewed by your Holy Spirit; through our Lord
Jesus Christ, who lives and reigns with you and the same
Spirit, one God, now and for ever.

The Readings

Isaiah 52:7-10	Good tidings of salvation
Psalm 98	
Hebrews 1:1-12	God now speaks to us through the Son
John 1:1-14 (or 1-18)	The Word is made flesh
Proper Preface 2	Canticle The Song of the Church (Morning Prayer section 21), 5, 10, 11

THE FIRST SUNDAY AFTER CHRISTMAS   W
between 26 December and 1 January

The Collect

Heavenly Father
you sent your Son into the world to do your will:
keep the pattern of his life always before our eyes
and inspire us to work for the coming of his kingdom;
who is alive and reigns with you and the Holy Spirit
one God, for ever and ever.

or

Almighty God, you have given us your only begotten Son
to take our nature upon him and to be born of a pure
Virgin: grant that we, who have been born again and
made your children by adoption and grace, may daily
be renewed by your Holy Spirit; through our Lord
Jesus Christ, who lives and reigns with you and the same
Spirit, one God, now and for ever.

The Readings

YEAR A

Isaiah 63:7-9	He has become our Saviour
Psalm 111	
Hebrews 2:10-18	He has become one with us in every respect
Matthew 2:13-23	The escape into Egypt

YEAR B

Isaiah 61:10–62:3	God gives salvation and righteousness
Psalm 111	
Galatians 4:4-7	God adopts us as his children
Luke 2:22-40	The presentation of Jesus in the Temple

YEAR C

Ecclesiasticus 3:3-7, 14-17	Family life
or	
1 Samuel 2:18-20, 26	The boy Samuel grows up
Psalm 111	
Colossians 3:12-17	Life in Christ
Luke 2:41-52	The boy Jesus found in the Temple
Proper Preface 2	Canticle 10, 11, 14

THE SECOND SUNDAY AFTER CHRISTMAS   W
between 2 and 5 January

The Collect

God our Father
you wonderfully created us in your image
and yet more wonderfully restored us
   through your Son Jesus Christ:
grant that we may share his divine life
   as he shares our humanity;
who is alive and reigns with you
in the unity of the Holy Spirit
one God, for ever and ever.

or

Almighty Father, you wonderfully created us in your
own image and yet more wonderfully restored us: grant
that as your Son our Lord Jesus Christ shared our humanity, so we may be partakers of his divine nature; through
the same your Son Jesus Christ, who is alive and reigns
with you and the Holy Spirit, now and for ever.

The Readings

YEARS A, B, C

Jeremiah 31:7-14	The redemption of God's people
or	
Ecclesiasticus 24:1-12	The Wisdom of God comes to earth
Psalm 147:12-20	
Ephesians 1:1-6, 15-18	Chosen by God to be his children
John 1:1-18	We have seen his glory
Proper Preface 2	Canticle 10, 11, 15

The Collect and Readings for the Epiphany may be used instead of the above.

THE EPIPHANY OF OUR LORD   W
6 January

The Collect

Sovereign Lord
by a star you led the wise men
  to an Infant who is the Light of the world:
let his light shine on every nation
  and fill the whole world with your glory;
through Jesus Christ our Lord.

or

Almighty Father, by the leading of a star you revealed
your only-begotten Son to the peoples of the earth: in
your mercy grant that we who know you now by faith,
may after this life come to the vision of your glorious
Godhead; through Jesus Christ our Lord.

Collects and Readings

The Readings

YEARS A, B, C

Isaiah 60:1-6	The glory of the Lord
Psalm 72:1-14	
Ephesians 3:1-12	The whole universe is to know God's purpose
Matthew 2:1-12	The wise men come to worship Christ

Proper Preface 3   Canticle 1, 10, 15

On the weekdays following the Epiphany, the Collect for the Epiphany is used, unless other provision is made.

Between the Epiphany and Ash Wednesday the collects and readings are those of Sundays of the Year, beginning with the First Sunday of the Year on p. 247.

160

Ash Wednesday to Easter
Preface

The joyful commemoration of the events of the first Easter morning formed the centre and climax of the Church's liturgical year from the earliest times. The all-night vigil which preceded the Eucharist at dawn was originally a time of preparation, but soon became an integral part of the celebration of the resurrection of Christ and the redemption which he won for his people, so that it was seen as a most appropriate occasion to administer baptism, the sacrament of rebirth.

This preparation moved back to include first of all Holy Week, and then ultimately the whole Lenten Fast, recalling the forty days of our Lord's temptation in the wilderness. At the Reformation the ceremonies associated with particular days in this period (e.g. Ash Wednesday or Palm Sunday) were for the most part not included in the Book of Common Prayer, but have won wide acceptance over the years, and are now very much part of the liturgical tradition of our Communion. These services reflect that process and attempt to restore more fully the riches of our Christian heritage. This is especially true of the Easter Vigil, and the opportunity given to the congregation in the course of that service to renew their baptismal promises means that Lent can become a more meaningful time of preparation. The annual reaffirmation of our commitment to Christ is also a fitting response to the liturgical proclamation of our Saviour's death and resurrection.

Brief notes have been inserted into the texts to assist in an understanding of the background and meaning of particular services.

ASH WEDNESDAY P

Today as the Church sets out on its Lenten journey to the Easter Vigil the theme is penitence. Ashes are blessed and used as a symbol of repentance. Those who wish go to the altar rails to be marked with a cross of ashes on their forehead.

1 Ashes made from the palms of the previous Palm Sunday are placed in a bowl on the altar or on a table in a convenient place.

AT THE EUCHARIST

The Collect

2 Almighty and holy God
your Son, in obedience to the Spirit
   fasted forty days in the desert:
give us grace to discipline ourselves
that we may press on towards Easter
   with eager faith and love;
through Jesus Christ our Lord.

or

Almighty and everlasting God, you hate nothing you have made and forgive the sins of all who are penitent: create in us new and contrite hearts, that lamenting our sins and acknowledging our weakness, we may obtain from you, the God of all mercy, perfect remission and forgiveness; through Jesus Christ our Lord.

One of these collects may be used daily until Palm Sunday after the Collect of the Day.

The Readings

3 Joel 2:12-18   Return to God and repent
Psalm 51:1-12
2 Corinthians 5:17–6:2   Be reconciled to God
Matthew 6:1-6, 16-18   Give, pray and fast

or

Isaiah 58:1-8	Genuine fasting
1 Corinthians 9:24-27	The Christian athlete
Matthew 6:16-21	True fasting and heavenly treasure

Proper Preface 4   Canticle 3, 13, 14, 19

4   A sermon may be preached.

The Blessing and Giving of Ashes

5   The Priest addresses the congregation in these or similar words

Dear friends in Christ, at the Christian Passover we celebrate year by year our redemption through the death and
resurrection of our Lord Jesus Christ. Since early days the
Church has kept the season of Lent as a time of preparation for Easter. We begin Lent by remembering the need
for repentance. So let us ask God our Father to bless these
ashes to our use. They have been made from the palms
with which we greeted Christ our King with joy last Palm
Sunday. They are a sign that we mean to prepare ourselves with penitence for Easter.

6   Let us pray

Lord, bless these ashes to our use
and grant that they may remind us of our mortality
    and of our need of repentance
so that we may keep Lent faithfully
in preparation for the joy of Easter.
We ask this in the name of Christ our Lord.
Amen

7   The Priest addresses the congregation

Remember that you are dust, and to dust you shall
return.

8   The Priest places ashes on those who come forward, saying to each

Turn away from sin and believe the good news.

And each answers

Amen

When all have received ashes, the Priest facing the congregation says

Remember that you are dust, and to dust you shall return.

9   Having washed his hands, the Priest says

Return to the Lord with all your heart; leave the past in ashes and turn to God with tears and fasting, for he is slow to anger and ready to forgive.

10   The Prayers of the Church are offered in this form

God our Father, we praise you that you are always ready to forgive the penitent. Bring us by your Spirit to true repentance and the joy of knowing your forgiveness. Accept through Jesus Christ our Lenten acts of love and sacrifice. Prepare us to celebrate his Passover and to share his risen life.

Lord, in your mercy
Hear our prayer

Father, we pray for your Church throughout the world, for *N* our metropolitan, and in this diocese for *N* our bishop, the clergy and people. Free us from dependence on material goods and the worship of power, and from all that hinders our union with you.

Lord, in your mercy
Hear our prayer

Father, we pray for our country and all in authority. Purge our land of all that is contrary to your will. Bring us all to know Christ as the way, the truth and the life, that we may live in harmony with one another.

Lord, in your mercy
Hear our prayer

Father, we pray for all who suffer, and especially for victims of greed and violence. Make your love known to them and to those who cause suffering.

Lord, in your mercy
Hear our prayer

Heavenly Father, we commend to your loving care all who will die during this Lent. Bring them and all the departed (or Bring us all) through the passion and death of your Son to share in the glory of his resurrection.

We offer these prayers in the name of Jesus Christ our Lord.
Amen

The Eucharist continues with the Peace.

THE GIVING OF ASHES OUTSIDE THE EUCHARIST

1 Ashes may be given outside the Eucharist in the following way:

   Morning or Evening Prayer is said up to and including the Penitence. Then follow sections 1-10, the service ending with the Grace or with a blessing.

2 Ashes previously blessed by a priest, may be given by a deacon or lay minister as at 7-9 above, the blessing at 6 being omitted, and the introduction at 5 being altered to

Dear friends in Christ, at the Christian Passover we celebrate year by year our redemption through the death and resurrection of our Lord Jesus Christ. Since early days the Church has kept the season of Lent as a time of preparation for Easter.

We begin Lent by remembering the need for repentance. These ashes, made from last year's palms, have been blessed. They are a sign that we mean to prepare ourselves with penitence for Easter.

SUNDAYS IN LENT

THE FIRST SUNDAY IN LENT   P

The Collect

Merciful Father
your Son was tempted as we are
    yet without sin:
be with us in our weakness
    that we may know your power to save;
through Jesus Christ our Lord.

or

Almighty God, your Son fasted forty days and forty
nights in the desert: give us grace to use such discipline,
that our flesh being subdued to the Spirit, we may always
obey your will in righteousness and holiness, to your
honour and glory; through Jesus Christ our Lord.

The Readings

YEAR A

Genesis 2:7-9; 3:1-7	The creation and fall
Psalm 51:1-13	
Romans 5:12-19	The obedience of Christ, the new Adam
Matthew 4:1-11	Jesus conquers temptation

YEAR B

Genesis 9:8-17	God makes a covenant with Noah
Psalm 25:1-10	
1 Peter 3:18-22	Water the symbol of baptism which saves us
Mark 1:9-15	The baptism and temptation of Jesus

YEAR C

Deuteronomy 26:1-11	Thanksgiving for God's loving care
Psalm 91:9-16	
Romans 10:8-13	Salvation through Christ
Luke 4:1-13	Jesus conquers temptation
Proper Preface 4	Canticle 3, 14, 19

THE SECOND SUNDAY IN LENT   P

The Collect

Almighty Father
the disciples saw your Son in glory
  before he suffered on the cross:
grant that by faith
  in his death and resurrection
we may triumph
  in the power of his victory;
through Jesus Christ our Lord.

or

Almighty Father, your Son was revealed in majesty
before he suffered death upon the cross: give us faith to
perceive his glory and strengthen us to bear the
cross; through the same Jesus Christ our Lord.

The Readings

YEAR A

Genesis 12:1-9	The call of Abraham
Psalm 33:17-21	
Romans 4:1-5, 13-17	
(or 1-17)	The faith of Abraham
Matthew 17:1-9	The transfiguration of Jesus

YEAR B

Genesis 17:1-10, 15-19	The covenant with Abraham
Psalm 127	
Philippians 3:14–4:1	Our transfiguration
Mark 9:2-10	The beloved Son transfigured

YEAR C

Genesis 22:1-18	The sacrifice of Isaac
Psalm 116:11-16	
Romans 8:31b-34	God gave up his own Son
Luke 9:28-36	As he prayed, he was transfigured

Proper Preface 5   Canticle 3, 13, 19

THE THIRD SUNDAY IN LENT   P

The Collect

Gracious Father
your Son is the source of living water:
grant that the gift of his Spirit
    may be to us a spring of water
    welling up to eternal life;
through Jesus Christ our Lord.

or

Loving Lord, grant your people grace to resist the
temptations of the world, the flesh and the devil, and
with pure hearts to follow you the only God; through
Jesus Christ our Lord.

The Readings

YEAR A

Exodus 17:3-7	Water from the rock
Psalm 95	
Romans 5:1-11	Salvation through God's love in Christ

John 4:5-26	
(or 5-42)	Christ, the water of life

YEAR B

Exodus 20:1-17	The Ten Commandments
Psalm 19:7-14	
1 Corinthians 1:22-25	Christ crucified, the wisdom of God
John 2:13-22	The cleansing of the Temple

YEAR C

Exodus 3:1-15	The call of Moses at the burning bush
Psalm 103:1-13	
1 Corinthians 10:1-13	Warnings from the history of Israel
Luke 13:1-9	Repentance is our urgent need
Proper Preface 6	Canticle 3, 13, 14

THE FOURTH SUNDAY IN LENT   P

The Collect

Eternal Father
your Son is the Light of the world:
dispel the darkness of our sins
   with your celestial brightness;
through Jesus Christ our Lord.

or

Lord God, we cannot put our trust in anything that we do: mercifully grant that by your power we may be defended against all adversity; through Jesus Christ our Lord.

169

The Readings

YEAR A

1 Samuel 16:1-13	Samuel anoints David
Psalm 23	
Ephesians 5:8-14	Walking in the light of Christ
John 9:1-25 (or 1-41)	Christ gives sight to the man born blind

YEAR B

2 Chronicles 36:14-23	God's wrath and mercy towards Israel
Psalm 137:1-6	
Ephesians 2:4-10	The gift of salvation to those dead in sin
John 3:14-21	The Son is sent to save the world

YEAR C

Joshua 5:9-12	Passover in the Promised Land
Psalm 34:1-8	
2 Corinthians 5:16-21	Be reconciled to God
Luke 15:1-3, 11-32	The father and his two sons
Proper Preface 7	Canticle 7, 14, 19

THE FIFTH SUNDAY IN LENT　　　　P

The Collect

Holy God and Lord of life
by the death and resurrection
　of your Son Jesus Christ
you delivered and saved the world:
grant that by faith in him who suffered on the cross
　we may triumph in the power of his victory;
through Jesus Christ our Lord.

or

Loving Father, you delivered and saved us all by the cross and passion of your Son Jesus Christ: grant that by steadfast faith in the merits of his sacrifice we may find help and salvation, and may triumph in the power of his victory; through Jesus Christ our Lord.

The Readings

YEAR A

Ezekiel 37: 1-14 — New life through the Spirit of God

Psalm 116: 1-9

Romans 8: 6-11 — The life-giving Spirit

John 11: 17-45 (or 1-45) — Christ the resurrection and the life

YEAR B

Jeremiah 31: 31-34 — Promise of a new covenant

Psalm 51: 10-17

Hebrews 5: 7-9 — His obedience brings our salvation

John 12: 20-33 — Through death, a rich harvest

YEAR C

Isaiah 43: 16-21 — The salvation of God's people

Psalm 126

Philippians 3: 8-14 — I want only to know Christ

John 8: 1-11 — The woman taken in adultery

Proper Preface 8 — Canticle 10, 13, 19

PALM SUNDAY R

THE SUNDAY OF THE PASSION

Today the Church sets forth the opening event of Holy Week, Christ's triumphal entry into Jerusalem. The congregation joins in the procession where possible, as an act of loyalty to Christ. The Scripture readings which follow, and the solemn reading or singing of the Passion, take us to the heart of this week.

COMMEMORATION OF THE LORD'S ENTRY INTO JERUSALEM

The Procession

13 The congregation assembles in a suitable place away from the church to which the procession will go.

Where this is not possible, all is done inside the church, and if possible some or all of the congregation take part in the procession.

The people bring palm or other branches, or palm crosses, or else they are given them as they arrive.

The Priest goes to the place where the people have assembled.

14 This acclamation is sung

Hosanna to the Son of David, the King of Israel.
Blessed is he who comes in the name of the Lord.
Hosanna in the highest.

15 The Priest addresses the congregation in these or similar words

Dear friends in Christ, during Lent we have been preparing by works of love and self-sacrifice for the celebration of our Lord's Paschal Mystery. Today we come together to begin this solemn celebration in union with the whole Church throughout the world. Christ enters his own city to complete his work as our Saviour, to suffer, to die, and to rise again. Let us go with him in faith that, united with him in his sufferings, we may share his risen life.

16   The Priest blesses the palms which the people hold up before him.

Let us pray

Eternal God
bless these palms to our use:
grant that we who have received them
may ever hail as King, and love as Saviour
your Son Jesus Christ our Lord.
Amen

17   Then is announced

A reading from the Gospel according to *Matthew/Mark/ Luke*

Glory to Christ our Saviour

YEAR A	Matthew 21: 1-11
YEAR B	Mark 11: 1-10
YEAR C	Luke 19: 28-40

This is the Gospel of Christ
Praise to Christ our Lord

18   The Priest addresses the congregation in these or similar words

My brothers and sisters, we have heard how the crowds who welcomed Christ to Jerusalem cut branches from the trees to do him honour. During the procession, let us hold up our *palms/branches*, and praise Christ our King and Saviour.

Let us go forth in peace
In the name of the Lord

During the procession, hymns in honour of Christ the King, such as 'All glory, laud and honour', or psalms such as 24 and 47 may be sung.

19   The Eucharist follows the procession, beginning with the Collect of the Day.

The Service without Procession

20 The palm ceremonies take place in the church in which the Eucharist is to be celebrated. As they arrive the people are given branches or crosses.

During or after the entry of the Priest the acclamation at 14 is said.

The Priest greets the people, and sections 15-17 follow.

21 There is no procession. The Eucharist follows, beginning with the Penitence.

The Collect

22 Eternal Father
your Son our Saviour Jesus Christ
fulfilled your will by taking our nature
   and giving his life for us:
help us to follow the example of his humility
   by walking in the way of the cross;
through Jesus Christ our Lord.

or

Almighty and everlasting Father, in your tender love towards us you sent your Son our Saviour Jesus Christ to take upon him our nature and to suffer death upon the cross: grant that we may follow the example of his patience, and also be made partakers of his resurrection; through Jesus Christ our Lord.

The Readings

23 YEARS A, B, C

Isaiah 50:4-9a	The Lord's suffering Servant
Psalm 31:9-16	
Philippians 2:5-11	The obedience and exaltation of Christ
Proper Preface 9	Canticle 13, 14, 19

24 Then is announced without response

The Passion of our Lord Jesus Christ according to *Matthew/Mark/Luke*

YEAR A	Matthew 26:14–27:66	or	Matthew 27:11-54
YEAR B	Mark 14:1–15:47	or	Mark 15:1-39
YEAR C	Luke 22:14–23:56	or	Luke 23:1-49

25 After the Sermon and Creed, the Prayers of the Church follow in this form

Father, we pray for the Church throughout the world and especially for this diocese and *N* our bishop, together with *N* our metropolitan. Give your people power to witness in word and deed to the crucified Lord and bring many to acknowledge him as their King and Saviour.

Lord, in your mercy
Hear our prayer

Father, we pray for those who are suffering persecution for the name of Christ. Give them grace to remain faithful, to pray for their persecutors, and to overcome hatred by the power of the cross.

Lord, in your mercy
Hear our prayer

Father, we pray for the world's outcasts. Set us free to recognise Christ in them. Lead them by your Spirit to find their hope in him.

Lord, in your mercy
Hear our prayer

Father, we pray for ourselves and all in this parish. Forgive us our many betrayals and denials of Christ. Enable us to share his sufferings and to know the power of his resurrection.

We ask this for the sake of Jesus Christ our King and Saviour.
Amen

The Eucharist continues with the Peace.

MONDAY, TUESDAY, AND WEDNESDAY
IN HOLY WEEK   P or R

The Collect is that for Palm Sunday.

The Readings

MONDAY

Isaiah 42:1-7	The Servant of the Lord
Psalm 27:1-8	
Hebrews 9:11-15	Christ our eternal sacrifice
John 12:1-8	Mary anoints Jesus in Bethany

TUESDAY

Isaiah 49:1-6	The second Servant Song
Psalm 71:1-12	
1 Corinthians 1:18-31	Christ, the power and the wisdom of God
John 12:27-36	I will draw everyone to me

WEDNESDAY

Isaiah 50:4-9a	The third Servant Song
Psalm 70	
Hebrews 12:1-3	Our eyes fixed on Jesus
John 13:21-30	The betrayal of Jesus
or	
Mark 12:1-11	Tenants kill the son of the owner of the vineyard

Proper Preface 9	Canticle 13, 14, 19

The Passion narratives as set out in the readings for Palm Sunday may replace the Gospel readings provided above.

176

MAUNDY THURSDAY
THE CHRISM EUCHARIST W

Since early times the holy oils used by the Church have been blessed on this morning. This is the prerogative of the Bishop, and because Maundy Thursday is associated with the Eucharist and therefore with the priesthood, the Bishop has traditionally celebrated the Eucharist in company with the priests of his diocese. An opportunity is given during the Eucharist for the priests to renew their ordination vows.

26 During the morning, the Bishop celebrates the Chrism Eucharist (concelebrating, if he desires, with the priests of the diocese).

The Blessing of the Oils may be preceded by the Renewal of Priestly Vows.

At the discretion of the Bishop, the Blessing of Oils and the Renewal of Priestly Vows may take place at some other time.

The Gloria is said.

THE RENEWAL OF PRIESTLY VOWS

27 When the Renewal does not take place the service continues at 32.

The Collect

28 Father
you anointed your only Son
   high priest of the new covenant
and have given your priests a share
   in his consecration:
make them faithful witnesses
   to his saving work;
through Jesus Christ our Lord.

The Readings

29 Isaiah 61:1-9   The ministry given by the Spirit
                                        of the Lord

   Psalm 89:21-27
   Revelation 1:4b-8   The royal priesthood
   Luke 4:16-21   Christ's ministry in the power
                                        of the Spirit

Proper Preface 10(a)   Canticle 12

30 After the Gospel, or Sermon if there is one, the Bishop says to his priests

My brothers, with wisdom and love Christ planned that
his royal priesthood should continue in the Church after
his ascension.

He grants a share in this royal priesthood to all
whom he makes his own in baptism, and from them he
appoints by the laying on of hands some to a special
priestly ministry.

He has appointed us his priests to show forth in his
name the sacrifice of our redemption, as we set before
God's family his paschal meal. He has called us to lead
his holy people in love, nourishing them with his word,
and strengthening them with the sacraments.

Let us renew our dedication to his service.

I ask therefore

Do you now before God, in the presence of his Church,
commit yourself anew to the trust and responsibility of
the priesthood to which you are called?
I do

Do you believe the holy Scriptures as uniquely revealing
the word of God and containing all things necessary for
eternal salvation through faith in Jesus Christ?
I do

Do you believe the doctrine of the Christian faith which
this church has received, and will you expound and teach
it with diligence?
I believe it and will so do

Will you be ready to banish error in doctrine with sound
teaching based on the holy Scriptures?
With God's help, I will

Will you accept the discipline of this church, and
reverently obey your Bishop and other ministers set over
you in the Lord?
With God's help, I will

Will you be diligent in prayer, in reading holy Scripture, and in all studies that will deepen your faith and fit you to overcome error by the truth of the gospel?
With God's help, I will

Will you endeavour to minister the word of God and his sacraments with such reverence and joy that God's people may be built up in holiness and love?
With God's help, I will

Will you help those in your care to discover and use to God's glory the gifts and ministries he gives them?
With God's help, I will

Will you strive to fashion your own life and that of your household according to the way of Christ?
With God's help, I will

Will you promote unity, peace and love among God's people, and in all things seek the glory of the Lord Christ?
With God's help, I will

Almighty God who has given you the will to do all these things, give you the strength to perform them; that he may complete his work which he has begun in you; through Jesus Christ our Lord.
Amen

31 The Bishop calls the people to prayer

My brothers and sisters, pray for your priests. Ask the Lord to bless them with the fulness of his love and to make them faithful stewards of his mysteries and diligent teachers of his gospel, so that they may be leaders in the way of salvation.

Lord, in your mercy
Hear our prayer

Pray also for me that, despite my unworthiness, I may faithfully fulfil the office of bishop which the Lord has entrusted to me. Pray that I may become more like our

179

High Priest and Good Shepherd, the teacher and servant of all, and so be a genuine sign of Christ's loving presence among you.

Lord, in your mercy
Hear our prayer

Pray also for the wives and families of our priests. Ask the Lord to bless them and to sustain them in his love, that they may share in the fellowship of the gospel. Pray for the homes of all our clergy that Christ's presence may be found there.

Lord, in your mercy
Hear our prayer

May the Lord in his love keep you ever close to him, and may he bring us all to the fulness of eternal life.
Amen

THE BLESSING OF THE OILS

32 The Blessing of the Oils, which is reserved to the Bishop, follows the Renewal of Priestly Vows. If there is no Renewal, it follows the Gospel and Sermon. The Bishop, at his discretion, may bless the Oil of the Sick before the doxology of the Eucharistic Prayer, and the Chrism after the Communion.

Olive oil is used for the Oil of the Sick; olive oil which has previously been mixed with balsam or some other perfume is used for the Chrism.

A table is placed in some convenient position. The Oils are either placed on the table before the service, or else they are solemnly brought into church before they are to be blessed.

The Collect (when there is no Renewal of Vows)

33 Heavenly Father
you anointed your Son Jesus Christ
with the Holy Spirit and with power
to bring us the blessings of your kingdom:
grant that we, who share in his sufferings and victory
may receive the benefits of his anointing;
who lives and reigns with you and the Holy Spirit
one God, for ever and ever.

The Readings (when there is no Renewal of Vows)

34 Leviticus 8:10-12   Moses anoints Aaron and the
                                        altar

   Psalm 89:21-27
   James 5:13-16   Healing and forgiveness
   Mark 6:7-13   The mission of the Twelve

   Proper Preface 10(b)   Canticle 1

35 The Bishop goes to the table. If there are concelebrants they now stand
   around the Bishop in a semi-circle.

   A minister holds up the Oil of the Sick before the Bishop and says

   The Oil of the Sick

   He places the vessel of oil on the table.

   The Bishop blesses the Oil of the Sick as follows

   Lord God, our loving Father, you bring healing to the sick
   through your Son, Jesus Christ. Hear us as we pray in
   faith, and send your Holy Spirit, our helper and friend,
   upon this oil.

   We ask you to bless those who will be anointed with it,
   and heal them in body, mind and spirit.

   Merciful Father, bless this oil for the ministry of healing, in the name of our Lord Jesus Christ.
   Amen

36 A minister brings the Oil for the Chrism to the Bishop and says

   The Oil for the holy Chrism

   He places the vessel of oil on the table.

The Bishop consecrates the Chrism

Father, we thank you for the gifts you have given us in your love. We thank you for life itself and for the sacraments that strengthen it and give it fuller meaning.

Under the old covenant you inspired your servants to use oil to set men apart as kings and priests; in the fulness of time you anointed your perfect Son, Jesus Christ, as our eternal Priest and King.

By his suffering, dying and rising to life he saved the human race. He sent your Spirit to fill the Church with every gift needed to complete your saving work.

From that time forward, by anointing them with the Spirit, you strengthen all who are baptized. You transform them into the likeness of Christ your Son, and give them a share in his prophetic, priestly and kingly work.

Priests who concelebrate now extend their right hands towards the Chrism until the end of the prayer. They do not say any part of the prayer.

And so, Father, by the power of your love, bless to our use this mixture of oil and perfume as a sign and means of your heavenly grace. Pour out the gifts of your Holy Spirit on those who will be anointed with it. Let the splendour of your holiness shine on the world from every place and thing signed with this oil.

Above all, Father, we pray that through this sign of your anointing you will grant increase to your Church until it attains to the eternal glory where you, Father, will be all in all, together with Christ your Son, in the unity of the Holy Spirit, for ever and ever.
Amen

37 The Peace follows immediately, the Creed and the Prayers of the Church being omitted.

The Oils are solemnly carried to the sacristy at the end of the service.

THE EVENING EUCHARIST OF
THE LORD'S SUPPER W

At the evening Eucharist the Church remembers Christ's gift of the sacrament of Holy Communion. The white vestments express our joy and thanksgiving. After the Gospel which describes Christ washing the feet of his disciples, the Priest may wash the feet of twelve members of the congregation.

At the end of the service the altar may be stripped and the decorations removed; the church is left bare and stark for Good Friday.

38 The Gloria is said.

The Collect

39 God, our Father
your Son revealed his love
 by giving us this supper
 to celebrate the new and eternal sacrifice:
may he nourish us by his presence
 and unite us in his love;
who is alive and reigns with you and the Holy Spirit
one God, now and for ever.

or

Almighty God
your Son our Lord Jesus Christ
 gave us the wonderful sacrament
 of his body and blood
to represent his death
 and to celebrate his resurrection:
strengthen our devotion to him
 in these holy mysteries
and through them renew our unity with him
 and with one another
that we may grow in grace
 and in the knowledge of our salvation;
through Jesus Christ our Lord.

or

Father, your Son our Lord Jesus Christ, in a wonderful sacrament gave us a memorial of his passion: grant that we may venerate the sacred mysteries of his body and blood, and perceive within ourselves the fruit of his redemption; who lives and reigns with you, in the unity of the Holy Spirit, one God, world without end.

The Readings

40   Readings from Year A are used when the ceremony of the washing of the feet is performed.

YEAR A

Exodus 12:1-14	The Passover
Psalm 116:11-18	
1 Corinthians 11:23-26	The Last Supper
John 13:1-15	Jesus washes his disciples' feet

YEAR B

Exodus 24:3-8	Sacrifice and the Old Covenant
Psalm 116:11-18	
1 Corinthians 10:16-17	Sharing the body and blood of Christ
Mark 14:12-26	The Last Supper

YEAR C

Jeremiah 31:31-34	Looking for the New Covenant
Psalm 116:11-18	
Hebrews 10:16-25	The new and living way
Luke 22:7-20	The Last Supper

Proper Preface 10(c)   Canticle 15

41   A sermon is preached on the mysteries of the day, and particularly on our Lord's institution of the Holy Eucharist and his commandment to love one another.

THE WASHING OF THE FEET

42   The Priest may wash the feet of twelve members of the congregation.

Those who have been chosen go to their allotted places. The following hymn may be sung

Rejoice in Christ, and sing with one accord;
His tender love has brought us to one fold.
O let us love and fear the living Lord,
And may the love amongst us not grow cold.
  For we believe, O God, thou surely art
  Where charity and love possess the heart.

We are one fold, and our chief care must be
To shun the unconcern of lonely pride:
Let quarrels cease, let spiteful discord flee,
And Christ be the companion at our side.
  For we believe, O God, thou surely art
  Where charity and love possess the heart.

O may we too be gathered to the fold
Of those who see Christ's face exultingly;
Joy that is true and blessedness untold,
Where age succeeds to age eternally.
  For we believe, O God, thou surely art
  Where charity and love possess the heart.

43   The washing of the feet completed, the Priest says

Lord, you have declared your will
That we should faithfully keep your commandments

You have commanded us to love one another
As you have loved us

Lord, in your mercy
Hear our prayer

Most loving Lord
you stooped to wash the feet of your disciples:
accept this our act of obedience and humble service
wash us clean from all sin

and teach us to serve you in the least of your brothers and
 sisters
to the glory of the Father
who lives and reigns with you and the Holy Spirit
one God, for ever and ever.
Amen

44   The Prayers of the Church follow in this form, the Creed being omitted.

On this solemn evening, in union with Christ's prayer
that all may be one, as he and the Father are one, we pray
for the unity of all Christians.

Father, we pray for Christians throughout the world
That we may be one

We pray for the Roman Catholic Church and for *N* the
Pope
That we may be one

We pray for the Eastern Orthodox Churches and for their
Patriarchs and Archbishops
That we may be one

We pray for the Churches which have covenanted with
us and for their leaders
That we may be one

We pray for all other Churches
That we may be one

We pray for the Anglican Communion and for *N*
Archbishop of Canterbury
That we may be one

We pray for the Church of the Province of Southern
Africa and for *N* our metropolitan
That we may be one

We pray for this diocese and for *N* our bishop
That we may be one

We pray for this *parish* and for *N* our *rector*
That we may be one

We pray for the unity of all Christian people, that the world may believe
That we may be one

Heavenly Father, your Son our Lord Jesus Christ said to his apostles, Peace I leave with you, my peace I give you: regard not our sins but the faith of your Church, and grant her that peace and unity which is according to your will; through Jesus Christ our Lord.
Amen

The Eucharist continues with the Peace.

45 If the Sacrament is reserved, it is carried to the appointed place after the prayer at 88 in the Eucharist.

THE STRIPPING OF THE ALTAR

46 The altar may be stripped. While this is being done Psalm 22 may be said with this antiphon before and after

They part my garments among them: and cast lots for my clothing.

If 45 or 46 is used the Blessing and Dismissal are omitted.

GOOD FRIDAY
R or B

CELEBRATION OF THE LORD'S PASSION

Today the Church, while mourning the sins which were the cause of Christ's suffering, celebrates the triumph of his saving death.

The service is in four parts

*(1) **The Liturgy of the Word** in which God speaks through the Scriptures of his saving love for mankind.*

*(2) **The General Intercessions** in which the Church prays for the whole human race for whom Christ died.*

*(3) **The Solemn Adoration of Christ Crucified** in which devotion is centred on the cross, the symbol of Christ's redeeming death.*

*(4) **The Holy Communion** through which the faithful are sacramentally united to Christ, their crucified and risen Lord.*

THE LITURGY OF THE WORD

47   The altar is completely bare.

The procession enters in silence, the congregation standing.

After the Priest enters he prostrates himself or kneels.

There is a period of silence, the congregation kneeling.

The Priest alone standing, without a greeting or 'Let us pray', says

Almighty Father
hear our prayer
   and look with mercy on this your family
for which our Lord Jesus Christ
   was ready to be betrayed
   into the hands of sinners
and to suffer death on the cross;
who is alive, and reigns with you and the Holy Spirit
one God, now and for ever.

48   Isaiah 52:13–53:12   The suffering Servant

49 *From Psalm 31*

To you Lord have I I come for I shelter:
    let me I never · be I put to I shame.
O deliver me I in your I righteousness:
    incline your ear to me I and be I swift to I save me.
In|to your I hands: Lord I I com|mit my I spirit.

For my life wears out in sorrow ⌣
    and my I years with I sighing:
my strength fails me in my affliction
    and my I bones I are con|sumed.
I am become the scorn of I all my I enemies:
    and my neighbours I wag their I heads · in de|rision.
In|to your I hands: Lord I I com|mit my I spirit.

I am a thing of I horror · to my I friends:
    and those that see me in the I street I shrink I from me.
I am forgotten like a dead man I out of I mind:
    I have be|come · like a I broken I vessel.
In|to your I hands: Lord I I com|mit my I spirit.

For I hear the I whispering · of I many:
    and I fear · is on I every I side;
While they plot to|gether · a|gainst me:
    and scheme to I take a|way my I life.
In|to your I hands: Lord I I com|mit my I spirit.

But in you Lord have I I put my I trust:
    I have said I I 'You I are my I God.'
All my days are I in your I hand:
    O deliver me from the power of my I enemies ·
    and I from my I persecutors.
In|to your I hands: Lord I I com|mit my I spirit.

But you heard the voice of my I supplic|ation:
    when I I cried to I you for I help.
Be strong and let your I heart take I courage:
    all I you that I hope · in the I Lord.
In|to your I hands: Lord I I com|mit my I spirit.

The 'Glory to the Father' is not said.

If the psalm is to be sung, it is better to choose a single chant. If a double chant is used, the refrain must be sung to the second part.

Collects and Readings

50   Hebrews 4:14–5:10   or   13:8-16   Jesus our High Priest

Acclamation

51   **Christ humbled himself and became obedient unto death, even death on a cross. Therefore God has highly exalted him and bestowed on him the name which is above every name.**

52   Then is announced without response

The Passion of our Lord Jesus Christ according to John.

John 18:1–19:42   or   John 19:1-37

53   A sermon may be preached.

THE GENERAL INTERCESSIONS

54   The Minister addresses the congregation in these or similar words

Today Christ offers his life to the Father for the salvation of humankind. In union with him we now pray that all may receive the benefits of his passion.

For the Church

Let us pray, dear friends, for the holy Church of God throughout the world, that God the almighty Father may guide it and gather it together so that we may worship him in peace and tranquillity.

Silent prayer. Then the Minister says

Almighty and eternal God, you have shown your glory to all nations in Christ, your Son. Guide the work of your Church. Help it to persevere in faith, to proclaim your name, and to bring your salvation to people everywhere.

Lord, in your mercy
Hear our prayer

For the clergy and laity of the Church

Let us pray for N our bishop, together with N our metropolitan, for all bishops, priests and deacons; for those who have a special ministry in the Church; and for all God's people.

Silent prayer. Then the Minister says

Almighty and eternal God, your Spirit guides the Church and makes it holy. Listen to our prayers and help all in their own vocation to do your work more faithfully.

Lord, in your mercy
Hear our prayer

For those preparing for baptism and confirmation

Let us pray for those preparing for baptism and confirmation, that God in his mercy may make them responsive to his love.

Silent prayer. Then the Minister says

Almighty and eternal God, you continually add to your Church those whom you call. Increase the faith and understanding of those preparing for baptism and confirmation, and make them faithful members of your chosen family.

Lord, in your mercy
Hear our prayer

For the unity of Christians

Let us pray for all our brothers and sisters who share our faith in Jesus Christ, that God may gather and keep together in one Church all those who seek the truth.

Silent prayer. Then the Minister says

Almighty and eternal God, you keep together those you have united. Look kindly on all who follow Jesus your

Son. We are consecrated to you by our common baptism;
make us one in the fulness of faith, and keep us one in
the fellowship of love.

Lord, in your mercy
Hear our prayer

For the Jewish people

Let us pray for the Jewish people, the first to hear the
word of God, that they may continue to grow in the love
of his Name and confess Jesus as Messiah.

Silent prayer. Then the Minister says

Almighty and eternal God, you gave your promise
to Abraham and his descendants. Grant that the people
you first made your own may arrive at the fulness of
redemption.

Lord, in your mercy
Hear our prayer

For those who do not believe in Christ

Let us pray for those who do not believe in Christ, that
the light of the Holy Spirit may show them the way of
salvation.

Silent prayer. Then the Minister says

Almighty and eternal God, whom all seek, even unknow-
ingly: open the eyes of those who know not Christ, that
they may find in him alone, the way, the truth and the
life.

Lord, in your mercy
Hear our prayer

For those who do not believe in God

Let us pray for those who do not believe in God.

Silent prayer. Then the Minister says

Almighty and eternal God, you have made us for yourself and our hearts are restless until they find their rest in you. Have mercy on all who live in doubt and unbelief, that they may know you the one Creator God and Jesus Christ whom you have sent.

Lord, in your mercy
Hear our prayer

For all in public office

Let us pray for those who serve in public office, that God will guide their minds and hearts, so that all may live in true peace and freedom.

Silent prayer. Then the Minister says

Almighty and eternal God, in your goodness watch over those in authority so that people everywhere may enjoy true freedom, security and peace.

Lord, in your mercy
Hear our prayer

For those in special need

Let us pray, dear friends, that God the almighty Father may heal the sick, comfort the dying, give safety to travellers, free those unjustly deprived of liberty and rid the world of falsehood, hunger and disease.

Silent prayer. Then the Minister says

Almighty and eternal God, you give strength to the weary and new courage to those who have lost heart. Hear the prayers of all who call on you in any trouble, that they may have the joy of receiving your help in their need.

We ask all this through Jesus Christ our Lord.
Amen

THE SOLEMN ADORATION OF CHRIST CRUCIFIED

55   This is done according to one of the three forms following

   1 A veiled cross is carried to the altar. Facing the people, the Priest uncovers the upper part of it, elevates it and says

     Lord, by your holy cross you have redeemed the world

     and all respond

     We adore you, Christ, and we bless you

     He then uncovers the right arm, elevates the cross, and the words are repeated. Finally he uncovers the entire cross, elevates it and the words are again repeated.

   2 An uncovered cross is carried in procession through the church to the sanctuary. Near the entrance to the church, in the middle of the church, and again at the entrance to the sanctuary, the person carrying the cross stops, lifts it up and says

     Lord, by your holy cross you have redeemed the world

     and all respond

     We adore you, Christ, and we bless you

     In both the above forms the cross is then placed between lighted candles. The Priest and the congregation may make an act of reverence before the cross.

   3 In silence the congregation adores Christ crucified, after which, opportunity may be given for free prayer, concluding with the above versicle and response.

56   The Reproaches are said, all kneeling. The traditional form may be substituted when a musical setting requires it.

My people, what have I done to you? How have I offended you? Answer me!

I led you out of Egypt, from slavery to freedom, but you led your Saviour to the cross.

My people, what have I done to you? How have I offended you? Answer me!

Holy is God! Holy and strong! Holy immortal One, have mercy on us.

For forty years I led you safely through the desert. I fed you with manna from heaven, and brought you to a land of plenty; but you led your Saviour to the cross.

Holy is God! Holy and strong! Holy immortal One, have mercy on us.

What more could I have done for you? I planted you as my fairest vine, but you yielded only bitterness. When I was thirsty you gave me vinegar to drink, and you pierced your Saviour's side with a lance.

Holy is God! Holy and strong! Holy immortal One, have mercy on us.

I opened the sea before you, but you opened my side with a spear.

My people, what have I done to you? How have I offended you? Answer me!

I led you on your way in a pillar of cloud, but you led me to Pilate's court.

My people, what have I done to you? How have I offended you? Answer me!

I bore you up with manna in the desert, but you struck me down and scourged me.

My people, what have I done to you? How have I offended you? Answer me!

I gave you saving water from the rock, but you gave me gall and vinegar to drink.

My people, what have I done to you? How have I offended you? Answer me!

I gave you a royal sceptre, but you gave me a crown of thorns.

My people, what have I done to you? How have I offended you? Answer me!

I raised you to the height of majesty, but you have raised me high on a cross.

My people, what have I done to you? How have I offended you? Answer me!

We praise and adore you, O Christ.

By your cross and precious blood you have redeemed us.

Worthy is the Lamb, the Lamb that was slain, to receive all power and wealth, wisdom and might, honour and glory and praise!

We praise and adore you, O Christ. By your cross and precious blood you have redeemed us.

You are worthy, O Christ, for you were slain, and by your blood you purchased for God people of every tribe, language, nation and race; you have made them a royal house, to serve our God as priests; and they shall reign upon earth.

We praise and adore you, O Christ. By your cross and precious blood you have redeemed us.

To him who loves us and has freed us from our sins by his blood, and made us a kingdom, priests to his God and Father:

To him be glory and dominion for ever and ever. Amen

57 If the cross is at the entrance to the sanctuary, it is now placed on or near the altar.

58   This hymn may be sung unless it has been included in the Reproaches.

Sing, my tongue, the glorious battle,
Sing the ending of the fray;
Now above the cross, the trophy,
Sound the loud triumphant lay;
Tell how Christ, the world's Redeemer,
As a victim won the day.

Thirty years among us dwelling,
His appointed time fulfilled,
Born for this, he meets his passion,
For that this he freely willed,
On the cross the Lamb is lifted
Where his life-blood shall be spilled.

Faithful cross! above all other,
One and only noble tree!
None in foliage, none in blossom,
None in fruit thy peer may be;
Sweetest wood and sweetest iron!
Sweetest weight is hung on thee.

Bend thy boughs, O tree of glory!
Thy relaxing sinews bend;
For awhile the ancient rigour
That thy birth bestowed, suspend;
And the King of heavenly beauty
On thy bosom gently tend!

To the Trinity be glory
Everlasting, as is meet;
Equal to the Father, equal
To the Son, and Paraclete:
Trinal Unity, whose praises
All created things repeat.

59   If Holy Communion is not to be given, the service ends with the two
prayers at 66.

THE HOLY COMMUNION

60 If Holy Communion is given from the reserved sacrament, the Priest brings it in silence from the place of reservation to the altar.

61 The Priest says

As Christ has taught us we are bold to say

Our Father in heaven
hallowed be your Name
your kingdom come
your will be done
on earth as in heaven.
Give us today our daily bread.
Forgive us our sins
as we forgive those who sin against us.
Save us from the time of trial
and deliver us from evil.
For the kingdom, the power, and the glory are yours
now and for ever. Amen

62 **Jesus, Lamb of God: have mercy on us.**
Jesus, bearer of our sins: have mercy on us.
Jesus, redeemer of the world: give us your peace.

63 **We do not presume**
to come to this your table, merciful Lord
trusting in our own righteousness
but in your manifold and great mercies.
We are not worthy so much as to gather up
the crumbs under your table;
but you are the same Lord
whose nature is always to have mercy.
Grant us therefore, gracious Lord
so to eat the flesh of your dear Son Jesus Christ
and to drink his blood
that we may evermore dwell in him and he in us.

64 Draw near and receive the body of our Lord Jesus Christ which he gave for you, and his blood which he shed for you. Feed on him in your hearts by faith with thanksgiving.

65 The Priest and people receive the sacrament. Any authorized words of administration may be used.

66 The service concludes with these two prayers

Almighty and eternal God
you have restored us to life
  by the triumphant death
  and resurrection of Christ:
continue this healing work within us
and grant that we who participate in this mystery
  may never cease to give you dedicated service;
we ask this through Christ our Lord.
Amen

The Priest, facing the people and extending his hands towards them, dismisses them, saying

Lord
send down your abundant blessing on your people
who have devoutly recalled the death of your Son
in the sure hope of the resurrection:
grant them pardon, bring them comfort
may their faith grow stronger
  and their eternal salvation be assured.
Amen

No blessing or dismissal is added. The service ends in silence.

67 If the Eucharist is to be celebrated, the order begins with the Presentation of Gifts, or with the Taking of the Bread and Wine. The Proper Preface is 9. The two prayers at 66 replace the Conclusion.

HOLY SATURDAY   P

The Collect

68 God our Father
we have been baptized
      into the death of your Son
      our Saviour Jesus Christ:
grant that, by continually putting to death
      our sinful nature
we may be buried with him
and through the grave and gate of death
may pass to our joyful resurrection;
      through Jesus Christ our Lord.

69 There is no Eucharist of this day, but the Easter Vigil may begin in the evening.

Easter Day has no first Evening Prayer; Evening Prayer is of Holy Saturday.

THE EASTER VIGIL   W

In the Easter Vigil, which from early times has been the centre of the liturgical year, the Church celebrates the resurrection of Christ and the redemption which he won. Christians share the fruits of this redemption in the sacraments of baptism and the Eucharist.

It is called a Vigil because in early times the Church kept an all-night watch, meditating on the Scriptures and praying till dawn when Christ's resurrection was acclaimed.

The Easter Candle is an important symbol in this service, and throughout Eastertide is a constant reminder of the risen Christ, the Light of the world.

70   The service is as follows

The Service of Light during which fire is blessed and the Easter Candle is lit to represent the risen Christ.

The Liturgy of the Word in which, through readings from the Old Testament, the Church meditates on God's mighty acts in history.

The Liturgy of the Eucharist in which is included the Service of Baptism. In baptism the fruit of Christ's redeeming death and resurrection is brought to us. After the water has been solemnly blessed, baptism (with confirmation) is administered, and those who have already been baptized renew their baptismal promises.

THE SERVICE OF LIGHT

The Blessing of the Fire and the Lighting of the Easter Candle

The church is in darkness as was Calvary when Christ died on the cross. As God in the Old Testament made his presence known by the sign of the pillar of fire, so fire now represents the return of Christ, the Light of the world, from the darkness of the grave.

71   Candles are given to the people as they arrive.

The church lights are extinguished.

The Priest goes in procession to the place where a fire has been laid.

72   The Priest addresses the congregation in these or similar words

Dear friends in Christ, on this most holy night, when our Lord Jesus Christ passed from death to life, the Church invites her children throughout the world to come together in vigil and prayer.

This is the Passover of the Lord when we venerate him in the mystery of his death and resurrection. Through the celebration of the Paschal Mystery in word and sacrament he renews our faith and hope, and gives us a share in his victory over death and in his eternal life with the Father.

73   The fire is lit in silence. The Priest blesses it

Father
we share in the light of your glory
    through your Son, the Light of the world:
sanctify this new fire
    and inflame us with new hope
purify our minds by this Easter celebration
and bring us to the feast of eternal light.
We ask this through Christ our Lord.
Amen

74   The Easter Candle is brought to the Priest.

The lighted Candle represents the risen Christ. It may be marked with various signs. Five grains of incense stand for the five wounds, the cross for his death; Alpha and Omega (the first and last letters of the Greek alphabet) is a title given to him in the book of Revelation; the date shows that he, the Lord of all time, sanctifies the present year.

The Priest may trace symbolic signs on the Candle.

As he traces the vertical arm of the cross he says

Christ yesterday and today

the horizontal arm of the cross
the beginning and the end

above the cross
Alpha

below the cross
Omega

the first numeral of the year
all times belong to him

the second numeral
and all the ages

the third numeral
to him be glory and power

the fourth numeral
through every age for ever. Amen

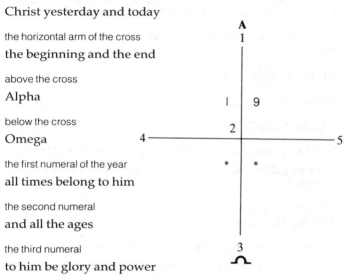

He inserts the grains of incense in the form of a cross saying

1 By his holy
2 and glorious wounds
3 may Christ our Lord
4 guard us
5 and keep us. Amen

The Candle is lit from the newly blessed fire, the Priest saying

May the light of Christ, rising in glory, dispel the darkness of our hearts and minds.

The Solemn Procession

The Candle is brought into church and its light is passed to all the people, a sign that every Christian must share in the Church's mission of carrying the light of Christ's gospel to every part of the world.

75 The Deacon, or if there is not one, a priest, lifts the Candle high and sings alone

Christ our light

and all respond

Thanks be to God

The Deacon bearing the Candle leads the procession into the church.

In the body of the church the Deacon lifts the Candle high and sings a second time

Christ our light
Thanks be to God

The candles of the congregation are lit from the Easter Candle.

When the Deacon arrives before the altar he faces the people and sings a third time

Christ our light
Thanks be to God

The Candle is put on a stand in a prominent position.

The Easter Proclamation (Exultet)

76 The Deacon sings the Easter Proclamation by the light of the Candle, the congregation standing holding lighted candles.

The Proclamation may be sung by a lay person. It may be shortened by omitting the bracketed sentences.

Rejoice, heavenly powers! Sing, choirs of angels! Exult, all creation around God's throne! Jesus Christ, our King, is risen! Sound the trumpet of salvation!

Rejoice, O earth, in shining splendour, radiant in the brightness of your King! Christ has conquered! Glory fills you! Darkness vanishes for ever!

Rejoice, O Mother Church! Exult in glory! The risen Saviour shines upon you! Let this place resound with joy, echoing the mighty song of all God's people!

(My dearest friends, standing with me in this holy light, join me in asking God for mercy, that he may give his unworthy minister grace to sing his Easter praises.)

The Lord be with you
And also with you

Lift up your hearts
We lift them to the Lord

Let us give thanks to the Lord our God
It is right to give him thanks and praise

It is truly right that with full hearts and minds and voices we should praise the unseen God, the all-powerful Father, and his only Son, our Lord Jesus Christ.

For Christ has ransomed us with his blood, and paid for us the price of Adam's sin to our eternal Father!

This is our passover feast, when Christ, the true Lamb, is slain, whose blood consecrates the homes of all believers.

This is the night when first you saved our forebears, you freed the people of Israel from their slavery and led them dry-shod through the sea.

(This is the night when the pillar of fire destroyed the darkness of sin!)

This is the night when Christians everywhere, washed clean of sin and freed from all defilement, are restored to grace and grow together in holiness.

This is the night when Jesus Christ broke the chains of death and rose triumphant from the grave.

(What good would life have been to us, had Christ not come as our Redeemer?)

Father, how wonderful your care for us! How boundless your merciful love! To ransom a slave you gave away your Son.

O happy fault, O necessary sin of Adam, which gained for us so great a Redeemer!

(Most blessed of all nights, chosen by God to see Christ rising from the dead!)

(Of this night Scripture says 'The night will be as clear as day; it will become my light, my joy.')

The power of this holy night dispels all evil, washes guilt away, restores lost innocence, brings mourners joy. (It casts out hatred, brings us peace, and humbles earthly pride.)

Night truly blessed when heaven is wedded to earth and the world reconciled to God!

Therefore, heavenly Father, in the joy of this night, receive our evening sacrifice of praise, your Church's solemn offering.

(Accept this Easter Candle, a flame divided but undimmed, a pillar of fire that glows to the honour of God.)

If this sentence is omitted then is sung

Accept this Easter Candle. May it always dispel the darkness of the night.

(Let it mingle with the lights of heaven and continue bravely burning to dispel the darkness of this night!)

May the Morning Star which never sets find this flame still burning: Christ, that Morning Star, who came back from the dead, and shed his peaceful light on

humankind, your Son who lives and reigns for ever and
ever.
Amen

THE LITURGY OF THE WORD

*The reading of Scripture has been an important part of vigils. Six read-
ings from the Old Testament follow, telling of God's acts in history, and
each is followed by verses from a psalm and a prayer.*

The church lights are put on. The people extinguish their candles and sit.
The Priest addresses them in these or similar words

Dear friends in Christ, we have begun our solemn vigil.
Let us listen attentively to the word of God, recalling how
again and again he saved his people and, in the fulness of
time, sent his Son to be our Redeemer.

The readings follow. Each is preceded by its introduction. The psalm
(without the 'Glory to the Father') and the prayer follow. It is desirable that
all the readings, with the accompanying psalms and prayers, should be
used in their entirety, but for good reason the Third and Fifth Readings
and some or all of the psalms may be omitted.

The First Reading

This story tells how God created Adam. Tonight we celebrate our new creation in Jesus Christ, who breathes the
Holy Spirit upon us.

Genesis 2:4-9

From Psalm 33

Rejoice in the | Lord you | righteous:
    for it be|fits the | just to | praise him.

By the word of the Lord were the | heavens | made:
    and their numberless | stars · by the | breath of · his |
      mouth.

He gathered the waters of the sea as | in a | water-skin:
    and laid up the | deep | in his | treasuries.

Let the whole earth I fear the I Lord:
    and let all the inhabitants of the I world I stand in I
      awe of him.

†For he spoke and I it was I done:
    he commanded I and it I stood I fast.

Let us pray

Almighty God
you wonderfully created
    and still more wonderfully redeemed us:
bring us to those lasting joys
which you have prepared for us
    through the sacrifice of Christ our Passover;
who lives and reigns with you and the Holy Spirit
one God, for ever and ever.
Amen

The Second Reading

This story witnesses to the common human experience of
separation from God through disobedience, and hints at
redemption through a descendant of the woman.

Genesis 3:1-19

From Psalm 32

Blessèd is he whose I sin · is forIgiven:
    whose inIiquity · is I put aIway.

Blessèd is the man to whom the Lord imIputes no I blame:
    and in whose I spirit · there I is no I guile.

Then I ackInowledged · my I sin to you:
    and my inIiquity · I I did not I hide;

I said 'I will confess my transIgressions · to the I Lord':
    and so you forgave the I wicked · ness I of my I sin.

†Great tribulations remain I for the · unIgodly:
    but whoever puts his trust in the Lord
      mercy emIbraces him · on I every I side.

Let us pray

Almighty Father
you sent your Son into the world
    to set us free from sin:
enable us to withstand temptation
and to abide in your presence;
through Jesus Christ our Lord.
Amen

The Third Reading

In obedience to God Abraham was prepared to sacrifice his only son, Isaac. But in response to Abraham's obedience God refused the sacrifice, though he would not refuse the sacrifice of his own Son Jesus, the Lamb of God.

Genesis 22:1-18   (verses 4-8 and 14 may be omitted)

From Psalm 40

Sacrifice and offering you do | not de|sire:
    but my | ears · you have | marked · for o|bedience;

Burnt-offering and sin-offering you have | not re|quired:
    then | said I | Lo I | come.

In the scroll of the book it is written of me ‿
        that I should | do your | will:
    O my God I long to do it* your | law de|lights my |
    heart.

I have declared your righteousness ‿
        in the | great · congre|gation:
    I have not restrained my lips O | Lord ‿
        and | that you | know.

I have not hidden your righteousness | in my | heart:
    I have spoken of your faithfulness | and of |
        your sal|vation.

I have not kept back your loving-kindness | and your |
        truth:
    from the | great | congre|gation.

Let us pray

Merciful Father
you accepted the sacrifice
  of your only beloved Son:
unite us with him in his self-offering
and make us obedient to you in all things;
through Jesus Christ our Lord.
Amen

The Fourth Reading

During their escape from Egypt, God led the Israelites
safely through the waters of the Red Sea in which the
pursuing Egyptians were destroyed, foreshadowing our
own deliverance through the waters of baptism.

Exodus 14:15–15:1a   (verses 17-20 may be omitted)

For the Psalm: Exodus 15: 1b-6

I will sing to the Lord for he has risen I up in I triumph:
  the horse and his rider he has I hurled inIto the I sea.

The Lord is my refuge and I my deIfence:
  he has shown himIself I my deIliverer.

He is my God and I I will I glorify him:
  he is my father's I God and I I · will exIalt him.

The I Lord · is a I warrior:
  the I Lord I is his I name.

The chariots of Pharaoh and his army he has cast I into ·
    the I sea:
  the flower of his officers are enIgulfed · in the I Red I
    Sea.

The watery aIbyss has I covered them:
  they sank into the I depths I like a I stone.

†Thy right hand O Lord is maIjestic · in I strength:
  thy right hand O I Lord I shattered · the I enemy.

Let us pray

Lord God
you made the Red Sea a symbol of our baptism
and the nation you redeemed
    a sign of your Christian people:
grant that people of every nation
    may come to the new birth
    of water and the Holy Spirit
and share by faith in the privilege of Israel;
through Jesus Christ our Lord.
Amen

The Fifth Reading

At Mount Sinai God established the Israelites as his
chosen people by making his covenant with them. This
first covenant was sealed in the blood of animal sacrifices.
The new covenant would be sealed in the blood of the
Lamb of God.

Exodus 24: 3-8

From Psalm 111

O praise the Lord
    I will praise the Lord with my l whole l heart:
in the company of the upright
    and al among the l congrel gation.

His marvellous acts have won him a name to l be
    rel membered:
    the l Lord is l gracious · and l merciful.

He gives food to l those that l fear him:
    he rel members · his l covenant · for l ever.

He showed his people the l power · of his l acts:
    in giving them the l herit · age l of the l heathen.

The works of his hands are l faithful · and l just:
    and l all · his com l mandments · are l sure;

They stand firm for | ever · and | ever:
     they are done in | faithful · ness | and in | truth.

He sent redemption to his people
          he ordained his | covenant · for | ever:
     holy is his name and | worthy | to be |feared.

The fear of the Lord is the beginning of wisdom
          and of good understanding are those that | keep ·
               his com|mandments:
     his | praise · shall en|dure for | ever.

Let us pray

Almighty Father
without your grace we cannot obey your law:
fill our hearts with love for you
that we may keep your commandments
     and do your will;
through Jesus Christ our Lord.
Amen

The Sixth Reading

God promised to purify the people of Israel, to renew
them in heart and spirit, and to make them his own
people. God did this not only for their own sake, but
that through them the world might come to know him.

Ezekiel 36:22-28

From Psalm 57

Be merciful to me O | God be | merciful:
     for I | come to | you for | shelter;

And in the shadow of your wings will | I take | refuge:
     until these | troubles · are | over-| past.

I will call to | God Most | High:
     to the God who will ful|fil his | purpose | for me.

He will send from | heaven · and | save me:
 he will send forth his faithfulness and his ⌣
  loving-kindness
  and rebuke | those · that would | trample · me |
  down.

For I lie amidst |raven · ing | lions:
 men whose teeth are spears and arrows
  and their | tongue a | sharpened | sword.

Be exalted O God a|bove the | heavens:
 and let your glory be | over | all the | earth.

Let us pray

Almighty Father
you have chosen us to be your own people:
take away our hearts of stone
 and give us hearts of flesh
that your holiness may be revealed in us;
through Jesus Christ our Lord.
Amen

THE LITURGY OF THE EUCHARIST

30 The altar candles are lit.

31 **Glory to God in the highest
and peace to his people on earth.**

**Lord God, heavenly King
almighty God and Father
we worship you, we give you thanks
we praise you for your glory.**

**Lord Jesus Christ, only Son of the Father
Lord God, Lamb of God
you take away the sin of the world:
have mercy on us;
you are seated at the right hand of the Father:
receive our prayer.**

For you alone are the Holy One
you alone are the Lord
you alone are the Most High
Jesus Christ
with the Holy Spirit
in the glory of God the Father. Amen

The Collect

82 Let us pray

Lord God
you have brightened this night
    with the radiance of the risen Christ:
may his light so shine within the Church
that we may be renewed in mind and body
and serve you with all our being;
through Jesus Christ our Lord.

New Testament Reading

83 Romans 6: 3-11   New life in Christ

84 All stand. The Priest may solemnly intone the Alleluia which is repeated
    by all present.

Then is sung from Psalm 118

O give thanks to the Lord for I he is I good:
    his I mercy · enIdures for I ever.

Let Israel I now proIclaim:
    that his mercy endures for I ever. I AlleIluia.

The right hand of the Lord does I mighty I things:
    the right hand of the I Lord I raises I up.

I shall not I die but I live:
    and proclaim the works of the I Lord. I AlleIluia.

The stone that the I builders · reIjected:
    has beIcome the I head · of the I corner.

This is the I Lord's I doing:
    and it is marvellous in our I eyes. I AlleIluia.

5   In place of 84 a hymn with Alleluias may be sung.

The Gospel

6   YEAR A   YEAR B   YEAR C
    Matthew 28:1-10   Mark 16:1-8   Luke 24:1-12

7   A sermon may be preached.

THE SERVICE OF BAPTISM

8   If there are no baptisms or confirmations, the service continues at 113.

    The Priest takes the Service of Baptism unless the Bishop is present.

9   The Priest, together with those to be baptized, their parents and their
    sponsors, stands before the font.

The Introduction

0   The Priest addresses the people

Our Lord Jesus Christ gave himself to death on the cross
and was raised again for the salvation of humankind.

Baptism is the sacrament in which, by repentance and
faith, we enter into this salvation: we are united with
Christ in his death; we are granted the forgiveness of
sins; we are made members of his Body and we are raised
with him to new life in the Spirit.

In Confirmation we come to be filled, through the
laying on of hands, with the power of the Spirit for
worship, witness and service.

The Renunciation

1   The Priest addresses the candidates, parents and godparents, omitting
    any paragraph not required.

You, who have come for baptism and confirmation,
must declare your rejection of all that is evil.

You, who present children for baptism, must promise
to bring them up to reject all that is evil. You are to
answer for yourselves and for your child.

You, who have already been baptized and have now come to be confirmed, must with your own lips and from your heart declare your rejection of all that is evil.

92 The Priest asks them

Do you renounce the devil and all the spiritual forces of wickedness that rebel against God?
I renounce them

Do you renounce the evil powers of this world which corrupt and destroy what God has created?
I renounce them

Do you renounce all sinful desires that draw you away from the love of God?
I renounce them

93 The Priest says to the congregation

Dear friends in Christ, let us pray for *these persons*

God of all mercy, look on *them*
Amen

Put to death *their* sinful desires
Amen
Grant *them* the life of your Spirit
Amen

Enable *them* to overcome the evil one
Amen
Give *them* every Christian virtue
Amen

Bring *them* with your saints to everlasting glory
Amen

94 The Priest, who may stretch out his hand towards the candidates, says

May almighty God deliver you from the powers of darkness and lead you into the light and obedience of Christ.
Amen

The Blessing of the Water

95 The Priest blesses the water as follows

Father, you give us grace through sacramental signs, which tell us of the wonders of your unseen power.

In baptism we use your gift of water, which you have made a rich symbol of the grace you give us in this sacrament.

At the very dawn of creation your Spirit breathed on the waters, making them the wellspring of all holiness.

The waters of the great flood you made a sign of the waters of baptism, that make an end of sin and a new beginning of goodness.

Through the waters of the Red Sea you led Israel out of slavery, to be an image of God's holy people, set free from sin by baptism.

In the waters of the Jordan your Son was baptized by John and anointed with the Spirit.

Your Son willed that water and blood should flow from his side as he hung upon the cross.

After his resurrection he told his disciples, 'Go out and make disciples of all nations, baptizing them in the name of the Father and of the Son and of the Holy Spirit'.

Father, look now with love upon your Church, and unseal for her the fountain of baptism.

†By the power of the Spirit and through the water of this font bestow the grace of your Son.

You created all people in your own likeness; cleanse them from sin in a new birth of innocence by water and the Spirit.

The Priest may lower the Easter Candle into the water once or three times.

We ask you, Father, with your Son, to send the Holy Spirit upon the waters of this font.

†These lines may be omitted.

May all who are buried with Christ in the death of baptism rise also with him to newness of life.

We ask this through Jesus Christ our Lord.

Amen

The Allegiance

96 The Priest addresses the candidates, parents and godparents, omitting any paragraph not required.

You, who are to be baptized and confirmed, must now in allegiance to Christ declare before God and his Church the Christian faith into which you are to be baptized and in which you will live and grow.

Parents and godparents, you must now in allegiance to Christ declare before God and his Church the Christian faith into which *these children are* to be baptized, and in which you will help *them* to live and grow. You are to answer for yourselves and for your child.

You, who have already been baptized and are to be confirmed, must now in allegiance to Christ declare before God and his Church that you accept the Christian faith into which you were baptized, and in which you will continue to live and grow.

97 Then the Priest says

Do you believe in God, the Father almighty, creator of heaven and earth?

Yes, I believe and trust in him

Do you believe in Jesus Christ, his only Son, our Lord, who was conceived by the Holy Spirit and born of the Virgin Mary, who suffered under Pontius Pilate, was crucified, died and was buried, and descended to the dead; who on the third day rose again, ascended into heaven and is seated at the right hand of the Father, and who will come to judge the living and the dead?

Yes, I believe and trust in him

Do you believe in the Holy Spirit, the holy catholic Church, the communion of saints, the forgiveness of sins, the resurrection of the body, and the life everlasting?
Yes, I believe

98 Alternatively, the candidates, parents and godparents may say together the Apostles' Creed

**I believe in God, the Father almighty
creator of heaven and earth.**

**I believe in Jesus Christ, his only Son, our Lord.
He was conceived by the Holy Spirit
and born of the Virgin Mary.
He suffered under Pontius Pilate
was crucified, died, and was buried.
He descended to the dead.
On the third day he rose again.
He ascended into heaven
and is seated at the right hand of the Father.
He will come to judge the living and the dead.**

**I believe in the Holy Spirit
the holy catholic Church
the communion of saints
the forgiveness of sins
the resurrection of the body
and the life everlasting. Amen**

99 To the candidates the Priest says

Will you, who are to be baptized into this faith, and will you, who are to be confirmed, live in obedience to God's laws, as a loyal member of his Church?
With God's help, I will

00 To parents and godparents he says

Parents and godparents, will you by your own example and teaching, bring up your child to live in

obedience to God's laws, as a loyal member of his Church?
With God's help, I will

The Baptism

(101) Each candidate is presented to the Priest by *his* parent or sponsor, who says

Reverend Father in God, I present to you *N* to be baptized.

102 The Priest baptizes the candidates, dipping each in the water three times, or pouring water on each three times, once at the mention of each Person of the Holy Trinity, and saying

N I baptize you in the name of the Father, and of the Son, and of the Holy Spirit.
Amen

The Welcome

103 The Priest makes the sign of the cross on the forehead of each one who has been baptized, saying

I sign you with the cross, the sign of Christ.

After the signing of each or all he says

Do not be ashamed to confess the faith of Christ crucified.

Fight valiantly under the banner of Christ
against sin, the world, and the devil
and continue his faithful *soldiers* and *servants*
to the end of your *lives*.

(104) A candle, lit from the Easter Candle if possible, is given to each, or to the godparents with the words

Christ our light

When a candle has been given to each one, the Priest says

By baptism into Christ you pass from darkness to light.

**Shine as a light in the world
to the glory of God the Father.**

05 The congregation, representing the whole Church, welcomes
the newly-baptized, the Priest saying

God has received you by baptism into his Church.

**We welcome you into the Lord's family.
We are members together of the Body of Christ;
we are children of the same heavenly Father;
we are inheritors together of the kingdom of God.
We welcome you.**

The Confirmation

06 The Bishop stands before those who are to be confirmed and
calls the congregation to prayer.

Silence is kept.

The hymn *Veni Creator*, or some other hymn addressed to the Holy Spirit,
is sung.

07 Come, Holy Ghost, our souls inspire,
And lighten with celestial fire;
Thou the anointing Spirit art,
Who dost thy sevenfold gifts impart.

Thy blessèd unction from above
Is comfort, life, and fire of love;
Enable with perpetual light
The dullness of our blinded sight.

Anoint and cheer our soilèd face
With the abundance of thy grace;
Keep far our foes, give peace at home;
Where thou art guide no ill can come.

Teach us to know the Father, Son,
And thee, of Both, to be but One;
That through the ages all along
This may be our endless song,

Praise to thy eternal merit,
Father, Son and Holy Spirit.   Amen

108 The Bishop stands and says

Our help is in the Name of the Lord
who has made heaven and earth

Blessed be the Name of the Lord
now and for ever.   Amen

109 The Bishop stretches out his hands towards those to be confirmed and says

Almighty and everliving God
you have given your *servants* new birth
   in baptism by water and the Spirit
and have forgiven *them* all *their* sins.
Let your Holy Spirit rest upon *them*:
the Spirit of wisdom and understanding;
the Spirit of discernment and inner strength;
the Spirit of knowledge and true godliness;
and fill *them* with the Spirit of the fear of the Lord
now and for ever.
Amen

110 The candidates kneel in order before the Bishop. The Bishop
may sign them on the forehead, using at his discretion the
Chrism, and may say

N I sign you with the sign of the cross and I lay my
hand upon you.

Or he may say

N I lay my hand upon you.

He lays his hand on their heads, saying

Lord, confirm and strengthen with your Holy Spirit
this your child *N*† and empower *him* for your service.
Amen

†The name may be omitted here if it has already been used.

111　When all have been confirmed, the Bishop leads the congregation in saying

Defend, O Lord, *these* **your** *servants* **with your
　　heavenly grace
that** *they* **may continue yours for ever
and daily increase in your Holy Spirit more and more
　　until** *they come* **to your everlasting kingdom.**

112　The Bishop says

Heavenly Father
we pray for your *servants*
　　upon whom we have now laid our hands.
May your fatherly hand ever be over *them*
your Holy Spirit ever be with *them*.
Sustain *them* continually
　　with the body and blood of your Son
and so lead *them* in the knowledge
　　and obedience of your word
that in the end
　　they may enjoy the fulness of eternal life;
through Jesus Christ our Lord.
Amen

THE RENEWAL OF BAPTISMAL PROMISES

13　The congregation may be sprinkled with water at the Renewal of Baptismal Promises, to remind them of their baptism. Baptismal water is used for this. If there have been no baptisms and it is desired to bless water, the following form is used

Dear friends, this water will be used to remind us of our baptism. Let us ask God to bless it and to keep us faithful to the Spirit he has given us.

Father, we give you thanks for your gift of life-giving water.

Through the waters of the Red Sea you brought your people out of slavery in Egypt, and in the waters of Jordan your Son was anointed with the Holy Spirit.

As he hung on the cross, water and blood flowed from his side.

Through the waters of baptism you delivered us from sin and raised us to newness of life.

We ask you now to bless this water to our use.

May it remind us of our baptism that, renewed by your Spirit, we may rejoice with all who are baptized this Easter.

Grant this through Jesus Christ our Lord.
Amen

114 The people stand. Their candles may be relighted. The Priest addresses the congregation in these or similar words

Dear friends in Christ, tonight is the night of nights for which we have been preparing during Lent. We have come to know more clearly the love of Christ for us. On Palm Sunday we went to Jerusalem with him. We followed him day by day until, on Good Friday, we stood at the foot of the cross as he died for us in the fulness of his love. Tonight we rejoice in that great love. As we celebrate the Paschal Mystery of his death and resurrection, we remember that, at our baptism, we were buried with Christ and raised with him to newness of life. (The lighted candles we hold remind us that we share in the light of Christ.) Let us now show our thankfulness by renewing the solemn pledges which were then made: to renounce the world, the flesh and the devil, to believe the Christian faith, and to keep God's holy will and commandments.

I ask you therefore

Do you renounce the wickedness of the world, its greed for possessions, power and status?
Yes, I renounce them all

Do you renounce all that corrupts our human nature, pride, selfishness and lust?
Yes, I renounce them all

Do you renounce the devil, the author of all evil and the father of lies?
Yes, I renounce him

Do you believe and trust in God the Father, the maker of all?
I believe and trust in him

Do you believe and trust in his Son, Jesus Christ, the redeemer of the world?
I believe and trust in him

Do you believe and trust in his Holy Spirit, the giver of life?
I believe and trust in him

This is the faith of the Church
This is our faith. We believe and trust in one God, Father, Son, and Holy Spirit.

Will you faithfully play your part in the life and fellowship of the Church?
With God's help I will

Will you gladly obey the commandments of God and seek to do his will?
With God's help I will

Will you by your life and witness share in the Church's mission to proclaim the gospel, and to set forward peace and justice among all people?
With God's help I will

Almighty God who gives you the will to do all these things, grant you also the power to perform them, that he may complete the work which he has begun in you; through Jesus Christ our Lord.
Amen

The Sprinkling

115 The congregation may be sprinkled with the newly blessed water, in which case the Priest says

You have renewed the vows which were made when you were baptized into Christ. Receive now the sprinkling of this water, as a reminder of your baptism.

116 During the sprinkling there may be sung one or more of the following

I saw | water | flowing: from the right side of the | temple | alle|luia.
It brought God's life and | his sal|vation: and the people sang in joyful praise   alle|luia | alle|luia.

or

A hymn, baptismal in character

or

The Litany of Redemption

O give thanks to the Lord for | he is | gracious:
   for his | mercy · en|dures for | ever.

Who has loved us from | all e|ternity:
   for his | mercy · en|dures for | ever.

Who only | does great | wonders:
   for his | mercy · en|dures for | ever.

Who by his excellent wisdom | made the | heavens:
   for his | mercy · en|dures for | ever.

Who laid out the earth a|bove the | waters:
   for his | mercy · en|dures for | ever.

Who has | made great | lights:
   for his | mercy · en|dures for | ever.

The sun to | rule the | day:
   for his | mercy · en|dures for | ever.

The moon and the stars to | govern · the | night:
    for his | mercy · en|dures for | ever.

Who gives food to | all | flesh:
    for his | mercy · en|dures for | ever.

Who called | Abraham · from | Haran:
    for his | mercy · en|dures for | ever.

Who brought out | Israel · from | Egypt:
    for his | mercy · en|dures for | ever.

With a mighty hand and a | stretched-out | arm:
    for his | mercy · en|dures for | ever.

Who divided the Red Sea in | two | parts:
    for his | mercy · en|dures for | ever.

And made Israel to go | through the | midst of it:
    for his | mercy · en|dures for | ever.

Who led his people | through the | wilderness:
    for his | mercy · en|dures for | ever.

Who remembered us * when | we were · in | trouble:
    for his | mercy · en|dures for | ever.

Who for us and for our salvation * came | down from |
    heaven:
    for his | mercy · en|dures for | ever.

And was incarnate by the Holy Spirit of the Virgin Mary *
    and | was made | man:
    for his | mercy · en|dures for | ever.

Who by his cross and passion has re|deemed the | world:
    for his | mercy · en|dures for | ever.

And has washed us from our sins in his | own | blood:
    for his | mercy · en|dures for | ever.

Who on the third day | rose · from the | dead:
    for his | mercy · en|dures for | ever.

And has given | us the | victory:
    for his | mercy · en|dures for | ever.

Who ascended | up on | high:
   for his | mercy · en|dures for | ever.

And opened wide for us the ever|lasting | doors:
   for his | mercy · en|dures for | ever.

Who sits on the right | hand of | God:
   for his | mercy · en|dures for | ever.

And ever lives to make inter|cession | for us:
   for his | mercy · en|dures for | ever.

For the Lord our God is a | merci · ful | God:
   who loves | all that | he has | made.

And to him is due all glory * | honour · and | worship:
   **to the Father and the Son and the Holy Spirit * now
   and for ever * | world with · out | end.   A|men**

The Prayers of the Church

117   The Prayers of the Church may be omitted; if used they are as follows

Father in heaven, we praise you that on this night Christ rose from the dead.

We thank you for his triumph over sin and death and for his gift of eternal life.

We remember before you those who have died in the great hope of the resurrection. Unite us with them in your unending joy.

Lord, in your mercy
Hear our prayer

We pray for ourselves and all Christian people, that we may live as those who believe in the victory of the cross.

Lord, in your mercy
Hear our prayer

We pray for those who at this season are receiving Christ's new life by water and the Spirit. May they be able to recognise the risen Christ in us, their brothers and sisters in the Lord.

Lord, in your mercy
Hear our prayer

Bless and guide all who govern the nations of the earth.
Help them to know what is right and to do it.

Lord, in your mercy
Hear our prayer

We pray for all who suffer or are troubled. Give them
good friends to comfort them, and grant them healing
and the knowledge of your Son in his victorious passion.

Lord, in your mercy
Hear our prayer

We praise you, Lord God, sovereign over all, because you
have taken your great power, and begun to reign.
Amen

THE PEACE

118   The Peace follows in this form

This is the day which the Lord has made. We will rejoice
and be glad in it.

The peace of the risen Christ be with you. Alleluia.
Alleluia
Peace be with you. Alleluia. Alleluia

The Peace is given according to local custom.

119   The Eucharist continues with the Presentation of Gifts and the Taking of
the Bread and Wine.

Proper Preface 11 is used.

120   In place of the prayer at (87) in the Conclusion, the Priest may say

Lord, you have nourished us with your Easter sacrament.
Fill us with your Spirit and make us one in peace and
love. We ask this through Jesus Christ our Lord.
Amen

121 It is appropriate that on Easter Day (provided adequate preparation has been made) opportunity be given for baptismal promises to be re-affirmed.

The Priest addresses the people in these or similar words

Dear friends in Christ, we have completed our Lenten observance and are come with great joy to celebrate the Paschal Mystery of Christ's death and resurrection.

We recall that at our baptism we were buried with Christ and raised with him to newness of life. Let us now show our thankfulness by renewing the solemn pledges which were then made: to renounce the world, the flesh and the devil, to believe the Christian faith and to keep God's holy will and commandments.

So I bid you stand and answer me

The people make their promises as at 114. The Creed may be omitted at the Eucharist and the Offices where this is done.

Easter to Corpus Christi

EASTER DAY   W

The Collect

Lord of all life and power
through the mighty resurrection of your Son
you overcame the old order of sin and death
    and made all things new in him:
grant that we, being dead to sin
    and alive to you in Jesus Christ
may reign with him in glory;
to whom with you and the Holy Spirit
    be praise and honour, glory and might
now and in all eternity.

or

Almighty Father, through your only begotten Son Jesus
Christ you overcame death and opened to us the gate of
everlasting life: we humbly pray that as by your grace you
put into our minds good desires, so by your continual
help we may bring them to fulfilment; through Jesus
Christ our Lord, who lives and reigns with you and the
Holy Spirit, ever one God, world without end.

The Readings

YEAR A

Acts 10:34-43	Peter preaches the resurrection of Christ
Psalm 118:14-24	
Colossians 3:1-4	Hidden with Christ in God
John 20:1-18	

or

Matthew 28:1-10	The first Easter day

(If an Old Testament reading is required, this passage is read

Jeremiah 31:1-6	God's faithfulness

Acts 10:34-43 is then the second reading)

YEAR B

Acts 10:34-43   Peter preaches the resurrection
                            of Christ

Psalm 118:14-24
1 Corinthians 15:1-11   The fact of the resurrection
John 20:1-18

or

Mark 16:1-8   The first Easter day

(If an Old Testament reading is required, this passage is read

  Isaiah 25:6-9   The salvation of God

Acts 10:34-43 is then the second reading)

YEAR C

Acts 10:34-43   Peter preaches the resurrection
                            of Christ

Psalm 118:14-24
1 Corinthians 15:19-26   Christ conquers death
John 20:1-18

or

Luke 24:1-9   The first Easter day

(If an Old Testament reading is required, this passage is read

  Isaiah 65:17-25   God's new creation

Acts 10:34-43 is then the second reading)

Proper Preface 12   Canticle 7, 8, 9

THE FIRST SUNDAY AFTER EASTER   W

The Collect

Heavenly Father
you have delivered us from the power of sin
and brought us into the kingdom of your Son:
grant that he whose death has recalled us to life
  may by his presence among us

raise us to eternal joys;
through Jesus Christ our Lord.

or

Almighty Father, you gave your Son to die for our sins and to rise again for our justification: grant that malice may not affect us nor evil corrupt us, so that we may serve you continually in holiness and truth; through Jesus Christ our Lord.

The Readings

YEAR A

Acts 2:14a, 22-32	Peter proclaims the resurrection of Christ
Psalm 16:5-11	
1 Peter 1:3-9	We receive a new birth through his resurrection
John 20:19-31	The risen Christ with his disciples

YEAR B

Acts 4:32-35	The apostles bear witness to the resurrection
Psalm 118:19-29	
1 John 1:1–2:2	Sin is conquered by the word of life
John 20:19-31	The risen Christ with his disciples

YEAR C

Acts 5:27-32	Forgiveness given by the exalted Christ
Psalm 2	
Revelation 1:9-19	John's vision of Christ
John 20:19-31	The risen Christ and his disciples
Proper Preface 12	Canticle 8, 9, 12, The Song of the Church (Morning Prayer section 21)

THE SECOND SUNDAY AFTER EASTER   W

The Collect

Merciful Lord
your Son is the resurrection and the life
   of all who believe in him:
raise us from the death of sin
   into the life of righteousness;
through Jesus Christ our Lord.

or

Almighty Father, you show to those in error the light of
your truth that they may return to the way of righteousness: may all who belong to Christ renounce what is
contrary to their profession and follow in his footsteps;
through Jesus Christ our Lord.

The Readings

YEAR A

Acts 2:14a, 36-41	Baptism in the name of the risen Christ
Psalm 116:11-18	
1 Peter 1:17-23	You were ransomed to become holy
Luke 24:13-35	The risen Jesus makes himself known

YEAR B

Acts 3:12-19	Peter preaches the risen Christ in the Temple
Psalm 4	
1 John 3:1-7	We are the children of God
Luke 24:35-48	The risen Jesus makes himself known

YEAR C

Acts 9:1-20	The risen Christ appears to Saul
Psalm 30:4-12	
Revelation 5:11-14	Worthy is the Lamb
John 21:1-19	Jesus meets his disciples by the lakeside

Proper Preface 12   Canticle 8, 9, 12, The Song of the Church (Morning Prayer section 21)

THE THIRD SUNDAY AFTER EASTER   W

The Collect

God of peace
you brought again from the dead
   our Lord Jesus Christ
   the great Shepherd of the sheep
   by the blood of the eternal covenant:
perfect us in all goodness
   that we may do your will
and make us what you would have us be;
through Jesus Christ our Lord.

or

Almighty Father, you have given your only Son to be for us a sacrifice for sin and an example of godly life: give us grace that we may always thankfully receive the immeasurable benefit of his sacrifice, and also daily endeavour to follow his holy life; through Jesus Christ our Lord.

The Readings

YEAR A

Acts 2:42-47   The common life of the Jerusalem Christians

Psalm 100
1 Peter 2:19-25   The passion of the Good
                                    Shepherd
John 10:1-10   The Gate of the sheepfold

YEAR B

Acts 4:8-12   By his name we are saved
Psalm 118:1-9
1 John 3:18-24   Believe in his name
John 10:11-18   The Good Shepherd lays down
                                    his life

YEAR C

Acts 13:15-16a, 26-33   Paul preaches the risen Christ
Psalm 23
Revelation 7:9-17   The Lamb is the Shepherd
John 10:22-30   He gives his sheep eternal life

Proper Preface 12   Canticle 7, 9, 12

THE FOURTH SUNDAY AFTER EASTER   W

The Collect

Sóvereign Lord and Father
through the death and resurrection of your Son
    all creation is renewed
and by faith we are born again:
make us grow up into him
and bring us to the fulness of Christ;
who is alive and reigns with you and the Holy Spirit
one God, now and for ever.

or

Almighty God, you only can control our disordered wills
and passions: grant that we may love what you command
and desire what you promise, that among the many and
varied changes of the world, our hearts may be firmly

fixed where true joys may be found; through Jesus Christ
our Lord.

The Readings

YEAR A

Acts 7:55-60 | Stephen sees a vision of Christ
Psalm 31:1-8
1 Peter 2:2-10 | You are God's own people
John 14:1-14 | The Way, the Truth and the Life

YEAR B

Acts 8:26-40 | The conversion of the Ethiopian
| eunuch
Psalm 22:26-32
1 John 4:7-12 | God loves us; we are to love one
| another
John 15:1-8 | He is the Vine, we are the
| branches

YEAR C

Acts 14:8-18 | Paul heals the cripple at Lystra
Psalm 145:14-21
Revelation 21:1-6 | God will wipe away all tears
John 13:31-35 | The new commandment

Proper Preface 12 | Canticle 7, 8, 9, 12

THE FIFTH SUNDAY AFTER EASTER   W

The Collect

Eternal Father
your kingdom extends beyond space and time:
grant that in this world of changing things
    we may hold fast to what endures for ever;
through Jesus Christ our Lord.

or

Loving Father, all that is good comes from you: give us your humble servants your inspiration, that we may be holy in thought and deed; through Jesus Christ our Lord.

The Readings

YEAR A

Acts 17:22-31   Paul preaches in Athens
Psalm 66:7-19
1 Peter 3:13-22   Christ died for us, once for all
John 14:15-21   The promise of the Holy Spirit

YEAR B

Acts 10:44-48   The Pentecost of the Gentiles
Psalm 98
1 John 5:1-6   To love God is to keep his
                              commandments
John 15:9-17   You are my friends

YEAR C

Acts 15:1-2, 22-29   Gentiles are welcomed into the
                              Church
Psalm 67
Revelation 21:10-11,
   22-27   The holy City
John 14:23-29   I go to the Father who will send
                              you the Spirit

Proper Preface 12   Canticle 4, 9, 12

ASCENSION EVE   W

The Collect

Eternal Father
your Son ascended far above the heavens
   and holds all authority in this world and the next:
grant us the faith to know

that he lives in his Church on earth
and at the end of time
the whole world will see his glory;
who lives and reigns with you and the Holy Spirit
one God, for ever and ever.

ASCENSION DAY   W

The Collect

Sovereign Lord
your Son ascended in triumph
to rule in love and glory
    over the whole universe:
grant that all peoples may acknowledge
    the authority of his kingdom;
through Jesus Christ our Lord.

or

Grant, we pray, Almighty Father, that as we believe your
only begotten Son our Lord Jesus Christ to have ascended
into heaven, so we may also in heart and mind thither
ascend, and with him continually dwell; who lives and
reigns with you and the Holy Spirit, one God, for ever
and ever.

The Readings

Acts 1:1-11	The Ascension
Psalm 47	
Ephesians 1:15-23	Christ, the Head of his Body, the Church

YEAR A

Matthew 28:16-20	The great commission

YEAR B

Mark 16:14-20	At the right hand of the Father

YEAR C

Luke 24:45-53   The promise of power from on
                                  high

Proper Preface 13   Canticle 8, 10, The Song of the
                                  Church (Morning Prayer section 21)

THE SIXTH SUNDAY AFTER EASTER   W

The Collect

Eternal Father
through Jesus Christ our ascended Lord
you sent your Holy Spirit
    to be the bond of fellowship in the Church:
unify the whole created order in Christ
who reigns supreme over all things
with you and the Holy Spirit
one God, for ever and ever.

or

O God, the king of glory, you have exalted your only Son
Jesus Christ with great triumph to your kingdom in
heaven: do not leave us desolate, but send your Holy
Spirit to strengthen us, and exalt us to that place
where our Saviour Christ has gone before; who lives and
reigns with you and the Holy Spirit, one God, in glory
everlasting.

The Readings

YEAR A

Acts 1:6-14   They gave themselves to prayer
Psalm 68:1-10
1 Peter 4:12-14; 5:6-11   Sharing Christ's sufferings
John 17:1-11   The high-priestly prayer

YEAR B

Acts 1:15-17, 21-26	Matthias is chosen to replace Judas
Psalm 1	
1 John 5:9-13	The gift of eternal life
John 17:11b-19	That they all may be one

YEAR C

Acts 16:16-34	The ministry of Paul and Silas in prison
Psalm 97	
Revelation 22:12-20	Come, Lord Jesus
John 17:20-26	May they be perfectly one
Proper Preface 13	Canticle 4, 8, 12

PENTECOST EVE R

The Collect

God our Father
when your Son ascended into heaven
he promised to send us the Holy Spirit:
grant that we, who have not been left as orphans
may abide always in that Spirit
and be loving and obedient disciples of your Son;
who lives and reigns with you and the Holy Spirit
one God, now and for ever.

THE DAY OF PENTECOST *Sunday* R
Weekdays G

The Collect

Almighty God
on the day of Pentecost
you sent your Holy Spirit to the disciples
with the wind from heaven and in tongues of flame:

inspire our hearts and set them on fire
   with his joy and power
and send us out as witnesses
   to the wonder of your love;
through Jesus Christ our Lord
who lives and reigns with you and the Holy Spirit
one God, now and for ever.

or

Almighty God, at this time you taught the hearts of your
faithful people by sending to them the light of your Holy
Spirit: grant us by the same Spirit to have a right judgement in all things, and evermore to rejoice in his holy
comfort; through the merits of Jesus Christ our Saviour,
who is alive and reigns with you in the unity of the Spirit,
one God, now and for ever.

The Readings

YEAR A

Acts 2:1-21	The outpouring of the Holy Spirit
Psalm 104:26-36	
1 Corinthians 12:3b-13	The Holy Spirit for each and all
John 20:19-23	The gift of the Spirit for mission

(If an Old Testament reading is required, this passage is read

| Isaiah 44:1-8 | The promise of the Spirit |

Acts 2:1-21 is then the second reading)

YEAR B

Acts 2:1-21	The outpouring of the Holy Spirit
Psalm 104:26-36	
Romans 8:22-27	The Spirit prays within us
John 15:26-27; 16:4b-15	The Spirit will guide you into all truth

(If an Old Testament reading is required, this passage is read

   Ezekiel 37:1-14   The Spirit gives life

Acts 2:1-21 is then the second reading)

YEAR C

Acts 2:1-21   The outpouring of the Holy
                                 Spirit

Psalm 104:26-36
Romans 8:14-17   Children of God by the Spirit
John 14:8-17, 25-27   The Father will send the Spirit
                                 in my name

(If an Old Testament reading is required, this passage is read

   Genesis 11:1-9   Disunity at Babel

Acts 2:1-21 is then the second reading)

Proper Preface 14   Canticle 4, 7, 14

TRINITY SUNDAY   *Sunday* W
                                      Weekdays G

The Collect

Eternal and infinite God
you have inspired us to acknowledge
   the glory of the Trinity
and in your divine power
   to worship the Unity:
keep us steadfast in this faith
and unite us in your boundless love;
that we may always praise you
Father, Son and Holy Spirit
one God, now and for ever.

or

Almighty and everlasting God, you have given us your servants grace, by the confession of a true faith, to acknowledge the glory of the eternal Trinity, and in the power of the divine Majesty to worship the Unity: keep us steadfast in this faith, that defended from all adversities, we may praise you, Father, Son and Holy Spirit, one God, for ever and ever.

The Readings

YEAR A

Deuteronomy 4:32-40	The Lord is God
Psalm 33:1-12	
2 Corinthians 13:11-14	The love of the Holy Trinity
Matthew 28:16-20	The threefold Name

YEAR B

Isaiah 6:1-8	Isaiah's vision of the holiness of God
Psalm 29	
Romans 8:12-17	Partakers of the divine nature
John 3:1-17	The love of God

YEAR C

Proverbs 8:22-31	The eternal divine Wisdom
Psalm 8	
Romans 5:1-5	Peace and love given us by the Holy Trinity
John 16:12-15	Jesus speaks of the Father and of the Spirit
Proper Preface 15	Canticle The Song of the Church (Morning Prayer section 21), 1, 5, 17

CORPUS CHRISTI   W
THE COMMEMORATION OF
THE HOLY COMMUNION

The Collect

Almighty God
your Son our Lord Jesus Christ
   gave us the wonderful sacrament
   of his body and blood
to represent his death
and to celebrate his resurrection:
strengthen our devotion to him
   in these holy mysteries
and through them renew our unity with him
   and one another;
through Jesus Christ our Lord.

or

Lord God, your Son Jesus Christ ordained this sacrament
as a pledge of his love and a continual remembrance of
his passion: grant that we may partake of it in faith and,
growing up into him in all things, may come to his eternal
joy; who with you and the Holy Spirit lives and reigns,
one God, now and for ever.

The Readings

YEAR A

Deuteronomy 8:2-3	Manna
Psalm 147:12-20	
1 Corinthians 10:16-17	The one loaf means we are one Body
John 6:51-58	My flesh is real food; my blood real drink

Collects and Readings

YEAR B

Exodus 24:3-8	The blood of the old covenant
Psalm 116:11-17	
Hebrews 9:11-15	The blood of Christ purifies us for service
Mark 14:12-16, 22-26	The Last Supper

YEAR C

Genesis 14:18-20	Melchizedek offers bread and wine
Psalm 110:1-4	
1 Corinthians 11:23-26	The Last Supper
Luke 9:11-17	The feeding of five thousand
Proper Preface 10(c)	Canticle 13, 15, 17

Sundays of the Year

The First to the Fourth Sundays of the Year are always Sundays after Epiphany, as the dates given for each indicate. Because the date of Easter varies, the Fifth to the Ninth Sundays of the Year sometimes occur after Epiphany, and sometimes after Pentecost.

The Sunday of the Year which is transferred because Lent has begun may coincide with Easter 6, in which case it is not used at all, or with the Day of Pentecost, in which case the Collect and Readings for Pentecost are used on the Sunday, and the collect of the Sunday of the Year on the weekdays following it.

THE FIRST SUNDAY OF THE YEAR
THE BAPTISM OF CHRIST   *Sunday* W
between 7 and 13 January   *Weekdays* G

This is always the first Sunday after the Epiphany.

The Collect

Heavenly Father
you revealed Jesus as your beloved Son
   when the Holy Spirit came upon him
   at his baptism in the Jordan:
grant that we, who have been baptized in him
   may rejoice to be your children
   and the servants of all;
through Jesus Christ our Lord

or

O God, your blessed Son was revealed that he might destroy the works of the devil, and make us your children and heirs of eternal life: purify us as he is pure, that when he appears again with power and great glory, we may become like him in his eternal and glorious kingdom; where with you, O Father, and you, O Holy Spirit, he lives and reigns, ever one God, world without end.

The Readings

YEAR A

Isaiah 42:1-9	The Lord's servant
Psalm 29	
Acts 10:34-43	The baptism of Christ, the beginning of his ministry
Matthew 3:13-17	The baptism of Jesus

YEAR B

Genesis 1:1-5	The Spirit of God moves over the waters
Psalm 29	
Acts 19:1-7	The baptism of John
Mark 1:4-11	John baptizes Jesus

YEAR C

Isaiah 61:1-4	Ministry given by the Spirit of the Lord
Psalm 29	
Acts 8:14-17	Peter and John lay hands on the Samaritans baptized by Philip
Luke 3:15-17, 21-22	John baptizes Jesus
Proper Preface 27	Canticle 10, 11, 13

THE SECOND SUNDAY OF THE YEAR   G
between 14 and 20 January

This is always the second Sunday after the Epiphany.

The Collect

Heavenly Father
by your grace alone
    you accepted us
and called us to your service:

strengthen us by your Spirit
and make us worthy of our calling;
through Jesus Christ our Lord.

or

Almighty Father, look on the heartfelt desires of your servants, and stretch forth your powerful right hand to be our defence against all our enemies; through Jesus Christ our Lord.

The Readings

YEAR A

Isaiah 49:1-7	The Lord's Servant to be a light to the nations
Psalm 40:1-14	
1 Corinthians 1:1-9	May God grant you grace and peace
John 1:29-34	Behold the Lamb of God

YEAR B

1 Samuel 3:1-10 (or 1-20)	Speak, Lord, your servant hears
Psalm 63:1-9	
1 Corinthians 6:12-20	Your bodies are members of Christ
John 1:35-42	John's disciples follow Christ

YEAR C

Isaiah 62:1-5	The Lord delights in you
Psalm 36:5-10	
1 Corinthians 12:1-11	The gifts of the Spirit
John 2:1-11	The wedding at Cana

Proper Preface 27	Any Canticle

THE THIRD SUNDAY OF THE YEAR G
between 21 and 27 January

This is always the third Sunday after the Epiphany.

The Collect

God our Father
in Christ you make all things new:
transform the poverty of our nature
    by the riches of your grace
and reveal your glory
    in the renewal of our lives;
through Jesus Christ our Lord.

or

Lord of all power and might, the author and giver of all
good things: graft in our hearts the love of your Name, increase in us true religion, nourish us with all goodness,
and bring forth in us the fruit of good works; through
Jesus Christ our Lord, who lives and reigns with you and
the Holy Spirit, one God, for ever and ever.

The Readings

YEAR A

Isaiah 9:1-4	From darkness to light
Psalm 27:1-8	
1 Corinthians 1:10-17	Agree among yourselves
Matthew 4:12-23	The hope of Isaiah is fulfilled

YEAR B

Jonah 3:1-5, 10	Nineveh repents at Jonah's preaching
Psalm 62:5-12	
1 Corinthians 7:29-31	We live in the last times
Mark 1:14-20	Repent and believe the good news

YEAR C

Nehemiah 8:1-4a, 5-10	Ezra reads the Law
Psalm 19:7-14	
1 Corinthians 12:12-30	You are the Body of Christ
Luke 4:14-21	Jesus in the synagogue at Nazareth

Proper Preface 27   Any Canticle

THE FOURTH SUNDAY OF THE YEAR   G
between 28 January and 3 February

This is always the fourth Sunday after the Epiphany.

The Collect

Merciful Lord
you are the only giver of pardon and peace:
cleanse us your faithful people from our sins
that we may serve you with a quiet mind;
through Jesus Christ our Lord.

or

Merciful Lord, grant to your faithful people pardon and
peace, that they may be cleansed from all their sins, and
serve you with a quiet mind; through Jesus Christ our
Lord.

The Readings

YEAR A

Micah 6:1-8	What does the Lord require?
Psalm 37:1-11	
1 Corinthians 1:18-31	Christ the power and wisdom of God
Matthew 5:1-12	True blessedness

Collects and Readings

YEAR B

Deuteronomy 18:15-20	The promised prophet of God
Psalm 111	
1 Corinthians 8:1-13	Food offered to idols and concern for others
Mark 1:21-28	A new teaching with authority

YEAR C

Jeremiah 1:4-10	The call of Jeremiah
Psalm 71:1-6	
1 Corinthians 13:1-13	Faith, hope, and love
Luke 4:21-30	The rejection of Jesus at Nazareth

Proper Preface 27   Any Canticle

THE FIFTH SUNDAY OF THE YEAR   G
between 4 and 10 February unless Lent has begun

The Collect

Lord God
we can do nothing good without you
but in your strength we can do all things:
grant us the spirit to think and do
    always whatever is right;
through Jesus Christ our Lord.

or

Grant to us, Lord, the spirit to think and do always what
is right, so that we, who cannot do anything good
without you, may be enabled to live according to your
will; through Jesus Christ our Lord.

The Readings

YEAR A

Isaiah 58:3-9a	True fasting
Psalm 112:4-9	
1 Corinthians 2:1-11	The proclamation of Christ crucified
Matthew 5:13-16	You are to be salt and light

YEAR B

Job 7:1-7	The problem of suffering
Psalm 147:1-11	
1 Corinthians 9:16-23	The necessity of preaching the gospel
Mark 1:29-39	Christ the healer

YEAR C

Isaiah 6:1-8 (or 1-13)	The call of Isaiah
Psalm 138	
1 Corinthians 15:1-11	The gospel of the resurrection
Luke 5:1-11	They left all and followed him

Proper Preface 27	Any Canticle

THE SIXTH SUNDAY OF THE YEAR　　G
*between 11 and 17 February,
or, if Lent has begun, between 8 and 14 May*

The Collect

Lord God of wisdom and truth
you made yourself known to the world
　in your Son Jesus Christ:
grant that we may know him and love him
and through him may share
　the fulness of eternal life;
who now lives and reigns with you and the Holy Spirit
one God, for ever and ever.

or

God our Father, you have prepared for those who love
you such good things as pass our understanding: pour
into our hearts such love towards you, that we, loving
you above all things, may obtain your promises which
exceed all that we can desire; through Jesus Christ our
Lord.

The Readings

YEAR A

Deuteronomy 30:15-20	The choice: life and good, death and evil

or

Ecclesiasticus 15:15-20	Keep the commandments and act faithfully
Psalm 119:1-8	
1 Corinthians 3:1-9	God gives the growth
Matthew 5:17-26	The fulfilment of the Law

YEAR B

2 Kings 5:1-14	Naaman is cured of leprosy
Psalm 32	
1 Corinthians 9:24-27	Running the race for an unfading wreath
Mark 1:40-45	Jesus heals a leper

YEAR C

Jeremiah 17:5-10	Trust not in human nature but in the Lord
Psalm 1	
1 Corinthians 15:12-20	Our hope is in the risen Christ
Luke 6:17-26	Blessings and woes
Proper Preface 27	Any Canticle

THE SEVENTH SUNDAY OF THE YEAR   G
between 18 and 24 February
or, if Lent has begun, between 15 and 21 May

The Collect

Merciful Lord
you have taught us through your Son
   that love is the fulfilling of the law:
grant that we may love you
   with our whole heart
and our neighbours as ourselves;
through Jesus Christ our Lord.

or

Almighty and everlasting God, increase in us the gifts of
faith, hope, and love; and, that we may obtain what you
promise, make us love what you command; through
Jesus Christ our Lord, who lives and reigns with you and
the Holy Spirit, one God, for ever and ever.

The Readings

YEAR A

Isaiah 49:8-13   The providence and
                                      compassion of God

Psalm 62:5-12
1 Corinthians 3:10-11,
   16-23   Belonging to Christ
Matthew 5:27-37   The fulfilment of the Law

YEAR B

Isaiah 43:18-25   God forgives his people
Psalm 41
2 Corinthians 1:18-22   Jesus, the fulfilment of God's
                                       promise
Mark 2:1-12   The paralysed man is forgiven
                                       and cured

YEAR C

Genesis 45:3-11, 15	Joseph's brothers find him lord of Egypt
Psalm 37:1-11	
1 Corinthians 15:35-38, 42-50	The resurrection of the dead
Luke 6:27-38	Love, not friends only, but also enemies
Proper Preface 27	Any Canticle

THE EIGHTH SUNDAY OF THE YEAR   G
between 25 February and 3 March (leap year 2 March)
or, if Lent has begun, between 22 and 28 May

The Collect

Gracious Father
you have taught us that love
  is the true bond of all virtues
and without it anything we do is worthless:
send your Holy Spirit
and pour this great gift into our hearts;
through Jesus Christ our Lord.

or

Lord, you have taught us that whatever we do without love is worth nothing: send your Holy Spirit and pour into our hearts that most excellent gift of love, the true bond of peace and of all virtues, without which whoever lives is counted dead before you; grant this for your only Son Jesus Christ's sake.

The Readings

YEAR A

Leviticus 19:1-2, 9-18	Love your neighbour as yourself
Psalm 119:33-40	

| 1 Corinthians 4:1-5 | The Lord judges his stewards |
| Matthew 5:38-48 | Be therefore perfect |

YEAR B

Hosea 2:14-20	God's love for his people
Psalm 103:1-13	
2 Corinthians 3:1-6	Confidence through Christ
Mark 2:18-22	Joy in Christ's presence

YEAR C

Ecclesiasticus 27:4-7	The test of a man is in his words
or	
Isaiah 55:10-13	God's word will accomplish its purpose
Psalm 92:1-4, 12-15	
1 Corinthians 15:51-58	Victory over death is ours through Christ
Luke 6:39-49	Hearing the Lord's words and doing them
Proper Preface 27	Any Canticle

THE NINTH SUNDAY OF THE YEAR   G
between 4 and 10 March (leap year, 3 and 9 March)
or, if Lent has begun, between 29 May and 4 June

The Collect

Lord of all wisdom
you have so ordered our life
   that we walk by faith and not by sight:
grant that in the darkness of this world
we may witness to our faith
   by the courage of our lives;
through Jesus Christ our Lord.

or

Graciously hear us, Lord God, and grant that we, to whom you have given the desire to pray, may by your mighty aid be defended and strengthened in all dangers and adversities; through Jesus Christ our Lord.

The Readings

YEAR A

Genesis 12:1-9	The call of Abraham
Psalm 33:12-21	
Romans 3:21-28	Righteousness through faith in Christ
Matthew 7:21-29	Hearing the Lord's words and doing them

YEAR B

1 Samuel 16:1-13	Samuel anoints David for kingship
Psalm 20	
2 Corinthians 4:5-12	The life of Jesus is to be seen in our life
Mark 2:23–3:6	The Lord of the sabbath

YEAR C

1 Kings 8:22-23, 41-43	The prayer of Solomon
Psalm 100	
Galatians 1:1-10	The gospel which Paul preached
Luke 7:1-10	The faith of the centurion
Proper Preface 27	Any Canticle

THE TENTH SUNDAY OF THE YEAR   G
between 5 and 11 June

The Collect

Heavenly Father
your Son has taught us
that in losing our life we save it:
put to death in us
all that keeps us
   from the life you alone can give;
through Jesus Christ our Lord.

or

Merciful God, it is by your gift alone that your faithful
people offer you true and acceptable service: grant that
we may so faithfully serve you in this life, that we fail not
finally to obtain your heavenly promises; through the
merits of Jesus Christ our Lord.

The Readings

YEAR A

Genesis 22:1-18	Abraham is ready to sacrifice Isaac
Psalm 13	
Romans 4:13-18	We receive God's promises by faith
Matthew 9:9-13	Matthew is called to be an apostle

YEAR B

1 Samuel 16:14-23	David is chosen to serve Saul
Psalm 57	
2 Corinthians 4:13–5:1	Looking to the unseen things which are eternal
Mark 3:20-35	Doing God's will

YEAR C

1 Kings 17:17-24	Elijah raises the widow's son
Psalm 113	
Galatians 1:11-24	Paul's spiritual pilgrimage
Luke 7:11-17	Jesus raises the widow's son in Nain

Proper Preface 27   Any Canticle

THE ELEVENTH SUNDAY OF THE YEAR   G
between 12 and 18 June

The Collect

Father of justice and love
you call your Church to witness
    that you are in Christ reconciling the world to yourself:
help us to proclaim boldly the good news of your love
that all who hear it may be reconciled to you
and work together for peace and justice;
through Jesus Christ our Lord.

or

Father in heaven, keep your household the Church steadfast in faith and love, that through your protection it may
be free from all adversities, and may devoutly serve you
in good works to the glory of your Name; through Jesus
Christ our Lord.

The Readings

YEAR A

Genesis 25:19-34	Esau sells his birthright
Psalm 46	
Romans 5:6-11	Through Christ we are reconciled to God
Matthew 9:35–10:8	Jesus is moved with compassion for the crowds

YEAR B

2 Samuel 1:17-27	David mourns the death of Saul and Jonathan
Psalm 46	
2 Corinthians 5:6-17	We make it our aim to please the Lord
Mark 4:26-34	Parables of the seed

YEAR C

1 Kings 19:1-8	Elijah flees to Horeb
Psalm 42	
Galatians 2:15-21	Justified by faith in the Son of God
Luke 7:36–8:3	She loved much and was forgiven much

Proper Preface 27	Any Canticle

THE TWELFTH SUNDAY OF THE YEAR   G
between 19 and 25 June

The Collect

Merciful Lord
you have called us to offer ourselves
   as a living sacrifice to you:
transform us by the renewal of our minds
that we may know and do your perfect will;
through Jesus Christ our Lord.

or

Almighty and everlasting God, mercifully look upon our infirmities, and in all our dangers and necessities stretch forth your right hand to help and defend us; through Jesus Christ our Lord.

The Readings

YEAR A

Genesis 28:10-17	God reveals himself to Jacob
Psalm 91:1-10	
Romans 5:12-19	The free gift of God's grace
Matthew 10:24-33	Fear not

YEAR B

2 Samuel 5:1-12	David becomes king over Israel
Psalm 48	
2 Corinthians 5:18–6:2	Now is the day of salvation
Mark 4:35-41	The stilling of the storm

YEAR C

1 Kings 19:9-14	Elijah hears the still small voice
Psalm 43	
Galatians 3:23-29	All are one in Christ
Luke 9:18-24	Taking up the cross

Proper Preface 27   Any Canticle

THE THIRTEENTH SUNDAY OF THE YEAR   G
between 26 June and 2 July

The Collect

Merciful Father
through the passion of your Son
you made an instrument of shameful death
   to be for us the way of life:
grant that we may glory in the cross of Christ
and gladly suffer for his sake;
who is alive and reigns with you and the Holy Spirit
one God, for ever and ever.

or

Grant, O Lord, that the course of this world may be so peaceably governed by your providence, that your Church may joyfully serve you in confidence and serenity; through Jesus Christ our Lord, who lives and reigns with you and the Holy Spirit, one God, for ever and ever.

The Readings

YEAR A

Genesis 32:22-32	Jacob wrestles with God
Psalm 17:1-7, 16	
Romans 6:3-11	Baptized into Christ's death and resurrection
Matthew 10:34-42	Christian discipleship

YEAR B

2 Samuel 6:1-15	David brings the Ark to Jerusalem
Psalm 24	
2 Corinthians 8:7-15	The generosity of Christ makes us rich
Mark 5:21-43	The daughter of Jairus; a woman with haemorrhage

YEAR C

1 Kings 19:15-21	Elijah is told what to do
Psalm 44:1-9	
Galatians 5:1, 13-25	Freedom in the Spirit; the fruit of the Spirit
Luke 9:51-62	The cost of discipleship
Proper Preface 27	Any Canticle

THE FOURTEENTH SUNDAY OF THE YEAR   G
between 3 and 9 July

The Collect

Heavenly Father
your Son revealed in signs and miracles
   the wonder of your saving love:
renew us by your heavenly grace
and in our weakness
   sustain us by your mighty power;
through Jesus Christ our Lord.

or

O God, the strength of all who put their trust in you: mercifully accept our prayers, and because in our weakness
we can do nothing good without you, give us the help of
your grace, that in keeping your commandments we may
please you in both will and deed; through Jesus Christ
our Lord, who lives and reigns with you and the Holy
Spirit, one God, for ever and ever.

The Readings

YEAR A

Exodus 1:6-14, 22–2:10	Israel suffers in Egypt and Moses is born
Psalm 124	
Romans 7:14-25a	The struggle with fallen human nature
Matthew 11:25-30	Come, I will give you rest

YEAR B

2 Samuel 7:1-17	David forbidden to build a temple
Psalm 89:21-38	
2 Corinthians 12:1-10	God's power made perfect in weakness
Mark 6:1-6	Jesus rejected at Nazareth

YEAR C

1 Kings 21:1-21	Ahab covets and seizes Naboth's vineyard
Psalm 5:1-7	
Galatians 6:7-18	The marks of the Lord Jesus
Luke 10:1-12, 17-20	The Lord commissions the seventy
Proper Preface 27	Any Canticle

THE FIFTEENTH SUNDAY OF THE YEAR　　G
between 10 and 16 July

The Collect

Almighty Father
you have broken the tyranny of sin
and sent the Spirit of your Son into our hearts:
take and receive our freedom
and bring us into the glorious liberty
　　of the children of God;
through Jesus Christ our Lord
who lives and reigns with you and the Holy Spirit
one God, now and for ever.

or

Loving Father, look with favour on the prayers of your
people, who are justly punished for their sins, and in
your goodness mercifully deliver them from all evil, for
the glory of your Name; through Jesus Christ our Lord.

The Readings

YEAR A

Exodus 2:11-22	Moses an exile in Midian
Psalm 69:6-14	
Romans 8:9-17	By the Spirit we cry 'Abba, Father'
Matthew 13:1-9, 18-23	The parable of the sower

YEAR B

2 Samuel 7:18-29	A prayer of David
Psalm 132:10-18	
Ephesians 1:1-10	God's plan for us
Mark 6:7-13	Jesus sends out the Twelve

YEAR C

2 Kings 2:1, 6-14	Elisha succeeds Elijah
Psalm 139:1-11	
Colossians 1:1-14	Paul gives thanks for the faith of the Colossians
Luke 10:25-37	Who is my neighbour?
Proper Preface 27	Any Canticle

THE SIXTEENTH SUNDAY OF THE YEAR　　G
between 17 and 23 July

The Collect

Eternal Lord
you spoke to the prophets
   to make your will and purpose known:
inspire the guardians of your truth
that through their witness
   all people may be made one with your saints;
through Jesus Christ our Lord.

or

Almighty and merciful God, in your goodness keep us
from all things that may hurt us, that we, being ready
both in body and mind, may accomplish with free hearts
those things agreeable to your will; through Jesus Christ
our Lord.

The Readings
YEAR A

Exodus 3:1-12

God commissions Moses at the burning bush

Psalm 103:1-13

Romans 8:18-25

Present suffering leads to future glory

Matthew 13:24-30, 36-43

The parable of the weeds

YEAR B

2 Samuel 11:1-15

The adultery of David and Bathsheba

Psalm 53

Ephesians 2:11-22

Christ is our peace

Mark 6:30-34

The compassion of Christ for unshepherded sheep

YEAR C

2 Kings 4:8-17

Elisha and the rich woman of Shunem

Psalm 139:12-18

Colossians 1:21-29

Christ our hope of glory

Luke 10:38-42

Mary and Martha at Bethany

Proper Preface 27

Any Canticle

THE SEVENTEENTH SUNDAY OF THE YEAR   G
between 24 and 30 July

The Collect

Lord of heaven and earth
you sent your Holy Spirit
   to be the life and power of your Church:
sow in our hearts the seeds of his grace
that we may bring forth the fruit of the Spirit
   in love and joy and peace;
through Jesus Christ our Lord.

or

Mercifully receive, O Lord, the prayers of your people who call upon you: grant that they may know what they ought to do, and may have grace faithfully to accomplish it; through Jesus Christ our Lord.

The Readings

YEAR A

Exodus 3:13-20	God charges Moses to liberate his people
Psalm 105:1-11	
Romans 8:26-30	God works for good with those who love him
Matthew 13:44-52	Parables of the kingdom

YEAR B

2 Samuel 12:1-14	David repents and is forgiven
Psalm 32	
Ephesians 3:14-21	Paul's prayer for the Ephesians
John 6:1-15	The feeding of the five thousand

YEAR C

2 Kings 5:1-15a (… in Israel)	Naaman cured of leprosy
Psalm 21:1-7	
Colossians 2:6-15	Fulness of life in Christ through baptism
Luke 11:1-13	Ask and it will be given you
Proper Preface 27	Any Canticle

THE EIGHTEENTH SUNDAY OF THE YEAR   G
between 31 July and 6 August

The Collect

Eternal God
your Son is the way, the truth and the life:
grant that we may walk in his way
rejoice in his truth
and share his risen life;
who is alive and reigns with you and the Holy Spirit
one God, for ever and ever.

or

Lord God, you declare your almighty power above all in
showing mercy and pity: grant us such a measure of your
grace that, running in the way of your commandments,
we may obtain your promises, and share in your heavenly treasure; through Jesus Christ our Lord.

The Readings

YEAR A

Exodus 12:1-14	The Passover
Psalm 143:1-10	
Romans 8:31-39	The love of God revealed in Christ
Matthew 14:13-21	Jesus feeds the five thousand

YEAR B

2 Samuel 12:15b-25	Solomon is born
Psalm 34:11-22	
Ephesians 4:1-6	One Lord, one faith, one baptism
John 6:24-35	The bread of life

YEAR C

2 Kings 13:14-20a	The death of Elisha
Psalm 28	
Colossians 3:1-11	Christ is all and in all
Luke 12:13-21	The parable of the rich fool

Proper Preface 27   Any Canticle

THE NINETEENTH SUNDAY OF THE YEAR   G
between 7 and 13 August

The Collect

Almighty God
you created the heavens and the earth
and made us in your own image:
teach us to discern your hand in all your works
and to serve you with reverence and thanksgiving;
through Jesus Christ our Lord
who with you and the Holy Spirit
    reigns supreme over all things
now and for ever.

or

Let your merciful ears, Lord God, be open to the prayers
of your people, and that they may obtain their petitions,
make them to ask such things as will please you; through
Jesus Christ our Lord.

The Readings

YEAR A

Exodus 14:19-31   God's people escape across the
                                   sea

Psalm 106:4-13
Romans 9:1-5   Paul protests his love for Israel
Matthew 14:22-33   Lord, save me

YEAR B

2 Samuel 18:1-15	The rebellion and the death of Absalom
Psalm 143:1-8	
Ephesians 4:25–5:2	Walk in love, as Christ loved us
John 6:35, 41-51	The living bread from heaven

YEAR C

Jeremiah 18:1-11	The potter and his clay
Psalm 14	
Hebrews 11:1-3, 8-19	The faith of Abraham and Sarah
Luke 12:32-40	Be ready and watch
Proper Preface 27	Any Canticle

THE TWENTIETH SUNDAY OF THE YEAR   G
between 14 and 20 August

The Collect

God our Saviour
your Son has promised
   that when two or three come together in his name
   he is there with them:
open our eyes that we may see him
and our hearts that we may love him;
through Jesus Christ our Lord.

or

O God of unchangeable power, in your loving providence you are carrying out the work of our salvation: look
mercifully on your Church, that wonderful and sacred
mystery, and let the whole world know that you are
bringing all things to perfection in Jesus Christ our Lord.

The Readings

YEAR A

Exodus 16:2-15	Manna and water given in the desert
Psalm 78:1-3, 10-19	
Romans 11:13-16, 29-32	God's mercy for all his people
Matthew 15:21-28	Great is your faith

YEAR B

2 Samuel 18:24-33	David's lament over Absalom
Psalm 102:1-12	
Ephesians 5:15-20	Be filled with the Spirit
John 6:51-58	My flesh is real food, my blood real drink

YEAR C

Jeremiah 20:7-13	Jeremiah unburdens his heart
Psalm 10:13-20	
Hebrews 12:1-2, 12-17	Looking to Jesus
Luke 12:49-56	I came not to bring peace but division

Proper Preface 27	Any Canticle

THE TWENTY FIRST SUNDAY OF THE YEAR   G
between 21 and 27 August

The Collect

Lord God
for the sake of the joy that lay ahead of him
your Son endured the cross and accepted the shame:
give us grace to bear our sufferings
and bring us to the glory that shall be revealed;
through Jesus Christ our Lord.

or

Almighty God, we have no power to help ourselves: keep us both outwardly in our bodies and inwardly in our souls, and defend us from all evil thoughts which may assault us; through Jesus Christ our Lord, who lives and reigns with you and the Holy Spirit, one God, for ever and ever.

The Readings

YEAR A

Exodus 17:1-7	The people are given water from the rock
Psalm 95	
Romans 11:33-36	The glory of God
Matthew 16:13-20	Peter confesses Jesus as the Christ

YEAR B

2 Samuel 23:1-7	The last words of David
Psalm 67	
Ephesians 5:21-33	Marriage in Christ
John 6:55-69	Jesus has the words of eternal life

YEAR C

Jeremiah 28:1-9	Jeremiah confronts a false prophet
Psalm 84	
Hebrews 12:18-29	The city of the living God
Luke 13:22-30	Enter by the narrow door
Proper Preface 27	Any Canticle

THE TWENTY SECOND SUNDAY OF THE YEAR   G
between 28 August and 3 September

The Collect

Gracious Father
your Son Jesus Christ offered himself
   in humble obedience to free us from our sins:
grant us grace to receive him with thankfulness
   as our Saviour and Lord
and in the freedom of your Spirit
   to follow the pattern of his holy life;
through Jesus Christ our Lord.

or

God our Father, you are our refuge and strength, the
author of all godliness: hear the devout prayers of your
Church, and grant that what we ask in faith we may
thankfully receive; through Jesus Christ our Lord.

The Readings

YEAR A

Exodus 19:1-9	The Covenant at Sinai
Psalm 114	
Romans 12:1-13	Life in the Body of Christ
Matthew 16:21-28	The way of the cross

YEAR B

1 Kings 2:1-4, 10-12	David's charge to Solomon and his death
Psalm 121	
Ephesians 6:10-20	The whole armour of God
Mark 7:1-23	What really makes people unclean

YEAR C

Ezekiel 18:1-9, 25-29	Individual responsibility
Psalm 15	
Hebrews 13:1-8	Continue in love to all
Luke 14:1, 7-14	Be ready to take the lowest place

| Proper Preface 27 | Any Canticle |

THE TWENTY THIRD SUNDAY OF THE YEAR   G
between 4 and 10 September

The Collect

Merciful Father
your Son Jesus Christ healed the sick
and restored them to fulness of life:
look with compassion on the anguish of the world
and heal the affliction of your people;
through our Lord and Saviour Jesus Christ.

or

Keep your Church, Lord God, with your continual
mercy, and because our human frailty without you cannot but fall, keep us always under your protection, and
lead us to those things that make for our salvation;
through Jesus Christ our Lord.

The Readings

YEAR A

Exodus 19:16-24	The Lord speaks to Moses at Sinai
Psalm 115:1-10	
Romans 13:1-10	The Christian and the state
Matthew 18:15-20	Disputes among God's people

YEAR B

Ecclesiasticus 5:8-15	The right use of speech
or	
Proverbs 2:1-8	The Lord gives wisdom
Psalm 119:129-136	
James 1:17-27	Hearing the word of God and doing it
Mark 7:31-37	The deaf hear, the dumb speak

YEAR C

Ezekiel 33:1-11	Ezekiel is called to be a watchman
Psalm 94:12-22	
Philemon 1-20	Your runaway slave is your brother
Luke 14:25-33	Counting the cost of discipleship
Proper Preface 27	Any Canticle

THE TWENTY FOURTH SUNDAY OF THE YEAR   G
between 11 and 17 September

The Collect

Gracious Father
Christ our Saviour in baptism
   made us one with him
   and assured us of eternal life:
free us from sin
   and raise us to new life in him;
who lives and reigns with you and the Holy Spirit
one God, now and for ever.

or

O God, without you we are not able to please you: mercifully grant that your Holy Spirit may in all things direct

and rule our hearts; through Jesus Christ our Lord, who lives and reigns with you and the Holy Spirit, one God, now and for ever.

The Readings

YEAR A

Exodus 20:1-20	The Ten Commandments
Psalm 19:7-14	
Romans 14:5-12	We live to the Lord, not to ourselves
Matthew 18:21-35	The servant who would not forgive

YEAR B

Proverbs 22:1-9	True blessedness
Psalm 125	
James 2:1-10, 14-17	The royal law of love
Mark 8:27-38	The necessity of the cross

YEAR C

Hosea 5:15–6:6	Let us return to the Lord
Psalm 77:11-20	
1 Timothy 1:12-17	The mercy and salvation of Christ
Luke 15:1-10	The lost coin and the lost sheep
Proper Preface 27	Any Canticle

THE TWENTY FIFTH SUNDAY OF THE YEAR   G
between 18 and 24 September

The Collect

Heavenly Father
your Son has taught us
    that anything we do
    for the least of our neighbours
    we do for him:

open our eyes to the needs of others
and give us the will
    to serve you in them;
through Jesus Christ our Lord.

or

Lord, let your continual pity cleanse and defend your
Church, and because it cannot continue in safety without
your aid, keep it evermore by your help and goodness;
through Jesus Christ our Lord.

The Readings

YEAR A

Exodus 32:1-14	The golden calf
Psalm 106:7-9, 20-24	
Philippians 1:21-27	Christ is to be honoured in every way
Matthew 20:1-16	The parable of the labourers in the vineyard

YEAR B

Job 28:20-28	The fear of the Lord is wisdom
Psalm 27:1-8	
James 3:13-18	Fruits of the wisdom from above
Mark 9:30-37	True greatness

YEAR C

Hosea 11:1-11	The Father's love for his disobedient child
Psalm 107:1-9	
1 Timothy 2:1-7	Salvation is for all
Luke 16:1-13	Shrewd manager, unjust steward

Proper Preface 27	Any Canticle

THE TWENTY SIXTH SUNDAY OF THE YEAR   G
between 25 September and 1 October

The Collect

God, mighty to save
you have given us the shield of faith
    and the sword of the Spirit:
strengthen us to resist all attacks of the enemy
and to fight at your side
    against the tyranny of evil;
through Jesus Christ our Lord.

or

Almighty and everlasting God, you are always more
ready to hear than we to pray, and you constantly give
more than either we desire or deserve: pour down on us
the abundance of your mercy, forgiving us those things
of which our conscience is afraid, and giving us those
good things which we are not worthy to ask, except
through the merits of Jesus Christ, your Son our Lord.

The Readings

YEAR A

Exodus 33:12-23   My presence will go with you
Psalm 99
Philippians 2:1-13   The mind of Christ
Matthew 21:28-32   Saying and doing

YEAR B

Job 42:1-6   I have seen you with my own
                       eyes
Psalm 27:9-17
James 5:1-11   The Lord is at hand
Mark 9:38-50   He who is not against us is for
                       us

YEAR C

Joel 2:23-29	Rejoice in God's goodness
Psalm 107:1, 33-43	
1 Timothy 6:6-19	Fight the good fight of faith
Luke 16:19-31	The rich man and Lazarus
Proper Preface 27	Any Canticle

THE TWENTY SEVENTH SUNDAY OF THE YEAR   G
between 2 and 8 October

The Collect

Eternal Father
you gave your only Son Jesus Christ
    that in him we might have eternal life:
reveal to us the greatness of your gift
and inspire us to give ourselves to you
    in thankful service for his sake;
who with you and the Holy Spirit
    is alive and reigns, one God, now and for ever.

or

O Lord, we pray that you will maintain your family the
Church in the true faith, that those who trust wholly in
your heavenly grace may always be defended by your
mighty power; through Jesus Christ our Lord.

The Readings

YEAR A

Numbers 27:12-23	Moses appoints Joshua to succeed him
Psalm 81:1-10	
Philippians 3:12-21	Pressing on toward the goal
Matthew 21:33-43	The parable of the vineyard and the tenants

YEAR B

Genesis 2:18-24	God institutes marriage
Psalm 128	
Hebrews 1:1-4; 2:9-11	God speaks through his Son, the pioneer of salvation
Mark 10:2-16	God's pattern for family life

YEAR C

Amos 5:6-7, 10-15	Hate evil, love good, establish justice
Psalm 101	
2 Timothy 1:1-14	Rekindle God's gift, guard the truth
Luke 17:5-10	Persevere in serving the Lord
Proper Preface 27	Any Canticle

THE TWENTY EIGHTH SUNDAY OF THE YEAR   G
between 9 and 15 October

The Collect

God, the source of all power
your Son prayed that you would keep his disciples
   from the evil one:
strengthen us to resist temptation
and to follow you the only God;
through Jesus Christ our Lord.

or

O God, your never-failing providence sets in order all
things both in heaven and earth: put away from us all
hurtful things, and give us those things which are best for
us; through Jesus Christ our Lord, who lives and reigns
with you and the Holy Spirit, one God, for ever and ever.

The Readings

YEAR A

Deuteronomy 34:1-12	The death of Moses
Psalm 135:1-14	
Philippians 4:1-9	Rejoice in the Lord always
Matthew 22:1-14	The wedding feast

YEAR B

Genesis 3:8-19	Adam and Eve rebel against God
Psalm 90:1-12	
Hebrews 4:1-3, 9-13	The word of God
Mark 10:17-30	The danger of riches

YEAR C

Micah 2:1-10	Judgement against oppressors
Psalm 26	
2 Timothy 2:8-15	Salvation in Christ Jesus
Luke 17:11-19	Jesus cures ten lepers; one is thankful
Proper Preface 27	Any Canticle

THE TWENTY NINTH SUNDAY OF THE YEAR   G
between 16 and 22 October

The Collect

Eternal God
in your loving mercy
you have planted within us the seed of faith:
grant that it may grow
    until we trust you with all our heart;
through Jesus Christ our Lord.

or

Almighty and everlasting God, you govern all things in heaven and earth; mercifully hear the prayers of your people, and grant us your peace all the days of our life; through Jesus Christ our Lord.

The Readings

YEAR A

Ruth:1:1-19a	Ruth goes home with Naomi
Psalm 146	
1 Thessalonians 1:1-10	Faith, love and hope
Matthew 22:15-22	Pay to Caesar what is his, to God what is his

YEAR B

Isaiah 53:7-12	The Lord's suffering Servant
Psalm 35:18-29	
Hebrews 4:14-16	Jesus our great High Priest
Mark 10:35-45	Christ's life a ransom for many

YEAR C

Habakkuk 1:1-3; 2:1-4	The righteous will live by his faithfulness
Psalm 119:137-144	
2 Timothy 3:14–4:5	A charge to Timothy
Luke 18:1-8	The widow and the judge
Proper Preface 27	Any Canticle

THE THIRTIETH SUNDAY OF THE YEAR   G
between 23 and 29 October

The Collect

Father of all
you gave your only Son Jesus Christ
    to take upon himself the form of a servant
and to be obedient, even to death on a cross:

give us the same mind that was in Christ Jesus
that sharing his humility
    we may come to be with him in his glory;
who lives and reigns with you and the Holy Spirit
one God, now and for ever.

or

Heavenly Father, grant that your grace may always
precede and follow us, that we may continually be given
to good works; through Jesus Christ our Lord, who lives
and reigns with you and the Holy Spirit, one God, now
and for ever.

The Readings

YEAR A

Ruth 2:1-13	Ruth meets Boaz
Psalm 128	
1 Thessalonians 2:1-8	Paul's love for the Thessalonians
Matthew 22:34-46	The two great commandments

YEAR B

Jeremiah 31:7-9	God promises to bring his people home
Psalm 126	
Hebrews 5:1-6	Jesus the gentle High Priest
Mark 10:46-52	Jesus gives sight to Bartimaeus

YEAR C

Zephaniah 3:1-9	The sin and restoration of Israel
Psalm 3	
2 Timothy 4:6-18	Paul's testimony to the Lord's faithfulness
Luke 18:9-14	The parable of the Pharisee and the tax collector

Proper Preface 27	Any Canticle

THE THIRTY FIRST SUNDAY OF THE YEAR   G
between 30 October and 5 November

The Collect

Eternal Father
your Son has opened for us
   a new and living way into your presence:
give us pure hearts and steadfast wills
   to worship you in spirit and in truth;
through Jesus Christ our Lord.

or

Merciful Lord, absolve your people from their offences,
that through your bountiful goodness we may be set free
from the chains of those sins which in our frailty we have
committed; grant this, heavenly Father, for the sake of
Jesus Christ, our Lord and Saviour.

The Readings

YEAR A

Ruth 4:7-17	Ruth is married to Boaz
Psalm 127	
1 Thessalonians 2:9-20	Paul's joy over the Thessalonians
Matthew 23:1-12	True greatness in being a servant

YEAR B

Deuteronomy 6:1-9	The great commandment
Psalm 119:33-48	
Hebrews 7:23-28	Jesus our eternal High Priest
Mark 12:28-34	Jesus gives us two great commandments

YEAR C

Haggai 2:1-9	The promise of a new temple
Psalm 65:1-7	

2 Thessalonians 1:5-12   May Jesus be glorified in you
Luke 19:1-10   Jesus and Zacchaeus

Proper Preface 27   Any Canticle

THE THIRTY SECOND SUNDAY OF THE YEAR   G
between 6 and 12 November

The Collect

God our Father
your Son came in love to deliver us
and to equip us for eternal life:
free us from all that hinders us
    from running the race you have set before us;
through Jesus Christ our Lord.

or

O God, you know we are surrounded by many great
dangers and that because of our weakness we often fall:
grant us your strength and protection to support us in all
dangers and to bring us through all temptation; through
Jesus Christ our Lord.

The Readings

YEAR A

Amos 5:18-24   Religious observance worthless
                           without justice

Psalm 50:7-15
1 Thessalonians
   4:13-18   The dead in Christ will rise
Matthew 25:1-13   The bridegroom is coming

YEAR B

1 Kings 17:8-16   The poor widow gives food to
                           Elijah

Psalm 146
Hebrews 9:24-28   Christ the sacrifice for sin

| Mark 12:38-44 | The widow's offering in the Temple |

YEAR C

Zechariah 7:1-10	Justice and mercy are to replace oppression
Psalm 9:11-20	
2 Thessalonians 2:13–3:5	The Lord is faithful
Luke 20:27-38	The God of the living

| Proper Preface 27 | Any Canticle |

THE THIRTY THIRD SUNDAY OF THE YEAR   G
between 13 and 19 November

The Collect

Gracious Lord
your Son came to bring us good news
    and power to transform our lives:
grant that when he comes again as judge
we may be ready to meet him with joy;
through Jesus Christ our Lord.

or

Stir up, O Lord, the wills of your faithful people, that
richly bearing the fruit of good works, they may by you
be richly rewarded; through Jesus Christ our Lord.

The Readings

YEAR A

Zephaniah 1:14-18	The day of the Lord
Psalm 76	
1 Thessalonians 5:1-11	Be ready for the coming of the Lord
Matthew 25:14-30	The parable of the talents

YEAR B

Daniel 7:9-14	One like a son of man
Psalm 145:8-14	
Hebrews 10:11-18	Christ's single offering for sin
Mark 13:24-32	The coming of the Son of Man

YEAR C

Malachi 4:1-6	The day of the Lord
Psalm 82	
2 Thessalonians 3:6-13	A warning against being idle
Luke 21:5-19	Endurance in the face of persecution

Proper Preface 27   Any Canticle

THE THIRTY FOURTH SUNDAY OF THE YEAR
CHRIST THE KING   *Sunday* W
between 20 and 26 November   *Weekdays* G

The Collect

Sovereign Lord
you are restoring all things in your Son
   the King of the universe:
free the peoples of the earth from sin
and bring them together
   under his gracious rule;
who lives and reigns with you and the Holy Spirit
one God, now and for ever.

or

Lord God, the protector of all who trust in you, without
you nothing is strong, nothing is holy: pour on us your
mercy that with you as our ruler and guide, we may pass
through things temporal and come to things eternal;
through Jesus Christ our Lord.

288

The Readings

YEAR A

Ezekiel 34:11-24	The Lord finds and feeds his sheep
Psalm 23	
1 Corinthians 15:20-28	The reign of Christ
Matthew 25:31-46	The Son of Man judges the nations

YEAR B

Jeremiah 23:1-6	He shall reign as King
Psalm 93	
Revelation 1:4b-8	Jesus Christ, the ruler of kings on earth
John 18:33-37	My kingship is not of this world

YEAR C

2 Samuel 5:1-5	David is anointed king
Psalm 95	
Colossians 1:11-20	All things were created by him and for him
John 12:9-19	The King of Israel enters Jerusalem, riding a donkey
Proper Preface 27	Canticle The Song of the Church (Morning Prayer section 21)

Festivals and Commemorations

All Saints' Day, which is a Great Festival, is included here for convenience.

Commemorations are optional and have no special readings provided in this book. Some have their own Collect, but most use one of the Common Collects (pages 319-323), indicated by CC and the number.

If a Commemoration is the Patronal Festival of a congregation, suitable readings may be chosen, together with a psalm and canticle.

If the Patron Saint does not appear in the Calendar, the same may be done, and an appropriate Common Collect used.

JANUARY

1 THE HOLY NAME OF JESUS: W
  THE CIRCUMCISION OF CHRIST

The Collect

Merciful Father
you have taught us
    that there is salvation in no other name
    than in the name of Jesus:
teach us to glorify his name
and make your salvation known
    to all the world;
through Jesus Christ our Lord.

The Readings

Isaiah 9:2-7	The Prince of the four names
Psalm 8	
Acts 4:8-12	Salvation in the name of Jesus
Luke 2:15-21	He was called Jesus
Proper Preface 2	Canticle 10

6 **THE EPIPHANY OF OUR LORD**
See under Advent to Epiphany

10 William Laud, Archbishop of Canterbury and
Martyr, 1645   CC1

11 The Holy Innocents may be kept on this day instead
of 28 December.

13 Hilary, Bishop of Poitiers and Teacher of the
Faith, 368   CC3

14 Richard Benson of Cowley, Religious, 1915   CC6

17 Antony of Egypt, Founder of the Religious
Life, 356   CC6

18 THE CONFESSION OF ST PETER   W

The Collect

Heavenly Father
you inspired Saint Peter
    first among the apostles
    to confess Jesus as the Messiah
    and Son of the living God:
keep your Church steadfast
    on the rock of this faith;
through Jesus Christ our Lord.

The Readings

Ezekiel 3:4-11	Sent to the house of Israel
Psalm 23	
Acts 4:8-13	Peter bears witness to faith in Jesus
Matthew 16:13-19	You are the Christ
Proper Preface 19	Canticle 16

21 Agnes, Virgin and Martyr at Rome, c. 304   CC2

23 Yona Kanamuzeyi, Deacon and Martyr in
Africa, 1964   CC2

24 Francis de Sales, Bishop of Geneva, 1622   CC5

25 THE CONVERSION OF ST PAUL W

The Collect

Heavenly Father
you caused the light of the gospel
    to shine throughout the world
    by the preaching of your apostle Saint Paul:
grant that we who celebrate
    his wonderful conversion
may follow him in bearing witness to your truth;
through Jesus Christ our Lord.

The Readings

Acts 26:9-23	I saw a light from heaven
Psalm 67	
Galatians 1:11-24	He preaches the faith he once tried to destroy
Mark 10:46-52	A blind man receives sight on the road

(If an Old Testament reading is required, this passage is read

Jeremiah 1:4-10	A call to be a prophet to the nations

Acts 26:9-23 is then the second reading.)

Proper Preface 19   Canticle 8

26 Timothy and Titus W

Heavenly Father
you sent your apostle Paul to preach the gospel
and gave him Timothy and Titus
    to be his companions in the faith:
grant that our fellowship in the Spirit
    may bear witness to the name of Jesus;
who is alive and reigns with you and the Holy Spirit
one God, now and for ever.

27 John Chrysostom, Bishop of Constantinople
    and Teacher of the Faith, 407   CC3

28 Thomas Aquinas, Teacher of the Faith, 1274   CC3

29 Charles Frederick Mackenzie, Bishop in Central
    Africa, 1862   CC4

FEBRUARY

2 THE PRESENTATION OF OUR LORD IN   W
   THE TEMPLE

The Collect

Almighty Father
your Son Jesus Christ was presented in the Temple
and was acclaimed the glory of Israel
    and the light of the nations:
grant that through him we may be presented to you
    and reflect his glory in the world;
through Jesus Christ our Lord.

The Readings

Malachi 3:1-4   The Lord comes suddenly
                             to his Temple
Psalm 24
Hebrews 2:14-18   He is like his people in every
                             respect, yet without sin
Luke 2:22-40   A light to the Gentiles and
                             the glory of Israel

Proper Preface 2   Canticle 2,   The Song of
                        Simeon (Evening Prayer
                        section 62)

3 Anskar, Bishop and Missionary in Denmark
   and Sweden, 864   CC4

4 Manche Masemola of Sekhukhuneland, Virgin
   and Martyr, 1928   CC2

5 The Martyrs of Japan, 1597   CC2

9 James Mata Dwane, Priest, 1916 — CC7

14 Cyril and Methodius, Missionaries to the
   Slavs, 9th century — CC4

15 Thomas Bray, Priest, 1730 — CC7

20 Mother Cecile of Grahamstown, Religious,
   1906 — CC6

21 Missionaries and Martyrs of Africa — R

Lord God
by the faithful witness
   of the missionaries and martyrs of Africa
you established your Church in this continent:
grant that by service and sacrifice
we may prove worthy of our inheritance;
through Jesus Christ our Lord.

23 Polycarp, Bishop of Smyrna and Martyr, 156 — CC1

27 George Herbert, Priest, 1632 — CC7

MARCH

1 David, Bishop and Missionary in Wales,
   6th century — CC4

2 Chad, Bishop of Lichfield, 672 — CC5

3 John and Charles Wesley, Priests,
   18th century — CC7

7 Perpetua and her Companions, Martyrs, 202 — CC2

9 Maqhamusela Khanyile of Zululand, Martyr,
   1877 — CC2

12 Gregory the Great, Bishop of Rome and
   Teacher of the Faith, 604 — CC3

17 Patrick, Bishop and Missionary in Ireland, 461 — CC4

18 Cyril of Jerusalem, Bishop and Teacher of
   the Faith, c. 386 — CC3

19 Thomas Ken, Bishop of Bath and Wells, 1711   CC5

20 Cuthbert, Bishop of Lindisfarne, 687   CC5

21 Thomas Cranmer, Archbishop of Canterbury
    and Martyr, 1556   CC1

25 THE ANNUNCIATION TO THE BLESSED VIRGIN MARY

W

The Collect

Father in heaven
you sent your angel to the Blessed Virgin Mary
  to announce the incarnation of your Son:
pour your grace into our hearts
and bring us through his cross and passion
  to the glory of his resurrection;
who is alive and reigns with you and the Holy Spirit
one God, for ever and ever.

The Readings

Isaiah 7:10-14	The promise of Emmanuel
Psalm 113	
Romans 5:12-17	God's free gift in Jesus Christ
Luke 1:26-38	Mary's obedience to the word of God
Proper Preface 2	Canticle 10

29 John Keble, Priest, 1866   CC7

APRIL

1 Frederick Denison Maurice, Priest, 1872   CC7

6 William Law, Priest, 1761   CC7

11 George Augustus Selwyn, Bishop and
    Missionary in New Zealand, 1878   CC4

21 Anselm, Archbishop of Canterbury and
   Teacher of the Faith, 1109   CC3

23 George, Martyr, 4th century   CC2

25 ST MARK   R

The Collect

Lord of glory
you enlightened your Church
    through the writings
    of your evangelist Saint Mark:
ground us firmly
    in the truth of the gospel
and make us faithful to its teaching;
through Jesus Christ our Lord.

The Readings

Ecclesiasticus 51:13, 23-30	I found for myself much instruction
or	
Isaiah 52:7-10	The good tidings of the gospel
Psalm 119:9-16	
Ephesians 4:7-16	God's gifts for the building of the whole Body
Mark 1:1-15	Mark proclaims the gospel
Proper Preface 19	Canticle 16

29 Catherine of Siena, 1380   CC8

MAY

1 ST JOSEPH   W

The Collect

God our Father
you chose Saint Joseph the carpenter
    as the guardian of your only Son:
bring nearer the day when all workers
    will find fulfilment in their work
    and rejoice in work well done;
through Jesus Christ our Lord.

The Readings

Deuteronomy
    33:13-16   The blessing of Joseph
Psalm 89:1-8
Philippians 4:5-8   Qualities pleasing to God
Matthew 13:53-58   The carpenter's son

Proper Preface 18   Canticle 6,   The Song of
                     Zechariah (Morning Prayer
                     section 17)

2 Athanasius, Bishop of Alexandria and Teacher
   of the Faith, 373   CC3

3 ST PHILIP AND ST JAMES   R

The Collect

Eternal Father
the apostles Saint Philip and Saint James
knew your Son to be
    the true and living way:
grant that we may follow them
    along that way
    which leads to eternal life;
through Jesus Christ our Lord.

The Readings

Wisdom 5:15-16	The reward of the righteous
or	
Proverbs 4:10-18	The path of the righteous
Psalm 84	
1 Corinthians 12:4-13	The Spirit is given in many ways in the one Body
John 14:1-14	The Son is the revelation of the Father

Proper Preface 19   Canticle 15

4 Monica, Mother of Augustine of Hippo, 387   CC8

6 St John may be kept on this day instead of 27 December.

12 Simon of Cyrene   W

Merciful Lord
Simon of Cyrene carried the cross
    of your Son our Saviour Jesus Christ:
grant that we who have been baptized
    into his death and resurrection
may daily take up our cross and follow him;
who lives and reigns with you and the Holy Spirit
one God, for ever and ever.

14 ST MATTHIAS   R

The Collect

Lord God
you chose your servant Saint Matthias
    to be an apostle in the place of Judas:
preserve your Church from false apostles
and by the ministry of faithful pastors and teachers
    keep us steadfast in your truth;
through Jesus Christ our Lord.

The Readings

Isaiah 22:15-22 — Eliakim is appointed to replace the disgraced Shebna

Psalm 16

Acts 1:15-26 — Matthias is chosen to take the place forfeited by Judas

John 13:12-30 — Any disciple may fail and betray the Lord

Proper Preface 19   Canticle 7

19 Dunstan, Archbishop of Canterbury, 988   CC5

21 Helena, Mother of the Emperor Constantine, 4th century   CC8

25 The Venerable Bede, Teacher of the Faith, 735   W

God our Father
you are the guardian of your Church from age to age
and you enriched it by the life and teaching
    of your servant Bede:
confirm our faith and hope
    by the story of your mercies in the past;
through Jesus Christ our Lord.

26 Augustine, First Archbishop of Canterbury and Missionary, 605   CC4

31 THE VISITATION OF THE BLESSED   W
VIRGIN MARY

The Collect
Merciful Father
Elizabeth rejoiced with Mary
and greeted her as the mother of the Lord:
fill us with your grace
    that we may acclaim her Son as our Saviour;
who lives and reigns with you and the Holy Spirit
one God, now and for ever.

The Readings

Zephaniah 3:14-18a	Rejoicing in the Lord
Psalm 113	
Ephesians 5:18b-20	Rejoicing with one another
Luke 1:39-49	Mary visits Elizabeth
Proper Preface 16	Canticle 10

JUNE

1	Justin Martyr, c. 165	CC2
2	The Martyrs of Lyons, 177	CC2
3	The Martyrs of Uganda, 1886	CC2
5	Boniface, Bishop and Martyr in Germany, c. 755	CC1
9	Columba of Iona, Missionary in Scotland, 597	CC4
11	ST BARNABAS	R

The Collect

Lord God
your Son Jesus Christ has taught us
   that it is more blessed to give than to receive:
help us by the example of your apostle Saint Barnabas
   to be generous in our judgements
   and unselfish in our service;
through Jesus Christ our Lord.

The Readings

Job 29:11-16	A man clothed in righteousness
Psalm 112	
Acts 11:19-30	Barnabas brings Saul to Antioch
John 15:12-17	The new commandment to love
Proper Preface 19	Canticle 16

13 Antony of Lisbon, Religious, 1231   CC6

14 Basil and his Companions, Teachers of the
Faith, 4th century   CC3

18 Bernard Mizeki, Martyr in Mashonaland, 1896   R

Lord of all nations
by the conversion of Bernard Mizeki
   you raised up from the people of Africa
   a missionary faithful even to death:
fill your people with love
   in the face of hatred and fear
and make us ready to live or die
   for the name of Jesus;
who is alive and reigns with you and the Holy Spirit
one God, now and for ever.

22 Alban, First Martyr in Britain, c. 304   CC2

24 THE BIRTH OF ST JOHN THE BAPTIST   W

The Collect

Lord God
Saint John the Baptist was wonderfully born
and he prepared the way for the coming of your Son:
help us to know Jesus Christ as our Saviour
and to obtain forgiveness of our sins through him;
who is alive and reigns with you and the Holy Spirit
one God, for ever and ever.

The Readings

Isaiah 40:1-11	A herald of good tidings
Psalm 119:161-168	
Acts 13:16-25	John's baptism of repentance
Luke 1:57-66, 80	The birth of John
Proper Preface 18	Canticle The Song of Zechariah(Morning Prayer section 17)

28 Irenaeus, Bishop of Lyons and Teacher of the
Faith, c. 202 CC3

29 ST PETER AND ST PAUL R

The Collect

Almighty God
your apostles Peter and Paul
    glorified you in life and death:
inspire your Church to follow their example
and to stand firm on the one foundation
    which is Christ our Lord;
to whom with you and the Holy Spirit
be all honour and glory, now and for ever.

The Readings

Jonah 3	A prophet is sent to Gentiles
Psalm 34:1-9	
2 Timothy 4:1-8	St Paul's good fight
John 21:15-19	The charge to St Peter
Proper Preface 19	Canticle 7

JULY

3 ST THOMAS R

The Collect

Eternal God
your apostle Saint Thomas
    was doubtful of your Son's resurrection
    until word and sight convinced him:
grant that we who have not seen
    may be not faithless but believing;
through Jesus Christ our Lord.

The Readings

Job 42:1-6	I have seen you with my own eyes
Psalm 126	
Hebrews 10:35–11:1	Your confidence has a great reward
John 20:24-29	My Lord and my God
Proper Preface 19	Canticle 17

6 Thomas More, Martyr, 1535   CC2

11 Benedict of Monte Cassino, Religious, c. 540   CC6

13 Silas   W

Lord God
you blessed Silas with the gift of prophecy
and made him a faithful brother
   of the apostles Peter and Paul:
give prophetic power to those you call
   to speak in the name of Christ;
who is alive and reigns with you and the Holy Spirit
one God, for ever and ever.

22 ST MARY MAGDALENE   W

The Collect

Merciful Lord
your Son restored Saint Mary Magdalene
   to health of body and mind
and called her to be a witness of his resurrection:
cleanse us and make us new
that we may serve you in the power of his risen life;
who with you and the Holy Spirit is alive and reigns
one God, now and for ever.

The Readings

Song of Songs 3:1-4a	The beloved is found
Psalm 63:1-9	
2 Corinthians 5:14-17	The love of Christ controls us
John 20:1-18	The risen Christ appears to Mary

Proper Preface 18   Canticle 11

25 ST JAMES   R

The Collect

Lord God
your apostle Saint James
   consented to leave his father
   and all that he had
and to suffer for the name of your Son:
mercifully grant that no earthly ties
   may keep us from your service;
through Jesus Christ our Lord.

The Readings

Jeremiah 45	Seek not great things
Psalm 15	
Acts 11:27– 12:3	The martyrdom of James
Mark 10:35-45	True greatness in service

Proper Preface 19   Canticle 15

29 William Wilberforce, Philanthropist, 1833   CC8

30 Mary and Martha of Bethany   W

Loving Father
your Son blessed with his presence
   the home of Mary and Martha

and brought back their brother from the grave:
make our homes your dwelling place
and raise us to newness of life;
through Jesus Christ our Lord.

AUGUST

3 St Stephen may be kept on this day instead of 26 December.

6 THE TRANSFIGURATION OF OUR LORD   W

The Collect

Almighty Father
your Son was revealed in glory
    before he suffered on the cross:
grant that by faith
    in his death and resurrection
we may triumph in the power of his victory;
through Jesus Christ our Lord.

The Readings

Exodus 34:29-35	His face shone when he talked with God
Psalm 99	
2 Corinthians 3:4-18	Through the Spirit, we are transfigured
Luke 9:28-36	He went up on the mountain to pray
Proper Preface 5	Canticle The Song of the Church (Morning Prayer section 21)

7 Dominic, Religious, 1221   CC6
10 Laurence, Deacon and Martyr at Rome, 258   CC2

15 ST MARY THE VIRGIN   W

The Collect

God our Saviour
you looked on the lowliness
   of the Blessed Virgin Mary
and received her into your glory:
teach us to humble ourselves before you
and bring us also to the splendour
   of your eternal kingdom;
through Jesus Christ our Lord.

The Readings

Genesis 3:8-15	From the fall comes the promise of redemption
Psalm 113	
Galatians 4:4-7	God sent his Son, born of a woman
Luke 11:27-28	Blessed in hearing God's word and keeping it
Proper Preface 16	Canticle 10

20 Bernard of Clairvaux, Religious, 1153   CC6

24 ST BARTHOLOMEW   R

The Collect

Eternal God
you gave your apostle Saint Bartholomew
   grace to believe and preach your word:
grant that your Church
   may love the word which he believed
   and faithfully preach and obey it;
through Jesus Christ our Lord.

The Readings

Genesis 28:10-17	Jacob's vision
Psalm 103:1-8	
Acts 5:12-16	The ministry of the apostles
John 1:43-51	A vision promised to the one without guile

Proper Preface 19   Canticle 16

28 Augustine, Bishop of Hippo, 430   W

Merciful Lord
you turned Augustine from his sins
   to be a faithful bishop and teacher:
grant that we may follow him
   in penitence and discipline
till our restless hearts find their rest in you;
through Jesus Christ our Lord.

29 The Beheading of St John the Baptist   R

Sovereign Lord
you called Saint John the Baptist
to be in death as in birth
   the forerunner of your Son:
grant that, after his example
we may contend for truth and justice;
through Jesus Christ our Lord.

SEPTEMBER

1 Robert Gray, First Bishop of Cape Town, 1872   W

Merciful Lord
you sent your servant Robert Gray
to lay firm foundations
   for the Church of this Province:
grant that, thankfully remembering
   the constancy of his labour and zeal
we may build up and strengthen your Church;
through Jesus Christ our Lord.

2 The Martyrs of New Guinea, 1942   CC2

8 The Birth of the Blessed Virgin Mary   W

Heavenly Father
source of all perfection
you gave the grace of sanctity
    to the Blessed Virgin Mary, mother of our Lord:
make us, like her, holy in body and soul;
through Jesus Christ our Lord.

13 Cyprian, Bishop of Carthage and Martyr, 258   CC1

14 Holy Cross Day   R

Eternal Lord
you revealed your love
when your Son was lifted up
    in splendour on the cross:
illuminate our world
and draw us out of darkness
    into his glorious light;
who reigns supreme with you and the Holy Spirit
one God, now and for ever.

16 Ninian, Bishop and Missionary in Scotland,
c. 432   CC4

19 Theodore of Tarsus, Archbishop of Canterbury,
690   CC5

20 John Coleridge Patteson, Bishop of Melanesia
and Martyr, 1871   CC1

21 ST MATTHEW   R

The Collect

God our Saviour
your Son called Saint Matthew
    to be an apostle and evangelist:
free us from possessiveness
    and love of money

and inspire us to follow Jesus Christ;
who is alive and reigns with you and the Holy Spirit
one God, now and for ever.

The Readings

Proverbs 3:9-18	Wisdom is greater than riches
Psalm 19	
2 Timothy 3:14-17	The inspiration of Scripture
Matthew 9:9-13	The call of Matthew

Proper Preface 19   Canticle 15

26 Lancelot Andrewes, Bishop of Winchester,
1626   CC5

29 ST MICHAEL AND ALL ANGELS   W

The Collect

Lord God of hosts
you created the angels to worship and serve you:
grant that as they inspire us
    in our worship
they may also strengthen us
    in our fight against evil;
through Jesus Christ our Lord.

The Readings

Job 38:1-7	The angels rejoice at the creation
Psalm 148:1-6	
Revelation 12:7-12	Michael and his angels defeat the dragon
Matthew 18:1-10	Their angels behold the face of the Father

Proper Preface 17   Canticle 5

30 Jerome, Priest and Teacher of the Faith, 420   CC3

OCTOBER

1 Remigius, Bishop and Missionary to the
Franks, 530   CC4

2 Anthony, Earl of Shaftesbury, Philanthropist,
1885   CC8

4 Francis of Assisi, Religious, 1226   CC6

7 William Tyndale, Priest and Martyr, 1536   CC2

11 Philip the Deacon   W

Lord God
your Spirit guided Philip the Deacon
to show how ancient prophecies
   are fulfilled in Jesus Christ:
open our minds to understand the Scriptures
and deepen our faith in him;
who is alive and reigns with you and the Holy Spirit
one God, for ever and ever.

15 Teresa of Avila, Religious, 1582   CC6

16 Hugh Latimer and Nicholas Ridley, Bishops
and Martyrs, 1555   CC1

17 Ignatius of Antioch, Bishop and Martyr,
c. 110   CC1

18 ST LUKE   R

The Collect

Gracious Father
you inspired Saint Luke the physician
to proclaim the love and healing power of your Son:
give your Church, by the grace of the Spirit
the same love and power to heal;
through Jesus Christ our Lord.

The Readings

Isaiah 61:1-6	The good tidings of the gospel
Psalm 147:1-7	
Acts 1:1-8	Luke continues the story he began in his Gospel
Luke 10:1-9	The mission of the Seventy

Proper Preface 19   Canticle 14

19 Henry Martyn, Missionary to the East, 1812   CC4

23 ST JAMES THE BROTHER OF THE LORD   R

The Collect

Lord God of peace:
grant that after the example of your servant
   Saint James the brother of our Lord
your Church may give itself continually to prayer
and to the reconciliation of all
   who are caught up in hatred or enmity;
through Jesus Christ our Lord.

The Readings

Isaiah 49:1-6	The Lord's servant
Psalm 1	
Acts 15:12-22	James presides at the Jerusalem Council
Mark 3:31-35	Who are the Lord's brothers?

Proper Preface 18   Canticle 2

28 ST SIMON AND ST JUDE   R

The Collect

Lord God
you built your Church on the foundation
   of the apostles and prophets

with Jesus Christ as the chief corner stone:
join us together in unity of spirit by their doctrine
and make us a holy temple acceptable to you;
through Jesus Christ our Lord.

The Readings

Ecclesiasticus 2:1-6	Face calamity by trusting God
or	
Isaiah 28:9-16	A foundation stone laid in Zion
Psalm 119:89-96	
Revelation 21:9-14	The holy city and its foundation
Luke 6:12-23	The call and mission of the Twelve

Proper Preface 19   Canticle 18

31 Evening Prayer is the first Evening Prayer of All Saints' Day.

NOVEMBER

1 **ALL SAINTS**   W

The Collect

Gracious Lord
you have bound your saints together
    in the fellowship of your Church
and have prepared for them
    joys beyond our understanding:
help us to follow them in our daily lives
and bring us with them to everlasting glory;
through Jesus Christ our Lord.

The Readings

2 Esdras 2:42-47	Praise of those who have stood valiantly for God
or	
Jeremiah 31:31-34	They shall all know the Lord

Psalm 150
Revelation 7:2-4,   The great multitude standing
   9-12   before the Lamb
Matthew 5:1-12   The truly blessed people of God

Proper Preface 18   Canticle 5

2   THE COMMEMORATION
    OF THE FAITHFUL DEPARTED   P or B

The Collect

God, the maker and redeemer of all believers:
grant to the souls of the faithful departed
   all the unsearchable benefits
   of your Son's death and resurrection
that at his coming again
   they may be revealed as your children;
through Jesus Christ our Lord.

or

Eternal Lord God
creator and sustainer of all life:
we entrust to you the souls
   of your servants who have died
and we rejoice with them in the sure hope
   of resurrection to the fulness of eternal life;
through Jesus Christ our Lord.

The Readings

Wisdom 3:1-5   The souls of the righteous are in
                            the hand of God

or

Isaiah 25:6-9   The conquest of death
Psalm 23 or 130
1 Thessalonians   God's care for those who have
   4:13-18   fallen asleep

or

Revelation 20:11-13	The judgement	
John 5:24-29	The dead will hear the voice of the Son of God	

or

John 6:37-40	All that the Father gives me will come to me	

Proper Preface 21   Canticle 9, 12

3 The Martyrs of Mbokotwana, 1880   CC2

4 Martin de Porres, Religious, 1639   CC6

7 Willibrord, Bishop and Missionary in Holland, 739   CC4

8 Martyrs and Confessors of our Time   R

Eternal Lord
throughout the world, in our own day
many have bravely borne witness to your Son:
grant that when faced by persecution
   or the challenge to do what is right
we too may be found faithful;
through Jesus Christ our Lord.

10 Leo the Great, Bishop of Rome and Teacher
    of the Faith, 461   CC3

11 Martin, Bishop of Tours, 397   CC5

12 Charles Simeon, Priest, 1836   CC7

14 Samuel Seabury, Bishop in America, 1784   CC4

16 Margaret, Queen of Scotland, 1093   CC8

18 Hilda of Whitby, Religious, 680   CC6

22 Cecilia, Virgin and Martyr at Rome, c. 230   CC2

23 Clement, Bishop of Rome and Martyr, c. 100   CC1

30 ST ANDREW R

The Collect

Lord God
by your grace the apostle Saint Andrew
    obeyed the call of your Son Jesus Christ
and followed him without delay:
grant that we may offer ourselves to you
    in joyful obedience;
through Jesus Christ our Lord.

The Readings

Zechariah 8:20-23   Many people come to seek
                          the Lord in Jerusalem

Psalm 47
Romans 10:8b-18   Faith through the preaching
                          of the gospel

John 1:35-42   Andrew brings his brother
                          to Jesus

Proper Preface 19   Canticle 2

DECEMBER

1 Nicholas Ferrar, Deacon and Religious, 1637   CC6

3 Francis Xavier, Priest and Missionary to the
    East, 1552   CC4

4 John of Damascus, Teacher of the Faith,
    c. 760   CC3

5 Peter Masiza, Priest, 1907   CC7

7 Ambrose, Bishop of Milan and Teacher of the
    Faith, 397   CC3

24 Christmas Eve   See under Advent to Epiphany

25 **CHRISTMAS DAY**   See under Advent to Epiphany

26 ST STEPHEN   R

This Festival may be transferred to 3 August.

The Collect

Heavenly Father
you gave your martyr Saint Stephen
   grace to pray for those who stoned him:
grant that when we suffer for the truth
we may follow his example of forgiveness;
through Jesus Christ our Lord.

The Readings

2 Chronicles 24:17-22	The stoning of the prophet Zechariah
Psalm 31:1-5	
Acts 6:8-10; 7:54-60	The stoning of Stephen
Matthew 10:17-22	He who endures to the end will be saved
Proper Preface 18	Canticle 13

27 ST JOHN   W

This Festival may be transferred to 6 May.

The Collect

Merciful Lord
you have enlightened your Church
   by the teaching of Saint John:
shed your bright beams of light upon us
that we may walk in the light of your truth
and finally come to your eternal splendour;
through Jesus Christ our Lord.

The Readings

Isaiah 6:1-8	Isaiah's vision of God's holiness

Psalm 97
1 John 1   St John sets forth the
                              Christian faith
John 21:20-24   The witness of John

Proper Preface 19   Canticle 14

28 THE HOLY INNOCENTS   R

This Festival may be transferred to 11 January.

The Collect

Heavenly Father
children suffered at the hands of Herod
though they had done no wrong:
give us grace not to be indifferent
    in the face of cruelty or oppression
but to defend the weak
    from the tyranny of the strong;
through Jesus Christ our Lord.

The Readings

Baruch 4:21-23   Gladness and joy follow
                              sorrow and weeping

or

Jeremiah 31:15-17   The children will return
                              home

Psalm 124
1 Peter 4:12-16   Christ's people share his
                              suffering
Matthew 2:13-18   The massacre at Bethlehem

Proper Preface
    27(c)   Canticle 12

29 Thomas Becket, Archbishop of Canterbury and
Martyr, 1170   CC1

THE DEDICATION FESTIVAL   W

The Collect

Lord God
your Son blessed with his presence
    the feast of the Dedication in Jerusalem:
as we thank you for the many blessings
    given to those who have worshipped here
we pray that all who seek you in this place
    may find you
and become a living temple acceptable to you;
through Jesus Christ our Lord.

The Readings

1 Kings 8:22-30	Solomon's dedication prayer
Psalm 84	
1 Peter 2:4-9	Living stones in God's house
Matthew 21:12-16	Jesus in the Temple

or

2 Chronicles 7:11-18	I have chosen this house
Psalm 122	
Revelation 21:1-4	God's dwelling is with his people
Luke 19:1-10	Today salvation has come to this house
Proper Preface 22	Canticle 5, 17

Common Collects

1 Of a Martyr Bishop R

Merciful Lord
you strengthened your Church
by the steadfast courage
   of your bishop and martyr ...:
make us faithful in our sufferings
   that with him we may receive the crown of life;
through Jesus Christ our Lord.

Jan 10	William Laud
Feb 23	Polycarp
Mar 21	Thomas Cranmer
Jun 5	Boniface
Sep 13	Cyprian
Sep 20	John Coleridge Patteson
Oct 16	Hugh Latimer and Nicholas Ridley
Oct 17	Ignatius of Antioch
Nov 23	Clement of Rome
Dec 29	Thomas Becket

2 Of a Martyr (not a Bishop) R

Eternal God
by whose grace your martyr(s) ...
   triumphed over suffering and *was* faithful unto death:
move us by *his* example to deeper devotion
   and perseverance in our Christian calling;
through Jesus Christ our Lord.

or

Lord God
your martyr(s) ... defied *his* persecutors
and through *his* great love for you
   endured the pain of death:
grant that we may love you daily more and more
and faithfully bear witness to the name of Jesus;

who is alive and reigns with you and the Holy Spirit
one God, for ever and ever.

Jan 21	Agnes
Jan 23	Yona Kanamuzeyi
Feb 4	Manche Masemola
Feb 5	The Martyrs of Japan
Mar 7	Perpetua and her Companions
Mar 9	Maqhamusela Khanyile
Apr 23	George
Jun 1	Justin Martyr
Jun 2	The Martyrs of Lyons
Jun 3	The Martyrs of Uganda
Jun 22	Alban
Jul 6	Thomas More
Aug 10	Laurence
Sep 2	The Martyrs of New Guinea
Oct 7	William Tyndale
Nov 3	The Martyrs of Mbokotwana
Nov 22	Cecilia

3 Of a Teacher of the Faith   W

God our Father
you enlightened your Church
  by the teaching of your servant …:
enrich it with your heavenly grace
and raise up faithful witnesses
  who by their life and teaching
  may proclaim the truth of your salvation;
through Jesus Christ our Lord.

Jan 13	Hilary
Jan 27	John Chrysostom
Jan 28	Thomas Aquinas
Mar 12	Gregory the Great
Mar 18	Cyril of Jerusalem
Apr 21	Anselm
May 2	Athanasius
Jun 14	Basil and his Companions

Jun 28	Irenaeus
Sep 30	Jerome
Nov 10	Leo the Great
Dec 4	John of Damascus
Dec 7	Ambrose

4 Of a Missionary   W

God our Father
you called us out of darkness
   into your marvellous light
and you gave us your servant ...
   to shine as a light in the world:
shine in our hearts
and enable us to proclaim your love;
through Jesus Christ our Lord.

Jan 29	Charles Frederick Mackenzie
Feb 3	Anskar
Feb 14	Cyril and Methodius
Mar 1	David
Mar 17	Patrick
Apr 11	George Augustus Selwyn
May 26	Augustine of Canterbury
Jun 9	Columba
Sep 16	Ninian
Oct 1	Remigius
Oct 19	Henry Martyn
Nov 7	Willibrord
Nov 14	Samuel Seabury
Dec 3	Francis Xavier

5 Of a Bishop   W

Almighty God
the light of the faithful and shepherd of souls
you set ... to be a bishop in the Church
   to feed your sheep by his word
   and guide them by his example:
give us grace to keep the faith he taught
and to follow in his footsteps;
through Jesus Christ our Lord.

Jan 24	Francis de Sales
Mar 2	Chad
Mar 19	Thomas Ken
Mar 20	Cuthbert
May 19	Dunstan
Sep 19	Theodore
Sep 26	Lancelot Andrewes
Nov 11	Martin

6 Of a Religious   W

God our Father
you inspired … with your love
   to accept your calling
   and become a burning and shining light
   in your Church:
grant that we too may be on fire
   with the same spirit of discipline and love;
through Jesus Christ our Lord.

Jan 14	Richard Benson
Jan 17	Antony of Egypt
Feb 20	Mother Cecile of Grahamstown
Jun 13	Antony of Lisbon
Jul 11	Benedict
Aug 7	Dominic
Aug 20	Bernard
Oct 4	Francis
Oct 15	Teresa of Avila
Nov 4	Martin de Porres
Nov 18	Hilda
Dec 1	Nicholas Ferrar

7 Of a Priest W

Eternal God
you called ... to proclaim your glory
in a life of priestly prayer and pastoral zeal:
keep the leaders of your Church faithful to you
and bless your people through their ministry;
through Jesus Christ our Lord.

Feb 9	James Mata Dwane
Feb 15	Thomas Bray
Feb 27	George Herbert
Mar 3	John and Charles Wesley
Mar 29	John Keble
Apr 1	Frederick Denison Maurice
Apr 6	William Law
Nov 12	Charles Simeon
Dec 5	Peter Masiza

8 Of any Saint W

Gracious Lord
you have built up your Church
through the love and devotion of your saints:
help us to follow in the steps of your servant ...
and fill our hearts with love for you
and others for your sake;
through Jesus Christ our Lord.

Apr 29	Catherine of Siena
May 4	Monica
May 21	Helena
Jul 29	William Wilberforce
Oct 2	Anthony, Earl of Shaftesbury
Nov 16	Margaret, Queen of Scotland

Various Occasions

Collects and readings for the following subjects may be used at the discretion of the Priest. They do not displace the collects and readings set for Sundays, other Great Festivals or Festivals.

For the Guidance of the Holy Spirit
For the Unity of the Church
For the Mission of the Church
For Justice and Peace
For Those who have Authority, Influence or Power
For Schools, Colleges and Universities
For Rogation Days
For a Harvest Festival
For Those Going on a Journey
In any Necessity or Calamity
For Ember Days
For Vocations
   General
   Religious Communities
For a Synod, Elective Assembly, Council, Vestry or
   Conference
For the Admission of Church Officers

Collects and readings for a Eucharist at Baptism, Confirmation, Marriage, Ordination, Funerals and Requiems, or for the sick and dying, are provided in the relevant services. These collects and readings may also be used on anniversaries, when appropriate.

FOR THE GUIDANCE OF THE HOLY SPIRIT   R

The Collect

Eternal God
through your Holy Spirit
   you enlighten the hearts of your people:
teach us what we ought to do
and give us the power to do it;
through Jesus Christ our Lord
who is alive and reigns with you and the Holy Spirit
one God, for ever and ever.

Or either of the collects for Pentecost may be used.

The Readings

Jeremiah 31:31-34   All shall know the Lord
Psalm 139:1-11
1 Corinthians 12:4-13   Gifts of the Spirit
Canticle 4
John 14:15-26   Another Counsellor, the Spirit
                      of truth

FOR THE UNITY OF THE CHURCH   P

The Collect

Heavenly Father
your Son our Lord Jesus Christ
   said to his apostles
Peace I leave with you, my peace I give you:
regard not our sins but the faith of your Church
and grant her that peace and unity
   which is according to your will;
through Jesus Christ our Lord.

The Readings

Ezekiel 37:15-28   Two sticks become one stick
Psalm 122 or 133

Ephesians 4:1-6	Unity of the Spirit in the bond of peace

Canticle 14

John 17:11-23	That they all may be one

FOR THE MISSION OF THE CHURCH   R

The Collect

Heavenly Father
you revealed your love
   by sending your only Son into the world
   that all might live through him:
grant that by the power of the Spirit
your Church may obey his command
   to make disciples of all nations;
through Jesus Christ our Lord.

The Readings

Isaiah 49:1-6	God's people a light to the nations

Psalm 67

Ephesians 2:13-22	Salvation for all through the cross

Canticle 15

Matthew 28:16-20	Jesus sends his apostles to make disciples

FOR JUSTICE AND PEACE   P

The Collect

Righteous Father
your Son will come to be our judge:
break down the barriers that divide us
and disperse our suspicions and hatred
   that we may practise justice with mercy
   and live together in your peace;
through Jesus Christ our Lord.

The Readings

Isaiah 42:1-7	Faithfully bringing forth justice
Psalm 72:1-14 or 85	
James 2:5-17	The royal law of love for neighbour
Canticle 2	
Matthew 5:43-48	Perfection in love

FOR THOSE WHO HAVE AUTHORITY, INFLUENCE OR POWER

P

The Collect

Almighty Father
you have given all authority to your beloved Son:
govern the hearts and minds
    of all who have influence and power
and bring the peoples of the earth
divided and torn apart by the ravages of sin
to the justice and peace of his kingdom;
who is alive and reigns with you and the Holy Spirit
one God, now and for ever.

The Readings

1 Kings 3:5-14	A wise and discerning mind
Psalm 15	
1 Timothy 2:1-6	Prayer for those in authority
Canticle 1	
Matthew 22:15-22	What is Caesar's and what is God's

FOR SCHOOLS, COLLEGES AND UNIVERSITIES

R

The Collect

Eternal God
you are the source of all wisdom
and you want us to know and love you:

bless those who teach and those who learn
that in humility they may rejoice
    in the knowledge of your truth;
through Jesus Christ our Lord.

The Readings

Proverbs 9:9-12	The fear of the Lord is the beginning of wisdom
Psalm 119:105-112	
Galatians 6:2-10	The teachers and the taught
Canticle 3	
Matthew 13:44-52	Treasure new and old

FOR ROGATION DAYS   P

These may be used at appropriate seasons of the year according to local
conditions and needs.

The Collect

Almighty God
it is your will that the earth and the sea
should bear fruit in due season:
bless the labours of those
    who work on land and sea
grant us a good harvest
and the grace always to rejoice in your fatherly care;
through Jesus Christ our Lord.

or

Almighty God and Father
you have so ordered our life
    that we are dependent on one another:
prosper those engaged in commerce and industry
and direct their minds and hands
that they may rightly use your gifts
    in the service of others;
through Jesus Christ our Lord.

The Readings

Deuteronomy 8:1-10	God's abundant provision
Psalm 104:14-26	
2 Corinthians 9:6-15	Generosity and thanksgiving
Canticle 6	
Luke 11:5-13	Asking and receiving

or

Job 28:1-11	The riches of the earth
Psalm 121	
Philippians 4:4-9	Joy and peace in the Lord
Canticle 1	
Matthew 6:25-34	Do not be anxious

or

Joel 2:21-27	Judgement and mercy
Psalm 128	
2 Thessalonians 3:6-13	Do not be weary in well-doing
Canticle 5	
Luke 5:1-11	Peter the fisherman

FOR A HARVEST FESTIVAL W

The Collect

Eternal God
you crown the year with your goodness
    and you give us the fruits of the earth in their season:
grant that we may use them to your glory
    for the relief of those in need
    and for our own well-being;
through Jesus Christ our Lord.

The Readings

Deuteronomy 26:1-11	Offering the first fruits
Psalm 65	

James 5:7-11   Waiting for the fruit of the earth
Canticle 6
Matthew 13:1-9   The parable of the sower

FOR THOSE GOING ON A JOURNEY   R

The Collect

God of infinite majesty
neither time nor space can separate you
    from those you love:
bless all who travel
    by land, sea or air;
protect them in danger
and bring them in safety
    to the place where they would be;
through Jesus Christ our Lord.

The Readings

Numbers 6:22-27   Aaron's blessing
Psalm 121
Acts 16:6-12   Paul's journey with his
                             companions

Canticle 3
John 4:1-15   Jesus on a journey

IN ANY NECESSITY OR CALAMITY   P

The Collect

Sovereign Lord
you are the defence of those who trust in you
and the strength of those who suffer:
look with mercy on our affliction
and deliver us through our mighty Saviour Jesus Christ;
who lives and reigns with you and the Holy Spirit
one God, for ever and ever.

The Readings

Lamentations 3:19-26	Waiting for the Lord
Psalm 86:1-7	
Romans 5:1-5	The ground of hope
Canticle 19	
Mark 11:22-25	Have faith in God

FOR EMBER DAYS   *Colour of the Season*

Ember Days are the Third Sunday in Advent, the Second Sunday in Lent, Trinity Sunday and the Twenty Sixth Sunday of the Year, together with the preceding Wednesday and Friday.

On these days prayer is offered for those to be ordained at this time, for vocations to the ordained ministry, for theological colleges and those preparing for ordination, and for all serving in the ordained ministry.

An Ember Collect and Readings may be used except on a Great Festival or Festival, when an Ember Collect may follow the Collect of the Day.

The Collect

Heavenly Father
you have entrusted to your Church
a share in the ministry of your Son, our great High Priest:
call many through your Holy Spirit
    into the ordained ministry of your Church
and inspire them to respond to your call;
through Jesus Christ our Lord.

or

Eternal Father
through your Holy Spirit you have appointed
    many ministries in the Church:
bless those (now) called to be deacon(s), priest(s) and
    bishop(s)
maintain them in your truth
renew them in your holiness
and make them your ever-faithful servants;
through Jesus Christ our Lord.

or

Lord God
you have entrusted to your Church
    a share in your Son's priesthood:
guide the bishops in their choice
    of priests and deacons
and strengthen with your Spirit
    those who are called to this ministry;
through Jesus Christ our Lord.

The Readings

Isaiah 61:1-6a	Anointed by the Spirit
Psalm 132:1-9	
Acts 20:28-35	Keep watch over the flock
Canticle 13	
Luke 4:16-21	Proclaim good news to the poor

or

Isaiah 40:1-11	He will feed his flock
Psalm 132:10-18	
1 Peter 5:1-11	Tend the flock of God
Canticle 10	
Matthew 9:35-38	Pray for labourers to harvest the crop

The Collect and Readings for Schools, Colleges and Universities may also be used if the special intention is for theological colleges.

FOR VOCATIONS   R

GENERAL

The Collect

Everlasting Father
your Son came to earth to do your will
and in baptism you call us to love and serve you:

help us to discern what you now ask of us
and give us grace to respond
    in joyful obedience
in union with your beloved Son;
who now lives and reigns with you and the Holy Spirit
one God, for ever and ever.

The Readings

1 Samuel 3:1-10	Listening to God
Psalm 40:6-13	
Ephesians 4:7-16	Different gifts and ministries
Canticle 8	
John 15:12-17	Christ chooses us and calls us friends

FOR RELIGIOUS COMMUNITIES

The Collect

Heavenly Father
you are the source of living prayer and humble service:
call many to Religious Communities
that waiting upon you in contemplation
they may share with others
    what they have received from you;
through Jesus Christ our Lord.

The Readings

Ecclesiasticus 2:1-6, 15-18	Falling into the hands of God
Psalm 84	
1 John 4:7-12	Love for one another
Canticle 8	
Mark 10:17-31	Treasure in heaven

FOR A SYNOD, ELECTIVE ASSEMBLY, COUNCIL, VESTRY OR CONFERENCE   R

The Collect

Lord God
you have given your Holy Spirit to the Church
  that he may lead us into all truth:
bless with his grace and presence
  the members of ...
keep *us/them* steadfast in faith and united in love
  that *we/they* may advance your glory
  and the peace and unity of your Church;
through Jesus Christ our Lord.

The Readings

Exodus 18:13-27	Shared leadership
Psalm 19:7-14	
1 Corinthians 12:7-11	Spiritual gifts for each and for all
Canticle 3	
John 15:1-8	Abiding in the Vine

or

Isaiah 40:27-31	Wait for the Lord
Psalm 25:1-9	
Ephesians 4:1-7	Forbearing one another in love
Canticle	The Song of the Church (Morning Prayer section 21)
John 13:12-17	Washing one another's feet

FOR THE ADMISSION OF CHURCH OFFICERS R

The Collect

Almighty and everlasting God
by your Spirit the whole body of your faithful people
   is governed and sanctified:
receive our prayers which we offer before you
   for all members of your holy Church
that in their vocation and ministry
   they may truly serve you;
through our Lord and Saviour Jesus Christ.

The Readings

Joshua 1:1-9	Be strong and of good courage
Psalm 133	
1 Corinthians 12:27–13:3	Different ministries in a spirit of love
Canticle 17	
John 15:4-11	Fruit-bearing branches in the Vine

THE CANTICLES

The Canticles

These Canticles may be used as alternatives to the Canticles in the Offices of Morning and Evening Prayer

1 The Song of David (*1 Chronicles 29:10-13*)

2 Jerusalem, City of Peace (*Isaiah 2:2-5*)

3 We have a Strong City (*Isaiah 26:1-4, 7-8*)

4 A Song of Ezekiel (*Ezekiel 36:24-28*)

5 Bless the Lord (*Song of the Three 28-34*)

6 A Song of Creation (*Song of the Three 35-41, 52-65*)

7 A Song of Salvation (*Romans 5:1-8; 8:37-39*)

8 A Song of Assurance (*Romans 8:28-35, 37*)

9 The Easter Anthems (*1 Corinthians 5:7-8; Romans 6:9-11; 1 Corinthians 15:20-22*)

10 A Song of Christ's Glory (*Philippians 2:6-11*)

11 Christ the Firstborn (*Colossians 1:12-20*)

12 Death and Life with Christ (*2 Timothy 2:11-13*)

13 Christ the Servant (*1 Peter 2:21-24*)

14 A Song of Love (*1 John 4:7-8; 1 Corinthians 13:4-10, 12-13*)

15 Glory and Honour (*Revelation 4:11; 5:12, 9-10, 13*)

16 A Song of God's Judgement (*Revelation 11:17-18; 12:10-12*)

17 Great and Wonderful (*Revelation 15:3-4; 5:13*)

18 The Wedding Song of the Lamb (*Revelation 19:1-2, 5-8*)

19 Saviour of the World (*Salvator Mundi*)

These canticles are printed in the Offices

The Song of Zechariah (*Luke 1:68-79*) and **The Song of the Church** (*Te Deum*) in Morning Prayer

The Song of Mary (*Luke 1:46-55*) and **The Song of Simeon** (*Luke 2:29-32*) in Evening Prayer

Any of the Canticles may be used at the Eucharist.

For particular seasons the following Canticles are appropriate

Advent   2, 16, 18.

Christmas and Epiphany   5, 10, 11.

Lent and Fridays   3, 13, 14, 19.

Easter, Ascension, Saturdays   4, 7, 8, 9, 12.

The Day of Pentecost   4, 7, 14.

Saints' Days   7, 8, 15, 16, 17.

1 A Song of David

(*1 Chronicles 29:10-13*)

1 May you be blessed Lord God of our | father | Israel: from cre|ation | and for | ever.

2 Yours is the greatness Lord and the power and glory * the splendour | and the | majesty: for everything in | heaven and | earth is | yours.

3 Yours is the sovereignty Lord * and you are exalted as | head a · bove | all: from you come riches and honour and | you rule | over | all things.

4 In your hand lie | strength and | power: and yours it is to give | greatness · and | strength to | all.

†5 And now our God we | give you | thanks: and praise the | splendour | of your | name.

Glory to the Father and | to the | Son: and | to the | Holy | Spirit.

As it was | in the · be|ginning: is now and | will be · for | ever · A|men

2 Jerusalem, City of Peace

(*Isaiah 2:2-5*)

1 In the last days the mountain of the Lord's house shall I be exI alted: it shall be established as the I highest I of the I mountains.

2 It shall be raised aIbove the I hills: and all nations I shall come I flocking I to it.

3 Many peoples shall say * Let us go up to the I mountain · of the I Lord: to the I house · of the I God of I Jacob.

4 That he may I teach us · his I ways: and I we may I walk in · his I paths.

5 For out of Zion shall go I forth the I law: and the I word · of the I Lord · from JeIrusalem.

6 He shall be judge beItween the I nations: and I arbiter · beItween the I peoples.

†7 They shall beat their I swords · into I ploughshares: and their I spears I into I pruning-hooks.

8 Nation shall not lift up I sword a · gainst I nation: nor ever aIgain be I trained for I war.

9 All you of the I house of I Jacob: come let us I walk · in the I light · of the I Lord.

Glory to the Father and I to the I Son: and I to the I Holy I Spirit.

As it was I in the · beIginning: is now and I will be · for I ever · AImen

3 We have a Strong City

(*Isaiah 26:1-4, 7-8*)

1 We have a | strong | city: God has made sal|vation ·
its | walls and | ramparts.

2 Open the gates to let a righteous | nation | in: even a |
nation | that is | faithful.

3 You keep in peace the one whose mind is | stayed on |
you: the peace which | comes from | trust in | you.

4 Trust in the | Lord for | ever: for the Lord himself is
an | ever|lasting | rock.

5 The path of the | upright · is | straight: you who are
the righteous God * mark out the | right way | for the |
just.

6 We too seek the path prescribed in your | laws O |
Lord: your presence and your power are | all our |
hearts de|sire.

Glory to the Father and | to the | Son: and | to the |
Holy | Spirit.

As it was | in the · be|ginning: is now and | will be ·
for | ever · A|men

4 A Song of Ezekiel

(*Ezekiel 36:24-28*)

1 I will take you from the nations * and gather you from | all the | countries: and I will bring you | into · your | own | land.

2 I will sprinkle clean water upon you * and you shall be clean from | all · your de|filements: and from all your | idols | I will | cleanse you.

3 A new heart | I will | give you: and a new spirit | I will | put with|in you.

4 I will take out of your flesh the | heart of | stone: and I will | give you · a | heart of | flesh.

5 I will put my | Spirit · with|in you: and I will | cause you · to | keep my | laws.

6 You shall live in the land which I | gave · to your | forebears: and you shall be my people and | I will | be your | God.

Glory to the Father and | to the | Son: and | to the | Holy | Spirit.

As it was | in the · be|ginning: is now and | will be · for | ever · A|men

5 Bless the Lord

(Song of the Three 28-34)

1 Bless the Lord the ǀ God of · our ǀ forebears: bless his ǀ
   holy · and ǀ glori · ous ǀ Name.

2 Bless him in his holy and ǀ glori · ous ǀ temple: sing
   his ǀ praise · and exǀalt him · for ǀ ever.

3 Bless him who beǀholds the ǀ depths: bless him who ǀ
   sits beǀtween the ǀ cherubim.

4 Bless him on the ǀ throne of · his ǀ kingdom: sing his ǀ
   praise · and exǀalt him · for ǀ ever.

5 Bless him in the ǀ heights of ǀ heaven: sing his ǀ
   praise · and exǀalt him · for ǀ ever.

6 Bless the Father the Son and the ǀ Holy ǀ Spirit: sing
   his ǀ praise · and exǀalt him · for ǀ ever.

6 A Song of Creation

(*Song of the Three 35-41, 52-65*)

1 Bless the Lord all cre|ated | things: sing his | praise · and ex|alt him · for | ever.

2 Bless the | Lord you | heavens: sing his | praise · and ex|alt him · for | ever.

3 Bless the Lord you | angels · of the | Lord: bless the | Lord all | you his | hosts.

4 Bless the Lord you waters a|bove the | heavens: sing his | praise · and ex|alt him · for | ever.

5 Bless the Lord | sun and | moon: bless the | Lord you | stars of | heaven.

6 Bless the Lord all | rain and | dew: sing his | praise · and ex|alt him · for | ever.

7 O let the earth | bless the | Lord: bless the | Lord you | mountains · and | hills.

8 Bless the Lord all that | grows · in the | ground: sing his | praise · and ex|alt him · for | ever.

9 Bless the | Lord you | springs: bless the | Lord you | seas and | rivers.

10 Bless the Lord you whales and all that | swim · in the | waters: sing his | praise · and ex|alt him · for | ever.

11 Bless the Lord all | birds · of the | air: bless the | Lord you | beasts and | cattle.

12 Bless the Lord all who | live · on the | earth: sing his | praise · and ex|alt him · for | ever.

13 O people of God | bless the | Lord: bless the | Lord you | priests · of the | Lord.

14 Bless the Lord you | servants · of the | Lord: sing his | praise · and ex|alt him · for | ever.

15 Bless the Lord all you of | upright | spirit: bless the
Lord you that are | holy · and | humble · in | heart.

16 Bless the Father the Son and the | Holy | Spirit: sing
his | praise · and ex|alt him · for | ever.

7 A Song of Salvation

(*Romans 5:1-8; 8:37-39*)

1 Now that we have been | justified · through |
faith: we are at peace with God through | Jesus |
Christ our | Lord.

2 And so we exult in our hope of the | splendour · of |
God: and we even exult in the | suffer · ings | we
en|dure.

3 For our hope is | not in | vain: because God's love
has flooded our inmost | hearts · through the | Holy |
Spirit.

4 When we were still powerless * Christ | died ·
for the | wicked: he died for us while we were still
sinners * and so God | proves his | love to|wards
us.

†5 We are more than conquerors through | him who |
loved us: for nothing can separate us from God's
love in | Jesus | Christ our | Lord.

Glory to the Father and | to the | Son: and | to the |
Holy | Spirit.

As it was | in the · be|ginning: is now and | will be ·
for | ever · A|men

8 A Song of Assurance

(Romans 8:28-35, 37)

1 God works for good in everything with ǀ those who ǀ love him: who are called acǀcording ǀ to his ǀ purpose.

2 For those whom ǀ he foreǀknew: he also predestined to be conformed to the ǀ image ǀ of his ǀ Son.

3 And those whom he predestined he ǀ also ǀ called: and those whom he ǀ called he ǀ also ǀ justified.

4 And to those ǀ whom he ǀ justified: he has ǀ also ǀ given · his ǀ splendour.

5 If God is ǀ on our ǀ side: who can ǀ ever ǀ be aǀgainst us.

6 He who did not spare his own Son * but gave him ǀ up · for us ǀ all: will he not also with him ǀ freely ǀ give us ǀ all things.

7 It is ǀ God who ǀ justifies: who ǀ then can ǀ ever · conǀdemn us.

8 For it is Christ Jesus who died and was ǀ raised · from the ǀ dead: who is at God's right ǀ hand to ǀ plead our ǀ cause.

9 What can separate us from the ǀ love of ǀ Christ: can persecution or hunger * can ǀ peril ǀ or the ǀ sword.

10 No * in all these things we are ǀ more than ǀ conquerors: through him who loved us * even ǀ Jesus ǀ Christ our ǀ Lord.

Glory to the Father and ǀ to the ǀ Son: and ǀ to the ǀ Holy ǀ Spirit.

As it was ǀ in the · beǀginning: is now and ǀ will be · for ǀ ever · Aǀmen

9 The Easter Anthems

(1 Corinthians 5:7-8; Romans 6:9-11;
1 Corinthians 15:20-22)

1 Christ our passover has been | sacri · ficed | for
us: so let us | cele|brate the | feast.

2 Not with the old leaven of cor|ruption · and |
wickedness: but with the unleavened | bread of ·
sin|cerity · and | truth.

3 Christ once raised from the dead | dies no |
more: death has no | more do|minion | over him.

4 In dying he died to sin | once for | all: in | living · he |
lives to | God.

5 See yourselves therefore as | dead to | sin: and alive
to God in | Jesus | Christ our |Lord.

6 Christ has been | raised · from the | dead: the | first-
fruits · of | those who | sleep.

7 For as by | man came | death: by man has come also
the resur|rection | of the | dead.

8 For as in | Adam · all | die: even so in Christ shall | all
be | made a|live.

Glory to the Father and | to the | Son: and | to the |
Holy | Spirit.

As it was | in the · be|ginning: is now and | will be ·
for | ever · A|men

10 A Song of Christ's Glory

(*Philippians 2:6-11*)

1 Christ Jesus was in the I form of I God: but he did not I cling · to eIquality · with I God.

2 He emptied himself * taking the I form · of a I servant: and was I born in I human I likeness.

3 And being found in human form he I humbled · himIself: and became obedient unto death * I even I death · on a I cross.

4 Therefore God has I highly · exIalted him: and bestowed on him the I name a · bove I every I name.

5 That at the name of Jesus every I knee should I bow: in heaven and on I earth and I under · the I earth.

6 And every tongue confess that Jesus I Christ is I Lord: to the I glory · of I God the I Father.

Glory to the Father and I to the I Son: and I to the I Holy I Spirit.

As it was I in the · beIginning: is now and I will be · for I ever · AImen

11 Christ the Firstborn

(*Colossians 1:12-20*)

1 Let us give | thanks · to the | Father: who has enabled us to share the inheritance | of the | saints in | light.

2 He has delivered us from the do|minion · of | darkness: and transferred us to the kingdom of | his be|loved | Son.

3 In him we | have re|demption: we have the for|giveness | of our | sins.

4 He is the image of the in|visi · ble | God: he is the | firstborn · of | all cre|ation.

5 For in him all things were created * both in | heaven and | earth: all things whether | visi · ble | or in|visible.

6 All things were created | through him · and | for him: he is before all things * and in him | all things | hold to|gether.

†7 He is the head of the body the Church * he is | its be|ginning: the firstborn from the dead pre|emi · nent | over | all.

8 For in him all the fulness of God was | pleased to | dwell: and through him God chose to reconcile | all things | to him|self.

9 Through his beloved Son * God has reconciled all things in | heaven and | earth: by the blood of the cross he has made | ever|lasting | peace.

Glory to the Father and | to the | Son: and | to the | Holy | Spirit.

As it was | in the · be|ginning: is now and | will be · for | ever · A|men

12 Death and Life with Christ

(*2 Timothy 2:11-13*)

1 Christ has died | Christ is | risen: Christ the | Lord will | come a|gain.

2 If we have died with him we shall also | live with | him: if we endure we shall | also | reign with | him.

3 If we deny him he will | also · de|ny us: if we are faithless he remains faithful * for he | cannot · de|ny him|self.

4 Christ has died | Christ is | risen: Christ the | Lord will | come a|gain.

Glory to the Father and | to the | Son: and | to the | Holy | Spirit.

As it was | in the · be|ginning: is now and | will be · for | ever · A|men

13 Christ the Servant

(*1 Peter 2:21-24*)

1 Jesus Christ suffered for you * leaving | you an · ex|ample: that you should | follow | in his | steps.

2 He committed no sin * no guile was | found on · his | lips: when he was reviled he did | not re|vile in · re|turn.

3 When he suffered he | did not | threaten: but trusted in | him who | judges | justly.

4 He himself bore our sins in his | body · on the | tree: that we might die to | sin and | live to | righteousness.

5 By his wounds you | have been | healed: for | you were | straying · like | sheep.

6 But now you | have re|turned: to the shepherd and | guardian | of your | souls.

Glory to the Father and | to the | Son: and | to the |
Holy | Spirit.

As it was | in the · be|ginning: is now and | will be ·
for | ever · A|men

14 A Song of Love

(1 John 4:7-8; 1 Corinthians 13:4-10, 12-13)

1 Christians let us | love · one an|other: because | love |
comes from | God.

2 The one who loves is born of | God and | knows
him: but one who does not | love does | not know |
God.

3 Love does not insist on its own way * it is not quick to |
take of|fence: it does not rejoice at wrong * but
re|joices | in the | right.

4 Love is | patient · and | kind: love is not jealous or
boastful * it | is not | arrogant · or | rude.

†5 Love bears all things and be|lieves | all things: love |
hopes · and en|dures | all things.

6 Love will never | come · to an | end: but prophecy
will vanish * tongues cease and | knowledge | pass
a|way.

7 For our knowledge and our prophecy are | both
im|perfect: but   when   the   perfect   comes   the
im|perfect · will | pass a|way.

8 Now I | know in | part: but then I shall understand
fully * even as I have been | fully | under|stood.

9 There are three things that last for ever * faith | hope
and | love: but the | greatest · of | these is | love.

Glory to the Father and | to the | Son: and | to the |
Holy | Spirit.

As it was | in the · be|ginning: is now and | will be ·
for | ever · A|men

15 Glory and Honour

(*Revelation 4:11; 5:12, 9-10, 13*)

1 Glory and | honour · and | power: are yours by |
   right O | Lord our | God.

2 For you cre|ated | all things: and by your | will they |
   have their | being.

3 Glory and | honour · and | power: are yours by |
   right O | Lamb · who was | slain.

4 For by your blood you ransomed | us for | God: from
   every race and language * from | every | people · and |
   nation.

5 To make us a | kingdom · of | priests: to stand and |
   serve be|fore our | God.

6 To him who sits on the throne * | and · to the |
   Lamb: be praise and honour and might * for ever
   and | ever | A|men.

   Glory to the Father and | to the | Son: and | to the |
   Holy | Spirit.

   As it was | in the · be|ginning: is now and | will be ·
   for | ever · A|men

16 A Song of God's Judgement

(*Revelation 11:17-18; 12:10-12*)

1 We give thanks to you Lord God almighty * ever
   present ǀ and eǀternal: for you have taken your
   great ǀ power · and beǀgun to ǀ reign.

2 The nations raged * but the day of your ǀ wrath has ǀ
   come: and the ǀ time · for the ǀ dead · to be ǀ judged.

3 The time has come to reward your servants the ǀ
   prophets · and ǀ saints: and those who fear your ǀ
   name both ǀ small and ǀ great.

4 Now the salvation of God has come * his power and
   his ǀ glori · ous ǀ kingdom: now has come the
   auǀthori · ty ǀ of his ǀ Christ.

5 For their accuser has been ǀ thrown ǀ down: who
   accuses them day and ǀ night beǀfore our ǀ God.

6 And they have conquered him by the ǀ blood · of the ǀ
   Lamb: and ǀ by their ǀ word of ǀ witness.

†7 Rejoice ǀ then O ǀ heaven: and ǀ you that ǀ dwell
   thereǀin.

   Glory to the Father and ǀ to the ǀ Son: and ǀ to the ǀ
   Holy ǀ Spirit.

   As it was ǀ in the · beǀginning: is now and ǀ will be ·
   for ǀ ever · Aǀmen

17 Great and Wonderful Deeds

(*Revelation 15:3-4; 5:13*)

1 Great and wonderful are your deeds Lord ǀ God · the
  Allǀmighty: just and true are your ǀ ways O ǀ King · of
  the ǀ nations.

2 Who shall not revere and praise your ǀ Name O ǀ
  Lord: for ǀ you allone are ǀ holy.

3 All nations shall come and worship ǀ in your ǀ
  presence: for your just ǀ dealings · have ǀ been
  reǀvealed.

4 To him who sits on the throne and ǀ to the ǀ Lamb:
  be praise and honour * glory and ǀ might for ǀ
  ever · and ǀ ever.

  Glory to the Father and ǀ to the ǀ Son: and ǀ to the ǀ
  Holy ǀ Spirit.

  As it was ǀ in the · beǀginning: is now and ǀ will be ·
  for ǀ ever · Aǀmen

18 The Wedding Song of the Lamb

(*Revelation 19:1-2, 5-8*)

1 Salvation glory and power beǀlong · to our ǀ God: O ǀ
  praise him ǀ Alleǀluia.

2 His judgements are ǀ true and ǀ just: Alleǀluia ǀ
  Alleǀluia.

3 Praise our God all ǀ you his ǀ servants: you who ǀ
  fear him ǀ small and ǀ great.

4 The Lord our God the Almighty has beǀgun to ǀ
  reign: O ǀ praise him ǀ Alleǀluia.

5 Let us rejoice and exult and give ǀ him the ǀ
  glory: Alleǀluia ǀ Alleǀluia.

6 The marriage of the ǀ Lamb has ǀ come: and his ǀ
  bride has ǀ made her · self ǀ ready.

7 She is clothed with the ǀ garment · of ǀ
  righteousness: O ǀ praise him ǀ Alleǀluia.

8 With linen ǀ bright and ǀ pure: Alleǀluia ǀ Alleǀluia.

  Glory to the Father and ǀ to the ǀ Son: and ǀ to the ǀ
  Holy ǀ Spirit.

  As it was ǀ in the · beǀginning: is now and ǀ will be ·
  for ǀ ever · Aǀmen

19 Saviour of the World

(*Salvator Mundi*)

1 Jesus Saviour of the world * come to us | in your | mercy: we look to | you to | save and | help us.

2 By your cross and your life laid down * you set your | people | free: we look to | you to | save and | help us.

3 When they were ready to perish you | saved · your dis|ciples: we look to | you to | come to · our | help.

4 In the greatness of your mercy loose us | from our | chains: forgive the | sins of | all your | people.

5 Make yourself known as our Saviour and | mighty de|liverer: save and | help us · that | we may | praise you.

6 Come now and dwell with us | Lord Christ | Jesus: hear our | prayer · and be | with us | always.

†7 And when you | come in · your | glory: make us to be one with you * and to | share the | life of · your | kingdom.

Glory to the Father and | to the | Son: and | to the | Holy | Spirit.

As it was | in the · be|ginning: is now and | will be · for | ever · A|men

BAPTISM
AND
CONFIRMATION

Preface
Birth and Growth in Christ

The Baptism of Jesus
At his baptism Jesus heard the voice from heaven which identified him as the 'beloved Son' of God, the Christ. He experienced the anointing of the Holy Spirit and, led by the Spirit, he devoted his life to the salvation of the world. He saw his death as the atoning sacrifice for sin and the completion of his baptism (Luke 12:50).

Identification with Christ
   'Do you not know that all of us who have been baptized into Christ Jesus were baptized into his death? We were buried therefore with him by baptism into death, so that as Christ was raised from the dead by the glory of the Father, we too might walk in newness of life' (Romans 6:3-4).

The two main sacraments of Baptism and Holy Communion, together with Confirmation, all relate to identification with Jesus Christ in his Paschal Mystery: that is, his birth, death, resurrection and ascension, and the giving of the Holy Spirit, all understood in the light of the Passover. God saved Israel by the Passover Lamb and Jesus is the Lamb of God by whose death and resurrection his people are brought out of bondage to sin, into new life in him.

Baptism
'Baptism is to be understood not merely as the rite of a moment but as the principle of a lifetime' (Lambeth Conference, 1968). Just as ordinary life involves birth and growth, so our birth and growth as Christians is an on-going development towards maturity. On the other hand, the administration of baptism is once for all, like birth and death. Christ died once and

Christians are baptized once, either as infants or as adults.

The Apostles first proclaimed the gospel on the Day of Pentecost (Acts 2:14-36) and three thousand converts were baptized. Most of these must have been adults. Today there are also many, not baptized in infancy, who come to faith as adults and then seek baptism. It is likely that from the earliest times Christian parents brought their children to baptism, and in time this became the general practice. For them, as for the Jews before them, infants were regarded as committed with their parents to God's Covenant. When Gentile converts, or proselytes, were received into Israel their children were received with them and shared in proselyte baptism. It is likely that St Paul followed this practice when he baptized households (1 Corinthians 1:16; Acts 16:15, 33). The practice of infant baptism witnesses to the truth that God must first give his grace to his people before they can respond to it.

Whilst the response of faith has to be made by each individual, human life is always lived in community. Children are born into a human family and those who are baptized are brought into the family of God, the Church. St Paul says, 'By one Spirit we were all baptized into one body' (1 Corinthians 12:13). Those who are baptized into the Body of Christ share in his anointing by the Spirit. United in him, they are to serve God in the world in a ministry of caring and compassion.

Confirmation

At Confirmation the individual makes the response of faith, an act of commitment to Christ, by making or renewing the baptismal promises. This takes place in the presence of the Bishop who represents the whole Church and who is the sign of apostolic authority, as well as being the focus of unity in the diocese. The Bishop then lays hands on the candidate's head and, along with the people, prays that *he* will receive the strengthening gift of the Holy Spirit. By receiving this gift the candidate is commissioned and empowered to fulfil *his* vocation as a Christian within the fellowship of the Church.

The Holy Eucharist

Christian Initiation is fulfilled in the Holy Communion. Jesus said, 'Whoever eats my flesh and drinks my blood remains in me and I in him' (John 6:56). In this sacrament, under the outward signs of bread and wine, the faithful share in his very life. He offered his life in sacrifice once for all on the cross and, as our high priest, presents that sacrifice eternally in heaven, thereby giving the faithful who are identified with him access to the Father. In the Holy Eucharist the life given in baptism is fed and sustained with the heavenly food of the body and blood of Christ.

General Rubrics

1   The services of Baptism and Confirmation are appropriately celebrated at the Holy Eucharist with the Bishop as the principal minister. He alone confirms and normally himself baptizes but he may delegate parts of the service to other ministers.

2   By virtue of his office, the Bishop is the minister of baptism in his diocese. Nevertheless the usual minister at Baptism when there is no Confirmation is the Priest to whom the Bishop has committed the cure of souls in the pastoral charge. The Priest may invite another priest to baptize. If no priest can be present a deacon may baptize.

    Emergency Baptism (which may be administered by a lay person) is provided for in sections 89-93.

3   It is the intention of the church that Baptism and Confirmation should be public services. When they are used apart from the Eucharist or Morning and Evening Prayer, representatives of the congregation should be present.

4   When an adult is to be baptized the Bishop is to receive timely notice so that if he wishes, he may himself baptize, as well as confirm the candidate.

5   In these services, an adult is a person whom the minister considers able to answer responsibly for *himself*.

6   When children who are unable to answer responsibly for themselves are baptized at the same time as their parents, the parents answer the questions in the plural, both for themselves and for their children. Such children may be invited to respond with their parents.

7   When children and their parents are baptized on the same occasion, it is fitting that the children be baptized immediately after their own parents.

8   Each candidate for baptism shall have one or more sponsors who have been baptized. It is the intention that sponsors be communicants of the Anglican Church.

9   Sponsors of adults present their candidates and thereby promise to support them by prayer and example in their Christian life.

10 Together with parents, sponsors of children (usually called godparents) present their candidates, renew their own commitment to Christ and make the promises on behalf of the children.

11 Parents and godparents are to be instructed in the meaning of baptism and prepared for their responsibility of helping children to grow in the knowledge and love of God and in the fellowship of the Church.

12 The rite of Baptism may, if pastoral need require, and with the permission of the Bishop, take place elsewhere than in the church building or in a place commonly used for worship. Representatives of the congregation should always be present.

13 Hymns may be sung at appropriate places in the services.

The Collect

14 Almighty and merciful Father
giver of life and power:
fill your faithful people
    with the abundance of your grace
that all who are born again
    by water and the Spirit
may grow into the full stature
    of your Son, Jesus Christ;
who is alive, and reigns with you and the Holy Spirit
one God, now and for ever.
Amen

15 Readings, psalms and canticles are chosen from the following table, subject to the rubric at section 2, and the additional table for use at the Confirmation Service at section 65.

Old Testament Genesis 7:17-23; Exodus 14:19-31;
Deuteronomy 30:15-20; Jeremiah 31:31-34; Ezekiel 36:25-28.

Psalms 25:1-10; 27:1-8; 34:1-8; 43; 107:1-9.

New Testament Acts 16:16-34; Romans 6:3-11;
Romans 8:11-17; 1 Corinthians 12:12-13; Galatians 5:16-25;
1 Peter 2:4-10.

Canticles 7, 12, 15.

Gospel Matthew 28:16-20; Mark 1:1-11; Luke 24:44-49;
John 3:1-8; John 14:15-18; John 15:1-11.

16 A sermon is always preached at these services.

The Blessing

17 The Blessing may be given in this form

Go forth into the world in peace; be of good courage; fight the good fight of faith; that you may finish your course with joy; and the blessing of God almighty, the Father, the Son, and the Holy Spirit, be among you, and remain with you always.
Amen

Baptism and Confirmation

1   When there are candidates for confirmation who have previously been baptized, or when children are to be baptized but
not confirmed, the appropriate sections are used.

All candidates, whether for baptism and confirmation, or for confirmation
only, make their vows together immediately before the Baptism. Where
they cannot conveniently be accommodated at the font, a temporary font
is placed in a more suitable position. The precise ordering of the service
should be determined beforehand by consultation between the Bishop
and the Priest.

At the Welcome the Bishop may address the candidates by name.

It is sufficient if the people make their responses once only at 21 and 22
after the Signing, and the Giving of Candles. Before the Signing at 21 the
newly-baptized may be clothed with a white vesture, commonly called
the Chrysom.

AT THE EUCHARIST

2   Baptism and Confirmation (sections 7-30) follow the Gospel and Sermon.

At the discretion of the Bishop, on Sundays and Festivals the collect and
readings are those of the day and the Collect at General Rubric 14
follows that of the day. On other occasions, or when the collect and
readings of the Sunday or Festival have already been used in public
worship, the special collect alone may be used and the readings
chosen from the table at General Rubric 15.

The Eucharist continues after the prayer at 30 with the Peace, for which a
special sentence is provided on page 144.

Proper Preface 23 may be used.

An alternative Blessing is provided at General Rubric 17.

AT MORNING OR EVENING PRAYER

3   Baptism and Confirmation (sections 7-30) follow the Sermon.

The Collect at General Rubric 14 is used. The psalms and Scripture readings may be chosen from the table at General Rubric 15.

At the discretion of the Bishop, other prayers may follow the prayer at
section 30.

The service ends with the Blessing at General Rubric 17.

BAPTISM AND CONFIRMATION AS A SEPARATE SERVICE

4   The Bishop greets the people

The Lord be with you
And also with you

The Lord is my strength and my song
and has become my salvation

5   **Let us pray**

The Collect at General Rubric 14 is used.

6   One or more Scripture readings follow, chosen from the table at General Rubric 15. One of the psalms there may be used.

A sermon is preached.

Sections 7 to 30 follow.

At the discretion of the Bishop, other prayers may follow the prayer at section 30.

The service ends with the Lord's Prayer, and the Blessing at General Rubric 17.

The Service of Baptism and Confirmation

THE INTRODUCTION

7   After the Sermon, the Bishop addresses the people in these or similar words

Our Lord Jesus Christ gave himself to death on the cross and was raised again for the salvation of humankind.

Baptism is the sacrament in which, by repentance and faith, we enter into this salvation: we are united with Christ in his death; we are granted the forgiveness of sins; we are made members of his Body and we are raised with him to new life in the Spirit.

In Confirmation we come to be filled, through the laying on of hands, with the power of the Spirit for worship, witness and service.

THE RENUNCIATION

8   The Bishop addresses the candidates, parents and godparents, omitting any paragraph not required.

You, who have come for baptism and confirmation, must declare your rejection of all that is evil.

You, who present children for baptism, must promise to bring them up to reject all that is evil. You are to answer for yourselves and for your child.

You, who have already been baptized and have now come to be confirmed, must with your own lips and from your heart declare your rejection of all that is evil.

9   The Bishop asks them

Do you renounce the devil and all the spiritual forces of wickedness that rebel against God?
I renounce them

Do you renounce the evil powers of this world which corrupt and destroy what God has created?
I renounce them

Do you renounce all sinful desires that draw you away from the love of God?
I renounce them

10   The Bishop says to the congregation

Dear friends in Christ, let us pray for *these persons*

God of all mercy, look on *them*
Amen

Put to death *their* sinful desires
Amen
Grant *them* the life of your Spirit
Amen

Enable *them* to overcome the evil one
Amen
Give *them* every Christian virtue
Amen

Bring *them* with your saints to everlasting glory
Amen

11   The Bishop, who may stretch out his hand towards the candidates, says

May almighty God deliver you from the powers of darkness and lead you into the light and obedience of Christ.
Amen

THE BLESSING OF THE WATER

12 The Bishop, together with the candidates and their sponsors and parents, stands before the water of baptism and says

Praise God who made heaven and earth
who keeps his promise for ever

13 Almighty God, whose Son Jesus Christ was baptized in
     the river Jordan;
  we thank you for the gift of water to cleanse and revive
     us;
  we thank you that through the waters of the Red Sea,
     you led your people out of slavery to freedom in the
     promised land;
  we thank you that through the deep waters of death you
     brought your Son, and raised him to life in triumph.
  Bless this water, that your *servants* who *are* washed in it
     may be made one with Christ in his death and in his
     resurrection, to be cleansed and delivered from all sin.
  Send your Holy Spirit upon *them* to bring *them* to new
     birth in the family of your Church, and raise *them*
     with Christ to full and eternal life.
  For all might, majesty, authority, and power are yours,
     now and for ever.
  Amen

THE ALLEGIANCE

14   The Bishop addresses the candidates, parents and godparents, omitting any paragraph not required.

You, who are to be baptized and confirmed, must now in allegiance to Christ declare before God and his Church the Christian faith into which you are to be baptized, and in which you will live and grow.

Parents and godparents, you must now in allegiance to Christ declare before God and his Church the Christian faith into which *these children are* to be baptized, and in which you will help *them* to live and grow. You are to answer for yourselves and for your child.

You, who have already been baptized and are to be confirmed, must now in allegiance to Christ declare before God and his Church that you accept the Christian faith into which you were baptized, and in which you will continue to live and grow.

15   The Bishop asks the candidates, parents and godparents

Do you believe and trust in God the Father
who made the world?
I believe and trust in him

Do you believe and trust in his Son Jesus Christ
who redeemed humankind?
I believe and trust in him

Do you believe and trust in his Holy Spirit
who gives life to the people of God?
I believe and trust in him

16   The Bishop says to the congregation

This is the faith of the Church.

**This is our faith.
We believe and trust in one God
Father, Son, and Holy Spirit.**

17   To the candidates he says

Will you, who are to be baptized into this faith, and will you, who are to be confirmed, live in obedience to God's laws, as a loyal member of his Church?
With God's help, I will

18   To the parents and godparents he says

Parents and godparents, will you by your own example and teaching, bring up your child to live in obedience to God's laws, as a loyal member of his Church?
With God's help, I will

THE BAPTISM

(19)   Each candidate is presented to the Bishop by *his* parent or sponsor, who says

Reverend Father in God, I present to you *N* to be baptized.

20   The Bishop baptizes the candidates, dipping each in the water three times, or pouring water on each three times, once at the mention of each Person of the Holy Trinity, and saying

N I baptize you in the name of the Father, and of the Son, and of the Holy Spirit.
Amen

THE WELCOME

21   The Bishop makes the sign of the cross on the forehead of each one who has been baptized, saying

I sign you with the cross, the sign of Christ.

After the signing of each or all he says

Do not be ashamed to confess the faith of Christ crucified.

Fight valiantly under the banner of Christ
against sin, the world, and the devil
and continue his faithful *soldiers* **and** *servants*
to the end of your *lives*.

(22)   A candle, lit from the Easter Candle if possible, is given to each, or to the godparents, with the words

Christ our light

When a candle has been given to each one, the Bishop says

By baptism into Christ you pass from darkness to light.

Shine as a light in the world
to the glory of God the Father.

23   The congregation, representing the whole Church, welcomes the newly-baptized, the Bishop saying

God has received you by baptism into his Church.

We welcome you into the Lord's family.
We are members together of the Body of Christ;
we are children of the same heavenly Father;
we are inheritors together of the kingdom of God.
We welcome you.

THE CONFIRMATION

24   The Bishop stands before those who are to be confirmed and calls the congregation to prayer.

Silence is kept.

The hymn *Veni Creator*, or some other hymn addressed to the Holy Spirit, is sung.

25   Come, Holy Ghost, our souls inspire,
And lighten with celestial fire;
Thou the anointing Spirit art,
Who dost thy sevenfold gifts impart.

Thy blessèd unction from above
Is comfort, life, and fire of love;
Enable with perpetual light
The dullness of our blinded sight.

Anoint and cheer our soilèd face
With the abundance of thy grace;
Keep far our foes, give peace at home;
Where thou art guide no ill can come.

Teach us to know the Father, Son,
And thee, of Both, to be but One;
That through the ages all along
This may be our endless song,

Praise to thy eternal merit,
Father, Son and Holy Spirit.   Amen

26   The Bishop stands and says

Our help is in the Name of the Lord
who has made heaven and earth

Blessed be the Name of the Lord
now and for ever.   Amen

27 The Bishop stretches out his hands towards those to be confirmed and says

Almighty and everliving God
you have given your *servants* new birth
   in baptism by water and the Spirit
and have forgiven *them* all *their* sins.
Let your Holy Spirit rest upon *them*:
the Spirit of wisdom and understanding;
the Spirit of discernment and inner strength;
the Spirit of knowledge and true godliness;
and fill *them* with the Spirit of the fear of the Lord
now and for ever.
Amen

28 The candidates kneel in order before the Bishop. The Bishop may sign them on the forehead, using at his discretion the Chrism, and may say

N I sign you with the sign of the cross and I lay my hand upon you.

Or he may say

N I lay my hand upon you.

He lays his hand on their heads, saying

Lord, confirm and strengthen with your Holy Spirit this your child *N*† and empower *him* for your service.
Amen

†The name may be omitted here if it has already been used.

29 When all have been confirmed, the Bishop leads the congregation in saying

Defend, O Lord, *these* your *servants* with your
   heavenly grace
that *they* may continue yours for ever
and daily increase in your Holy Spirit more and more
until *they come* to your everlasting kingdom.

30   The Bishop says

Heavenly Father
we pray for your *servants*
   upon whom we have now laid our hands.
May your fatherly hand ever be over *them*
your Holy Spirit ever be with *them*.
Sustain *them* continually
   with the body and blood of your Son
and so lead *them* in the knowledge
   and obedience of your word
that in the end
they may enjoy the fulness of eternal life;
through Jesus Christ our Lord.
Amen

Baptism

31   This service is used both for adults and for children who are not able to answer responsibly for themselves. Children who are able to do so may, at the discretion of the Priest, answer with their parents and godparents. If children alone, or adults alone, are to be baptized, certain sections of the service are omitted.

At the Welcome the Priest may address the candidates by name.

It is sufficient if the people make their responses once only at 56 and 57 after the Signing, and the Giving of Candles. Before the Signing at 56 the newly-baptized may be clothed with a white vesture, commonly called the Chrysom.

AT THE EUCHARIST

32   Baptism (sections 37-63), follows the Gospel and Sermon.

At the discretion of the Bishop, on Sundays and Festivals the collect and readings are those of the day and the Collect at General Rubric 14 follows that of the day. On other occasions, or when the collect and readings of the Sunday or Festival have already been used in public worship, the special collect alone may be used and the readings chosen from the table at General Rubric 15.

The Eucharist continues after the optional prayers at 59-63, with the Peace, for which a special Sentence is provided on page 144.

Proper Preface 23 may be used.

An alternative Blessing is provided at General Rubric 17.

AT MORNING OR EVENING PRAYER

33   Baptism (sections 37 to 63) follows the Sermon.

The Collect at General Rubric 14 is used. The psalms and Scripture readings may be chosen from the table at General Rubric 15. The Service ends with the Blessing at General Rubric 17, or the Grace.

BAPTISM AS A SEPARATE SERVICE

34 The Priest greets the people

The Lord be with you
And also with you

The Lord is my strength and my song
And has become my salvation

35 Let us pray

The Collect at General Rubric 14 is used.

36 One or more Scripture readings follow, chosen from the table at General Rubric 15. One of the psalms there may be used.

A sermon is preached.

Sections 37 to 63 follow.

At the discretion of the Priest, other prayers may follow the prayer at section 63.

The service ends with the Lord's Prayer, and with the Blessing at General Rubric 17 or the Grace.

The Service of Baptism

THE GREETING

37   The Priest addresses those who have come for baptism, and their parents, godparents and sponsors, in these or similar words

On behalf of this parish and of the whole Church of God, we greet you in the name of the Lord and we rejoice with you.

THE INTRODUCTION

38   The Priest says

Our Lord Jesus Christ gave himself to death on the cross and was raised again for the salvation of humankind.

Baptism is the sacrament in which, by repentance and faith, we enter into this salvation: we are united with Christ in his death; we are granted the forgiveness of sins; we are made members of his Body and we are raised with him to new life in the Spirit.

39   Sections 40-42 are used only when children are to be baptized.

40   Children who are too young to profess the Christian faith are baptized on the understanding that they will be brought up as Christians within the family of the Church. As they grow up, they need the support of that family, so that they may learn to live by trust in God. They need encouragement to be faithful in public worship and personal prayer, to come to confirmation and to continue in obedience to the commandments of God all the days of their life.

41 Parents and godparents, the *children* whom you have brought for baptism *depend* chiefly on you for the help *they need*. Will you help and encourage your child by your prayers, by your example and by your teaching?

42 The parents and godparents answer

With God's help, I will

THE RENUNCIATION

43 The Priest addresses the candidates, parents and godparents, omitting any paragraph not required.

You, who present children for baptism, must promise to bring them up to reject all that is evil. You are to answer for yourselves and for your child.

You, who have come to be baptized, must declare your rejection of all that is evil.

44 The Priest asks the parents and the godparents and the adult candidates

Do you renounce the devil and all the spiritual forces of wickedness that rebel against God?
I renounce them

Do you renounce the evil powers of this world which corrupt and destroy what God has created?
I renounce them

Do you renounce all sinful desires that draw you away from the love of God?
I renounce them

45 The Priest says to the congregation

Dear friends in Christ, let us pray for *these persons*

God of all mercy, look on *them*
Amen

Put to death *their* sinful desires
Amen
Grant *them* the life of your Spirit
Amen

Enable *them* to overcome the evil one
Amen
Give *them* every Christian virtue
Amen

Bring *them* with your saints to everlasting glory
Amen

46 The Priest, who may stretch out his hand towards the candidates, says

May Almighty God deliver you from the powers of darkness and lead you into the light and obedience of Christ.
Amen

THE BLESSING OF THE WATER

47 The Priest, together with the parents, sponsors and candidates, stands before the water of baptism and says

Praise God who made heaven and earth
who keeps his promise for ever

48 Almighty God, whose Son Jesus Christ was baptized in the river Jordan;
we thank you for the gift of water to cleanse and revive us;
we thank you that through the waters of the Red Sea, you led your people out of slavery to freedom in the promised land;
we thank you that through the deep waters of death you brought your Son, and raised him to life in triumph.

Bless this water, that your *servants* who *are* washed in it
may be made one with Christ in his death and in his
resurrection, to be cleansed and delivered from all sin.

Send your Holy Spirit upon *them* to bring *them* to new
birth in the family of your Church, and raise *them*
with Christ to full and eternal life.

For all might, majesty, authority, and power are yours,
now and for ever.

Amen

THE ALLEGIANCE

49 The Priest addresses the parents and godparents and the adult
candidates, omitting any paragraph not required.

Parents and godparents, you must now in allegiance to
Christ declare before God and his Church the Christian
faith into which *these children are* to be baptized,
and in which you will help *them* to live and grow. You
are to answer for yourselves and for your child.

You who have come to be baptized must now in
allegiance to Christ declare before God and his Church
the Christian faith into which you are to be baptized, and
in which you will live and grow.

50 The Priest asks the parents and godparents and the adult
candidates

Do you believe and trust in God the Father
who made the world?
I believe and trust in him

Do you believe and trust in his Son Jesus Christ
who redeemed humankind?
I believe and trust in him

Do you believe and trust in his Holy Spirit
who gives life to the people of God?
I believe and trust in him

51 The Priest says to the congregation

This is the faith of the Church.

**This is our faith.
We believe and trust in one God
Father, Son, and Holy Spirit.**

52 To the parents and godparents he says

Parents and godparents, will you by your own example and teaching, bring up your child to live in obedience to God's laws, as a loyal member of his Church?
With God's help, I will

53 To the adults who are to be baptized he says

Will you, who are to be baptized into this faith, live in obedience to God's laws, as a loyal member of his Church?
With God's help, I will

THE BAPTISM

(54) Each candidate is presented to the Priest by *his* parent or sponsor, who says

I present to you *N* to be baptized.

55 The Priest baptizes the candidates, dipping each in the water three times, or pouring water on each three times, once at the mention of each Person of the Holy Trinity, and saying

N I baptize you in the name of the Father, and of the Son, and of the Holy Spirit.
Amen

THE WELCOME

56 The Priest makes the sign of the cross on the forehead of each one who has been baptized, saying

I sign you with the cross, the sign of Christ.

After the signing of each or all he says

Do not be ashamed to confess the faith of Christ crucified.

**Fight valiantly under the banner of Christ
against sin, the world, and the devil
and continue his faithful** *soldiers* **and** *servants*
to the end of your *lives*.

57 A candle, lit from the Easter Candle if possible, is given to the godparents or to the candidate, with the words

Christ our light

When a candle has been given to each one, the Priest says

By baptism into Christ you pass from darkness to light.

**Shine as a light in the world
to the glory of God the Father.**

58 The congregation, representing the whole Church, welcomes the newly-baptized, the Priest saying

God has received you by baptism into his Church.

**We welcome you into the Lord's family.
We are members together of the Body of Christ;
we are children of the same heavenly Father;
we are inheritors together of the kingdom of God.
We welcome you.**

THE PRAYERS

59 One or more of the prayers which follow may be used.

60 Lord God our Father, maker of heaven and earth
we thank you that by your Holy Spirit
these your *children have* been born again into new life
adopted for your own
and received into the fellowship of your Church:
grant that *they* may grow in the faith
    into which *they have* been baptized
that *they* may profess it for *themselves*
    when *they come* to be confirmed
and that all things belonging to the Spirit
    may live and grow in *them*;
through Jesus Christ our Lord.
Amen

61 Merciful Father
we thank you for your gift in holy baptism:
grant that *these children* may worthily receive
    your gracious favour
and grow into the full maturity of Christ your Son;
who is alive and reigns with you and the Holy Spirit
one God, now and for ever.
Amen

62 Heavenly Father
we pray for the parents of *these children*.
Give them the spirit of wisdom and love
that *their homes* may reflect the joy
    of your eternal kingdom;
through Jesus Christ our Lord.
Amen

53 Almighty God
we thank you for our fellowship
   in the household of faith
with all those who have been baptized in your name.
Keep us faithful to our baptism
and so make us ready for that day
when the whole creation shall be made perfect
   in your Son, our Saviour Jesus Christ.
Amen

Confirmation

64   This service is used only when none of the candidates is to be baptized; otherwise the Service of Baptism and Confirmation is used.

65   Readings and psalms may be chosen from the following table instead of the one at General Rubric 15.

Old Testament   Isaiah 11:1-9;   Isaiah 44:1-8;   Isaiah 61:1-3; Ezekiel 36:25-27;   Ezekiel 37:1-10;   Joel 2:28-32.

Psalms   46;   51:9-13;   65;   139:1-13.

New Testament   Acts 1:1-8;   Acts 2:1-21;   Acts 2:22-39; Acts 8:4-8, 14-17;   Acts 19:1-7;   Romans 15:13-21; 1 Corinthians 12:3-13;   Ephesians 3:14-21;   Ephesians 5:8-21; Colossians 1:1-14;   2 Thessalonians 2:13-17;   1 Timothy 6:12-16; 2 Timothy 1:1-7;   Hebrews 2:1-4.

Gospel   Luke 4:14-21;   Luke 11:9-13;   John 4:5-14; John 7:37-39;   John 14:15-26;   John 15:26—16:15.

AT THE EUCHARIST

66   Confirmation (sections 71-83) follows the Gospel and Sermon.

At the discretion of the Bishop, on Sundays and Festivals the collect and readings are those of the day and the Collect at General Rubric 14 follows that of the day. On other occasions, or when the collect and readings of the Sunday or Festival have already been used in public worship, the special collect alone may be used and the readings chosen from the tables at 65 and General Rubric 15.

The Eucharist continues after the prayer at 83, with the Peace, for which a special sentence is provided on page 144.

Proper Preface 23 may be used.

An alternative Blessing is provided at General Rubric 17.

AT MORNING OR EVENING PRAYER

67 Confirmation (sections 71 to 83) follows the Sermon.

The Collect at General Rubric 14 is used. The psalms and Scripture readings may be chosen from the tables at 65 and General Rubric 15.

At the discretion of the Bishop, other prayers may follow the prayer at 83.

The service ends with the Blessing at General Rubric 17.

CONFIRMATION AS A SEPARATE SERVICE

68 The Bishop greets the people

The Lord be with you
And also with you

The Lord is my strength and my song
and has become my salvation

69 Let us pray

The Collect at General Rubric 14 is used.

70 One of more Scripture readings follow, chosen from the tables at 65 and General Rubric 15. One of the psalms there may be used.

A sermon is preached.

Sections 71 to 86 follow.

At the discretion of the Bishop, other prayers may follow the prayer at 86.

The service ends with the Lord's Prayer, and the Blessing at General Rubric 17.

The Service of Confirmation

THE INTRODUCTION

71 The Bishop may address the people in these or similar words

Our Lord Jesus Christ gave himself to death on the cross and was raised again for the salvation of humankind.

Baptism is the sacrament in which, by repentance and faith, we enter into this salvation: we are united with Christ in his death; we are granted the forgiveness of sins; we are made members of his Body and we are raised with him to new life in the Spirit.

In Confirmation we come to be filled, through the laying on of hands, with the power of the Spirit for worship, witness and service.

THE RENEWAL OF BAPTISMAL VOWS

THE RENUNCIATION

72 The Bishop addresses the candidates

You, who are to be confirmed, must renew the vows of your baptism, and first, with your own lips and from your heart you must declare your rejection of all that is evil.

73 Do you renounce the devil and all the spiritual forces of wickedness that rebel against God?
I renounce them

Do you renounce the evil powers of this world which corrupt and destroy what God has created?
I renounce them

Do you renounce all sinful desires that draw you away
from the love of God?
I renounce them

THE ALLEGIANCE

74 Now, in allegiance to Christ, you must declare before
    God and his Church that you accept the Christian faith
    into which you were baptized, and in which you will
    continue to live and grow.

    Do you believe and trust in God the Father
    who made the world?
    I believe and trust in him

    Do you believe and trust in his Son Jesus Christ
    who redeemed humankind?
    I believe and trust in him

    Do you believe and trust in his Holy Spirit
    who gives life to the people of God?
    I believe and trust in him

75 The Bishop says to the congregation

    This is the faith of the Church.

    This is our faith.
    We believe and trust in one God
    Father, Son, and Holy Spirit.

76 The Bishop asks the candidates

    Will you, who are now to be confirmed, live in obedience
    to God's laws, as a loyal member of his Church?
    With God's help, I will

THE CONFIRMATION

77 The Bishop stands before those who are to be confirmed and calls the congregation to prayer.

Silence is kept.

The hymn *Veni Creator*, or some other hymn addressed to the Holy Spirit, is sung.

78 Come, Holy Ghost, our souls inspire,
And lighten with celestial fire;
Thou the anointing Spirit art,
Who dost thy sevenfold gifts impart.

Thy blessèd unction from above
Is comfort, life, and fire of love;
Enable with perpetual light
The dullness of our blinded sight.

Anoint and cheer our soilèd face
With the abundance of thy grace;
Keep far our foes, give peace at home;
Where thou art guide no ill can come.

Teach us to know the Father, Son,
And thee, of Both, to be but One;
That through the ages all along
This may be our endless song,

Praise to thy eternal merit,
Father, Son and Holy Spirit. **Amen**

79 The Bishop stands and says

Our help is in the Name of the Lord
who has made heaven and earth

Blessed be the Name of the Lord
now and for ever. Amen

The Bishop stretches out his hands towards those to be confirmed and says

Almighty and everliving God
you have given your *servants* new birth
  in baptism by water and the Spirit
and have forgiven *them* all *their* sins.
Let your Holy Spirit rest upon *them*:
the Spirit of wisdom and understanding;
the Spirit of discernment and inner strength;
the Spirit of knowledge and true godliness;
and fill *them* with the Spirit of the fear of the Lord
now and for ever.
Amen

The candidates kneel in order before the Bishop. The Bishop may sign them on the forehead, using at his discretion the Chrism, and may say

N I sign you with the sign of the cross and I lay my hand upon you.

Or he may say

N I lay my hand upon you.

He lays his hand on their heads, saying

Lord, confirm and strengthen with your Holy Spirit this your child *N*† and empower *him* for your service.
Amen

†The name may be omitted here if it has already been used.

When all have been confirmed, the Bishop leads the congregation in saying

**Defend, O Lord, *these* your *servants* with your
  heavenly grace
that *they* may continue yours for ever
and daily increase in your Holy Spirit more and more
until *they come* to your everlasting kingdom.**

83 The Bishop says

Heavenly Father
we pray for your *servants*
   upon whom we have now laid our hands.
May your fatherly hand ever be over *them*
your Holy Spirit ever be with *them*.
Sustain *them* continually
   with the body and blood of your Son
and so lead *them* in the knowledge
   and obedience of your word
that in the end
they may enjoy the fulness of eternal life;
through Jesus Christ our Lord.
Amen

84 Prayers may follow, at the discretion of the Bishop.

For all Christian people

85 Almighty Father, we thank you for our fellowship in
the household of faith with all who have been baptized
in your name. Keep us faithful to our baptism, and so
make us ready for that day when the whole creation
shall be made perfect in your Son, our Saviour Jesus
Christ.
Amen

For the Church's witness

86 Almighty God, whose Holy Spirit equips the Church
with a rich variety of gifts; grant that we may use them
to bear witness to Christ by lives built on faith and
love. Make us ready to live his gospel and eager to do
his will, that we may share with all your Church in the
joys of eternal life; through Jesus Christ our Lord.
Amen

Associated Services

CONDITIONAL BAPTISM

7 Conditional baptism is administered where there is reasonable doubt that a person has been validly baptized (with water and 'In the name of the Father, and of the Son, and of the Holy Spirit').

The absence of a baptismal certificate is not in itself a reason for conditional baptism. It may be possible to establish by other means that a valid baptism has already taken place. In this case, it is desirable that a signed statement be obtained from parents, or a member of the family, or a godparent, or a member of the congregation, or a minister. This statement should be attached to the register of baptisms.

It is important that conditional baptism be administered as no mere formality but with the solemnity proper to all the rites of Christian Initiation.

8 The usual service of baptism is used but the form of words at the Baptism (20 and 55) is

N **if you have not already been baptized, I baptize you in the name of the Father, and of the Son, and of the Holy Spirit.**
Amen

EMERGENCY BAPTISM AND RECEPTION INTO THE CONGREGATION

THE BAPTISM

89   Emergency baptism may be administered to anyone in danger of dying unbaptized, provided that in the case of an adult there is evidence to show that *he* is desirous of it.

     Parents or others requesting emergency baptism should be assured that questions of ultimate salvation or of the provision of a Christian funeral do not depend upon whether or not the person has been baptized.

     In an emergency, a lay person may administer baptism. However, the Priest must be notified of this without delay.

     When the name of the person is unknown, the baptism can be administered without the use of the name. The identity of the person should be subsequently established, so that an entry may be recorded in the register of baptisms.

90   The person administering the sacrament pours water upon the person being baptized, saying

N I baptize you, in the name of the Father, and of the Son, and of the Holy Spirit.
Amen

There follow the Lord's Prayer and the Grace.

91   If the person so baptized lives, *he* shall come (or be brought) to church as soon as possible in order to be received into the congregation, after appropriate preparation.

92   When the person was baptized by someone other than the Priest, the Priest shall satisfy himself that the baptism has been properly administered. He may, if necessary, question those responsible in these or similar words

Who baptized this *child/person?*
Who was present at the baptism?
Was *he* baptized with water?
What words were used for the baptism?

93   If there is uncertainty as to whether the person was baptized with water, 'In the name of the Father, and of the Son, and of the Holy Spirit', the Priest administers baptism using the formula for conditional baptism at 88.

Where the Priest is satisfied that there was no valid baptism, he uses the Service of Baptism.

If the Priest himself baptized the person, or if he is satisfied that *he* was duly baptized, he arranges for *him* to be received into the congregation, as provided below.

RECEPTION INTO THE CONGREGATION

94   This ceremony most appropriately takes place at the time of a public baptism. It is desirable that an adult who is received into the congregation be confirmed either at the same service or as soon as may be convenient afterwards. If there are no candidates for baptism, the Blessing of the Water (sections 12-13 or 47-48) and the Baptism (sections 19-20 or 54-55) are omitted. Otherwise the Service of Baptism or the Service of Baptism and Confirmation is used, subject to the changes set out below.

95   Before proceeding with the Reception the Priest says to the congregation

I declare that all has been well done and according to due order, concerning the baptism of this *child/person, N.*

96   At the Renunciation the wording is changed as follows in addressing the parents and godparents at 8 and 43

You must promise to bring up this child to reject all that is evil. You are to answer for yourselves and for this child who has been baptized.

An adult candidate who is not being confirmed at the same service is addressed as follows at 8 and 43

You, who have been baptized, must declare your rejection of all that is evil.

97 At the Allegiance the wording is changed as follows in addressing the parents and godparents at 14 and 49

Parents and godparents, you must now in allegiance to Christ declare before God and his Church the Christian faith in which you will help this child to live and grow. You are to answer both for yourselves and for *him*.

An adult candidate not being confirmed at the same service is addressed as follows at 14 and 49

You, who have been baptized, must now in allegiance to Christ declare before God and his Church the Christian faith into which you have been baptized, and in which you will live and grow.

and as follows at 17 and 53

Will you, who have been baptized into this faith, live in obedience to God's laws, as a loyal member of his Church?

THE ADMISSION
OF BAPTIZED COMMUNICANTS

*from other Churches
into Communicant Membership of the
Church of the Province of Southern Africa*

98 This service is intended for those who have been confirmed in other Churches and is used at a Confirmation after 30 or 83 or on some other suitable occasion, at the discretion of the Bishop.

The Bishop is the minister of this rite. When there is a delay, the person who wishes to be admitted may be allowed to receive the Holy Communion before *his* formal admission.

99 Those to be admitted are brought to the Bishop by the Priest, who says

Reverend Father in God, I present to you *N* and *N* (or *these persons*) who *wish* to be admitted into the Church of the Province of Southern Africa.

00 The Bishop says to them

Dear *brothers and sisters* in Christ, peace be with you. Before I admit you, I invite you to declare publicly your faith in God in whose name you were baptized

Do you believe in God, Father, Son and Holy Spirit, and accept the Christian faith as contained in the Apostles' Creed?
I do

01 We praise God that together we know his saving grace in Jesus Christ. We rejoice that God has given you the desire to express your Christian discipleship within the fellowship of the Anglican Communion and in the family of this Diocese and Province. We pray that we may be mutually encouraged and enriched by each other's faith and learn from each other's heritage.

102 Do you acknowledge the Church of the Province of Southern Africa to be a true part of the one, holy, catholic and apostolic Church?
I do

Do you accept its ministry of bishops, priests and deacons, and believe its sacraments of Baptism and Holy Communion to be those which Christ appointed?
I do

Will you be a loyal member of the Church of the Province of Southern Africa, accepting its discipline as well as its teaching, and will you faithfully share in its worship, work and witness?
I will

103 Almighty God who gives you the will to do all these things, grant you grace and power to perform them, that he may complete the good work he has begun in you, through Jesus Christ our Lord.
Amen

104 Those who are to receive Episcopal Confirmation kneel before the Bishop. He lays his hand on the head of each, and may sign *him* with the sign of the cross, using chrism if he desires, and says

N be confirmed and strengthened with the Holy Spirit.
Amen

105 The Bishop invites the congregation to join with him in praying for *those* who *have* been confirmed.

Defend, O Lord, *these* **your** *servants,* **with your heavenly grace**
that *they* **may continue yours for ever**
and daily increase in your Holy Spirit more and more
until *they come* **to your everlasting kingdom.**

06 The Bishop gives to all those who are to be admitted the right hand of fellowship, saying

N we receive you into the Church of the Province of Southern Africa and into the fellowship of the Anglican Communion.

He may add a blessing.

07 The Bishop and the congregation welcome those who have been admitted.

We welcome you into our fellowship.
We are members together of the Body of Christ;
we are children of the same heavenly Father;
we are inheritors together of the kingdom of God.
We welcome you.

RENEWAL OF BAPTISMAL PROMISES

108 The Minister of this service is the Priest or any other person duly authorized and instructed by him.

Baptismal promises may be renewed on appropriate occasions when the
people have been duly prepared.

Such renewal normally takes place during public worship, but not at
services of Christian Initiation (apart from the Easter Vigil, when the
form on pages 223-225 is used), unless the Bishop gives permission.

Since the circumstances of this service will vary greatly, the Minister may
explain its purpose and may invite those renewing their promises to give
testimony to the work of God's grace in their lives.

109 The Minister and the congregation may offer free and spontaneous
prayer.

All say together

**Grant, Lord
that we who have been baptized
may never be ashamed
to confess the faith of Christ crucified
to fight valiantly under his banner
    against sin, the world and the devil
and to continue his faithful soldiers and servants
    to the end of our lives.**

110 The Minister addresses those who wish to renew their promises
in these or similar words

In our baptism we died with Christ and were buried
with him, so that we might rise with him to a new life
within the family of his Church.

We can never be baptized again, but we can, in
response to a movement of God's Spirit, and after careful
preparation, renew the promises made at our baptism.

So I invite you who are ready to do so to affirm your
rejection of all that is evil.

11 Do you renounce the devil and all the spiritual forces of wickedness that rebel against God?
I renounce them

Do you renounce the evil powers of this world which corrupt and destroy what God has created?
I renounce them

Do you renounce all sinful desires that draw you away from the love of God?
I renounce them

12 The Minister says

Now in allegiance to Christ you must declare before God and his Church that you accept the Christian faith into which you were baptized, and in which you will continue to live and grow.

Do you believe and trust in God the Father
who made the world?
I believe and trust in him

Do you believe and trust in his Son Jesus Christ
who redeemed humankind?
I believe and trust in him

Do you believe and trust in his Holy Spirit
who gives life to the people of God?
I believe and trust in him

13 The Minister says

This is the faith of the Church.

This is our faith.
We believe and trust in one God
Father, Son and Holy Spirit.

14 The Minister says

Will you live in obedience to God's laws, as a loyal member of his Church?
With God's help, I will

115 Almighty God who gives you the will to do all these things, grant you grace and power to perform them, that he may complete the good work he has begun in you, through Jesus Christ our Lord.
Amen

116 The Minister says one or both of these prayers

117 Almighty God, we thank you for our fellowship in the household of faith with all those who have been baptized in your name. Keep us faithful to our baptism, and so make us ready for that day when the whole creation shall be made perfect in your Son, our Saviour Jesus Christ.
Amen

118 Almighty God, whose Holy Spirit equips the Church with a rich variety of gifts, grant that we may use them to bear witness to Christ by lives built on faith and love. Make us ready to live his gospel and eager to do his will, that we may share with all your Church in the joys of eternal life; through Jesus Christ our Lord.
Amen

119 The Minister and the congregation may offer free and spontaneous prayer.

120 All say together

Eternal God
you have declared in Christ
   the completion of your purpose of love.
May we live by faith, walk in hope
   and be renewed in love
until the world reflects your glory
   and you are all in all.
Even so; come, Lord Jesus.   Amen

121 The service may end with the Lord's Prayer, and the Blessing or the Grace.

THANKSGIVING FOR THE BIRTH OF A CHILD

This is a great occasion for thanksgiving, both for joy that a child is born into the world and for the safe delivery of the mother. Essentially a family occasion, it may suitably take place at home and is a prelude to baptism.

There are, however, those who are unable or unwilling to make a commitment to the obligations which baptism demands. They may find in this service a helpful way of giving thanks and praying for their child. It is definitely not baptism, nor a substitute for it; it may, however, lead some people to seek baptism for their children.

The gospel reading shows Jesus as the one who blesses all children brought to him, and the optional giving of a Gospel is a signpost on the way to a greater knowledge of God's love.

22 Since this service is a family occasion it is fitting that it take place in the home.

If it takes place in church, it should not take place at the font, nor during any service of Christian Initiation.

The minister is the Priest, but he may invite some other person to take his place.

INTRODUCTION

23 The Minister addresses the people in these or similar words

We have come together to rejoice with N and N (and their family) in the birth of this child and, with them, to give thanks to our heavenly Father. When children were brought to our Lord Jesus Christ he welcomed them, took them in his arms and blessed them. We thank God for this assurance of his love.

God so loved the world that he sent his Son Jesus Christ to live, to die and rise from the dead, so that those who believe in him might have eternal life. Baptism is the sacrament in which by repentance and faith we enter into this life. It is the Church's desire that all may come to baptism and to a living faith in Jesus Christ.

PRAISE

124 It is good to give thanks to the Lord
His love endures for ever

125 Psalm 100 may follow, or a hymn may be sung.

> 1 O shout to the Lord in triumph, all the earth:
>   serve the Lord with gladness,
>   and come before his face with songs of joy.
>
> 2 Know that the Lord he is God:
>   it is he who made us and we are his;
>   we are his people and the sheep of his pasture.
>
> 3 Come into his gates with thanksgiving
>   and into his courts with praise:
>   give thanks to him, and bless his holy name.
>
> 4 For the Lord is good, his loving mercy is for ever:
>   his faithfulness throughout all generations.
>
>   Glory to the Father and to the Son:
>   and to the Holy Spirit.
>   As it was in the beginning:
>   is now and will be for ever.   Amen

126 The Minister says

God the maker of heaven and earth, creator of life:
we praise you that in the birth of children
   you give parents a share
   in the work and joy of creation.
Amen

127 We glorify you for your creative power and love
through which *N* and *N* have been granted
   the gift of this child.
Amen

28 We bless you for preserving *N* in childbirth
    and for the skill and care of all
       who have guarded the health of mother and child.
    Amen

29 We thank you for all the blessings of this life
    and all opportunities for growth
       in body, mind and spirit.
    Amen

30 We thank you that you have given us human birth
    and that you call us to be born again
       as your children
    through faith in your beloved Son, Jesus Christ.
    Amen

31 **Blessing and honour and thanksgiving and praise**
    more than we can utter
    more than we can understand
    be to you, O holy and glorious Trinity
    Father, Son and Holy Spirit
    from all angels
    all people
    all creatures
    for ever and ever.

THE WORD OF GOD

132 The Minister says

Hear these words from the Gospel according to St Mark

People were bringing little children to Jesus to have him touch them, but the disciples rebuked them. When Jesus saw this, he was indignant. He said to them, 'Let the little children come to me, and do not hinder them, for the kingdom of God belongs to such as these. I tell you the truth, anyone who will not receive the kingdom of God like a little child will never enter it'. And he took the children in his arms, put his hands on them and blessed them.   *(Mark 10:13-16)*

(133) The Minister hands a copy of one of the Gospels to the parents with these or similar words

Take this book; in it is the good news of God's love. Read it, for it tells how we can share in the eternal life which God extends to all who repent and who put their faith in Jesus Christ.

THE BLESSING

134 The Minister takes the child in *his* arms and says

May the Lord bless you.
May you grow and become strong;
may you be filled with wisdom;
may the favour of God be upon you.

135 The parents receive the child and they may say

God our Father, we thank you
    for this child you have given us:
help us to be good parents
and grant that by our love for *him*

he may learn to know and love you
   his heavenly Father;
through Jesus Christ our Lord.

THE PRAYERS

Our Father in heaven
hallowed be your Name
your kingdom come
your will be done
on earth as in heaven.
Give us today our daily bread.
Forgive us our sins
   as we forgive those who sin against us.
Save us from the time of trial
and deliver us from evil.
For the kingdom, the power, and the glory are yours
now and for ever.   Amen

One or more of these prayers may be said

Heavenly Father, from whom every family in heaven
and on earth is named: bless *N* and *N*, the parents of this
child, and give to them and to all in whose charge *he*
may be, the spirit of wisdom and love, that *his* home
may be to *him* an image of your kingdom, and the care
of *his* parents a likeness of your love; through Jesus
Christ our Lord.
Amen

Almighty Father
we pray for this child
that in due time
he may be received by baptism
   into the family of your Church
and become an inheritor of your kingdom;
through Jesus Christ our Lord.
Amen

140 **Almighty God, the fountain of all wisdom**
you know our needs before we ask
and our ignorance in asking:
have compassion on our weakness
and those things which for
    our unworthiness we dare not
and for our blindness we cannot ask
grant us through your Son Jesus Christ our Saviour.

CONCLUSION

141 **May the Lord bless us and watch over us.**
May the Lord make his face shine on us
    and be gracious to us.
May the Lord look kindly on us
and give us peace.

142 Or, if a priest is present, he may pronounce the Blessing.

Thanksgiving for the Mother's Safety after the Death of a Child

143 When a child has died at birth and it is desired to give thanks for the safety of the mother, suitable parts of the foregoing service may be used, together with one or more of the following prayers.

144 Almighty Father, we thank you that your servant *N* has been brought in safety through the pain and peril of child-birth: give to her your continuing help, that she may live faithfully according to your will and share in your everlasting glory; through Jesus Christ our Lord.
Amen

God of loving kindness, comfort N (*and N*) in *their* distress, that *they* may hold to you through good and ill, and always trust in your unfailing love; through Jesus Christ our Lord.
Amen

Let us commend this child to the love of God our Father.

Heavenly Father, by your mighty power you gave us life, and in your love you have given us new life in Christ Jesus. We entrust this child to your merciful keeping, in the faith of Jesus Christ your Son our Lord, who died and rose again to save us, and is now alive and reigns with you and the Holy Spirit in glory for ever.
Amen

God is our refuge and strength:
a very present help in trouble.
Though my flesh and my heart fail me:
you, O God, are my portion for ever.
Forsake me not, O Lord
go not from me, my God:
hasten to my help, O Lord my salvation.
Why are you so full of heaviness, my soul:
and why so unquiet within me?
O put your trust in God:
for I will praise him yet
who is my deliverer and my God.

Glory to the Father, and to the Son
and to the Holy Spirit:
As it was in the beginning, is now
and will be for ever.
Amen

THANKSGIVING AFTER ADOPTION

This service is similar to the Thanksgiving for the Birth of a Child, with the account of Jesus blessing children brought to him, an optional giving of a Gospel and a selection of prayers.

The circumstances of adoption and the age at which a child is adopted vary so widely that the wording of any Introduction that may seem necessary has been left to the Minister.

The reality of the given parenthood is stressed. So the parents, together with the family (which may include other children and various relatives), declare their joy and love as they receive the child into their number. The parents may also use a prayer of thanksgiving.

The child may have already been baptized but if not, a prayer may be used which looks forward to the great blessing of baptism.

148   This service may be used either at home or in church.

PRAISE

149   The Minister may greet the people, leading them to thanks-giving and prayer for the child who has been adopted.

It is good to give thanks to the Lord
His love endures for ever

150   Psalm 100 may follow, or a hymn may be sung.

> 1 O shout to the Lord in triumph, all the earth:
>   serve the Lord with gladness,
>   and come before his face with songs of joy.
>
> 2 Know that the Lord he is God:
>   it is he who made us and we are his;
>   we are his people and the sheep of his pasture.
>
> 3 Come into his gates with thanksgiving
>   and into his courts with praise:
>   give thanks to him, and bless his holy name.
>
> 4 For the Lord is good, his loving mercy is for ever:
>   his faithfulness throughout all generations.

Glory to the Father and to the Son:
  and to the Holy Spirit.
As it was in the beginning:
  is now and will be for ever.   Amen

1 The Minister says

God our Father
maker of all that is living
we praise you for the wonder and joy of creation.
We thank you from our hearts
  for the life of this child
and for the privilege of parenthood.
Accept our thanks and praise
through Jesus Christ our Lord.
Amen

2 **Blessing and honour and thanksgiving and praise**
more than we can utter
more than we can understand
be to you, O holy and glorious Trinity
Father, Son and Holy Spirit
from all angels
all people
all creatures
for ever and ever.

THE WORD OF GOD

3 The Minister says

Hear these words from the Gospel according to St Mark

People were bringing little children to Jesus to have
him touch them, but the disciples rebuked them.
When Jesus saw this, he was indignant. He said to
them, 'Let the little children come to me, and do not
hinder them, for the kingdom of God belongs to such
as these. I tell you the truth, anyone who will not

receive the kingdom of God like a little child will never enter it'. And he took the children in his arms, put his hands on them and blessed them. *(Mark 10:13-16)*

(154) The Minister hands a copy of one of the Gospels to the parents with these or similar words

Take this book; in it is the good news of God's love. Read it, for it tells how we can share in the eternal life which God extends to all who repent and who put their faith in Jesus Christ.

THE BLESSING

155 The Minister may take the child in *his* arms, or by the hand, and *he* says

May the Lord bless you.
May you grow and become strong;
may you be filled with wisdom;
may the favour of God be upon you.

156 The parents receive the child and, together with members of the family, they say

We receive this child into our family
    with thanksgiving and joy.
Through the love of God we receive *him*;
with the love of God we will care for *him*;
by the love of God we will guide *him*;
and in the love of God
    may we all abide for ever.

7 The parents may say

God our Father, we thank you
  for this child you have given us:
help us to be good parents
and grant that by our love for *him*
he may learn to know and love you
  his heavenly Father;
through Jesus Christ our Lord.

THE PRAYERS

8 **Our Father in heaven
hallowed be your Name
your kingdom come
your will be done
on earth as in heaven.
Give us today our daily bread.
Forgive us our sins
  as we forgive those who sin against us.
Save us from the time of trial
and deliver us from evil.
For the kingdom, the power, and the glory are yours
now and for ever.   Amen**

9 One or more of these prayers may be said.

10 Heavenly Father, from whom every family in heaven and on earth is named: bless *N* and *N*, the parents of this child, and give to them and to all in whose charge *he* may be, the spirit of wisdom and love, that *his* home may be to *him* an image of your kingdom, and the care of *his* parents a likeness of your love; through Jesus Christ our Lord.
Amen

For an unbaptized child

161 Almighty Father
we pray for this child
that in due time
he may be received by baptism
    into the family of your Church
and become an inheritor of your kingdom;
through Jesus Christ our Lord.
Amen

162 **Almighty God, the fountain of all wisdom**
you know our needs before we ask
and our ignorance in asking:
have compassion on our weakness
and those things which for
    our unworthiness we dare not
and for our blindness we cannot ask
grant us through your Son Jesus Christ our Saviour.

CONCLUSION

163 **May the Lord bless us and watch over us.**
May the Lord make his face shine on us
    and be gracious to us.
May the Lord look kindly on us
and give us peace.

164 Or, if a priest is present, he may pronounce the Blessing.

THE ADMISSION OF CATECHUMENS
(Adult Candidates for Baptism)

The Catechumenate is a period of pre-baptismal instruction for adults who desire to become Christians.

The preparation of those who are to receive Christian Initiation is traditionally the responsibility of the Bishop. In practice, he usually delegates this to his priests, deacons and catechists.

The candidates and their sponsors are to be encouraged to pray and fast, and to read and study Holy Scripture and the Church's teaching. They are to participate in the corporate worship of the Church.

After an initial period of teaching, candidates are enrolled in the Catechumenate. This service normally takes place at a Sunday celebration of the Eucharist.

It is followed by continuing instruction in the Christian faith and life.

The baptism and confirmation of catechumens takes place most appropriately at the Easter Vigil. In this case, the first Sunday in Lent is suitable for the admission of catechumens. They may also be admitted at other times.

Care should be taken to ensure the continuing nurture of adult converts after baptism and confirmation.

465 This service may be used during a celebration of the Eucharist immediately before the Peace at section 44, or during Morning or Evening Prayer after the Collects.

466 The *sponsors bring* the *candidates* to the church and they are seated near the entrance. At the appropriate point in the service, the Priest goes to them, invites them to come forward and leads them to stand before the congregation.

467 He faces them and says

Friends, what do you seek?

468 The *candidates answer*

We seek life in Christ.

417

169   The Priest addresses the *candidates*

Our Lord Jesus Christ said: the Lord our God is Lord alone, and you shall love the Lord your God with all your heart, and with all your soul, and with all your mind; and your neighbour as yourself.

170   Do you want to know the one true and living God, to love, obey and serve him?
I do

Do you want to be further instructed in the faith of Christ?
I do

Do you renounce the devil and every form of evil?
I do

171   Peace be with you

The *candidates* and *sponsors* reply

And also with you

172   The *candidates* kneel and the Priest stretches out his hands towards *them*, saying

Most merciful God, behold and sustain *these Catechumens* who *seek* to know you more fully. Deliver *them* from the power of the Evil One. Make *them* bold to renounce all sinful desires that entice *them* from loving you. Grant that, coming in faith to the sacrament of baptism, *they* may commit *themselves* to you, receive the seal of the Holy Spirit, and share with us in the eternal priesthood of Jesus Christ our Lord.
Amen

73 The Priest makes the sign of the cross on the forehead of each Catechumen, saying

Receive Christ in your heart and take up his cross.

The Catechumen replies

Amen

74 Let us pray

75 One or both of the following prayers may be said

76 Almighty and merciful Father, creator of all: look with favour on *these* your *servants*, and bring *them* by your grace to rebirth in baptism, that *they* may be numbered among the children of promise; through Jesus Christ your only Son our Lord.
Amen

77 Holy and eternal Lord, we pray for *these* your *servants* whom you have called from darkness into light. Cleanse *them* from sin, grant *them* regeneration by the Holy Spirit in the waters of baptism and grace to grow into the likeness of your Son, our Saviour Jesus Christ.
Amen

78 The Priest says to the *Catechumens*

Almighty God who has called you to the knowledge of his grace, grant you entrance into his kingdom.
Amen

79 The names of the *Catechumens are* inscribed in the church roll.

A CATECHISM

A Catechism

Human Nature

1 What are we by nature?
We are part of God's creation, made in the image of God.

2 What does it mean to be created in the image of God?
It means that we are free to make choices: to love, to create, to reason, and to live in harmony with creation and with God.

3 Why then do we live apart from God and out of harmony with creation?
From the beginning, human beings have misused their freedom and made wrong choices.

4 Why do we not use our freedom as we should?
Because we rebel against God, and we put ourselves in the place of God.

5 What help is there for us?
Our help is in God.

6 How did God first help us?
God first helped us by revealing himself and his will, through nature and history, through many seers and saints, and especially through the prophets of Israel.

God the Father

7 What do we learn about God as creator from the revelation to Israel?
We learn that there is one God, the Father almighty, creator of heaven and earth, of all that is, seen and unseen.

8 What does this mean?
This means that the universe is good, that it is the work of a single loving God who creates, sustains, and directs it.

9 What does this mean about our place in the universe?
  It means that the world belongs to its creator; and that
  we are called to enjoy it and to care for it in accordance
  with God's purposes.

10 What does this mean about human life?
  It means that all people are worthy of respect and
  honour, because all are created in the image of God,
  and all can respond to the love of God.

11 How was this revelation handed down to us?
  This revelation was handed down to us through a
  community created by a covenant with God.

The Old Covenant

12 What is meant by a covenant with God?
  A covenant is a relationship initiated by God, to which
  a body of people responds in faith.

13 What is the Old Covenant?
  The Old Covenant is the one given by God to the
  Hebrew people.

14 What did God promise them?
  God promised that they would be his people to bring
  all the nations of the world to him.

15 What response did God require from the chosen
  people?
  God required the chosen people to be faithful; to do
  justice, to love mercy, and to walk humbly with
  their God.

16 Where is this Old Covenant to be found?
  The covenant with the Hebrew people is to be found
  in the books which we call the Old Testament.

17 Where in the Old Testament is God's will for us
  shown most clearly?
  God's will for us is shown most clearly in the Ten
  Commandments.

The Ten Commandments

18 What are the Ten Commandments?
The Ten Commandments are the laws given to Moses and the people of Israel.

19 Recite the Ten Commandments.

I   You shall have no other gods before me.
II   You shall not make for yourself a graven image, or any likeness of anything that is in heaven above, or that is in the earth beneath, or that is in the water under the earth.
III   You shall not take the name of the Lord your God in vain.
IV   Remember the sabbath day, to keep it holy.
V   Honour your father and your mother.
VI   You shall not kill.
VII   You shall not commit adultery.
VIII You shall not steal.
IX   You shall not bear false witness against your neighbour.
X   You shall not covet.

20 What do we learn from these commandments?
We learn two things: our duty to God, and our duty to our neighbours.

21 What is our duty to God?
Our duty is to believe and trust in God;
I   To love and obey God and to bring others to know him;
II   To put nothing in the place of God;
III   To show God respect in thought, word, and deed;
IV   And to set aside regular times for worship, prayer, and the study of God's ways.

22 What is our duty to our neighbours?
Our duty to our neighbours is to love them as ourselves, and to do to other people as we wish them to do to us;

V   To love, honour, and help our parents and family; to honour those in authority, and to meet their just demands;

VI   To show respect for the life God has given us; to work and pray for peace; to bear no malice, prejudice or hatred in our hearts; and to be kind to all the creatures of God;

VII   To use all our bodily desires as God intended;

VIII To be honest and fair in our dealings; to seek justice, freedom, and the necessities of life for all people; and to use our talents and possessions as ones who must answer for them to God;

IX   To speak the truth, and not to mislead others by our silence;

X   To resist temptations to envy, greed, and jealousy; to rejoice in other people's gifts and graces; and to do our duty for the love of God, who has called us into fellowship with him.

23 What is the purpose of the Ten Commandments?
The Ten Commandments were given to define our relationship with God and our neighbours.

24 Since we do not fully obey them, are they useful at all?
Since we do not fully obey them, we see more clearly our sin and our need for redemption.

Sin and Redemption

25 What is sin?
Sin is the seeking of our own will instead of the will of God, thus distorting our relationship with God, with other people, and with all creation.

26 How does sin have power over us?
Sin has power over us because we lose our liberty when our relationship with God is distorted.

27 What is redemption?
Redemption is the act of God which sets us free from the power of evil, sin, and death.

28 How did God prepare us for redemption?
God sent the prophets to call us back to himself, to show us our need for redemption, and to announce the coming of the Messiah.

29 What is meant by the Messiah?
The Messiah is one sent by God to free us from the power of sin, so that with the help of God we may live in harmony with God, within ourselves, with our neighbours, and with all creation.

30 Who do we believe is the Messiah?
The Messiah, or Christ, is Jesus of Nazareth, the only Son of God.

God the Son

31 What do we mean when we say that Jesus is the only Son of God?
We mean that Jesus is the only perfect image of the Father, and shows us the nature of God.

32 What is the nature of God revealed in Jesus?
God is love.

33 What do we mean when we say that Jesus was conceived by the Holy Spirit and became incarnate from the Virgin Mary?
We mean that by God's own act, his divine Son received our human nature from the Virgin Mary, his mother.

34 Why did he take our human nature?
The divine Son became human, so that in him human beings might be adopted as children of God, and be made heirs of God's kingdom.

35 What is the great importance of Jesus' suffering and death?
By his obedience, even to suffering and death, Jesus made the offering which we could not make; in him we are freed from the power of sin and reconciled to God.

36 What is the significance of Jesus' resurrection?
By his resurrection, Jesus overcame death and opened for us the way of eternal life.

37 What do we mean when we say that he descended to the dead?
We mean that he went to the departed and offered them also the benefits of redemption.

38 What do we mean when we say that he ascended into heaven and is seated at the right hand of the Father?
We mean that Jesus took our human nature into heaven where he now reigns with the Father and intercedes for us.

39 How can we share in his victory over sin, suffering, and death?
We share in his victory when we are baptized into the New Covenant and become living members of Christ.

The New Covenant

40 What is the New Covenant?
The New Covenant is the new relationship with God given by Jesus Christ, the Messiah, to the apostles; and, through them, to all who believe in him.

41 What did the Messiah promise in the New Covenant?
Christ promised to bring us into the kingdom of God and give us life in all its fulness.

42 What response did Christ require?
Christ commanded us to believe in him and to keep his commandments.

43 What are the commandments taught by Christ?
Christ taught us the Summary of the Law and gave us the New Commandment.

44 What is the Summary of the Law?
You shall love the Lord your God with all your heart, with all your soul, and with all your mind. This is the

first and the great commandment. And the second is
like it: You shall love your neighbour as yourself.

45 What is the New Commandment?
The New Commandment is that we love one another
as Christ loved us.

46 Where may we find what Christians believe about
Christ?
What Christians believe about Christ is found in the
Scriptures and summed up in the creeds.

The Creeds

47 What are the creeds?
The creeds are statements of our basic beliefs about
God.

48 How many creeds does this church use in its
worship?
This church uses two creeds: The Apostles' Creed and
the Nicene Creed.

49 What is the Apostles' Creed?
The Apostles' Creed is the ancient creed of baptism; it
is used in the church's daily worship to recall our
baptismal covenant.

50 Recite the Apostles' Creed.

I believe in God, the Father almighty
creator of heaven and earth.

I believe in Jesus Christ, his only Son, our Lord.
He was conceived by the Holy Spirit
and born of the Virgin Mary.
He suffered under Pontius Pilate
was crucified, died, and was buried.
He descended to the dead.
On the third day he rose again.
He ascended into heaven
and is seated at the right hand of the Father.
He will come to judge the living and the dead.

I believe in the Holy Spirit
the holy catholic Church
the communion of saints
the forgiveness of sins
the resurrection of the body
and the life everlasting.   Amen

51 What is the Nicene Creed?
   The Nicene Creed is the creed of the universal Church
   and is used at the Eucharist.

52 What, then, is the Athanasian Creed?
   The Athanasian Creed is an ancient document pro-
   claiming the nature of the Incarnation and of God as
   Trinity.

53 What do we mean by speaking of God as Trinity?
   We mean that we believe in God the Father, God the
   Son and God the Holy Spirit, three Persons and yet
   one God.

God the Holy Spirit

54 Who is the Holy Spirit?
   The Holy Spirit is the Third Person of the Trinity, God
   at work in the world and in the Church even now.

55 How is the Holy Spirit revealed in the Old Covenant?
   The Holy Spirit is revealed in the Old Covenant as
   the giver of life, the One who spoke through the
   prophets.

56 How is the Holy Spirit revealed in the New Covenant?
   The Holy Spirit is revealed as the Lord who leads us
   into all truth and enables us to grow in the likeness of
   Christ.

57 How do we recognize the presence of the Holy Spirit
   in our lives?
   We recognize the presence of the Holy Spirit when we
   confess Jesus Christ as Lord and are brought into love
   and harmony with God, with ourselves, with our
   neighbours, and with all creation.

58 How do we recognize the truths taught by the Holy Spirit?
We recognize truths to be taught by the Holy Spirit when they are in accord with the Scriptures.

The Holy Scriptures

59 What are the holy Scriptures?
The holy Scriptures, commonly called the Bible, are the books of the Old and New Testaments; other books, called the Apocrypha, are often included in the Bible.

60 What is the Old Testament?
The Old Testament consists of books written by the people of the Old Covenant, under the inspiration of the Holy Spirit, to show God at work in nature and history.

61 What is the New Testament?
The New Testament consists of books written by the people of the New Covenant, under the inspiration of the Holy Spirit, to set forth the life and teachings of Jesus and to proclaim the good news of the kingdom for all people.

62 What is the Apocrypha?
The Apocrypha is a collection of additional books written by people of the Old Covenant, and used in the Christian Church.

63 Why do we call the holy Scriptures the word of God?
We call them the word of God because God inspired their human authors and because God still speaks to us through the Bible.

64 How do we understand the meaning of the Bible?
We understand the meaning of the Bible by the help of the Holy Spirit, who guides the Church in the true interpretation of the Scriptures.

The Church

65 What is the Church?
    The Church is the community of the New Covenant.

66 How is the Church described in the Bible?
    The Church is described as the Body of which Jesus Christ is the Head and of which all baptized persons are members. It is called the people of God, the new Israel, a holy nation, a royal priesthood, and the pillar and ground of truth.

67 How is the Church described in the creeds?
    The Church is described as one, holy, catholic and apostolic.

68 Why is the Church described as one?
    The Church is one, because it is one Body, under one Head, our Lord Jesus Christ.

69 Why is the Church described as holy?
    The Church is holy, because the Holy Spirit dwells in it, consecrates its members, and guides them to do God's work.

70 Why is the Church described as catholic?
    The Church is catholic, because it proclaims the whole faith to all people, to the end of time.

71 Why is the Church described as apostolic?
    The Church is apostolic, because it continues in the teaching and fellowship of the apostles and is sent to carry out Christ's mission to all people.

72 What is the Anglican Communion?
    The Anglican Communion is a family of churches within the universal Church of Christ, maintaining apostolic doctrine and order and in full communion with one another and with the see of Canterbury.

73 What is the Church of the Province of Southern Africa?
    The Church of the Province of Southern Africa is a self-governing Province of the Anglican Communion.

It proclaims and holds fast the doctrine and ministry of the one, holy, catholic and apostolic Church.

74 What is the mission of the Church?
The mission of the Church is to restore all people to unity with God and each other in Christ.

75 How does the Church pursue its mission?
The Church pursues its mission as it prays and worships, proclaims the gospel, and promotes justice, peace and love.

76 Through whom does the Church carry out its mission?
The Church carries out its mission through the ministry of all its members.

The Ministry

77 Who are the ministers of the Church?
The ministers of the Church are lay persons, bishops, priests, and deacons.

78 What is the ministry of the laity?
The ministry of lay persons is to represent Christ and his Church; to bear witness to him wherever they may be; and according to the gifts given them, to carry on Christ's work of reconciliation in the world; and to take their place in the life, worship, and governance of the Church.

79 What is the ministry of a bishop?
The ministry of a bishop is to represent Christ and his Church, particularly as apostle, chief priest, and pastor of a diocese; to guard the faith, unity, and discipline of the whole Church; to proclaim the word of God; to act in Christ's name for the reconciliation of the world and the building up of the Church; and to ordain others to continue Christ's ministry.

80 What is the ministry of a priest or presbyter?
The ministry of a priest is to represent Christ and his Church, particularly as pastor to the people; to share

with the bishop in the overseeing of the Church; to proclaim the gospel; to administer the sacraments; and to bless and declare pardon in the name of God.

81 What is the ministry of a deacon?
The ministry of a deacon is to represent Christ and his Church, particularly as a servant of those in need; and to assist bishops and priests in the proclamation of the gospel and the administration of the sacraments.

82 What is the duty of all Christians?
The duty of all Christians is to follow Christ; to come together week by week for corporate worship; and to work, pray, and give for the spread of the kingdom of God.

The Bishops of the Church of the Province of Southern Africa described the duty of all Anglican Christians of our church thus:
The Father expects all his people to witness to the Lord Jesus Christ, and in the power of the Holy Spirit to bring others to a knowledge of him.

The Anglican Church in Southern Africa shares in this call, and every baptized and confirmed member must share in God's mission to the world.

To this end your life-style as a Christian should include these responses to God's love for you:

to –come to God in personal prayer every day
  –read the Bible daily
  –receive Holy Communion frequently and in expectant faith
  –follow the example of Jesus in daily life
  –speak about Jesus openly, as the Lord whom you know
  –work for justice and reconciliation
  –uphold Christian standards in marriage
  –bring up children to love and serve the Lord
  –give money for God's work and to consider the claims of tithing

–give personal service to the Church and to your
  neighbour
–let your life be marked with self-denial and
  simplicity

Stewardship

83 What is Christian Stewardship?
  Christian stewardship is the way in which Christians
  exercise their duty to administer what God has entrusted to them and to serve him gladly in his Church.

84 What has God entrusted to human beings to administer?
  God has entrusted to human beings material possessions, time and talents and made us stewards of his
  creation.

Prayer and Worship

85 What is prayer?
  Prayer is responding to God, by thought and by
  deeds, with or without words.

86 What is Christian Prayer?
  Christian prayer is response to God the Father,
  through Jesus Christ, in the power of the Holy Spirit.

87 What prayer did Christ teach us?
  Our Lord gave us the example of prayer known as the
  Lord's Prayer.

88 Recite the Lord's Prayer.

  Our Father in heaven
  hallowed be your Name
  your kingdom come
  your will be done
  on earth as in heaven.
  Give us today our daily bread.
  Forgive us our sins
    as we forgive those who sin against us.

Save us from the time of trial
and deliver us from evil.
For the kingdom, the power, and the glory are yours
now and for ever.   Amen

89 What are the principal kinds of prayer?
The principal kinds of prayer are adoration, praise,
thanksgiving, penitence, oblation, intercession,
petition, meditation and contemplation.

90 What is adoration?
Adoration is the lifting up of the heart and mind to
God, asking nothing but to enjoy God's presence.

91 Why do we praise God?
We praise God, not to obtain anything, but because
God's Being draws praise from us.

92 For what do we offer thanksgiving?
Thanksgiving is offered to God for all the blessings of
this life, for our redemption, and for whatever draws
us closer to God.

93 What is penitence?
In penitence, we confess our sins and make restitution
where possible, with the intention to amend our lives.

94 What is prayer of oblation?
Oblation is an offering of ourselves, our lives and
labours, in union with Christ, for the purposes of
God.

95 What are intercession and petition?
Intercession brings before God the needs of others; in
petition, we present our own needs, that God's will
may be done.

96 What is corporate worship?
In corporate worship, we unite ourselves with others
to acknowledge the holiness of God, to hear God's
word, to offer prayer, and to celebrate the sacraments.

97 What is meditation?
Meditation is a form of prayer in which we reflect on a

portion of Scripture, or some truth or experience, and ponder it in our hearts.

98 What is contemplation?
Contemplation is a form of prayer in which we keep our hearts and minds still and attentive to God, allowing him to work in us as he will.

Fasting

99 What is fasting?
Fasting is a voluntary act of denying oneself food for a certain length of time.

100 Why do Christians fast?
Fasting is a means of self-denial, repentance, intercession and identification with the needy, and a way of listening to what God has to tell his people.

101 Why is fasting often associated with prayer?
Our Lord's example and other scriptural sources teach us that this form of self-discipline is an aid to prayer.

102 What is abstinence?
Abstinence is a voluntary act of lessening the quantity of food one eats or of denying oneself other pleasures.

103 When do Christians fast?
Provincial Synod enacted the following:

Days of Fasting and Self-denial
Fast Days
Ash Wednesday and Good Friday are Fast Days, when the amount of food eaten is reduced.

Days of Self-denial
The weekdays of Lent.

Other Fridays of the year (except Christmas Day, the Fridays following Christmas, Easter and Ascension Day, and also public holidays falling on a Friday).
 On these days remembrance is made of the suffering and death of our Lord.

They may be observed in one or more of these ways:

1 By giving more time to prayer, Bible study, or spiritual reading;
2 By eating less or simpler food;
3 By giving up some pleasure or luxury, and using the money saved to help other people.

(Act of Provincial Synod)

Many Christians keep a fast at other times in response to a call from their Bishop. Christians also fast at other times, such as before receiving Holy Communion or on Fridays.

The Sacraments

104 What are the sacraments?
The sacraments are outward and visible signs of inward and spiritual grace, given by Christ as sure and certain means by which we receive that grace.

105 What is grace?
Grace is God's favour towards us, unearned and undeserved; by grace God forgives our sins, enlightens our minds, stirs our hearts, and strengthens our wills.

106 What are the two great sacraments of the gospel?
The two great sacraments given by Christ to his Church are Baptism and the Holy Eucharist.

Baptism

107 What is Baptism?
Baptism is the sacrament by which God adopts us as his children and makes us members of Christ's Body, the Church, and inheritors of the kingdom of God.

108 What is the outward and visible sign in baptism?
The outward and visible sign in baptism is water, in which the person is baptized in the name of the Father, and of the Son, and of the Holy Spirit.

109 What is the inward and spiritual grace in baptism?
The inward and spiritual grace in baptism is union with Christ in his death and resurrection, birth into God's family the Church, forgiveness of sins, and new life in the Holy Spirit.

110 What is required of us at baptism?
It is required that we renounce Satan, repent of our sins, and accept Jesus as our Lord and Saviour.

111 Why then are infants baptized?
Infants are baptized so that they can share citizenship in the Covenant, membership in Christ, and redemption by God.

112 How are the promises for infants made and carried out?
Promises are made for them by their parents and sponsors, who guarantee that the infants will be brought up within the Church, to know Christ and be able to follow him.

The Holy Eucharist

113 What is the Holy Eucharist?
The Holy Eucharist is the sacrament commanded by Christ for the continual remembrance of his life, death, and resurrection, until his coming again.

114 Why is the Eucharist called a sacrifice?
Because the Eucharist, the Church's sacrifice of praise and thanksgiving, is the way by which the sacrifice of Christ is made present, and in which he unites us to his one offering of himself.

115 By what other names is this service known?
The Holy Eucharist is called the Lord's Supper, and Holy Communion; it is also known as the Divine Liturgy, the Mass, and the Great Offering.

116 What is the outward and visible sign in the Eucharist?
The outward and visible sign in the Eucharist is
bread and wine, given and received according to
Christ's command.

117 What is the inward and spiritual grace given in the
Eucharist?
The inward and spiritual grace in the Holy Communion is the body and blood of Christ given to his
people, and received by faith.

118 What are the benefits which we receive in the Lord's
Supper?
The benefits we receive are the forgiveness of our
sins, the strengthening of our union with Christ and
one another, and the foretaste of the heavenly
banquet which is our nourishment in eternal life.

119 What is required of us when we come to the
Eucharist?
It is required that we should examine our lives,
repent of our sins, and be in love and charity with
all people.

Other Sacramental Rites

120 What other sacramental rites evolved in the Church
under the guidance of the Holy Spirit?
Other sacramental rites which evolved in the
Church include Confirmation, Ordination, Christian
Marriage, Confession and Absolution, and the
Anointing of the Sick.

121 How do they differ from the two sacraments of the
gospel?
Although they are means of grace, they are not
necessary for all persons in the same way that Baptism and the Eucharist are.

122 **What is Confirmation?**
Confirmation is the rite in which we express a mature commitment to Christ, and receive strength from the Holy Spirit through prayer and the laying on of hands by a bishop.

123 **What is required of those to be confirmed?**
It is required of those to be confirmed that they have been baptized, are sufficiently instructed in the Christian faith, are penitent for their sins, and are ready to affirm their confession of Jesus Christ as Saviour and Lord.

124 **What is Ordination?**
Ordination is the rite in which God gives authority and the grace of the Holy Spirit to those being made bishops, priests and deacons, through prayer and the laying on of hands by bishops.

125 **What is Christian Marriage?**
Christian Marriage, sometimes called Holy Matrimony, is a lifelong union into which the woman and the man enter when they make their vows before God and the Church, and receive the grace and blessing of God to help them fulfil their vows.

126 **What is Confession and Absolution?**
Confession and Absolution, sometimes called the Reconciliation of a Penitent, or Penance, is the rite in which those who repent of their sins may confess them to God in the presence of a priest, and receive the assurance of pardon and the grace of absolution.

127 **What is the Anointing of the Sick?**
The Anointing of the Sick, sometimes called Unction, is the anointing of the sick with oil. By this God's grace is given for the healing of spirit, mind and body.

128 Is God's activity limited to these rites?

God does not limit himself to these rites; they are patterns of countless ways by which God uses material things to reach out to us.

129 How are the sacraments related to our Christian hope?

Sacraments sustain our present hope and anticipate its future fulfilment.

Angels

130 What is an angel?

An angel is a spiritual creature and part of God's great unseen world. The word angel means messenger.

131 Why are angels important to us?

Beyond being messengers of God they are guardians to human beings against danger and temptations, and they watch over children. They remind us that we are part of a great spiritual world that is bound up with our material world.

132 Is belief in angels scriptural?

Yes. Mention of angels is found frequently in both the Old and the New Testaments. The Bible refers to cherubim, seraphim, archangels and guardian angels. Angels played a significant role in the life and teaching of Jesus Christ.

133 Are all angels good?

All angels were created good by God but some rebelled against him and became his enemies. These are called demons and their leader is Satan or the devil.

134 Have demons power to harm Christians?

The power of God is always stronger than the power of demons. Those who trust in God and call on Jesus as Lord and Saviour have the victory.

135 What is the Church called to do for people who are afflicted or possessed by evil spirits?
In the power of Jesus the Church can put to flight all forces that enslave people, so that peace and health can be fully established in people and places. The individual Christian is called to trust at all times in the protection of the blood of Jesus.

The Christian Hope

136 What is the Christian hope?
The Christian hope is to live with confidence in newness and fulness of life, and to await the coming of Christ in glory, and the completion of God's purpose for the world.

137 What do we mean by the coming of Christ in glory?
By the coming of Christ in glory, we mean that Christ will come, not in weakness but in power, and will make all things new.

138 What do we mean by heaven and hell?
By heaven, we mean eternal life in our enjoyment of God; by hell, we mean eternal death in our rejection of God.

139 Why do we remember the dead in prayer?
We remember them, because we still hold them in our love and because we trust that in God's presence those who have chosen to serve him will grow in his love, until they see him as he is.

140 What do we mean by the last judgement?
We believe that Christ will come in glory and judge the living and the dead.

141 What do we mean by the resurrection of the body?
We mean that God will raise us from death in the fulness of our being, that we may live with Christ in the communion of the saints.

142 What is the communion of saints?
   The communion of saints is the whole family of God,
   the living and the dead, those whom we love and
   those whom we hurt, bound together in Christ by
   sacrament, prayer and praise.

143 What do we mean by everlasting life?
   By everlasting life, we mean a new existence, in
   which we are united with all the people of God, in
   the joy of fully knowing and loving God and each
   other.

144 What, then, is our assurance as Christians?
   Our assurance as Christians is that nothing, not even
   death, shall separate us from the love of God which
   is in Christ Jesus our Lord.   Amen

CONFESSION
AND
ABSOLUTION

Preface

God our loving Father has shown his love for the world by reconciling it to himself through the blood of Jesus. In his life among us, Jesus preached repentance. He called men and women to turn away from sin, believe in him and amend their lives. He entrusted this ministry of reconciliation to his Church. By our baptism we enter into the Church and become sharers in all the benefits of his death and resurrection.

But we are weak; we sin after baptism. Christ our Head remains pure and undefiled; his Body, the Church, is constantly weakened by sin. Its members therefore need continual purification; they need to repent and be renewed in him.

Sin is an offence against God. It disrupts and can ultimately destroy our relationship with him.

Sin is an offence against the Church. Even if it is secret and unknown to others, the spiritual life of the Church is harmed and its effectiveness is diminished.

Sin is an offence against our neighbour and so against all humanity. It hinders the coming of God's kingdom, the doing of his will and the hallowing of his Name.

Sin is an offence against ourselves. It defiles the image of God in us and can ultimately destroy us.

If we are to return to God in true penitence, we must be cut to the heart (Acts 2:37). There must be sorrow and a desire to amend. 'A broken and contrite heart, O God, you will not despise' (Ps 51:17). In addition there must be a willingness to open our hearts, with all the darkness to be found there, to the light of the Holy Spirit. We must be willing to accept the fact and the gravity of sin with no attempt to conceal it. Furthermore, there must be a desire to live the new life in Christ.

We may receive God's forgiveness and be reconciled to him in various ways, one of which is confession to God in the presence of a priest.

Every priest in exercising this ministry of reconciliation, committed by Christ to his Church, is solemnly bound to observe secrecy concerning all those matters which are confessed before him.

The Church does not require anyone to confess in the presence of a priest in order to receive forgiveness. It requires only that all may be honestly assured in their own conscience of their duty in this matter.

Those who are satisfied with a private confession to God in prayer ought not to be offended with those who use confession to God in the presence of a priest; nor ought those who think it necessary to confess their sins in the presence of a priest be offended with those who are satisfied with their confession to God in prayer together with the general confession of the Church. All should remember to follow and keep the rule of love and not to judge other people's conscience since there is no warrant for this in God's word.

Rite 1

1   The Priest says to the penitent

The Lord be in your heart and on your lips, that you
may truly and humbly confess your sins.

2   The penitent makes confession of sin in these or similar words

I confess to God almighty, the Father, the Son, and the
Holy Spirit, before the whole company of heaven, and
before you, that I have sinned in thought, word, and
deed, and in what I have left undone, through my own
fault. And especially (since my last confession) I have
sinned in these ways ...

For these and all my other sins which I cannot now
remember, or of which I am not aware, I am truly
sorry, firmly mean to do better, and humbly ask
pardon of God, and of you penance, (advice), and
absolution. Wherefore I pray God to have mercy on
me, and you to pray for me to the Lord our God.

3   The Priest may offer prayer on behalf of the penitent, and he may give
    advice if it is requested or if he judges it appropriate. He suggests
    some prayer or action as a token of repentance and thanksgiving. He
    asks the penitent whether this is acceptable.

4   He absolves the penitent as follows

Our Lord Jesus Christ, who has left power to his
Church to absolve all sinners who truly repent and
believe in him, of his great mercy forgive you your
offences; and by his authority committed to me, I
absolve you from all your sins: in the name of the
Father, and of the Son, and of the Holy Spirit.

5   The penitent says

Amen

Confession and Absolution

6   The Priest dismisses the penitent with these or similar words. He may
    add a blessing.

Go in peace, the Lord has put away your sins. Pray for
me, also a sinner.

Rite 2

The Welcome

7 The Priest welcomes the penitent in these or similar words

The Lord be in your heart and on your lips that you may truly and humbly confess your sins.

or

God graciously welcomes you to this sacrament, which is given by him to enable us to be restored to communion with him and his Church, and to bring inner peace. God acts through this sacrament and is able to restore you.

or

May the grace of the Holy Spirit fill your heart with light, that you may confess your sins with loving trust, and come to know that God is merciful.

Reading of Scripture

8 One of the following or another suitable passage may be read by the Priest or the penitent. The passage may be discussed.

Psalm 32:1-9;   Psalm 51;   Psalm 130;   Isaiah 53:4-6;
Luke 6:31-38;   Luke 15:1-9;   John 20:19-23;   Romans 5:8-9;
1 Corinthians 13:4-7;   Galatians 5:16-25;   Ephesians 5:1-12;
Colossians 3:8-17; 1 Peter 1:18-21;   1 John 1:6-9.

The Confession

9　The penitent makes his confession in these or similar words

Most merciful God, have mercy upon me. In your compassion forgive my sins both known and unknown, things done and left undone (especially ...). O God, uphold me by your Spirit, that I may live and serve you in newness of life to the honour and glory of your Name; through Jesus Christ our Lord.

Amen

10　The penitent may make an act of contrition in these or similar words

O my God, I am truly sorry for my sins.

or

Wash me from my wickedness and cleanse me from my faults.

or

Lord Jesus Christ, Son of God, have mercy on me.

Spiritual Guidance

11　The Priest may offer prayer on behalf of the penitent, and he may give advice if he judges it appropriate. He suggests some prayer or action as a token of repentance and thanksgiving. He asks the penitent whether this is acceptable.

The Absolution

12　The Priest declares God's forgiveness to the penitent, using one of the following

Our Lord Jesus Christ, who has left power to his Church to absolve all sinners who truly repent and believe in him, of his great mercy forgive you your offences; and by his authority committed to me, I absolve you from all your sins: in the name of the Father, and of the Son, and of the Holy Spirit.

or

God, the Father of mercies, through the death and resurrection of his Son has reconciled the world to himself and forgives all who repent and believe in him. Through this ministry of reconciliation and by his authority committed to me you are absolved from all your sins: in the name of the Father, and of the Son, and of the Holy Spirit.

13 The penitent says

Amen

14 A prayer for healing with the laying on of hands may follow. In special circumstances the penitent may be anointed.

The Conclusion

15 Give thanks to the Lord for he is gracious
His mercy endures for ever

16 Prayers of thanksgiving may follow.

17 The Priest and penitent may make an act of commitment, using the following prayer or some other

Father almighty
we offer ourselves to you
as a living sacrifice
　　in Jesus Christ our Lord.
Send us out into the world
　　in the power of the Holy Spirit
to live and work
　　to your praise and glory.

18 The Priest dismisses the penitent with these or similar words. He may add a blessing.

Go in peace, the Lord has put away your sins. Pray for me, also a sinner.

God, the Father of Jesus ... his ...
resurrection of Jesus has reconciled the world to
himself and forgives all who repent, believe ... him ...
through that ministry of reconciliation sent by the
authority committed to us in the name of the Father
and ... in the name of the Father and of the Son and
of the Holy Spirit.

15 *Silent prayer.*

Amen.

16 *A prayer in traditional language should be ... occasion may be or special ... conclude ... prayer not previously used ...*

The Eucharist

17 Give thanks to the Lord for he is gracious.
   His mercy endures for ever.

18 Have your hearts among you lifted ...

19 *The Priest and others may prepare ... table ... during the singing of a hymn, or otherwise proceeds as follows:*

Father, accept us
we offer ourselves to you
as a living sacrifice.
to Jesus Christ our Lord.
Send us out into the world
in the power of the Holy Spirit
to live and work
to your praise and glory.

18 *The Priest takes the bread and ... wine and ... maybe ... the wine to be ... used ...*

19 In peace, the Lord has put away your sins. Pray for
me, also a sinner.

MARRIAGE

MARRIAGE

Preface
Christian Marriage

'The Church of the Province of Southern Africa affirms that marriage by divine institution is a lifelong and exclusive union and partnership between one man and one woman.' (*Canon on Holy Matrimony in the Constitution and Canons of the C.P.S.A.*)

This affirmation is grounded on the teaching in Genesis which is reflected and emphasized in the teaching of Jesus, 'Therefore a man leaves his father and his mother and cleaves to his wife, and they become one flesh' (Genesis 2:24; Mark 10:7). The bodily union of man and wife is an expression of the totality of their union, each with the other.

The Marriage Service marks the beginning of this union, as the bride and the bridegroom make their life-long and exclusive vows to each other. The giving of the ring is a profound symbol of their commitment to an unending love within the love of God. As they live out this love day by day, they come to understand more of the nature of God, who is Love, and they glimpse something of the mystery of the unity of Father, Son and Holy Spirit. In founding a Christian home where their love flows out to children and friends they share in some measure the joy of God in his creation.

Another symbol of deep meaning in the Marriage Service is contained in the action whereby the Priest joins the right hands of the newly wedded couple (usually by binding their hands with the stole which is a symbol of his office) and says, 'Those whom God has joined together, let not man put asunder'.

No possibility of doubt remains as to the divine intention for marriage.

Christian marriage is also a sign of the union between Christ and his Church (Ephesians 5:21-33). In Scripture the Church is described in a variety of ways and one image portrays her as the bride of Christ (Revelation 21:9). The inseparable bond between a man and his wife thus mirrors the relationship between Jesus and his bride the Church. Jesus gave himself completely for the Church in a sacrificial love that the bridegroom is to imitate. As the Church responds to Christ's self-giving in wonder and awe that he should love so much, so, according to this pattern, the bride is to love her husband. For both husband and wife the high calling of Christian married life is this total self-giving. It is communion of the deepest sort.

For this reason it is appropriate that the first action of a newly wedded couple should be to receive the body and blood of Christ in the Eucharist, which is the celebration of Christ's sacrificial love. Thereafter, by regularly coming to be fed at the Lord's table, they will be strengthened to fulfil their vocation.

Customs in regard to married life may vary in different cultures, but for the Christian the three chief purposes of marriage are unchangeable:

Marriage is given that the couple may know each other in mutual love and find in each other the lifelong companionship and support which is God's intention for them.

In marriage God's gifts of sex and affection find their true and lasting expression in an indissoluble relationship.

In the security of this relationship, children are born and brought up in the love and fear of God, being entrusted by him as a sacred charge to their parents.

Rightly, therefore, the Introduction to the service stresses that no one should enter into the holy state of matrimony without much careful thought and prayer.

In this service, with its prayers and the outward signs

of the joining of hands and the giving and receiving of a ring (or rings), there is the promise of God's continuing grace to the man and his wife. They need and can rely on this help as, day by day, they strive to realize in their marriage the love and mutual sacrifice which is God's plan for them.

General Rubrics

1 Care shall be taken to observe the provisions of the Canons and Acts of Provincial Synod in respect of marriage.

2 If, in response to the Introduction (section 2), an impediment to the marriage is alleged, the marriage may not proceed until or unless the allegations made are found to be without substance and the truth is established.

3 It is appropriate that marriage be celebrated in the context of the Eucharist.

4 Hymns may be sung at suitable points in the service.

5 In these services the Word of God is placed before the vows or the reaffirmation of vows. It is permissible for this order to be reversed, as indicated in each service.

6 Readings and psalms are chosen from the following table. When there is no Eucharist, one or two readings are used and a psalm may be said.

   When there is a Eucharist, two or three readings are used, one of which is always from a Gospel. A psalm is said. Suitable sentences for the Peace are provided at 106 of the Eucharist.

Old Testament Readings
Genesis 1:24-31a;   Genesis 2:7, 15-24;   Tobit 8:5b-8.

Psalms
Psalms 37:3-6;   67;   128.

New Testament Readings
Romans 12:1-2, 9-13;   Ephesians 3:14-19;   Ephesians 5:21-33;
Colossians 3:12-17.

Gospel Readings
Matthew 7:21, 24-27;   Mark 10:2-9;   John 2:1-11;   John 15:7-12.

Proper Preface 24   Canticle 14

The Marriage Service

1 When the Eucharist is celebrated, it is combined with the Marriage Service in either of two ways:

    1 The first part of the Eucharist up to the Sermon (sections 1-22) follows section 2 of the Introduction and precedes the Marriage (7-23). The second part of the Eucharist, beginning with the Peace, follows the Marriage.

    2 The Eucharist as a whole follows the Marriage (after section 23).

In both instances the Creed and Prayers (sections 23-42) are omitted. The Collect is the prayer at 4 in the Marriage Service. The Word of God and Proper Preface can be found from the table at General Rubric 6.

The Nuptial Blessing (sections 27-31) may precede the Invitation at 82 of the Eucharist or follow the giving of Communion at 84.

INTRODUCTION

2 The Priest addresses the bride and bridegroom and the congregation

We have come together in the presence of God to witness the marriage of *N* and *N*, to ask his blessing on them and to rejoice with them. Our Lord Jesus Christ, by his presence at the marriage in Cana of Galilee, blessed this way of life.

Marriage is a gift of God and a means of grace, in which man and woman become one flesh. It is God's purpose that, as husband and wife give themselves to each other in love, they shall grow together and be united in that love, as Christ is united with his Church.

The union of husband and wife in heart, mind and body is given for their mutual comfort and help in prosperity and adversity. It is given that they may know each other with delight and tenderness in acts of love. It is given that they may have children and bring them up in the knowledge and love of the Lord.

In marriage husband and wife are linked to each other's families and they begin a new life together in the community. This is a way of life that all should reverence and none should lightly undertake. Those who are called by God to this holy state, should continue in mutual fidelity and love.

Into this way of life *N* and *N* come now to be joined. If any of you can show just cause why they may not lawfully be married you must now declare it.

N and *N*, I charge you both, as you will answer before God who is the judge of all, that if either of you knows any reason why you may not be united in marriage lawfully in accordance with God's word, you now declare it.

3 The Lord be with you
And also with you

4 Let us pray

Heavenly Father
you have taught us through your Son
that love is the fulfilling of the law:
grant that your Holy Spirit may lead
   your servants *N* and *N*
in the way of eternal life
and that they may continue together
   in your love
until their lives' end;
through Jesus Christ our Lord.
Amen

THE WORD OF GOD

5   If preferred, the Word of God may follow the Marriage. In that case it will immediately precede 25.

6   One or more Scripture readings follow, chosen from the table at General Rubric 6. One of the psalms there may be used.

A sermon may be preached.

THE MARRIAGE

7   The bride and bridegroom stand before the Priest, the congregation standing.

8   The Priest asks the bridegroom for his consent

> *N*, will you take *N* to be your wife? Will you love her, comfort her, honour and protect her, and, forsaking all others, be faithful to her as long as you both shall live?

Answer   **I will**

9   The Priest asks the bride for her consent

> *N*, will you take *N* to be your husband? Will you love him, comfort him, honour and protect him, and, forsaking all others, be faithful to him as long as you both shall live?

Answer   **I will**

10) The Priest asks

> Who gives this woman to be married to this man?

Answer   **I do**

11) The Priest receives the woman from the hand of her father (or other relative or friend).

12 The bridegroom takes the bride's right hand in his and they turn towards
each other. He says

I, *N*, take you, *N*
to be my wedded wife
to have and to hold
from this day forward;
for better, for worse
for richer, for poorer
in sickness and in health
to love and to cherish
and to honour in the Lord
till death us do part
according to God's holy law;
and this is my solemn vow.

13 They loose hands. The bride takes the bridegroom's right hand in hers.
She says

I, *N*, take you, *N*
to be my wedded husband
to have and to hold
from this day forward;
for better, for worse
for richer, for poorer
in sickness and in health
to love and to cherish
and to honour in the Lord*
till death us do part
according to God's holy law;
and this is my solemn vow.

*Here may be inserted the words

and in all things lawful to obey

14   They loose hands. The Priest receives the ring(s). He says

Heavenly Father, by your blessing let *this ring* be to N and
N a symbol of unending love and faithfulness, to remind
them of the vow and covenant which they have made this
day; through Jesus Christ our Lord.
Amen

15   The bridegroom places the ring on the fourth finger of the bride's left
hand and, holding it there, says

I give you this ring
as a sign of our marriage.
With my body I honour you
all that I am I give to you
and all that I have I share with you
within the love of God
Father, Son, and Holy Spirit.

16   If only one ring is used, before they loose hands the bride says

I receive this ring
as a sign of our marriage.
With my body I honour you
all that I am I give to you
and all that I have I share with you
within the love of God
Father, Son, and Holy Spirit.

17   If rings are exchanged, they loose hands and the bride places a ring on
the fourth finger of the bridegroom's left hand and, holding it there, says

I give you this ring
as a sign of our marriage.
With my body I honour you
all that I am I give to you
and all that I have I share with you
within the love of God
Father, Son, and Holy Spirit.

18 The bride and bridegroom kneel, whilst the congregation remains standing. The Priest says

Eternal God, creator and preserver of all
giver of spiritual grace and author of everlasting life:
send your blessing upon *N* and *N*
    whom we bless in your name
that living faithfully together
they may fulfil the vow and covenant they have made
of which the *ring* given and received
    is a token and pledge
and may ever remain
    in perfect love and peace together
and live according to your laws;
through Jesus Christ our Lord.
Amen

19 Now that *N* and *N* have given their consent and made their vows to each other before God and this congregation, with the joining of hands and the giving and receiving of *a ring*, in the name of God I declare that they are husband and wife.

20 The Priest joins their right hands together and says

Those whom God has joined together, let not man put asunder.
Amen

21 The Priest blesses them

God the Father
God the Son
God the Holy Spirit
bless, preserve and keep you;
the Lord pour upon you the riches of his grace
that you may faithfully live together
and receive the blessings of eternal life.
Amen

22 These acclamations may be used

Priest   Blessed are you, heavenly Father
You give joy to bridegroom and bride

Priest   Blessed are you, Lord Jesus Christ
You have brought new life to humankind

Priest   Blessed are you, Holy Spirit of God
You bring us together in love

Priest   Blessed be Father, Son, and Holy Spirit
One God, to be praised for ever.   Amen

23 The signing of the register takes place here or at the end of the service.

24 The Eucharist may begin here.

If the first part of the Eucharist has been used before the Marriage, the second part of the Eucharist follows here, beginning with the Peace. Appropriate sentences for use at the Peace are provided at 106 of the Eucharist.

25 The Priest and the couple go to the Lord's table. A psalm may be used, or a hymn may be sung.

26 **Our Father in heaven**
hallowed be your Name
your kingdom come
your will be done
on earth as in heaven.
Give us today our daily bread.
Forgive us our sins
   as we forgive those who sin against us.
Save us from the time of trial
and deliver us from evil.
For the kingdom, the power, and the glory are yours
now and for ever.   Amen

THE NUPTIAL BLESSING

27 The Priest, standing before the couple, gives the Nuptial Blessing as
   follows

(28) Merciful Lord and heavenly Father, by your gracious gift
   humankind is increased: bestow upon *N* and *N* the gift of
   children; and grant that they may so live together in
   godly love and honesty, that they may bring up their
   children in faith and virtue, to your praise and honour;
   through Jesus Christ our Lord.
   Amen

29 God our maker, you have consecrated marriage
       as a wonderful mystery
   a sign of the spiritual unity
       between Christ and his Church:
   look in mercy on these your servants
   that *N* may love his wife
       as Christ loved his bride the Church
   and also that *N* may love her husband
       as the Church is called to love her Lord.
   Bless them both
   that they may inherit your eternal kingdom;
   through Jesus Christ our Lord.
   Amen

30 The Priest may add further prayers at his discretion.

31 Almighty God the Father of our Lord Jesus Christ
   sanctify and bless you
   that you may please him both in body and soul
   and live together in holy love to your lives' end.
   Amen

32 The Priest blesses the congregation.

Thanksgiving for a Marriage
or
the Reaffirmation of Vows

33 This service may be used for:

a thanksgiving on an anniversary or for a recent church marriage solemnised elsewhere

b the reaffirmation of vows on an anniversary or other suitable occasion

c the reaffirmation of vows by a couple who, after a church marriage, have been divorced from each other and now wish to come together again

Counselling is required before the reaffirmation of vows after a divorce.

Before the reaffirmation of vows after a divorce, a civil ceremony and the entry in the State's records is required. This may be undertaken by the Priest if he is a State-appointed Marriage Officer.

The ring or rings are not blessed, unless new ones are given.

34 The emphasis is on thanksgiving, so the service may appropriately take place during the Eucharist.

It is combined with the Eucharist in either of two ways:

1 The first part of the Eucharist up to the Sermon (sections 1-22) follows section 35 of the Introduction and precedes the Reaffirmation of Vows. The second part of the Eucharist, beginning with the Peace, follows the Reaffirmation.

2 The Eucharist as a whole follows the Reaffirmation (after section 51).

In both instances the Creed and Prayers (sections 23-42) are omitted. The Collect is the prayer at 37. The Word of God and Proper Preface can be found from the table at General Rubric 6.

The Nuptial Blessing (sections 55-59) may precede the Invitation at 82 of the Eucharist or follow the giving of Communion at 84.

INTRODUCTION

35　The Priest addresses the couple and the congregation

We have come together in the presence of God to give thanks for the marriage of *N* and *N* and to ask his blessing upon it as they continue their married life together. Our Lord Jesus Christ, by his presence at the marriage in Cana of Galilee, blessed this way of life.

Marriage is a gift of God and a means of grace, in which man and woman become one flesh. It is God's purpose that, as husband and wife give themselves to each other in love, they shall grow together and be united in that love, as Christ is united with his Church.

The union of husband and wife in heart, mind and body is given for their mutual comfort and help in prosperity and adversity. It is given that they may know each other with delight and tenderness in acts of love. It is given that they may have children and bring them up in the knowledge and love of the Lord.

In marriage husband and wife are linked to each other's families and they begin a new life together in the community. This is a way of life that all should reverence and none should lightly undertake.

We rejoice with *N* and *N* as they give thanks that they are called by God to this holy state and as they ask his blessing that they may continue in it in mutual fidelity and love.

36　The Lord be with you
And also with you

37　Let us pray

Heavenly Father
you have taught us through your Son
that love is the fulfilling of the law:
grant that your Holy Spirit may lead
　　your servants *N* and *N*

in the way of eternal life
and that they may continue together
   in your love
until their lives' end;
through Jesus Christ our Lord.
Amen

THE WORD OF GOD

38 If preferred, the Word of God may follow the Reaffirmation of Vows. In that case it will immediately precede 53.

39 One or more Scripture readings follow, chosen from the table at General Rubric 6. One of the psalms there may be used.

A sermon may be preached.

THE REAFFIRMATION OF VOWS

40 Sections 41-42 may be omitted in a service of thanksgiving for a marriage.

41 The married couple stand before the Priest, who says to the man

         N, do you acknowledge *N* as your wedded wife?
Answer   **I do**

         Will you love her, comfort her, honour and protect her, and, forsaking all others, be faithful to her as long as you both shall live?
Answer   **I will**

42 The Priest says to the woman

         N, do you acknowledge *N* as your wedded husband?
Answer   **I do**

         Will you love him, comfort him, honour and protect him, and, forsaking all others, be faithful to him as long as you both shall live?
Answer   **I will**

43 The husband takes his wife's right hand in his and they turn towards each other. He says

> I, *N*, renew my vow to you, *N*
> my wedded wife
> to have and to hold you
> for better, for worse
> for richer, for poorer
> in sickness and in health
> to love and to cherish
> and to honour in the Lord
> till death us do part
> according to God's holy law.

44 They loose hands. The wife takes her husband's right hand in hers. She says

> I, *N*, renew my vow to you, *N*
> my wedded husband
> to have and to hold you
> for better, for worse
> for richer, for poorer
> in sickness and in health
> to love and to cherish
> and to honour in the Lord*
> till death us do part
> according to God's holy law.

*Here may be inserted the words

> and in all things lawful to obey

45 Sections 46-49 are used only if a new ring is given or new rings are exchanged.

46 They loose hands. The Priest receives the ring(s). He says

> Heavenly Father, by your blessing let *this ring* be to *N* and *N* a symbol of unending love and faithfulness, to remind them of the vow and covenant which they have renewed this day; through Jesus Christ our Lord.
> **Amen**

47 The husband places the ring on the fourth finger of his wife's left hand and, holding it there, says

I give you this ring
as a sign of our marriage.
With my body I honour you
all that I am I give to you
and all that I have I share with you
within the love of God
Father, Son, and Holy Spirit.

48 If only one ring is used, before they loose hands the wife says

I receive this ring
as a sign of our marriage.
With my body I honour you
all that I am I give to you
and all that I have I share with you
within the love of God
Father, Son, and Holy Spirit.

49 If rings are exchanged, they loose hands and the wife places a ring on the fourth finger of her husband's left hand and, holding it there, says

I give you this ring
as a sign of our marriage.
With my body I honour you
all that I am I give to you
and all that I have I share with you
within the love of God
Father, Son, and Holy Spirit.

50 The Priest blesses the couple

God the Father
God the Son
God the Holy Spirit
bless, preserve and keep you;
the Lord pour upon you the riches of his grace
that you may continue faithful together
and receive the blessings of eternal life.
Amen

51 These acclamations may be used

> *Priest* Blessed are you, heavenly Father
> **You give joy to bridegroom and bride**

> *Priest* Blessed are you, Lord Jesus Christ
> **You have brought new life to humankind**

> *Priest* Blessed are you, Holy Spirit of God
> **You bring us together in love**

> *Priest* Blessed be Father, Son, and Holy Spirit
> **One God, to be praised for ever.   Amen**

52 The Eucharist may begin here.

If the first part of the Eucharist has been used before the Reaffirmation, the second part of the Eucharist follows here, beginning with the Peace. Appropriate sentences for use at the Peace are provided at 106 of the Eucharist.

53 The Priest and the couple go to the Lord's table. A psalm may be used, or a hymn may be sung.

54 **Our Father in heaven**
hallowed be your Name
your kingdom come
your will be done
on earth as in heaven.
Give us today our daily bread.
Forgive us our sins
   as we forgive those who sin against us.
Save us from the time of trial
and deliver us from evil.
For the kingdom, the power, and the glory are yours
now and for ever.   Amen

THE NUPTIAL BLESSING

55 The Priest, standing before the couple, gives the Nuptial Blessing as follows

56) Merciful Lord and heavenly Father, by your gracious gift humankind is increased: bestow upon *N* and *N* the gift of children; and grant that they may so live together in godly love and honesty, that they may bring up their children in faith and virtue, to your praise and honour; through Jesus Christ our Lord.
   Amen

57 God our maker, you have consecrated marriage
      as a wonderful mystery
   a sign of the spiritual unity
      between Christ and his Church:
   look in mercy on these your servants
   that *N* may love his wife
      as Christ loved his bride the Church
   and also that *N* may love her husband
      as the Church is called to love her Lord.
   Bless them both
   that they may inherit your eternal kingdom;
   through Jesus Christ our Lord.
   Amen

58 The Priest may add further prayers at his discretion.

59 Almighty God the Father of our Lord Jesus Christ
   sanctify and bless you
   that you may please him both in body and soul
   and live together in holy love to your lives' end.
   Amen

60 The Priest blesses the congregation.

The Blessing of a Civil Marriage or Customary Union

61 It is appropriate that this service take place during the Eucharist.

It is combined with the Eucharist in either of two ways:

1 The first part of the Eucharist up to the Sermon (sections 1-22) follows section 62 of the Introduction and precedes the Blessing of the Marriage. The second part of the Eucharist, beginning with the Peace, follows the Blessing of the Marriage.

2 The Eucharist as a whole follows the Blessing of the Marriage (after section 77).

In both instances the Creed and Prayers (sections 23-42) are omitted. The Collect is the prayer at 64. The Word of God and Proper Preface can be found from the table at General Rubric 6.

The Nuptial Blessing (sections 82-86) may precede the Invitation at 82 of the Eucharist or follow the giving of Communion at 84.

The church marriage register is used to record the blessing of a civil marriage or customary union.

There should be careful preparation of the couple to ensure that they understand the nature of Christian marriage.

The normal accompaniments to a wedding in church may have their place, such as bridal dress, flowers and attendants.

INTRODUCTION

62 The Priest addresses the couple and the congregation

We have come together in the presence of God to give thanks for the marriage of N and N and to ask his blessing upon it as they continue their married life together. Our Lord Jesus Christ, by his presence at the marriage in Cana of Galilee, blessed this way of life.

Marriage is a gift of God and a means of grace, in which man and woman become one flesh. It is God's purpose that, as husband and wife give themselves to each other in love, they shall grow together and be united in that love, as Christ is united with his Church.

The union of husband and wife in heart, mind and body is given for their mutual comfort and help in prosperity and adversity. It is given that they may know each other with delight and tenderness in acts of love. It is given that they may have children and bring them up in the knowledge and love of the Lord.

In marriage husband and wife are linked to each other's families and they begin a new life together in the community. This is a way of life that all should reverence and none should lightly undertake.

We rejoice with N and N as they give thanks that they are called by God to this holy state and as they ask his blessing that they may continue in it in mutual fidelity and love.

63 The Lord be with you
And also with you

64 Let us pray

Heavenly Father
you have taught us through your Son
that love is the fulfilling of the law:
grant that your Holy Spirit may lead
   your servants *N* and *N*
in the way of eternal life
and that they may continue together
   in your love
until their lives' end;
through Jesus Christ our Lord.
Amen

THE WORD OF GOD

65 If preferred, the Word of God may follow the Blessing of the Marriage. In that case it will immediately precede 79.

66 One or more Scripture readings follow, chosen from the table at General Rubric 6. One of the psalms there may be used.

A sermon may be preached.

THE BLESSING OF THE MARRIAGE

67 The married couple stand before the Priest, who says

The Church of the Province of Southern Africa affirms that marriage by divine institution is a lifelong and exclusive union and partnership between one man and one woman.

Do you accept this Affirmation to be binding on your marriage?

The couple answer together

We do

68   The Priest says to the man

> *N*, do you acknowledge *N* as your wedded wife?

Answer   **I do**

> Will you love her, comfort her, honour and protect her, and, forsaking all others, be faithful to her as long as you both shall live?

Answer   **I will**

69   The Priest says to the woman

> *N*, do you acknowledge *N* as your wedded husband?

Answer   **I do**

> Will you love him, comfort him, honour and protect him, and, forsaking all others, be faithful to him as long as you both shall live?

Answer   **I will**

70   The husband takes his wife's right hand in his and they turn towards each other. He says

Before God and his Church
I, *N*, take you, *N*
my wedded wife
to have and to hold
for better, for worse
for richer, for poorer
in sickness and in health
to love and to cherish
and to honour in the Lord
till death us do part
according to God's holy law;
and this is my solemn vow.

71   They loose hands. The wife takes her husband's right hand in hers. She says

Before God and his Church
I, *N*, take you, *N*
my wedded husband
to have and to hold
for better, for worse
for richer, for poorer
in sickness and in health
to love and to cherish
and to honour in the Lord*
till death us do part
according to God's holy law;
and this is my solemn vow.

*Here may be inserted the words

and in all things lawful to obey

72   They loose hands. The Priest receives the ring(s). He says

Heavenly Father, by your blessing let *this ring* be to *N* and
***N* a symbol of unending love and faithfulness, to remind**
them of the vow and covenant which they have made this
day; through Jesus Christ our Lord.
Amen

73   The husband places the ring on the fourth finger of his wife's left hand and, holding it there, says

I give you this ring
as a sign of our marriage.
With my body I honour you
all that I am I give to you
and all that I have I share with you
within the love of God
Father, Son, and Holy Spirit.

74   If only one ring is used, before they loose hands the wife says

> I receive this ring
> as a sign of our marriage.
> With my body I honour you
> all that I am I give to you
> and all that I have I share with you
> within the love of God
> Father, Son, and Holy Spirit.

75   If rings are exchanged, they loose hands and the wife places a ring on the fourth finger of her husband's left hand and, holding it there, says

> I give you this ring
> as a sign of our marriage.
> With my body I honour you
> all that I am I give to you
> and all that I have I share with you
> within the love of God
> Father, Son, and Holy Spirit.

76   The Priest blesses the couple

> God the Father
> God the Son
> God the Holy Spirit
> bless, preserve and keep you;
> the Lord pour upon you the riches of his grace
> that you may continue faithful together
> and receive the blessings of eternal life.
> **Amen**

77 These acclamations may be used

Priest Blessed are you, heavenly Father
You give joy to bridegroom and bride

Priest Blessed are you, Lord Jesus Christ
You have brought new life to humankind

Priest Blessed are you, Holy Spirit of God
You bring us together in love

Priest Blessed be Father, Son, and Holy Spirit
One God, to be praised for ever.   Amen

78 The Eucharist may begin here.

If the first part of the Eucharist has been used before the Blessing of the Marriage, the second part of the Eucharist follows here, beginning with the Peace. Appropriate sentences for use at the Peace are provided at 106 of the Eucharist.

79 The Priest and the couple go to the Lord's table. A psalm may be used, or a hymn may be sung.

80 **Our Father in heaven
hallowed be your Name
your kingdom come
your will be done
on earth as in heaven.
Give us today our daily bread.
Forgive us our sins
    as we forgive those who sin against us.
Save us from the time of trial
and deliver us from evil.
For the kingdom, the power, and the glory are yours
now and for ever.   Amen**

THE NUPTIAL BLESSING

81 The Priest, standing before the couple, gives the Nuptial Blessing as follows

82) Merciful Lord and heavenly Father, by your gracious gift humankind is increased: bestow upon *N* and *N* the gift of children; and grant that they may so live together in godly love and honesty, that they may bring up their children in faith and virtue, to your praise and honour; through Jesus Christ our Lord.
Amen

83 God our maker, you have consecrated marriage
      as a wonderful mystery
   a sign of the spiritual unity
      between Christ and his Church:
   look in mercy on these your servants
   that *N* may love his wife
      as Christ loved his bride the Church
   and also that *N* may love her husband
      as the Church is called to love her Lord.
   Bless them both
   that they may inherit your eternal kingdom;
   through Jesus Christ our Lord.
   Amen

84 The Priest may add further prayers at his discretion.

85 Almighty God the Father of our Lord Jesus Christ
   sanctify and bless you
   that you may please him both in body and soul
   and live together in holy love to your lives' end.
   Amen

86 The Priest blesses the congregation.

Introduction for the
Remarriage of Divorced Persons

87 This form of service is used for the solemnization of matrimony or the blessing of a civil marriage when one (or both) of the partners to the marriage is divorced and the spouse of a former marriage is still living.

This form is used only when the Bishop's licence has been given in accordance with the Canon *Of Holy Matrimony*.

INTRODUCTION

88 The Priest addresses the bride and bridegroom and the congregation.

The congregation sits.

We are met together in the presence of God to celebrate the marriage of *N* and *N*, to ask his blessing on them and to share in their joy.

The Church of the Province of Southern Africa affirms that marriage by divine institution is a lifelong and exclusive partnership between one man and one woman. The union of husband and wife in heart, mind and body is a gift from God for their mutual joy.

Marriage is given for the companionship, help and comfort that the one ought to have of the other in prosperity and adversity.

It is given, that the natural instincts and desires, bestowed by God, should be hallowed and ordered aright.

It is given, that they may have children and nurture them in the knowledge and love of the Lord.

A Christian marriage is both a civil contract and a spiritual union into which the couple enter by the exchange of solemn vows made before God. It is a serious matter to break a civil contract. It is a much more serious matter to break a vow which one has made for life before God.

Those of you who are aware that N (and N) *has* been married before and that the partner(s) of the marriage(s) *is* still alive may wonder how it is that this marriage can have the church's blessing. It is not a matter which has been lightly decided. The breakdown of a marriage is always a falling short of the ideal of marriage which God sets before us in the Scriptures.

The Bishop himself is satisfied that in this instance there is no prospect of re-establishing a true marriage relationship between the partners of the former marriage(s). N and N have been interviewed and the Bishop is assured that there is due penitence for the failure of the previous marriage(s) and a knowledge of God's forgiveness as well as a readiness to forgive. They are pledged to live their married life within the worshipping and witnessing community of the Church.

St John says:

If we say we have no sin, we deceive ourselves, and the truth is not in us. If we confess our sins, God is just, and may be trusted to forgive our sins and cleanse us from every kind of wrong.

We all need to know the forgiving and healing power of God's love, for God's forgiveness brings healing of all the hurts of the past which sin has inflicted.

Let us therefore together ask God's pardon. Then, in the joy of his forgiveness, we can ask his blessing on the marriage of N and N.

89   Silence may be kept. All kneel and say

Almighty God, our heavenly Father
in penitence we confess
    that we have sinned against you
    through our own fault
in thought, word, and deed
and in what we have left undone.

For the sake of your Son, Christ our Lord
forgive us all that is past
and grant that we may serve you
   in newness of life
to the glory of your Name.

90   The Priest says

Almighty God, who forgives all who truly repent, have mercy on *you*; pardon *your* sins and set *you* free from them; confirm and strengthen *you* in all goodness, and keep *you* in eternal life; through Jesus Christ our Lord.
Amen

91   A hymn may be sung.

92   This section is not used if a civil marriage is being blessed.

The congregation stands and the Priest says

N and *N* come now to be joined in the holy state of marriage. If any of you can show just cause why they may not lawfully be married you must now declare it.

   N and *N*, if either of you knows a reason why you may not lawfully marry, you must declare it now.

93   The Marriage Service follows, omitting section 2 of the Introduction.

If there has been a civil marriage, the Blessing of a Civil Marriage follows, omitting section 62 of the Introduction.

94   When there is a Eucharist sections 10-14 of the Eucharist are omitted.

MINISTRY TO
THE SICK AND DYING

Preface
Healing in Christ

Our Lord Jesus Christ proclaimed the coming of the kingdom of God not only by preaching but also by healing the sick. He brought healing in all its fulness: physical cures, the healing brought by forgiveness of sin, restoration of broken relationships, assurance of salvation, acceptance of the sinner by God. His miracles are evidence of God's desire that his people should be completely whole: healthy in body, mind and spirit, holy in life.

In the ministry of healing the Church has a role to play which has not always been clear in her teaching. It is right and fitting to pray for healing of the body, of the mind, of the emotions, of the memories; for healing too of relationships and of society. In prayer and in the sacraments, in the rites of laying on of hands and of anointing, the Church continues the Lord's gracious work, banishing fear and division, bringing unity, wholeness and peace. Sometimes it is possible to co-operate with the medical profession in such work, but always the Church witnesses to the fact that true healing has a spiritual dimension which is far deeper than any merely physical cure. Earthly life is not intended to last for ever, and the Christian knows that death is not the end of everything, but only the prelude to a healing more perfect than any we can know in this life.

Christians may at any time be faced with the need to minister to family, friends or strangers who are sick, injured or dying. Sickness varies from mild childhood diseases to painful terminal illness, and the sufferer may need reassurance and hope more than physical relief. The services and prayers provided here seek to offer something for all needs. Lay people can use much of this material, and it is hoped that they will make themselves familiar with the services so that they know where to turn to find help for others or for themselves.

There is a wide selection of Scripture references, grouped under headings. These and the 'Considerations for the Sick' are chiefly resource material. Those who do much sick visiting will find it helpful to study them in depth. They may also be useful to those who, during a protracted illness or convalescence, are able to read their prayer books. Such people may make many of the prayers their own by changing the pronouns from 'he' and 'him' to 'I' and 'me'.

Visitors to the sick should bear in mind that someone who is very ill or in great pain can bear only a short visit, and cannot concentrate for long. Great sensitivity is required in selecting appropriate readings and prayers of suitable brevity. Sometimes the presence of a visitor praying silently can be of greater support than any words. Sometimes spontaneous prayer in the visitor's own words is more appropriate. It is also valuable to commit to memory prayers from these services or from other sources.

A seemingly unconscious person, or someone in a coma, can usually hear and understand what is being said, even if response is impossible. It is helpful to speak to such a patient, to read slowly a verse or two of Scripture, and to pray aloud. With a dying person, especially if death comes slowly, verses can be repeated at intervals, and the Prayers for the Dying used with silences. A group of family or friends praying quietly at a Christian deathbed is a powerful witness to the presence and the love of God, even in the valley of the shadow of death. The miracle of that healing love which is with us always is part of the glorious truth of the gospel which the Ministry to the Sick proclaims.

Those who bring to God in Christ the pain and brokenness of human life, small or great, know that whether we live or die, we are the Lord's, and nothing can separate us from his love.

General Rubrics

1 These services do not include any form of exorcism. When a priest believes such a ministry to be required, he must refer to the Bishop, who will supply the necessary form to be used, or refer the priest to someone specially appointed to minister exorcism. Prayer 45 is not intended for use when there is actual possession.

2 Except where otherwise indicated, a lay person may use any of the sections.

3 Free and spontaneous prayer may be used at the Minister's discretion.

Ministry to the Sick

GREETING

1   On entering the house or other place where the sick person is, the Minister may say

Peace be to this house, and to all who live here

or

The peace of the Lord be with you always

SUITABLE PASSAGES OF SCRIPTURE

2   **Confidence in God:** Psalms 27;   46;   91;   121;   139:1-13;
     Proverbs   3:11-26;   Isaiah 26:1-9;   40:1-11;   40:25-end;
     Lamentations 3:22-33;
     Hosea 6:1-3;   Matthew 6:24-end;   11:25-30;
     Romans 8:31-end.

Healing in answer to prayer: 2 Kings 20:1-5;   Psalms 30;   34;   138.

Prayer for divine aid: Psalms 13;   43;   86;   143;   James 5:10-end.

Penitence: Psalms 51;   130.

Praise and thanksgiving: Psalms 103;   146;   Isaiah 12.

A simple girl spreads the good news about God's healing:
     2 Kings 5:1-14.

God's dealing with his people through affliction:
     Job 33:14-30;   Hebrews 12:1-11.

Christ our example in suffering: Isaiah 53;   Matthew 26:36-46;
     Luke   23:26-49.

Jesus, the Lord's servant, is to bring healing and good news for the afflicted: Isaiah 61:1-3.

Healing is a sign of the coming of the kingdom of God:
     Matthew 10:1, 7-8;   Luke 7:20-23.

It is associated with preaching: Mark 6:7-13.

Jesus Christ heals in many different ways:
– **by a word:** Mark 10:46-52.
– **by touch:** Matthew 8:1-4;   Luke 4:40.
– **by gesture and word:** Mark 7:32-37.

– by other physical means: Mark 7:32-37;   John 9:1-7.

– gradually: Mark 8:22-25.

– at a distance: John 4:46-53.

– by rebuke: Luke 4:38-41.

– after long-standing illness: Mark 5:25-34;   John 5:2-9.

– when others bring a sick person: Mark 2:1-12.

– various healings: Matthew 15:29-31.

Healing connected with prayer and repentance: James 5:14-16.

Healing in response to faith and prayer: Mark 9:14-29.

The response to healing:

– the need to stay with Jesus and sin no more: Mark 10:46-52;   John 5:1-15.

– the need for thanksgiving: Luke 17:11-19.

Christ's followers are also called to heal:

– through the name of Jesus: John 14:12-14;   Acts 3:1-10;   4:8-12;   9:32-35;   16:16-18.

– by a word: Acts 14:8-10.

– by touch: Acts 28:7-9.

If physical healing does not happen: Psalm 73:21-26;   Luke 22: 42;   2 Corinthians 12:7-10.

God's call to repentance and faith: Isaiah 55.

The Beatitudes: Matthew 5:1-12.

Watchfulness: Luke 12:32-40.

Christ the good shepherd: Psalm 23;   John 10:1-18.

The Resurrection: John 20:1-18;   20:19-end;   2 Corinthians 4:13–5:9.

The Redemption: Romans 5:1-11;   8:14-end;   1 John 1:1-9.

Christian love: 1 Corinthians 13.

Growth in grace: Ephesians 3:13-end;   6:10-20;   Philippians 3:7-14.

Patience in suffering: 2 Corinthians 4:16-18;   James 5:10-end.

God's love for us: 1 John 3:1-7;   4:9-end.

The life of the world to come: Revelation 7:9-end;   21:1-7;   21:22-end;   22:1-5.

Our Lord's last discourse before his passion: John 14, 15, 16, 17.

CONSIDERATIONS FOR THE SICK

3 Our Lord Jesus Christ came to give us life in all its fulness. The Gospels relate that he forgave sins; restored sight, hearing, speech and movement; cured all kinds of diseases and sickness, and healed those who were mentally afflicted. The power of the risen Christ has not changed: for us today he still brings health, life, joy and peace.

Christ heals in many ways, especially through those who dedicate their lives to the service of the sick. These include Christian priests and laity as well as doctors, surgeons, psychiatrists, nurses and other hospital staff. God works through prayer and the sacraments of Baptism and the Eucharist, through the rites of Confession, of Laying on of Hands and Anointing, as well as through those who are engaged in medical research and technology and the day to day running of hospital and nursing services. It is for us, trusting in God's unfailing love, to make use of all available means by which we may be brought to that wholeness and holiness which is God's will for us.

Our heavenly Father, in his love for us, gives spiritual strength through Jesus Christ our Lord to enable us to use sickness for our profit and to his glory.

All illness, whether mild or serious, reminds us to give thought to our relationship with God, and to make no delay in seeking reconciliation with those from whom we may be estranged.

Our Lord himself, as is taught in Scripture, was made perfect through suffering, and we are to regard all sickness as an opportunity for spiritual growth.

There is no easy answer to the problem of pain and suffering. Those who ponder the gospel will find comfort and help in the assurance of Christ's healing power and his love, and also in the mystery of redemption, in which the suffering and death of Jesus bring a deeper and more complete healing to the world.

Scripture teaches us that we are the Body of Christ, that Christ lives in us and we in him, that whatever is done to the least of us is done to him. On the cross he conquered the power of sin and death, once and for all, by bearing the worst that could be done to him without bitterness or resentment. When, in his strength, we bear our sufferings in the way he bore his, he can use us as channels of his redemptive love.

The aim of the Christian, in sickness or in health, is to give glory to God through Jesus Christ our Lord.

PRAYERS

4 Lord of all grace and blessing, look with mercy on your servant *N*. Strengthen *his* faith, defend *him* against all evil, and keep *him* in peace and in the awareness of your loving presence, now and always.
Amen

5 Heavenly Father, during his life on earth your Son Jesus Christ healed the sick and brought peace to those who were distressed and sorrowful. We commend to your loving care our *brother N*: grant *him* relief from pain and healing of body, mind and spirit; to those who are anxious about *him* give your peace and comfort; and to those who tend *him* give wisdom, skill and compassion; for the sake of Jesus Christ your Son our Saviour.
Amen

For a sick child

6 Heavenly Father, you are always close to us; bless your child *N*, take away *his* pain, keep *him* in your love and make *him* well and strong again; for Jesus' sake.
Amen

7 *N*, may you know the presence of the Lord Jesus with you, giving you his peace and love. May he help you to bear your illness bravely; may he help you sleep and make you well again; for his dear Name's sake.
Amen

Before an operation

8 Heavenly Father, help *N* to trust you and not be afraid. May *he* cast all *his* care upon you, knowing that you care for *him*. Take from *him* all anxiety. As *he* becomes unconscious may *he* know that underneath are the everlasting arms. Guide and use the surgeon and all others who minister to *N* and grant them success in their labours; for Jesus Christ's sake.
Amen

N, may the Lord bless you as you face your operation. May he take from you all fear and anxiety and keep you in his peace. May he give (*N*) your surgeon and all others who minister to you skill, wisdom and compassion, and may you be speedily restored to health; through Jesus Christ our Lord.
Amen

During prolonged illness

Heavenly Father, sanctify this time of sickness that it may become a blessing for *N*, and in your good time restore *him* to health, that *he* may spend the rest of *his* life in your service and finally dwell with you in the fulness of eternal life.
Amen

Lord Jesus Christ, by your cross and passion you redeemed the world: to all who face long-continued suffering grant patience, courage, and an unshakeable trust in your love; help them to offer their weakness with thanksgiving to you; strengthen them to go on seeking your perfect will, that having endured with you they may also live and reign with you, now and for ever.
Amen

For one in great pain

Almighty Father, grant to *N* healing and release from pain, and your gifts of peace and hope, of courage and endurance. Cast out from *him* the spirit of anxiety and fear, and grant *him* perfect confidence and trust in you; through Jesus Christ our Lord.
Amen

For one with chronic or terminal illness

13 Lord God almighty, your thoughts are not our thoughts, neither are your ways our ways. We stand in awe and humility before the mystery of suffering. Grant *N* the faith and courage to accept *his* suffering in the spirit of Christ, and the grace to offer it in union with his passion to be used according to your eternal purposes. Fill *him* with your peace and support *him* with your love, that *he* may give glory to your Name; through Jesus Christ your Son our Saviour.
Amen

For one who is troubled in mind or spirit

14 Blessed Lord, Father of all mercy and giver of all comfort, look with compassion on *N* in *his* present distress. Give *him* a clearer understanding of *himself* and of your love for *him*; reveal your will to *him*; cast out all fear and doubt and grant *him* that peace which passes understanding; for the sake of Jesus Christ our Lord.
Amen

For one who is losing hope

15 Gracious Father, give *N* the gift of hope amidst *his* perplexity and pain, that in quietness and trust *he* may find *his* rest in you; through Jesus Christ our Lord.
Amen

16 *N*, may God renew in you his gifts of faith and hope and love, and may he give you his joy and his peace; through Jesus Christ.
Amen

For a convalescent

17 Heavenly Father, we give you thanks and praise for the healing *N* has already received. Continue your gracious work in *him*, that rejoicing in the knowledge of your love and goodness, *he* may be fully restored to health and strength; through Jesus Christ our Lord.
Amen

For those who tend the sick

Almighty God, your Son Jesus Christ went about doing good and healing all kinds of illness: continue his gracious work among us in hospitals and homes and wherever his people gather. Give wisdom, sympathy and patience to those who minister to the sick, and prosper all that is being done to prevent suffering and to forward the purposes of your love; through the same Jesus Christ our Lord.
Amen

For the family of the sick person

God our Father, be with all who love *N*. Watch over and protect them, strengthen their faith, unite them in your love and fill them with peace and confidence in your goodness; for Jesus Christ's sake.
Amen

For sleep

Heavenly Father, you give your children sleep for the refreshing of body and soul: grant *N* this gift; keep *him* in that perfect peace which you have promised to those whose minds are fixed on you; and grant that in the hours of silence *he* may enjoy the assurance of your love; through Jesus Christ our Saviour.
Amen

An evening prayer

Watch, Lord, with those who wake or watch or weep this night. Tend the sick, give rest to the weary, comfort the dying, relieve the suffering and calm the distressed; for your dear Name's sake.
Amen

THE LAYING ON OF HANDS

22   The Laying on of Hands is the most suitable rite for repeated ministration to the same sick person, and is normally administered by the Priest.

Under the guidance and direction of the Priest, lay persons may also use this rite, either in healing services or in homes or hospitals.

The rite may be used on its own, or within one of the other services of the Church.

23   The Minister may sprinkle the sick person and the room with holy water, saying

Remember that in your baptism you died to sin and rose again to new life in Christ.

or

Purge me with hyssop, and I shall be clean:
wash me, and I shall be whiter than snow.   *(Ps 51: 7)*

24   The Minister prays with the sick person, using prayers from sections 4-21 or other suitable forms of prayer. *He* then says

Our help is in the name of the Lord
who has made heaven and earth

Almighty God, giver of life and health, grant healing to N, that rejoicing in your love *he* may be made whole and live to your glory; through Jesus Christ our Lord.
Amen

25   The Minister may invite others to join *him* as *he* lays hands on the sick person. *He* says

In the name of God most high, Father, Son and Holy Spirit, may release be given you from your pain according to his will; may new life quicken your mind and body; and may perfect health abound in you.
Amen

or

26 In the name of God most high, may release from all
    your pain be given you;
  in the name of our Lord Jesus Christ, may new life
    quicken your body;
  in the name of the Holy Spirit, may you be filled
    with all inward joy and peace in believing;
  and the God of peace sanctify you and make you
    entire
  unto the coming of his kingdom.
  Amen

27) May the God who gives us peace make you holy in
  every way and keep your whole being – spirit, soul and
  body – free from every fault at the coming of our Lord
  Jesus Christ.   *(1 Thess 5: 23)*
  Amen

28 Or the Priest pronounces the Blessing.

THE ANOINTING OF THE SICK

29   The Priest is the proper minister of the rite, but the Bishop may authorize deacons or may license lay ministers to administer unction.

In cases of extreme necessity, 46 and 47 alone may be used.

The oil used is the Oil of the Sick, blessed by the Bishop. In cases of grave necessity, the Priest may bless natural vegetable oil, as follows

**Almighty God, giver of health and salvation, sanctify this oil for the healing of your people; through Jesus Christ our Lord.
Amen**

30   Anointing is always associated with a call to penitence. If the sick person wishes to make a private confession, the rite of Confession precedes the Anointing, which begins at section 38 below.

If the Anointing is given in the context of the Eucharist or an Office, the General Confession is sufficient preparation, and the rite of Anointing begins at section 38.

If the rite of Anointing is celebrated without private confession, and outside the Eucharist or an Office, the Preparation below (sections 31-37) is used.

PREPARATION

31   The Minister says

Peace be to this house and to all who live here

or

The peace of the Lord be with you always

32 The Minister may sprinkle the sick person and the room with holy water, saying

Remember that in your baptism you died to sin and rose again to new life in Christ.

or

Purge me with hyssop, and I shall be clean:
wash me, and I shall be whiter than snow. *(Ps 51: 7)*

33 St James writes,
'Is any one of you sick? He should call the elders of the church to pray over him and anoint him with oil in the name of the Lord. And the prayer offered in faith will make the sick person well; the Lord will raise him up. If he has sinned, he will be forgiven.' *(James 5: 14-15)*

As a preparation for the anointing, let us call to mind and confess our sins.

34 Silence may be kept. Then is said

Almighty God, our heavenly Father
in penitence we confess
that we have sinned against you
through our own fault
in thought, word, and deed
and in what we have left undone.
For the sake of your Son, Christ our Lord
forgive us all that is past
and grant that we may serve you
in newness of life
to the glory of your Name.

35 Almighty God, who forgives all who truly repent, have mercy on *you*; pardon *your* sins and set *you* free from them; confirm and strengthen *you* in all goodness and keep *you* in eternal life; through Jesus Christ our Lord.
Amen

36 If Communion follows the Anointing, section 38 follows and 37 is omitted.

37 As Christ has taught us we are bold to say

Our Father in heaven
hallowed be your Name
your kingdom come
your will be done
on earth as in heaven.
Give us today our daily bread.
Forgive us our sins
 as we forgive those who sin against us.
Save us from the time of trial
and deliver us from evil.
For the kingdom, the power, and the glory are yours
now and for ever.   Amen

THE LAYING ON OF HANDS
AND ANOINTING

38 Our help is in the name of the Lord
who has made heaven and earth

39 **Saviour of the world, by your cross and precious blood**
you have redeemed us; save us and help us, we humbly
beseech you, O Lord.

40 **I lift up my eyes to the hills:**
but where shall I find help?

My help comes from the Lord:
who has made heaven and earth.

He will not suffer your foot to stumble:
and he who watches over you will not sleep.

Be sure he who has charge of Israel:
will neither slumber nor sleep.

The Lord himself is your keeper:
the Lord is your defence upon your right hand;

The sun shall not strike you by day:
nor shall the moon by night.

The Lord will defend you from all evil:
it is he who will guard your life.

The Lord will defend your going out and your
   coming in:
from this time forward for evermore.   *(Ps 121)*

41 **Saviour of the world, by your cross and precious blood
you have redeemed us; save us and help us, we humbly
beseech you, O Lord.**

42 A passage of Scripture may be read

Matthew 8:1-4;   Matthew 11:25-30;   Matthew 15:29-31;   Mark 2:1-12;
Mark 7:32-37;   Mark 10:46-52;   Luke 17:11-19;   John 4:46-53,
or other suitable passages.

If the rite takes place during the Eucharist or an Office, one of the following verses may be read here instead of a longer passage

'The apostles drove out many demons and anointed
many sick people with oil and healed them.'   *(Mark 6:13)*

'Is any one of you sick? He should call the elders of the
church to pray over him and anoint him with oil in the
name of the Lord.'   *(James 5:14)*

43 The Minister says to the sick person

Do you give yourself to God, that his will may be done
in you?
I do

All things are possible to those who believe. Do you
believe in God's power to help you?
I do

44 The Minister may invite others present to join *him* as *he* lays hands on the sick person. *He* may pray in silence, or say

In the name of God most high, Father, Son and Holy Spirit, may release be given you from your pain according to his will; may new life quicken your mind and body; and may perfect health abound in you.
Amen

45 If the Priest considers it appropriate, he may use the following form

N, may Christ, the Light of the world, drive away from you all darkness and all assaults of evil. In the name of God, Father, Son and Holy Spirit, I lay my hands upon you: may he fill you with his healing, his light and his peace.

46 The Minister then anoints the sick person, saying

N, I anoint you with oil in the name of our Lord Jesus Christ. May our heavenly Father make you whole in body and mind, and grant you the inward anointing of his Holy Spirit, the Spirit of strength and joy and peace.
Amen

47 The Almighty Lord, who is a strong tower to all who put their trust in him, be now and evermore your defence, and make you believe and trust that the only name under heaven given for health and salvation is the name of our Lord Jesus Christ.
Amen

48 Praise the Lord, O my soul
and all that is within me, praise his holy Name
Praise the Lord, O my soul
and forget not all his benefits
Who forgives all your sin
and heals all your infirmities.   *(Ps 103: 1-3)*

49 **Blessing and honour and thanksgiving and praise**
more than we can utter
more than we can understand
be to you, O holy and glorious Trinity
Father, Son and Holy Spirit
from all angels
all people
all creatures
for ever and ever.

50 A minister who is not a priest may conclude the rite with the Grace. If the Minister is a priest he says the following or some other suitable blessing

To God's gracious mercy and protection we commit
you.
The Lord bless you and watch over you.
The Lord make his face shine on you
and be gracious to you.
The Lord look kindly on you
and give you peace.
Amen

THE EUCHARIST OF THE SICK

51 The Eucharist may fittingly be celebrated for the sick, using the Propers provided below in sections 52-56, at a healing service or during a healing mission; in a hospital chapel or ward, or in a private house, if the sick person is strong enough for a full service. The Propers may also be used at a votive Eucharist for the sick and suffering.

When the Eucharist is celebrated with a sick person, a shortened form may be used consisting of the Communion of the Sick (sections 58-72), together with Prayers D, the fifth Eucharistic Prayer and the Breaking of the Bread (sections 42, 95-99 and 79 of the Eucharist) which are inserted at the appropriate places.

A form for the Communion of the Sick from the reserved sacrament is also provided (sections 57-72).

A form of Preparation for Communion is provided in sections 73-79 for the use of those who are to receive the Communion of the Sick. Those who are unable to receive the sacrament physically may make use of this form of preparation with sections 80-82 to make a spiritual communion.

The Collect

52 **Heavenly Father**
giver of life and health:
comfort and restore (*N* and) all who are sick
that they may be strengthened in their weakness
and have confidence in your unfailing love;
through Jesus Christ our Lord.
Amen

or

53 **Almighty and everlasting God**
mercifully look upon our infirmities
and in all our dangers and necessities
stretch forth your right hand to help and defend us;
through Jesus Christ our Lord.
Amen

54 A gospel reading and one or two other readings from those listed below are used.

Old Testament
2 Kings 20:1-5;   Isaiah 53:3-5;   Isaiah 61:1-3;   Hosea 6:1-3;
Ecclesiasticus 38:1-4.

New Testament
Acts 3:1-10;   Acts 4:8-12;   Romans 8:14-17;   Romans 8:31-39;
2 Corinthians 4:16-18.

Gospel
Matthew 8:1-4;   Matthew 11:25-30;   Matthew 15:29-31;
Mark 2:1-12;   Mark 7:32-37;   Mark 10:46-52;   Luke 17:11-19;
John 4:46-53.

55 **Psalm and Canticle**
Psalm 13   *or*   23   *or*   86:1-7   *or*   138   *or*   139:1-13.
Canticle 14   *or*   15   *or*   16.

56 The following Proper Preface may be used

And now we give you thanks because you sent your Son
Jesus Christ to share our sufferings and bear our sorrows,
and revealed through him your power to make us whole.

COMMUNION OF THE SICK

57 When the sick person is communicated outside the Eucharist, *he* may receive the consecrated bread and wine either in both kinds separately, or by intinction (in which case the Minister says, 'The body and blood of Christ ...'), or in one kind only.

If the sick person is anointed immediately before receiving, sections 58-61 are omitted.

58 The Minister greets the sick person and others present

Peace be to this house and to all who live here

or

The peace of the Lord be with you always

59 **Almighty God**
to whom all hearts are open
all desires known
and from whom no secrets are hid:
cleanse the thoughts of our hearts
    by the inspiration of your Holy Spirit
that we may perfectly love you
and worthily magnify your holy Name;
through Christ our Lord.

60 **Almighty God, our heavenly Father**
in penitence we confess
    that we have sinned against you
    through our own fault
in thought, word, and deed
and in what we have left undone.
For the sake of your Son, Christ our Lord
forgive us all that is past
and grant that we may serve you
    in newness of life
to the glory of your Name.

61 Almighty God, who forgives all who truly repent, have mercy on *you*; pardon *your* sins and set *you* free from them; confirm and strengthen *you* in all goodness and keep *you* in eternal life; through Jesus Christ our Lord. **Amen**

62 A collect is said, either the Collect for the day or one chosen from sections 52-53.

63 A reading chosen from section 54, or the Gospel of the day, or one of the following verses is read

Jesus said 'Whoever eats my flesh and drinks my blood remains in me, and I in him.' *(John 6: 56)*

or

Jesus said 'Do not let your hearts be troubled. Trust in God, trust also in me.' *(John 14: 1)*

or

Jesus said 'As the Father has loved me, so have I loved you; abide in my love.' *(John 15: 9)*

or

Jesus said 'I am with you always, to the end of time.' *(Matt 28: 20)*

or any other suitable verse.

64 **Our Father in heaven**
hallowed be your Name
your kingdom come
your will be done
on earth as in heaven.
Give us today our daily bread.
Forgive us our sins
   as we forgive those who sin against us.
Save us from the time of trial
and deliver us from evil.
For the kingdom, the power, and the glory are yours
now and for ever.   Amen

(65) **Jesus, Lamb of God: have mercy on us.**
Jesus, bearer of our sins: have mercy on us.
Jesus, redeemer of the world: give us your peace.
or

Lamb of God, you take away the sin of the world:
have mercy on us.
Lamb of God, you take away the sin of the world:
have mercy on us.
Lamb of God, you take away the sin of the world:
grant us peace.

(66) **We do not presume**
to come to this your table, merciful Lord
trusting in our own righteousness
but in your manifold and great mercies.
We are not worthy so much as to gather up
   the crumbs under your table;
but you are the same Lord
   whose nature is always to have mercy.
Grant us therefore, gracious Lord
so to eat the flesh of your dear Son Jesus Christ
and to drink his blood
that we may evermore dwell in him and he in us.

67 *Minister*   The body of our Lord Jesus Christ, which was
given for you, keep you in eternal life.
Amen

Minister   The blood of our Lord Jesus Christ, which was
shed for you, keep you in eternal life.
Amen

68 Give thanks to the Lord for he is gracious
His mercy endures for ever

69) Almighty and eternal God, we thank you for feeding us
in these holy mysteries with the body and blood of your
Son, our Saviour Jesus Christ; and for keeping us by your
grace in the Body of your Son, the company of all faithful
people. Help us to persevere as living members of that
holy fellowship, and to grow in love and obedience according to your will; through Jesus Christ our Lord, who
lives and reigns with you and the Holy Spirit, one God,
now and for ever.
Amen

70) **Father almighty**
we offer ourselves to you
as a living sacrifice
   in Jesus Christ our Lord.
In the power of the Holy Spirit
enable us to live
   to your praise and glory.   Amen

71 Prayers from sections 4-21 may also be used.

72 The Blessing or the Grace.

513

A PREPARATION FOR COMMUNION

73 Personal preparation for Communion may be made in one's own words, but the following suggestions are given for those who prefer a set form.

Recollection of God's presence

74 The Lord is close to all who call upon him   *(Ps 145: 18)*

Be still and know that I am God   *(Ps 46: 10)*

Lord, silence all voices in my heart but yours

Thanksgiving: recollection of all one has received or enjoyed

75 Praise the Lord, O my soul, and forget not all his benefits
(Ps 103: 2)

Penitence: recollection of ways one has sinned in thought, word and deed

76 Lord Jesus Christ, Son of the living God, have mercy on me

Prayers for others and oneself

77 Some of the prayers from sections 4-21 may be used.

Reflection on Christ's gift of himself in the sacrament

78 'Whoever eats my flesh and drinks my blood has eternal life, and I will raise him up at the last day. For my flesh is real food and my blood is real drink. Whoever eats my flesh and drinks my blood remains in me, and I in him.'   *(John 6: 54-56)*

79 Almighty and everlasting God
 we approach the sacrament
  of your only begotten Son
  our Lord Jesus Christ;
 as sick, we come to the physician of life;
 as unclean, to the fountain of mercy;
 as blind, to the light of eternal splendour;
 as needy, to the Lord of heaven and earth;
 as naked, to the King of glory.
 Amen

SPIRITUAL COMMUNION

80 One who is unable to receive the Sacrament physically may make a spiritual communion, and be certain that Christ comes to *him* in this way as surely as he does in the Sacrament. The act of spiritual communion is made by concluding the prayers of preparation with an invitation to our Lord to enter, for example

Come into my heart, Lord Jesus

or

81 Jesus, may all that is you flow into me.
May your body and blood be my food and drink.
May your passion and death be my strength and life.
Jesus, with you by my side enough has been given.
May the shelter I seek be the shadow of your cross.
Let me not run from the love which you offer
but hold me safe from the forces of evil.
On each of my dyings shed your light and your love.
Keep calling to me until that day comes
when, with your saints, I may praise you for ever.
Amen

or the more traditional form of this prayer

82 Soul of Christ, sanctify me.
Body of Christ, save me.
Blood of Christ, refresh me.
Water from the side of Christ, wash me.
Passion of Christ, strengthen me.
O good Jesus, hear me.
Within your wounds hide me.
Let me never be separated from you.
From the malicious enemy defend me.
In the hour of my death call me
    and bid me come to you
that with your saints I may praise you
    for ever and ever.   Amen

Ministry to the Dying

THE EUCHARIST

83   If the Eucharist is celebrated in the home of the dying person, the following Collect is used

Lord Jesus Christ, in your last hour you commended your spirit into the hands of your heavenly Father: have mercy on your servant *N*. Give *him* the assurance of your presence even in the dark valley, and may death be to *him* the gate of paradise; for you are the Resurrection and the Life, to whom be glory for ever and ever.
Amen

84   The following readings may be used

Isaiah 25:8-9;   2 Corinthians 1:3-5   *or*   Romans 14:7-9; John 10: 14-15 *and* 27-29.

Psalm 121 and Canticle 14 are suitable.

85   The Collect at 83 and the gospel reading at 84 may be used if the dying person receives the Communion of the Sick.

PRAYERS FOR THE DYING

86   This service, or any part of it, may be said either by the Priest or by relatives or friends of the sick person, or by any lay person. One or more verses of Scripture may be selected and repeated.

87   **Peace be to this house and to all who live here**

or

The peace of the Lord be with you always

88   The eternal God is your refuge and underneath are the everlasting arms

89   Let us pray

Our Father in heaven
hallowed be your Name
your kingdom come
your will be done
on earth as in heaven.
Give us today our daily bread.
Forgive us our sins
   as we forgive those who sin against us.
Save us from the time of trial
and deliver us from evil.
For the kingdom, the power and the glory are yours
now and for ever.   Amen

90   Heavenly Father, grant us the assurance of your loving
        presence
     and fill us with your peace.
     Amen

91   Our Lord on the cross turned to his Father, using the words of Scripture. Let us follow his example and find comfort and strength in God's word.

Scripture Verses

From the Psalms

92   O Lord, be not far off:
     O my Strength, come quickly to help me.   *(Ps 22:20)*

     O Lord, do not forsake me:
     be not far from me, O my God.
     Come quickly to help me,
     O Lord my Saviour.   *(Ps 38: 21)*

     The Lord is my light and my salvation:
     whom then shall I fear?   *(Ps 27: 1)*

The Lord is my shepherd, therefore can I lack nothing.
(Ps 23: 1)

Though I walk through the valley of the shadow of
    death, I will fear no evil: for you are with me,
    your rod and your staff comfort me. *(Ps 23: 4)*

Though heart and body fail, yet God is my possession
for ever. *(Ps 73: 26)*

With you is the fountain of life:
and in your light we see light. *(Ps 36: 9)*

The darkness is no darkness with you
but the night is as clear as the day:
the darkness and the light are both alike. *(Ps 139: 11)*

You will show me the path of life:
in your presence is the fulness of joy,
and at your right hand there is pleasure for
    evermore. *(Ps 16: 11)*

When I awake and see you as you are I shall be
    satisfied. *(Ps 17: 16)*

From the Gospels

Father, into your hands I commend my spirit.
(Luke 23: 46)

God so loved the world that he gave his only Son, that
whoever believes in him should not perish but have
eternal life. *(John 3: 16)*

I am the light of the world. *(John 8: 12)*

I am the good shepherd. The good shepherd lays down
his life for the sheep. *(John 10: 11)*

Peace I leave with you; my peace I give you.

(John 14: 27)

Let not your heart be troubled. Trust in God; trust also in me. I go to prepare a place for you. *(John 14: 1, 2b)*

From the Epistles

I consider that our present sufferings are not worth comparing with the glory that will be revealed in us.

(Rom 8: 18)

I am sure that neither death, nor life, nor angels, nor principalities, nor things present, nor things to come, nor powers, nor height, nor depth, nor anything else in all creation, will be able to separate us from the love of God in Christ Jesus our Lord. *(Rom 8: 38-39)*

From the Revelation

God shall wipe away all tears from their eyes; and there shall be no more death, neither sorrow, nor crying, neither shall there be any more pain; for the former things are passed away. *(Rev 21: 4)*

Night shall be no more; they need no light of lamp or sun, for the Lord God will be their light, and they shall reign for ever and ever. *(Rev 22: 5)*

The Song of Simeon *(Luke 2: 29-32)*

93 Lord, now you let your servant go in peace:
       your word has been fulfilled.
    My own eyes have seen the salvation:
       which you have prepared in the sight of every
          people.
    A light to reveal you to the nations:
       and the glory of your people Israel.

94 Lord, to you we commend N. In your loving mercy forgive *his* sins, that dying in this world *he* may be raised to life in the world to come; through Jesus Christ our Lord.
Amen

95 Faithful Creator and most merciful Saviour, we commend into your hands our dear *brother N*. May *he* know that *he* is precious in your sight. Wash *him* in the blood of the Lamb who was slain to take away the sins of the world; purge *him* of all defilement, that *he* may be presented pure and spotless in your sight; through the merits of Jesus Christ your only Son our Lord.
Amen

For a child

96 Almighty Father, your Son our Lord Jesus Christ for our sake lived among us as a child. We commend N to your loving care. Send your holy angels to lead *him* to those heavenly places where those who rest in you have everlasting joy. Enfold *him* in the arms of your unfailing love that *he* may live with you for ever.
Amen

Litany

97 Lord, remember not our
offences **Spare us, good Lord**
From all evil and sin **Good Lord, deliver** *him*
From the assaults of the
devil **Good Lord, deliver** *him*
In the hour of death
and in the day of
judgement **Good Lord, deliver** *him*
By your holy incarnation **Save** *him*, **Lord**
By your cross and
passion **Save** *him*, **Lord**

By your resurrection and final triumph	**Save** *him*, **Lord**
Grant *him* relief from pain and deliver *him*	**Lord, hear us**
Cleanse *him* from *his* sin and receive *him* to yourself	**Lord, hear us**
Give *him* light and peace and number *him* with your saints	**Lord, hear us**
Jesus, Lamb of God	**Have mercy on us**
Jesus, bearer of our sins	**Have mercy on us**
Jesus, redeemer of the world	**Give us your peace**

At the point of death

98 Go forth, Christian soul, on your journey from this world:

In the name of the almighty Father who created you.
Amen

In the name of Jesus Christ who suffered for you.
Amen

In the name of the Holy Spirit who strengthens you.
Amen

In communion with the holy apostles, confessors and martyrs, and all the blessed saints, and aided by angels and archangels and all the armies of the heavenly host.
Amen

May you enter this day into the new Jerusalem, the abode of peace, and dwell with God for ever.
Amen.   Alleluia

FUNERAL SERVICES

Preface
Death and Life in Christ

The services which are provided for use in connection with death and the reverent disposal of a human body are part of the Church's continual celebration of the incarnation, death, resurrection and ascension of Jesus and the giving of the Holy Spirit which together constitute what has been called the Paschal Mystery of Christ.

Christians are incorporated in this Paschal Mystery through baptism, and for one who has already died with Christ in that sacrament, and now lives with him in faith (Romans 6:3-11), death marks but a necessary stage in the journey towards the fulness of eternal life with the risen Lord (1 Corinthians 15:50-58).

For this reason the services which mark a Christian's death provide an occasion for the proclamation of the resurrection of Jesus and there is a proper joy about them.

But whilst there is joy, there is also a certain solemnity about a funeral. For there is the natural human sadness at parting from one who is loved (see John 11:35). There is also the sobering reminder that for every one of us death is inescapable, as is the certainty of judgement.

No guarantee of salvation is provided by belief in a person's virtue or claims that the deceased has led a 'good' life, for eternal life and acceptance by God (justification) are the result of faith in Jesus rather than the rewards of human righteousness (John 11:25-26; Romans 3:21-24).

Moreover, even those who know themselves to have been justified by God through Jesus Christ (Romans 5:1) are aware of many a fall from grace in 'working out' their salvation (Philippians 2:12).

For these reasons and because none is in a position to be able to judge the faith of another, the deceased person is commended to God's mercy; and many would wish to pray for him or her to be granted the forgiveness which Jesus came to bring (Mark 2:17).

This is not to deny that it is sometimes appropriate to rehearse the good qualities and achievements of the deceased. But where a tribute is paid at a funeral, it needs to be honest and should have the purpose of moving those present to thank God for what he has accomplished by his grace in and through the person concerned. Thus it is a matter not so much of paying one's last respects, or even of saying goodbye to the deceased, as of giving him or her back to God with thanksgiving and confidence in his mercy.

But as the dead are commended to the care of a loving Father, so too are those who have been bereaved. Their need at this time is for strength and solace in accepting their loss. The proclamation of the resurrection and the assurance of life with Jesus (John 14:1-3) goes much of the way in meeting this need. But the bereaved also need to be allowed to face the reality of death, perhaps to weep, and certainly to be prayed for as they face the days ahead.

An assertion of faith in the resurrection life which leaves no room for grief or which ignores the fact of death and certainty of judgement does no service to those who mourn, even if it spares their feelings for the time being. There is an important distinction between insensitive heartiness and the quiet assertion of confidence together with sympathy which reflects the gentleness of the risen Lord with Mary in the garden (John 20:11-18).

At most funerals there are those who do not feel the loss of a dead person so personally as those who were near and dear. Nevertheless, they are not without the need of prayer and they are therefore included in an approach to God which is made on behalf of all who are present: both that his grace should enable Christians to rejoice in their unity with all who are in Christ, whether living or departed; and that the Church should live and witness to her faith in the death and resurrection of Jesus – for this is at the heart of her existence (1 Corinthians 15:14) and is most truly tested when her members face the fact of death.

Thus, many elements combine in the Christian liturgy for death. Always there should be held together the opposites of joy and sorrow, mercy and judgement, the reality of sin and the vision of heaven.

General Rubrics

1 Several services are provided to meet various needs. The Priest may consult the family to select which services are to be used and to make a choice from the options included in each service.

2 The Priest may authorize a deacon or lay minister to take any of these services or any part of a service, except for those sections of the Eucharist which are reserved to a priest. The Service for Use before a Funeral (sections 1 to 6) and A Memorial Service (sections 63-79), when used in the home, may be conducted by any lay person.

3 The Committal may immediately follow the Funeral in the church only when the body is to be cremated. Otherwise the Committal takes place at the grave (or at sea). Both the Funeral and the Committal may take place at the cemetery or crematorium or at sea.

4 A Memorial Service is not an alternative to the Funeral Service. It is an additional service which may be used in the home when custom requires, or in church. It may precede the Interment of Ashes.

When the circumstances of death do not leave a body that can be committed, the Funeral Service and Committal are held, but the words committing the body to the ground are omitted from the prayers at 27, 28, 55 and 56.

5 Both the Funeral Service and A Memorial Service may appropriately take place within the Eucharist. Rubrics in these services indicate how this may be done.

6 The Collect for a Eucharist is as follows

For an Adult

God our Father
your Son Jesus Christ died and rose again
 for our salvation:
we entrust to you the soul of your servant *N*
praying that *he* and all the faithful departed
may be revealed as your children
when Christ shall come again;
to whom, with you and the Holy Spirit
be honour and glory, now and for ever.

For a Child

Heavenly Father
your Son, our Saviour
took little children into his arms and blessed them:
receive your child *N*
 in your never failing care and love
comfort those who have loved *him* on earth
and bring us all to your everlasting kingdom;
through Jesus Christ our Lord
who lives and reigns with you and the Holy Spirit
one God, now and for ever.

At a requiem, one of the collects for the Commemoration of the Faithful Departed may be used.

The liturgical colour is white, purple or black.

7 Sentences, psalms, lessons and prayers are provided for each service. The Minister may use any of those set for one service at another. He may use other prayers from sections 107 to 124, and choose alternative lessons and psalms from the following table, or substitute others which are particularly appropriate.

Old Testament
Isaiah 35: 1-2, 8-10; Isaiah 63: 7-9.

For a child 2 Kings 4: 18-26.

Psalms
27; 42:1-7; 103; 121; 130; 139:1-18; 147:1-7.

New Testament
Romans 8:31-39; 2 Corinthians 4:7-18; Philippians 3:7-21;
1 Thessalonians 4:13-18; 2 Timothy 1:8-12; 1 Peter 1:3-9;
2 Peter 1:1-11; Revelation 7:9-17 *or* 21:1-7 *or* 21:22–22:5.

For a child Ephesians 3:14-19.

Gospel
Matthew 5:3-10; Luke 23:33, 39-43; John 5:24-29 *or* 6:37-40
or 14:1-6 *or* 20:1-18.

For a child Matthew 11:25-30; John 11:17-27.

8 During a procession from the home or from the church any of these psalms may be used

Psalms 116; 121; 123; 126; 132; 134; 139:1-18.

9 Hymns may also be sung during the procession and at appropriate places in the services.

10 If the person died unbaptized, excommunicate, in the act of committing or in a state of grave sin, or by suicide, it is appropriate that the reading should be John 5: 25-29, the prayer at 114 and the form of committal at 28/84 being used. In cases of doubt, time permitting, the Bishop should be consulted.

11 The ashes after cremation are placed either in a grave or in some place set apart for that purpose.

A Service for Use before the Funeral

This service may be used at the home or other appropriate place where family and friends gather at any time before the funeral. It may also be used if the body is brought to the church some time before the funeral.

The Minister at this service is a priest, deacon or lay minister. When used in the home, the service may be taken by any lay person.

The Minister reads one or more of the sentences following

The steadfast love of the Lord never ceases, his mercies never come to an end; they are new every morning.

(Lam 3:22-23)

God so loved the world that he gave his only Son, that whoever believes in him should not perish, but have eternal life. *(John 3:16)*

Come to me, all you who are weary and burdened, and I will give you rest. *(Matt 11:28)*

A psalm is said, either the following or one chosen from the table at General Rubric 7. More than one psalm may be said.

Psalm 42:1-7

1 As a deer longs for the I running I brooks:
   so longs my I soul for I you O I God.

2 My soul is thirsty for God * thirsty for the I living I God:
   when shall I I come and I see his I face?

3 My tears have been my food I day and I night:
   while they ask me all day long I 'Where now I is your I God?'

4 As I pour out my soul by myself I reImember I this:
   how I went to the house of the Mighty One I ‿ into · the I temple · of I God,

† 5 To the shouts and | songs of · thanks|giving:
    a multitude | keeping | high | festival.

6 Why are you so full of | heaviness · my | soul:
    and | why · so un|quiet · with|in me?

7 O put your | trust in | God:
    for I will praise him yet
      who is my de|liver · er | and my | God.

4 A lesson or lessons chosen from the table at General Rubric 7 may be read.

5 A time of prayer follows. The Minister may use prayers from sections 107-124; *he* and others may offer free prayer.

6 The prayers conclude with

Father, we come to you in our grief, trusting in your love for *N* and for ourselves. We know that death cannot separate us from your love in Jesus Christ our Lord.

This is our faith
Lord, increase our faith

Father, your Son Jesus wept at the tomb of Lazarus. We believe that you share our grief and will give us strength in our loss.

This is our faith
Lord, increase our faith

Father, Jesus died that we might be forgiven. We trust in your forgiveness for *N* and for ourselves.

This is our faith
Lord, increase our faith

Father, you gave your only Son, that all who have faith in him may not die, but have eternal life.

This is the faith of the Church
This is our faith   Amen.   Alleluia

The Funeral of an Adult

7   The Priest meets the body at the entrance to the church and leads the procession into church saying one or more of the Sentences at 8. If the body is brought into church sometime before the service, Sentences may be used at the beginning of the service.

When the Eucharist is celebrated, the Priest begins the Eucharist after section 8 below. He may omit sections 1-5 of the Eucharist, the Sermon, the Creed and the Peace. Sections 18-22 or sections 107 or 108 are used for the Prayers. The Collect for the Eucharist is to be found in General Rubric 6. A psalm and two or three readings are chosen from the table at General Rubric 7. Canticle 7 or 9 and Proper Preface 21 may be used. The Funeral Service continues from section 23 below after sections 86-(87) of the Eucharist.

The Easter Candle may be placed by the coffin and lit.

Sentences

8   I am the resurrection, and I am the life; he who believes in me, though he die, yet shall he live, and whoever lives and believes in me shall never die.
(John 11:25-26)

I know that my Redeemer lives, and that in the end he will stand upon the earth. I myself will see him with my own eyes – I, and not another.   *(Job 19:25, 27)*

Do not bring your servant into judgement, for no one living is righteous before you.   *(Ps 143:2)*

I am sure that neither death, nor life, nor angels, nor principalities, nor powers, nor things present, nor things to come, nor height, nor depth, nor anything else in all creation, will be able to separate us from the love of God in Christ Jesus our Lord.   *(Rom 8:38-39)*

Remember not the sins of my youth nor my transgressions: but according to your mercy think on me.
(Ps 25:7)

We brought nothing into the world, and we take nothing out. The Lord gives, and the Lord takes away: blessed be the name of the Lord. *(1 Tim 6:7; Job 1:21)*

For now we see in a mirror, dimly; but then face to face: now I know in part; but then shall I know even as also I am known. *(1 Cor 13:12)*

None of us lives to himself, and none of us dies to himself. If we live, we live to the Lord, and if we die, we die to the Lord: so then, whether we live or whether we die, we are the Lord's. *(Rom 14:7-8)*

The eternal God is your refuge, and underneath are the everlasting arms. *(Deut 33:27)*

In my Father's house are many mansions; if it were not so, I would have told you. I am going there to prepare a place for you. *(John 14:2)*

Eye has not seen, nor ear heard, nor the heart of man conceived, what God has prepared for those who love him. *(1 Cor 2:9)*

We believe that Jesus died and rose again, and so it will be for those who died as Christians; God will bring them to life with Jesus. Thus we shall always be with the Lord. Comfort one another with these words. *(1 Thess 4:14, 18)*

9 Heavenly Father, in your Son Jesus Christ you have given us a true faith and a sure hope: help us to live as those who believe in the communion of saints, the forgiveness of sins, and the resurrection to eternal life, and strengthen this faith and hope in us all the days of our life; through the love of your Son Jesus Christ our Saviour.
Amen

10 A psalm is said, either one of the following or one chosen from the table at General Rubric 7. More than one psalm may be said.

Psalm 23

11 1 The Lord I is my I shepherd:
      therefore I can I I lack I nothing.

2 He will make me lie down in I green I pastures:
  and I lead me · belside still I waters.

3 He will relfresh my I soul:
  and guide me in right pathways I for his I name's I sake.

4 Though I walk through the valley of the shadow of ⌣
      death   I will I fear no I evil:
  for you are with me
      your I rod · and your I staff I comfort me.

5 You spread a table before me
      in the face of I those who I trouble me:
  you have anointed my head with oil I and my I cup · will be I full.

6 Surely your goodness and loving-kindness ⌣
      will follow me * all the I days · of my I life:
  and I shall dwell in the I house · of the I Lord for I ever.

Psalm 90

12 1 Lord you have I been our I refuge:
      from one generlation I to anlother.

2 Before the mountains were born
      or the earth and the world were I brought to I be:
  from eternity to etlerni · ty I you are I God.

3 You turn man I back · into I dust:
  saying   'Return to I dust you I sons of I Adam.'

4 For a thousand years in your sight ⌣
    are like | yester · day | passing:
    or | like one | watch · of the | night.

5 You cut them | short · like a | dream:
    like the fresh | grass | of the | morning;

6 In the morning it is | green and | flourishes:
    at evening it is | withered · and | dried | up.

7 And we are con|sumed · by your | anger:
    because of your indig|nation · we | cease to | be.

8 You have brought our in|iquities · be|fore you:
    and our secret | sins · to the | light of · your |
    countenance.

9 Our days decline be|neath your | wrath:
    and our years | pass a|way · like a | sigh.

10 The days of our life are three score years and ten
    or if we have | strength   four | score:
    the pride of our labours is but toil and sorrow
    for it passes quickly a|way and | we are | gone.

11 Who can know the | power of · your | wrath:
    who can know your indig|nation · like | those that |
    fear you?

12 Teach us so to | number · our | days:
    that we may ap|ply our | hearts to | wisdom.

13 Relent O Lord * how long will | you be | angry?:
    take | pity | on your | servants.

14 O satisfy us early | with your | mercy:
    that all our days we | may re|joice and | sing.

15 Give us joy for all the days you | have af|flicted us:
    for the | years · we have | suffered · ad|versity.

16 Show your | servants · your | work:
    and let their | children | see your | glory.

†17 May the gracious favour of the Lord our | God · be
    up|on us:
    prosper the work of our hands
        O | prosper · the | work · of our | hands!

Psalm 130

1 Out of the depths have I called to | you O | Lord:
    Lord | hear | my | voice;

2 O let your ears con|sider | well:
    the | voice · of my | suppli|cation.

3 If you Lord should note what | we do | wrong:
    who | then O | Lord could | stand?

4 But there is for|giveness · with | you:
    so that | you | shall be | feared.

5 I wait for the Lord * my | soul | waits for him:
    and | in his | word · is my | hope.

6 My soul | looks · for the | Lord:
    more than watchmen for the morning
        more I say than | watchmen | for the | morning.

7 O Israel trust in the Lord * for with the | Lord ·
        there is | mercy:
    and with | him is | ample · re|demption.

8 He will re|deem | Israel:
    from the | multi · tude | of his | sins.

A lesson is read, either the following or one chosen from the table at
General Rubric 7. More than one lesson may be read.

Christ has been raised from the dead, the first fruits of
those who have fallen asleep. For as by a man came
death, by a man has come also the resurrection of the
dead. For as in Adam all die, so also in Christ shall all
be made alive. But each in his own order: Christ the
first fruits, then at his coming those who belong to
Christ. Then comes the end, when he delivers the
kingdom to God the Father after destroying every rule

and every authority and power. For he must reign until he has put all his enemies under his feet. The last enemy to be destroyed is death.

But someone will ask, 'How are the dead raised? With what kind of body do they come?' You foolish man! What you sow does not come to life unless it dies. And what you sow is not the body which is to be, but a bare kernel, perhaps of wheat or of some other grain. But God gives it a body as he has chosen, and to each kind of seed its own body.

So it is with the resurrection of the dead. What is sown is perishable, what is raised is imperishable. It is sown in dishonour, it is raised in glory. It is sown in weakness, it is raised in power. It is sown a physical body, it is raised a spiritual body.

For this perishable nature must put on the imperishable, and this mortal nature must put on immortality. When the perishable puts on the imperishable, and the mortal puts on immortality, then shall come to pass the saying that is written: 'Death is swallowed up in victory'. 'O death, where is thy victory? O death, where is thy sting?' The sting of death is sin, and the power of sin is the law. But thanks be to God, who gives us the victory through our Lord Jesus Christ.

Therefore, my beloved brethren, be steadfast, immovable, always abounding in the work of the Lord, knowing that in the Lord your labour is not in vain.

(1 Cor 15:20-26, 35-38, 42-44a, 53-58)

15 A sermon may be preached in exposition of the Scripture reading.

16 The Lord be with you
And also with you

Let us pray

Lord, have mercy
Lord, have mercy

Christ, have mercy
Christ, have mercy

Lord, have mercy
Lord, have mercy

7 **Our Father in heaven
hallowed be your Name
your kingdom come
your will be done
on earth as in heaven.
Give us today our daily bread.
Forgive us our sins
   as we forgive those who sin against us.
Save us from the time of trial
and deliver us from evil.
For the kingdom, the power, and the glory are yours
now and for ever. Amen**

The Prayers

8 Appropriate prayers from sections 107-124 may be used in addition to those from 20 to 22 below.

9 The Minister may say

Let us commend our *brother N* to the mercy of God our maker and redeemer

0 Heavenly Father, by your mighty power you gave us life, and in your love you have given us new life in Christ Jesus. We entrust *N* to your merciful keeping: in the faith of Jesus Christ your Son our Lord, who died and rose again to save us, and is now alive and reigns with you and the Holy Spirit in glory for ever.
Amen

For the bereaved

21 Almighty God, Father of all mercies and giver of all comfort, deal graciously with those who mourn, that casting all their care on you, they may know the consolation of your love; through Jesus Christ our Lord.
Amen

For ourselves

22 Grant us, Lord, the wisdom and grace to use aright the time that is left to us here on earth. Lead us to repent of our sins, both the evil we have done and the good we have not done; and strengthen us to follow in the steps of your Son, in the way that leads to the fulness of eternal life; through Jesus Christ our Lord.
Amen

23 May God in his infinite love and mercy bring the whole Church, living and departed in the Lord Jesus, to a joyful resurrection and the fulfilment of his eternal kingdom.
Amen. Alleluia

24 The service ends with the Grace or a blessing given by a priest.

As the coffin is taken out of church, sections 35-37 may be used or a hymn sung.

If the body is to be cremated, the Committal may follow here.

The Committal

25 When the body is to be buried in unconsecrated ground this prayer is used

Almighty God, your Son Jesus Christ by his burial sanctified the grave to be a bed of hope to your people: bless this grave that it may be a resting place, peaceful and secure, for the body of your servant N; for the sake of him who died and was raised and is alive for evermore.
Amen

26 Man born of a woman has but a short time to live.
Like a flower he blossoms and then withers;
like a shadow he flees and never stays.   (*Job* 14:1-2)

In the midst of life we are in death: to whom can we turn for help, but to you, Lord, who are justly angered by our sins?

Lord God, holy and mighty, holy and immortal, holy and most merciful Saviour, deliver us from the bitter pains of eternal death. You know the secrets of our hearts: in your mercy hear our prayer, forgive us our sins, and at our last hour let us not fall away from you.

or

The Lord is full of compassion and mercy:
slow to anger and of great goodness.
As a father is tender towards his children:
so is the Lord tender to those that fear him.
For he knows of what we are made:
he remembers that we are but dust.
The days of man are but as grass:
he flourishes like a flower of the field;
when the wind goes over it, it is gone:
and its place will know it no more.

But the merciful goodness of the Lord
 endures for ever and ever
 toward those that fear him:
and his righteousness upon their
 children's children.   *(Verses from Ps 103)*

27 Into the Lord's most gracious mercy and protection
   we have entrusted our *brother N*
 and we now commit *his* body
   to the ground, earth to earth
   ashes to ashes, dust to dust;
 (*or,* to be cremated);
 (*or,* to the deep);
 in sure and certain hope of the resurrection
   to eternal life;
 through our Lord Jesus Christ
 who died, was buried, and rose again for us.
 To him be glory for ever and ever.
 Amen. Alleluia. Alleluia

 or

28 We commit the body of our dear *brother N*
 to the ground, earth to earth
   ashes to ashes, dust to dust;
 (*or,* to be cremated);
 (*or,* to the deep);
 and we commend *him*
   to the just and merciful judgement
   of him who alone has perfect understanding
 even Jesus Christ our Lord.
 Amen

29 I heard a voice from heaven saying, 'Write this:
 Blessed are the dead who die in the Lord henceforth.'
 'Blessed indeed,' says the Spirit, 'that they may rest
 from their labours, for their deeds follow them!'
             (Rev 14:13)

Additional prayers from sections 107-124 may be used here.

God will show us the path of life;
in his presence is the fulness of joy:
and at his right hand
there is pleasure for evermore.   *(Ps 16:11)*

Now unto him that is able to keep you from falling,
and present you faultless before the presence of his
glory with exceeding joy, to the only wise God our
Saviour, be glory and majesty, dominion and power,
both now and ever.   *(Jude 24-25)*
Amen

The Priest may pronounce a blessing or the Grace may be said.

As the coffin is taken out of church, one or more of the following may
be said or a hymn sung.

May the angels lead you into paradise;
may the martyrs come to welcome you
and take you to the holy city
the new and eternal Jerusalem.
May the choir of angels welcome you.
Where Lazarus is poor no longer
may you have eternal rest.

Give rest, O Christ, to your servants with your saints
where sorrow and pain are no more
neither sighing but life everlasting.
You only are immortal
the creator and maker of all
and we are mortal, formed of the earth
and to the earth we shall return
as you ordained when you created us
saying
'Dust you are, to dust you shall return.'
We all go down to the dust
and weeping at the grave we make our song
alleluia, alleluia, alleluia.

37 1 Lord now you let your servant I go in I peace:
your I word has I been ful|filled.

2 My own eyes have I seen the · sal|vation: which
you have prepared in the I sight of I every I people.

3 A light to re|veal you · to the I nations: and the I
glory · of your I people I Israel.

The Funeral of a Child

The Priest meets the body at the entrance to the church and leads the procession into church saying one or more of the Sentences at 39. If the body has been brought to church some time before the service, Sentences may be used at the beginning of the service.

When the Eucharist is celebrated, the Priest begins the Eucharist after section 39 below. He may omit sections 1-5 of the Eucharist, the Sermon, the Creed and the Peace. Sections 48-51 or section 107 or 108 are used for the Prayers. The Collect for the Eucharist is to be found in General Rubric 6. A psalm and two or three readings are chosen from the table at General Rubric 7. Canticle 7 or 9 and Proper Preface 21 may be used. The Funeral Service continues from section 52 below after sections 86-(87) of the Eucharist

The Easter Candle may be placed by the coffin and lit.

Sentences

I am the resurrection and I am the life; he who believes in me, though he die, yet shall he live, and whoever lives and believes in me shall never die. *(John 11:25-26)*

God shows his love for us in that while we were yet sinners Christ died for us. *(Rom 5:8)*

The Lord gave, and the Lord has taken away; blessed be the name of the Lord. *(Job 1:21)*

Jesus called them to him saying, 'Let the children come to me and do not hinder them; for to such belongs the kingdom of God'. *(Luke 18:16)*

Blessed are the pure in heart, for they shall see God. *(Matt 5:8)*

See that you do not despise one of these little ones; for I tell you that in heaven their angels always behold the face of my Father who is in heaven. *(Matt 18:10)*

545

He will feed his flock like a shepherd, he will gather the lambs in his arms, he will carry them in his bosom.

(Isaiah 40:11)

The eternal God is your refuge, and underneath are the everlasting arms. *(Deut 33:27)*

40 A psalm is said, either one of the following or one chosen from the table at General Rubric 7. More than one psalm may be said.

Psalm 23

41   1 The Lord | is my | shepherd:
      therefore | can I | lack | nothing.

  2 He will make me lie down in | green | pastures:
      and | lead me · be|side still | waters.

  3 He will re|fresh my | soul:
      and guide me in right pathways | for his | name's | sake.

  4 Though I walk through the valley of the shadow of ‿ death I will | fear no | evil:
      for you are with me
      your | rod · and your | staff | comfort me.

  5 You spread a table before me
      in the face of | those who | trouble me:
      you have anointed my head with oil | and my | cup · will be | full.

  6 Surely your goodness and loving-kindness ‿
      will follow me * all the | days · of my | life:
      and I shall dwell in the | house · of the | Lord for | ever.

Psalm 121

42 1 lift up my | eyes · to the | hills:
but | where · shall I | find | help?

2 My help | comes · from the | Lord:
who has | made | heaven · and | earth.

3 He will not suffer your | foot to | stumble:
and he who watches | over · you | will not | sleep.

4 Be sure he who has | charge of | Israel:
will | neither | slumber · nor | sleep.

5 The Lord him|self is · your | keeper:
the Lord is your defence up|on your | right | hand;

6 The sun shall not | strike you · by | day:
nor | shall the | moon by | night.

7 The Lord will defend you from | all | evil:
it is | he · who will | guard your | life.

8 The Lord will defend your going out and your | coming | in:
from this time | forward · for | ever|more.

43 A lesson is read, either one of the following or one chosen from the table at General Rubric 7. More than one lesson may be read.

44 Go, my children, go your way!
I must stay bereft and lonely;
I will cry to the Eternal all my life
for I look to the Eternal for your rescue
and joy has come to me from the Holy One
at the mercy soon to reach you
from your saviour, the Eternal.
In sorrow and tears I watched you go away
but God will give you back to me in joy and gladness
for ever.   *(Baruch 4:19, 20b, 22, 23a)*

or

They were bringing children to Christ, that he might touch them; and the disciples rebuked them. But when Jesus saw it he was indignant, and said to them, 'Let the children come to me, do not hinder them; for to such belongs the kingdom of God. Truly, I say to you, whoever does not receive the kingdom of God like a child shall not enter it'. And he took them in his arms and blessed them, laying his hands upon them.

(Mark 10:13-16)

45 A sermon may be preached in exposition of the Scripture reading.

46 The Lord be with you
And also with you

Let us pray

Lord, have mercy
Lord, have mercy

Christ, have mercy
Christ, have mercy

Lord, have mercy
Lord, have mercy

47 **Our Father in heaven**
hallowed be your Name
your kingdom come
your will be done
on earth as in heaven.
Give us today our daily bread.
Forgive us our sins
    as we forgive those who sin against us.
Save us from the time of trial
and deliver us from evil.
For the kingdom, the power, and the glory are yours
now and for ever.   Amen

Appropriate prayers from sections 107-124 below may be used in addition to those from 49-51 below.

Lord Jesus Christ, you took little children into your arms and blessed them. In perfect confidence we commit *N* to your infinite love, for you live and reign with the Father and the Holy Spirit, one God, now and for ever.
Amen

or

Lord Jesus Christ, your heart was moved with compassion for Jairus and his wife, and for the widow of Nain, and you restored their children to life on earth. To your love and compassion we commit *N*, believing that you will raise *him* to eternal life in heaven, where you live and reign with the Father and the Holy Spirit, one God, now and for ever.
Amen

Lord God, your ways are beyond our understanding, and your love for those whom you create is greater by far than ours; comfort these parents whose hearts are full of grief for the child they have lost. Give them the faith to endure the darkness of bereavement and bring them in the fulness of time to share with *N* the light and joy of your eternal presence; through Jesus Christ our Lord.
Amen

The service ends with the Grace or a blessing given by a priest.

As the coffin is taken out of church, sections 61-62 may be used or a hymn sung.

If the body is to be cremated, the Committal may follow here.

The Committal of a Child

53 When the body is to be buried in unconsecrated ground this prayer is
used

Almighty God, your Son Jesus Christ by his burial
sanctified the grave to be a bed of hope to your people:
bless this grave that it may be a resting place, peaceful
and secure, for the body of your servant *N*; for the sake
of him who died and was raised and is alive for
evermore.
Amen

54 Man born of a woman has but a short time to live.
Like a flower he blossoms and then withers;
like a shadow he flees and never stays.   *(Job 14:1-2)*

While the child was still alive, I fasted and wept; for I
said, 'Who knows whether the Lord will be gracious to
me that the child may live?' But now he is dead, why
should I fast? Can I bring him back again? I shall go to
him, but he will not return to me.   *(2 Sam 12:22-23)*

Thus says the Lord:
'A voice is heard in Ramah
lamentation and bitter weeping.
Rachel is weeping for her children;
she refuses to be comforted for her children
because they are not.'
Thus says the Lord:
'Keep your voice from weeping
and your eyes from tears;
for your work shall be rewarded
says the Lord
and they shall come back from the land of the enemy.
There is hope for your future
says the Lord
and your children shall come back
to their own country.'   *(Jer 31:15-17)*

55 We believe that God in his mercy
    has received N to himself
and we commit *his* body
    to the ground;
    (*or* to be cremated);
    (*or* to the deep);
in sure and certain hope of the resurrection
    to eternal life;
through our Lord Jesus Christ.
Amen.   **Alleluia**

or

56 To God's loving mercy we commend N
that he may grant *him* a share
    in the unsearchable riches of the redemption
    won for us by his Son
our Lord and Saviour Jesus Christ;
and we commit the body of N
    to the ground;
    (*or* to be cremated);
    (*or* to the deep);
in the name of God, Father, Son, and Holy Spirit.
Amen

57 Therefore are they before the throne of God
and serve him day and night within his temple;
and he who sits upon the throne will shelter them with
    his presence.
They shall hunger no more, neither thirst any more;
the sun shall not strike them, nor any scorching heat.
For the Lamb in the midst of the throne will be their
    shepherd
and he will guide them to springs of living water;
and God will wipe away every tear from their eyes.
(Rev 7:15-17)

58 Additional prayers from sections 107-124 may be used here.

59 The Priest may pronounce a blessing or the Grace may be said.

60 As the coffin is taken out of the church, one or both of the following may be said, or a hymn sung.

61 May the angels lead you into paradise;
may the martyrs come to welcome you
and take you to the holy city
the new and eternal Jerusalem.
May the choir of angels welcome you.
Where Lazarus is poor no longer
may you have eternal rest.

62 Give rest, O Christ, to your servant with your saints
where sorrow and pain are no more
neither sighing but life everlasting.
You only are immortal
the creator and maker of all
and we are mortal, formed of the earth
and to the earth we shall return
as you ordained when you created us
saying
'Dust you are, to dust you shall return.'
We all go down to the dust
and weeping at the grave we make our song
alleluia, alleluia, alleluia.

A Memorial Service

63 This service is not to be used instead of the Funeral Service. It is an additional service which may be used in church, in the home or in some other convenient place. It may precede the Interment of Ashes.

When the Eucharist is celebrated, the Priest begins the Eucharist after section 65 below. He may omit sections 1-5 of the Eucharist, the Sermon, the Creed and the Peace. Sections 75-77 or sections 107 or 108 are used for the Prayers. The Collect for the Eucharist is to be found in General Rubric 6. A psalm and two or three readings are chosen from the table at General Rubric 7. Canticle 7 or 9 and Proper Preface 21 may be used. The Memorial Service continues from section 78 below after sections 86-(87) of the Eucharist.

64 If there is to be an address commemorating the deceased, it follows section 65.

65 One or more of these Sentences is used

The eternal God is your refuge
and underneath are the everlasting arms.   *(Deut 33:27)*

The steadfast love of the Lord never ceases,
his mercies never come to an end;
they are new every morning.   *(Lam 3:22-23)*

Eye has not seen, nor ear heard, nor the heart of man conceived, what God has prepared for those who love him.   *(1 Cor 2:9)*

We believe that Jesus died and rose again, and so we believe that God will bring with Jesus those who have fallen asleep in him. Therefore comfort one another with these words.   *(1 Thess 4:14,18)*

66 The Lord be with you
And also with you

Let us pray

Lord, have mercy
Lord, have mercy

Christ, have mercy
Christ, have mercy

Lord, have mercy
Lord, have mercy

67 **Our Father in heaven
hallowed be your Name
your kingdom come
your will be done
on earth as in heaven.
Give us today our daily bread.
Forgive us our sins
    as we forgive those who sin against us.
Save us from the time of trial
and deliver us from evil.
For the kingdom, the power, and the glory are yours
now and for ever.   Amen**

68 Almighty God, neither death nor life can separate us from your love: with the whole company of the redeemed in heaven and earth we praise and magnify your glorious Name, Father, Son and Holy Spirit, one God, blessed for ever.
Amen

69 A psalm is said, either one of the following or one chosen from the table at General Rubric 7. More than one psalm may be said.

Psalm 16

70 1 Preserve | me O | God:
  for in | you · have I | taken | refuge.

 2 I have said to the Lord | You are | my lord:
  and all my | good de|pends on | you.

 5 The Lord is my appointed portion | and my | cup:
  you | hold my | lot · in your | hands.

 6 The share that has fallen to me is in | pleasant |
   places:
  and a fair | land is | my pos|session.

†11 You will show me the | path of | life:
  in your presence is the fulness of joy * and from ‿
   your right hand flow de|lights for | ever|more.

Psalm 34

71 1 I will bless the | Lord con|tinually:
  his praise shall be | always | in my | mouth.

 2 Let my soul | boast · of the | Lord:
  the humble shall | hear it | and re|joice.

 3 O praise the | Lord with | me:
  let us ex|alt his | name to|gether.

 4 For I sought the Lord's | help · and he | answered:
  and he | freed me · from | all my | fears.

 5 Look towards him and be | bright with | joy:
  your | faces · shall | not · be a|shamed.

 6 Here is a wretch who cried and the | Lord | heard
   him:
  and | saved him · from | all his | troubles.

 7 The angel of the Lord encamps round | those who |
   fear him:
  and de|livers · them | in their | need.

 8 O taste and see that the | Lord is | good:
  happy the | man who | hides in | him!

9 Fear the Lord all | you his | holy ones:
  for those who | fear him | never | lack.

10 Lions may suffer | want · and go | hungry:
  but those who seek the | Lord lack | nothing |
  good.

72 A lesson chosen from the table at General Rubric 7 is read. More than one lesson may be read.

73 A sermon may be preached in exposition of the Scripture reading.

74 The Prayers which follow may be replaced or supplemented by prayers from sections 107-124 or as allowed for in General Rubric 7.

75 Eternal God and Father
whose love is stronger than death
we rejoice that the dead as well as the living
are in your love and care;
and as we remember with thanksgiving N
and all those who have gone before us
  in the way of Christ
we pray that we may be counted worthy
  to share with them the life of your kingdom;
through Jesus Christ our Lord.
Amen

76 Lord Christ, you spoke words of comfort to your friends Martha and Mary in their hour of sorrow. Give consolation and courage to those who mourn today, and may they find their peace and hope in you, the Resurrection and the Life, for your tender mercies' sake.
Amen

77 Lord Jesus Christ
you are the image of the invisible God
the first-born from the dead;
in you we have redemption
  and the forgiveness of sins.

Keep us firm in this faith
setting our hearts on things above
so that, when you appear
    we too may appear with you in glory.
Amen

78 To God the Father, who loved us, and made us
    accepted in the Beloved:
To God the Son, who loved us, and loosed us from our
    sins by his own blood:
To God the Holy Spirit, who sheds the love of God
    abroad in our hearts:
To the one true God be all love and all glory for time
    and for eternity.
Amen.   **Alleluia**

79 The Priest may pronounce a blessing or the Grace may be said.

The Interment of Ashes

80   The ashes after a funeral service and cremation are placed either in a grave, or in some place set apart for the purpose.

At the place of interment one or more of the Sentences at 8 or 65 may be used.

81   This prayer is used when the place of interment is not consecrated

Almighty God, by his burial your Son Jesus Christ sanctified the grave to be a bed of hope to your people; bless this resting place for the ashes of your servant *N*, that it may be peaceful and secure; for the sake of him who died and was raised and is alive for evermore.
Amen

82   Either 83 or 84 is said as the ashes are deposited.

83   Into the Lord's most gracious mercy and protection we have entrusted our *brother N*, and we now commit *his* ashes to their resting place, in sure and certain hope of the resurrection to eternal life through our Lord Jesus Christ, who died, was buried, and rose again for us. To him be glory for ever and ever.
Amen.   **Alleluia**

or

84   We commit the ashes of our dear *brother N* to their resting place and we commend *him* to the just and merciful judgement of him who alone has perfect understanding, even Jesus Christ our Lord.
Amen

85 Let us pray

Our Father in heaven
hallowed be your Name
your kingdom come
your will be done
on earth as in heaven.
Give us today our daily bread.
Forgive us our sins
  as we forgive those who sin against us.
Save us from the time of trial
and deliver us from evil.
For the kingdom, the power, and the glory are yours
now and for ever.   Amen

86 Almighty God, grant that we, with all those who have
believed in you, may be united in the full knowledge of
your love and the unclouded vision of your glory;
through Jesus Christ our Lord.
Amen

87 **The grace of our Lord Jesus Christ, and the love of**
God, and the fellowship of the Holy Spirit be with us
all for ever.   Amen

88 Or, if a priest is present, he may pronounce a blessing.

The Dedication and Unveiling of a Tombstone

89   This is a joyous occasion. The Scripture readings and address should proclaim the Paschal Mystery and stress the Christian hope of resurrection and the communion of saints.

There shall be no speeches between sections 90 and 106.

Preferably on a day when the death of the departed is remembered at the Eucharist, the Priest and congregation assemble at the graveside.

If the Priest is unable to be present he may appoint a lay minister to conduct the service.

90   The Priest welcomes the people

**The Lord is risen
He is risen indeed, alleluia**

91   Let us pray

**Almighty God, Father of the living and the dead, we worship and adore you, we give you thanks for calling us into the communion of saints. We remember before you your servant *N*, who, like us, was baptized into the death and resurrection of your Son. Bring us all through death to life by the merits of Jesus Christ your Son our Lord, who lives and reigns with you and the Holy Spirit, one God, now and for ever.
Amen**

92   One of the following lessons or some other suitable passage is read

Genesis 28:10-22	Genesis 35:16-20
Romans 8:31-39	1 Corinthians 15:20-26

93   A short exposition of the Scripture reading may follow.

94   The tombstone is unveiled.

95 Our help is in the name of the Lord
Who has made heaven and earth

The Lord be with you
And also with you

96 **Our Father in heaven
hallowed be your Name
your kingdom come
your will be done
on earth as in heaven.
Give us today our daily bread.
Forgive us our sins
  as we forgive those who sin against us.
Save us from the time of trial
and deliver us from evil.
For the kingdom, the power, and the glory are yours
now and for ever.   Amen**

97 Let us pray

Eternal God, you hold all souls in life: shed forth upon your Church in paradise and on earth the bright beams of your light and heavenly comfort. Help us to follow the example of those who have loved and served you here on earth and are now at rest, and bring us with them into the fulness of your unending joy; through Jesus Christ our Lord.
Amen

98 Almighty God, through your only Son Jesus Christ you have overcome death and opened to us the gate of eternal life: as you put into our minds good desires, so by your continual help may we bring them to good effect; through Jesus Christ our Lord, who is alive and reigns with you and the Holy Spirit, one God, now and for ever.
Amen

99 Believing that *N* is at rest in Christ, and rejoicing in the communion of saints, we ask you, heavenly Father, to bless this stone which has been erected to *his* memory.

561

100   If the Priest is present he adds

In the name of God, Father, Son and Holy Spirit, we
dedicate this stone to the memory of *N*.
Amen

101   The service continues with one or more of the following, or prayers
from sections 107-124.

102   We praise you, heavenly Father, that nothing can separate us from your love in Christ Jesus our Lord, who
died and rose again that, awake or asleep, we may live
with him. Keep us in that love and in the sure hope of
the resurrection of the dead; through Jesus Christ our
Lord.
Amen

103   Eternal God and Father, whose love is stronger than
death: we rejoice that the dead and the living are in
your keeping. As we remember with thanksgiving
those who have gone before us in the way of Christ,
we pray that we may be counted worthy to share with
them the life of your kingdom; through Jesus Christ
our Lord.
Amen

104   Rest eternal grant unto *him* O Lord
And let light perpetual shine upon *him*

105   The following may be said

May the God of peace make you perfect and holy; and
may you all be kept safe and blameless, spirit, soul and
body, for the coming of our Lord Jesus Christ. God has
called you and he will not fail you.

106   The Priest may pronounce a blessing.

Prayers for Use at Any of the Services

The Prayers at the Eucharist

107 Almighty God, our heavenly Father, we celebrate this holy Eucharist with praise and thanksgiving for the hope of everlasting life which is ours in Christ Jesus. Keep us steadfast in this faith during the time of sorrow and bereavement.

Lord, in your mercy
Hear our prayer

We give thanks for your love reflected in *N*'s life and for the joys we have shared with *him*. Free us from all bitterness and regret.

Lord, in your mercy
Hear our prayer

We thank you that our Lord Jesus came to share our sufferings and enter into our sorrows; may all who mourn know his compassion and be filled with his peace.

Lord, in your mercy
Hear our prayer

We thank you for those who tend the sick and dying, (especially those who cared for *N*); may your gentleness and love be always revealed through them.

Lord, in your mercy
Hear our prayer

We thank you for our unity in Christ which even death cannot destroy. Increase our faith in the communion of saints.

Lord, in your mercy
Accept these our prayers for the sake of your Son, our Saviour Jesus Christ.

108 Let us pray with confidence to God our Father, who raised Christ his Son from the dead for the salvation of all. Grant, Lord, that your servant may know the fulness of life which you have promised to those who love you.

Lord, in your mercy
Hear our prayer

Be close to those who mourn: increase their faith in your undying love.

Lord, in your mercy
Hear our prayer

May we be strengthened in our faith, live the rest of our lives in following your Son, and be ready when you shall call us to the fulness of eternal life.

Lord, in your mercy
Hear our prayer

Show your mercy to the dying; strengthen them with hope, and fill them with the peace and joy of your presence.

Lord, in your mercy
Hear our prayer

Lord, we commend all those who have died to your unfailing love, that in them your will may be fulfilled; and we pray that we may share with them in your eternal kingdom; through Jesus Christ our Lord.
Amen

109 Merciful Father and Lord of all life, we praise you that we are made in your image and reflect your truth and light. We thank you for the life of your *son N*, for the love and mercy *he* received from you and showed among us. Above all, we rejoice at your gracious promise to all your servants, living and departed: that we shall rise again at the coming of Christ. And we ask that we may share with our *brother* that clearer vision, when we shall see your face in Jesus Christ our Lord.
Amen

110 Almighty God, you are the source of all good thoughts and deeds. We praise you for the life of *N*, for *his* concern for others and for *his* many acts of kindness, and we commend *him* to your love and mercy; through Jesus Christ our Lord.
Amen

111 Father of all, by whose mercy and grace your saints remain in everlasting light and peace: we remember with thanksgiving those whom we love but see no longer; and we pray that in them your perfect will may be fulfilled; through Jesus Christ our Lord.
Amen

12 Remember, O Lord, this your servant, who has gone before us with the sign of faith, and now rests in the sleep of peace. According to your promises, grant to *him* and to all who rest in Christ, refreshment, light, and peace; through Jesus Christ our Lord.
Amen

13 We commend all people to your unfailing love, that in them your will may be fulfilled; and we rejoice at the faithful witness of your saints in every age, praying that we may share with them in your eternal kingdom; through Jesus Christ our Lord.
Amen

*For one who has died after long-continued illness
or in tragic circumstances*

114 Father in heaven
you gave your Son Jesus Christ
   to suffering and death on the cross
and you raised him to life in glory.
We commend *N* to your mercy
praying that you may use for good
   the pain and agony
   the suddenness
   the violence
   of *his* death
and that your Name
   may be glorified for ever;
through Jesus Christ our Lord.
Amen

For a child

115 Father, you love all whom you have made; to you we
entrust this child. Comfort *his* parents in their grief and
uphold *his* family with your love; through Jesus Christ
your Son, our Lord.
Amen

For one with no family or close friends

116 Heavenly Father, without your knowledge no sparrow
falls to the ground. We thank you that you have
watched over *N* your *son* through *his* life and that your
unfailing love is *his* for ever.
Amen

For the bereaved

117 Heavenly Father, we pray for those who are bereaved.
May they not grieve as those who have no hope, but
believing that Jesus died and rose again, know that you
will bring with Jesus those who have fallen asleep in
him.
Amen

118 Father in heaven, you gave your Son Jesus Christ to suffering and to death on the cross, and raised him to life in glory. Grant to those who mourn a patient faith in time of darkness, and strengthen their hearts with the knowledge of your love; through Jesus Christ our Lord.
Amen

For those who care for the dying and the dead

119 Almighty Father, you caused the body of your Son to be lovingly placed in a tomb by Joseph of Arimathea. We praise you for those who care for the dying and provide for the needs of the dead. May they show compassion to the living and reverence for the mortal body you created, that in serving others they may serve Jesus Christ our Lord; who lives and reigns with you and the Holy Spirit, one God, now and for ever.
Amen

For ourselves

120 Eternal God, you hold all souls in life: shed forth upon your Church in paradise and on earth the bright beams of your light and heavenly comfort. Help us to follow the example of those who have loved and served you here on earth and are now at rest, and bring us with them into the fulness of your unending joy; through Jesus Christ our Lord.
Amen

121 O Lord, support us all the day long of this troubled life, until the shadows lengthen, and the evening comes, and the busy world is hushed, the fever of life is over, and our work is done. Then, Lord, in your mercy grant us safe lodging, a holy rest, and peace at the last; through Jesus Christ our Lord.
Amen

*For use after a miscarriage, a still birth
or the death of a new-born infant*

122 Gracious Father
in darkness and in light
in trouble and in joy
help us to trust your love
to serve your purpose
and to praise your Name;
through Jesus Christ our Lord.
Amen

123 God of loving kindness, comfort *N* (and *N*) in *their*
distress that *they* may hold to you through good and ill,
and always trust in your unfailing love; through Jesus
Christ our Lord.
Amen

124 Let us commend this child to the love of God our
Father.

Heavenly Father, by your mighty power you gave us
life, and in your love you have given us new life in
Christ Jesus. We entrust this child to your merciful
keeping, in the faith of Jesus Christ your Son our Lord,
who died and rose again to save us, and is now alive
and reigns with you and the Holy Spirit in glory for
ever.
Amen

ORDINATION

Preface

At Mount Sinai God made a covenant with the people of Israel and called them to be a kingdom of priests and a holy nation (Exodus 19:5-6). He appointed from among them a high priest together with priests and Levites to represent and lead them in the yearly round of worship and sacrifice (Numbers 3:5-10).

The Old Testament sacrifices foreshadowed the day when our Lord, the great high priest, offered himself on the cross, one single sacrifice for sins, for all time. On Calvary the faithful remnant of God's people, spoken of by the prophets, was found in just one person, our Lord Jesus Christ. The new covenant in his blood replaced the old covenant of Sinai and a new people of God was constituted from those who through baptism would be united to Christ in his death and resurrection. This new people, drawn now from every nation, is also called a holy priesthood, appointed to offer spiritual sacrifices (1 Peter 2:5) and to be a kingdom of priests to God (Revelation 1:6).

Within this priestly body God has appointed ministers exercising a variety of gifts (1 Corinthians 12). The New Testament witnesses to ministries of apostolic oversight, of pastoral care and of service which by the second century emerged as the threefold ministry of bishop, priest (presbyter) and deacon.

This pattern of ministry, with some adaptation to meet local needs and customs, continued without interruption for fourteen hundred years. At the time of the Reformation, the Church of England, from which the Anglican Communion stems, deliberately retained the threefold ministry, and this ministry is reflected in these services of ordination.

The Bishop is the minister of ordination and the Church accepts as her bishops, priests and deacons those who have been ordained by a bishop. The central act of ordination consists of the imposition of hands by a bishop, together with prayer for the Holy Spirit to give grace for the particular order being bestowed.

The Bishop is ordained to be father in the diocesan family and in the Church of God, guardian of the faith and pastor of his clergy and people; the Priest shares with him in the ministration of word and sacraments and in pastoral care; the Deacon, as the title indicates, represents the Church in the service of all who need its help.

Each order takes its place within the total ministry of the priestly people of God, called to offer praise and worship to his glory, to win the world for his kingdom, and to be a sign for all of his justice and love.

General Rubrics

1   The Ordination of Deacons and Priests is normally held on a Sunday in Embertide. If there is good reason it may take place on some other Sunday, a Festival or some other convenient day at the discretion of the Bishop.

2   It is fitting that the Archbishop or Bishop conferring Holy Orders should preside from a place near the people so that all may see what is being done.

3   The Archbishop or Bishop may at his discretion substitute other readings for those set.

The Ordination of Deacons and Priests
(also called Presbyters)

1   If deacons only are to be ordained the words 'and priest(s)' are omitted at 11 and 24 and so are sections 8-10 and 39-50 and the suffrage for priests in the Litany.

If priests only are to be ordained the words 'deacon(s) and' are omitted at 11 and 24, and so are sections 5-7 and 28-38 and the suffrage for deacons in the Litany.

Representatives of family or friends may assist in the vesting of the deacon or priest being ordained.

2   *Bishop*   **The Lord be with you**
              And also with you

3   The people remain standing. The Bishop says

Let us pray

Almighty and everlasting God, by your Spirit the whole body of your faithful people is governed and sanctified: receive our prayers which we offer before you for all members of your holy Church that in their vocation and ministry they may truly serve you; through our Lord and Saviour Jesus Christ.
Amen

4   The Sermon may be preached here or after the Gospel.

THE PRESENTATION OF DEACONS

5 The Archdeacon or other person appointed presents those to be ordained deacon, saying

Reverend Father in God, we present these persons to be ordained to the office of deacon in the Church of God.

6 The full name of each person to be ordained and that of the parish where *he* is to serve may then be given.

7 The Bishop presents the candidates to the people, and says

Those whose duty it is to inquire about these persons and examine them have found them to be of godly life and sound learning, and believe them to be duly called to serve God in this ministry. Nevertheless, if any of you know any impediment or crime in any of them, on account of which *he* should not be ordained, come forward now, and make it known.

THE PRESENTATION OF PRIESTS

8 The Archdeacon or other person appointed presents those to be ordained priest, saying

Reverend Father in God, we present these persons to be ordained to the office of priest in the Church of God.

9 The full names of each person to be ordained and that of the parish where he is to serve may then be given.

10 The Bishop presents the candidates to the people, saying

Those whose duty it is to inquire about these persons
and examine them have found them to be of godly life
and sound learning, and believe them to be duly called
to serve God in this ministry. Nevertheless, if any of
you know any impediment or crime in any of them, on
account of which he should not be ordained, come
forward now, and make it known.

11 The Bishop calls the people to prayer, saying

Respect those who are to be ordained *deacon and priest*
and hold them in high esteem and affection for the
work they do.

I commend them to your prayers.

THE LITANY

12 A minister leads the Litany during which the candidates may be
prostrate.

13 O God the Father, of heaven
Have mercy upon us

O God the Son, Redeemer of the world
Have mercy upon us

O God the Holy Spirit, proceeding from the Father
through the Son
Have mercy upon us

O holy, blessed, and glorious Trinity, three Persons
and one God
Have mercy upon us

For your holy catholic Church, that it may be filled
with truth and love, and be found without fault at the
day of your coming
Hear us, good Lord

For all members of your Church, that they may find
and follow their true vocation and ministry
Hear us, good Lord

For *N* our bishop, and for all bishops, priests and
deacons, that they may hunger for truth, thirst after
righteousness and be filled with your love
Hear us, good Lord

The Bishop offers the suffrages for the candidates and their families

> For your servants now to be made deacon, that
> they may serve your Church and reveal your
> glory in the world
> **Hear us, good Lord**

> For your servants now to be ordained priest,
> that they may be faithful shepherds of your
> flock and glorify your holy Name
> **Hear us, good Lord**

> For their homes and families, that they may be
> adorned with all Christian virtues
> **Hear us, good Lord**

For all who love and fear your holy Name, that they
may be one as you are one
Hear us, good Lord

For those who do not believe, and for those who have
lost their faith, that they may receive the light of the
gospel
Hear us, good Lord

For the nations of the world, that they may live
together in justice and peace
Hear us, good Lord

For those in positions of public trust, that they may
love justice, and promote the dignity and freedom of
every person
Hear us, good Lord

For your blessing on the life and work to which you call us, for the right use of your gifts, that the world may be freed from poverty, famine and disaster
Hear us, good Lord

For the poor and the persecuted, the sick and the suffering; for prisoners, refugees and those in danger; that they may be relieved and protected
Hear us, good Lord

From all blindness of heart; from pride, vanity and hypocrisy; from envy, hatred and malice; and from all uncharitableness
Good Lord, deliver us

From disordered and sinful affections, and from the deceits of the world, the flesh and the devil
Good Lord, deliver us

That it may please you to give us true repentance; to forgive us all our sins; and to fill us with the grace of the Holy Spirit to amend our lives according to your holy word
Hear us, good Lord

That we may so serve you in this life, that finally we lose not the life eternal
Hear us, good Lord

14 *Bishop* Almighty God, you have promised to hear those who pray in the name of your Son. Grant that what we have asked in faith we may obtain according to your will; through Jesus Christ our Lord.
Amen

15   The Minister begins the Eucharist, saying

Praise the Lord
Praise him you servants of the Lord

Blessed be God, Father, Son and Holy Spirit
Blessed be his Name, now and for ever

16   **Glory to God in the highest**
and peace to his people on earth.

Lord God, heavenly King
almighty God and Father
we worship you, we give you thanks
we praise you for your glory.

Lord Jesus Christ, only Son of the Father
Lord God, Lamb of God
you take away the sin of the world:
have mercy on us;
you are seated at the right hand of the Father:
receive our prayer.

For you alone are the Holy One
you alone are the Lord
you alone are the Most High
Jesus Christ
with the Holy Spirit
in the glory of God the Father.   **Amen**

17   The Minister may say

Let us pray

18 **Almighty God**
to whom all hearts are open
all desires known
and from whom no secrets are hid:
cleanse the thoughts of our hearts
    by the inspiration of your Holy Spirit
that we may perfectly love you
and worthily magnify your holy Name;
through Christ our Lord.

(19) Lord, have mercy
Lord, have mercy

    Christ, have mercy
    Christ, have mercy

    Lord, have mercy
    Lord, have mercy

20 The Minister exhorts the congregation to penitence in these or similar words

Let us confess our sins (firmly resolved to keep God's commandments and to live in love and peace with our neighbour).

21 Silence may be kept.

22 **Almighty God, our heavenly Father**
in penitence we confess
    that we have sinned against you
    through our own fault
in thought, word, and deed
and in what we have left undone.
For the sake of your Son, Christ our Lord
forgive us all that is past
and grant that we may serve you
    in newness of life
to the glory of your Name.

23 *Bishop* Almighty God, who forgives all who truly repent, have mercy on *you*; pardon *your* sins and set *you* free from them; confirm and strengthen *you* in all goodness and keep *you* in eternal life; through Jesus Christ our Lord.
Amen

The Collect

24 *Bishop* Let us pray

Eternal Father
through your Holy Spirit you have appointed
    many ministries in the Church:
bless those now called to be *deacon(s) and*
    priest(s)
maintain them in your truth
renew them in your holiness
and make them your ever-faithful servants;
through Jesus Christ our Lord.
Amen

THE WORD OF GOD

25 Old Testament

Isaiah 6:1-8	for deacons, for deacons and priests
Isaiah 61:1-3a	
or	for priests
Malachi 2:5-7	

Psalm

119:33-38	for deacons
145:1-7	for deacons and priests, for priests

New Testament

Romans 12:1-12	for deacons, for deacons and priests
2 Corinthians 5:14-19	for priests

Canticle

3, 15 or The Song of the Church (Morning Prayer Section 21); or a hymn

Gospel

| Mark 10:35-45 | for deacons |
| John 20:19-23 | for deacons and priests, for priests |

26 The Sermon, if not already preached, may be preached here, or after the Nicene Creed.

THE NICENE CREED

27 **We believe in one God**
the Father, the Almighty
maker of heaven and earth
of all that is, seen and unseen.

We believe in one Lord, Jesus Christ
the only Son of God
eternally begotten of the Father
God from God, Light from Light
true God from true God
begotten, not made, of one Being with the Father;
through him all things were made.
For us and for our salvation
   he came down from heaven
was incarnate of the Holy Spirit
   and the Virgin Mary
and was made man.
For our sake he was crucified under Pontius Pilate;
he suffered death and was buried.
On the third day he rose again
   in accordance with the Scriptures;
he ascended into heaven
   and is seated at the right hand of the Father.
He will come again in glory
   to judge the living and the dead
and his kingdom will have no end.

We believe in the Holy Spirit, the Lord
the giver of life
who proceeds from the Father and the Son
who with the Father and the Son is worshipped
and glorified
who has spoken through the prophets.
We believe in one holy catholic and apostolic Church.
We acknowledge one baptism for the forgiveness of
sins.
We look for the resurrection of the dead
and the life of the world to come.   Amen

THE CHARGE TO THE DEACONS

28   The people sit. The candidates stand before the Bishop, who says

My *brothers*, every Christian is called to follow Jesus
Christ, serving God the Father, through the power of
the Holy Spirit. God now calls you to a special ministry
of humble service. In the name of Jesus Christ, you are
to serve all people, and to seek out particularly the
poor, the weak, the sick and the lonely.

As a deacon in the Church you are to study the holy
Scriptures, to seek nourishment from them, and to
model your life upon them. By your word and
example, you are to make Christ and his redemptive
love known to those among whom you live and work
and worship. You are to interpret to the Church
the needs, the concerns and hopes of the world. You are
to assist the Bishop and priests in public worship and in
the administration of God's word and sacraments, and
you are to carry out other duties assigned to you from
time to time. At all times your life and teaching are to
show Christ's people that in serving those in need,
they are serving Christ himself.

THE QUESTIONS

29 The Bishop asks the candidates

My *brothers*, do you believe that you are truly called by God and his Church to the life and work of a deacon?

Answer **I believe I am so called**

Bishop Do you now in the presence of God and his Church accept this trust and responsibility?

Answer **I do**

Bishop Do you believe the holy Scriptures as uniquely revealing the word of God and containing all things necessary for eternal salvation through faith in Jesus Christ?

Answer **I do**

Bishop Will you be faithful in prayer, and in the reading and study of the holy Scriptures?

Answer **With God's help, I will**

Bishop Will you seek for Christ in others, and be ready to help them in their need?

Answer **With God's help, I will**

Bishop Will you strive to fashion your own life and that of your household, according to the way of Christ?

Answer **With God's help, I will**

Bishop Will you reverently obey your Bishop and other ministers set over you in the Lord, gladly accepting their pastoral direction and leadership?

Answer **With God's help, I will**

Bishop Will you in all things seek not your own glory but the glory of the Lord Christ?

Answer **With God's help, I will**

Bishop May the Lord by his grace uphold you in the service to which he calls you.

People **Amen**

THE ORDINATION OF DEACONS

0   The Bishop commends those to be ordained deacon to the prayers of the people and silence is kept.

1   The hymn *Veni Creator* is sung, unless priests are also to be ordained, when some other hymn or anthem to the Holy Spirit is sung at this point.

2   Come, Holy Ghost, our souls inspire,
And lighten with celestial fire;
Thou the anointing Spirit art,
Who dost thy sevenfold gifts impart.

Thy blessèd unction from above
Is comfort, life, and fire of love;
Enable with perpetual light
The dullness of our blinded sight.

Anoint and cheer our soilèd face
With the abundance of thy grace;
Keep far our foes, give peace at home;
Where thou art guide no ill can come.

Teach us to know the Father, Son,
And thee, of Both, to be but One;
That through the ages all along
This may be our endless song,

Praise to thy eternal merit,
Father, Son and Holy Spirit.   Amen

3   The candidates kneel before the Bishop; he stretches out his hands towards them, and says

We praise and glorify you, most merciful Father, because in your great love you sent your only Son Jesus Christ to take the form of a servant; he came to serve and not to be served; and taught us that he who would be great among us must be the servant of all; he humbled himself for our sake, and in obedience accepted death, even death on a cross; therefore you highly exalted him and gave him the name which is above every name.

And now we give you thanks that you have called these your servants, whom we ordain in your name, to share this ministry entrusted to your Church.

Send down the Holy Spirit upon them for the office and work of a deacon in your Church.

Almighty Father, give them grace and power to fulfil their ministry. Make them faithful to serve, ready to teach, constant in advancing your gospel; and grant that, always having full assurance of faith, abounding in hope, and being rooted and grounded in love, they may continue strong and steadfast in your Son Jesus Christ our Lord, to whom, with you and your Holy Spirit, belong glory and honour, worship and praise, now and for ever.

34 The people respond in a loud voice

Amen

35 The candidates kneel in turn before the Bishop, who lays his hands on the head of each of them, saying

N, receive the Holy Spirit for the office and work of a deacon in the Church of God; in the name of the Father, and of the Son, and of the Holy Spirit.   Amen

36 The newly-ordained deacon is vested according to custom.

37 The Bishop gives *him* the New Testament, saying

Take authority to proclaim the gospel and to assist in the administration of the sacraments.

38 The Bishop may greet the newly-ordained.

The deacons go to their place.

A hymn or anthem may be sung.

THE CHARGE TO THE PRIESTS

9   The people sit. The candidates stand before the Bishop, who says

My brothers, you stand here today as God's dear children and members of the Body of Christ. By baptism you and every member of God's Church have been called to witness to Jesus Christ as Lord of life, to proclaim him to the world and to follow in his footsteps.

When you were made deacon, you accepted the call to be servant of God and of his people. Remember that you never cease to be a deacon, and be ready to offer service wherever God calls.

Today you have come to respond to the call from God heard in your heart and confirmed by the Church, to be priest, pastor and teacher, together with your Bishop and fellow presbyters, for God's glory and the strengthening of his people. Your answer to that call is a lifetime of ministry in the following of Christ. You will only be able to maintain that response by an ever-deepening practice of prayer, enriched by daily reading and study of holy Scripture. You will depend, not on your own strength, but on the Holy Spirit of God and his grace given in word and sacrament.

You are called to make disciples, bringing them to baptism and confirmation; to lead the people in prayer; faithfully to read the Scriptures and proclaim the word of God; and to preside at the Eucharist with reverence and wonder. Like Aaron, you will bear the names of your people on your breast in intercession before the Lord. You will teach and encourage them from the Scriptures, and bless them in the name of God. You will help God's people to discover and use to his glory the gifts he has given them. Like Moses, you will gladly receive counsel and share the burden of leadership with others. In love and mercy, remembering your own frailty, you will rebuke sin, pronounce God's forgiveness to the penitent and absolve them in the name of Christ. Following the Good Shepherd, you will care for the sick, bring back those who have strayed, guide his people through this life, and prepare them for death and for the life to come, that they may be saved through Christ for ever.

This ministry will be your great joy and privilege.

It is also a weighty responsibility which none would dare to undertake except for the call from God. To you whom he calls, he will always give his strength.

THE QUESTIONS

40 The Bishop asks the candidates

> My brothers, do you believe that you are truly called by God and his Church to the life and work of a priest?

Answer **I believe I am so called**

Bishop Do you now in the presence of God and of his Church accept this trust and responsibility?

Answer **I do**

Bishop Do you believe the holy Scriptures as uniquely revealing the word of God and containing all things necessary for eternal salvation through faith in Jesus Christ?

Answer **I do**

Bishop Do you believe the doctrine of the Christian faith which this church has received, and will you expound and teach it with diligence?

Answer **I believe it and will so do**

Bishop Will you be ready to banish error in doctrine with sound teaching based on the holy Scriptures?

Answer **With God's help, I will**

Bishop Will you accept the discipline of this church, and reverently obey your Bishop and other ministers set over you in the Lord?

Answer **With God's help, I will**

Bishop Will you be diligent in prayer, in reading holy Scripture, and in all studies that will deepen your faith and fit you to overcome error by the truth of the gospel?

Answer **With God's help, I will**

Bishop Will you endeavour to minister the word of God and his sacraments with such reverence and joy that God's people may be built up in holiness and love?

Answer **With God's help, I will**

Bishop Will you help those in your care to discover and use to God's glory the gifts and ministries he gives them?

Answer **With God's help, I will**

Bishop Will you strive to fashion your own life and that of your household according to the way of Christ?

Answer **With God's help, I will**

Bishop Will you promote unity, peace and love among God's people, and in all things seek the glory of the Lord Christ?

Answer **With God's help, I will**

Bishop Come then in his strength to this ministry with joy and courage, with dedication and perseverance, determined to give yourselves wholly to this one thing, and may the Lord who has given you the will to do these things, give you the grace and strength to perform them.

People **Amen**

THE ORDINATION OF PRIESTS

41   The Bishop commends those who are to be ordained priest to the prayers of the people and silence is kept.

42   The hymn *Veni Creator* is sung

Come, Holy Ghost, our souls inspire,
And lighten with celestial fire;
Thou the anointing Spirit art,
Who dost thy sevenfold gifts impart.

Thy blessèd unction from above
Is comfort, life, and fire of love;
Enable with perpetual light
The dullness of our blinded sight.

Anoint and cheer our soilèd face
With the abundance of thy grace;
Keep far our foes, give peace at home;
Where thou art guide no ill can come.

Teach us to know the Father, Son,
And thee, of Both, to be but One;
That through the ages all along
This may be our endless song,

    Praise to thy eternal merit,
    Father, Son and Holy Spirit.   Amen

43   The Bishop stands with the priests who assist him; the candidates kneel before him; he stretches out his hands towards them, and says

We praise and glorify you, almighty Father, because you have formed throughout the world a holy people for your own possession, a royal priesthood, a universal Church.

We praise and glorify you because you have given us your only Son Jesus Christ to be the Apostle and High Priest of our faith, and the Shepherd of our souls.

We praise and glorify you that by his death he has overcome death; and that, having ascended into heaven, he has given his gifts abundantly, making some, apostles; some, prophets; some, evangelists; some, pastors and teachers; to equip your people for the work of ministry and to build up his Body.

And now we give you thanks that you have called these your servants, whom we ordain in your name, to share this ministry entrusted to your Church.

Send down the Holy Spirit upon them for the office and work of a priest in your Church.

Almighty Father, give them grace and power to fulfil their ministry among those committed to their charge; to watch over them and care for them; to absolve and bless them in your name, and to proclaim the gospel of your salvation. Set them among your people to offer with them spiritual sacrifices acceptable in your sight and to minister the sacraments of the new covenant. As you have called them to your service, make them worthy of their calling. Give them wisdom and discipline to work faithfully with all their fellow-servants in Christ, that the world may come to know your glory and your love.

Accept our prayers, most merciful Father, through your Son Jesus Christ our Lord, to whom, with you and your Holy Spirit, belong glory and honour, worship and praise, now and for ever.

4 The people respond in a loud voice

Amen

45 The candidates kneel in turn before the Bishop. He and the priests who assist him lay their hands on the head of each of them, and he says

N, receive the Holy Spirit for the office and work of a priest in the Church of God, now committed to you by the laying on of our hands. Whose sins you forgive, they are forgiven; whose sins you retain, they are retained. Be a faithful minister of the word of God and of his holy sacraments: in the name of the Father, and of the Son, and of the Holy Spirit. Amen

46 The newly-ordained priest is vested according to custom.

47 The Bishop may anoint his palms with chrism saying

As the Father anointed his Son with the power of the Spirit, so may Jesus Christ preserve you to sanctify his people and to offer sacrifices of praise and thanksgiving.

48 The Bishop gives him the Bible, saying

Take authority to preach the word of God and to administer his holy sacraments.

49 The Bishop may also give him a chalice and paten.

50 The Bishop may greet the newly-ordained.

The priests go to their place.

THE PEACE

51 The Bishop says

The Son of Man came not to be served but to serve, and to give his life a ransom for many.

52 The peace of the Lord be with you always
Peace be with you

3 The Peace is given according to local custom.

4 The newly-ordained priests may join the Bishop at the Lord's table for the Eucharistic celebration.

5 The Bishop continues the Eucharist from the Presentation of Gifts using the following

The Proper Preface

And now we give you thanks because within the royal priesthood of your Church you ordain ministers to proclaim the word of God, to care for your people, to equip them for the work of ministry and to celebrate the sacraments of the new covenant.

The Post-Communion Prayer (in the place of section 87 in the Eucharist)

Almighty and eternal God, we thank you for feeding us with the body and blood of your Son, our Saviour Jesus Christ, and for uniting us in the Body of your Son, the company of all faithful people.

We thank you for raising up among us those whom we have now ordained for the ministry of your word and sacraments. Give them holiness of life, wisdom and gentleness in their ministry, and perseverance in prayer; through Jesus Christ our Lord.
Amen

The Blessing

God the Holy Trinity make you strong in faith and love, defend you on every side, and keep you in truth and peace; and the blessing of God almighty, the Father, the Son, and the Holy Spirit, be among you, and remain with you always.
Amen

593

The Ordination and Consecration of a Bishop

56   At the Presentation *NN* implies that the full names of the bishop are given; elsewhere *N* indicates the name by which he is to be known in the diocese.

The Oath of Allegiance is omitted at the consecration of an archbishop.

The suffrage for the diocesan bishop in the Litany is omitted when a diocesan bishop is consecrated in his own diocese.

The Archbishop presides. If need arise his place may be taken by a bishop duly appointed.

At least two other bishops lay hands on the Bishop-elect with the Archbishop.

57   The Archbishop begins the Eucharist.

58   The following collect is used

Eternal Father
through your Holy Spirit you have appointed
    many ministries in the Church:
bless your servant *N* now called to be a bishop
maintain him in your truth
renew him in your holiness
and make him your ever-faithful servant;
through Jesus Christ our Lord.
Amen

59   For the Word of God the following are used

Old Testament Lesson   Isaiah 6:1-8

Psalm   100

New Testament Lesson   2 Corinthians 4:1-10

Canticle 3   or a hymn

Gospel   John 21: 15-17

0 The Sermon may precede or follow the Nicene Creed. After the Creed or Sermon there follows

THE PRESENTATION

1 Two bishops present the Bishop-elect to the Archbishop and say

Most Reverend Father in God, we present *NN* to be ordained and consecrated bishop in the Church of God.

2 The Oath of Allegiance to the Archbishop is taken and the Canonical Declaration is made.

THE LITANY

3 A minister leads the Litany during which the Bishop-elect may be prostrate.

4 O God the Father, of heaven
Have mercy upon us

O God the Son, Redeemer of the world
Have mercy upon us

O God the Holy Spirit, proceeding from the Father through the Son
Have mercy upon us

O holy, blessed, and glorious Trinity, three Persons and one God
Have mercy upon us

For your holy catholic Church, that it may be filled with truth and love, and be found without fault at the day of your coming
Hear us, good Lord

For all members of your Church, that they may find and follow their true vocation and ministry
Hear us, good Lord

For *N* our bishop, and for all bishops, priests and deacons, that they may hunger for truth, thirst after righteousness and be filled with your love
Hear us, good Lord

The Archbishop offers the following two suffrages for the Bishop-elect and his family

> For your servant *N*, now to be consecrated bishop, that by the indwelling of your Spirit he may grow in holiness and serve your people in wisdom, truth and love
> **Hear us, good Lord**

> For his home and family, that they may be adorned with all Christian virtues
> **Hear us, good Lord**

For all who love and fear your holy Name, that they may be one as you are one
Hear us, good Lord

For those who do not believe, and for those who have lost their faith, that they may receive the light of the gospel
Hear us, good Lord

For the nations of the world, that they may live together in justice and peace
Hear us, good Lord

For those in positions of public trust, that they may love justice, and promote the dignity and freedom of every person
Hear us, good Lord

For your blessing on the life and work to which you call us, for the right use of your gifts, that the world may be freed from poverty, famine and disaster
Hear us, good Lord

For the poor and the persecuted, the sick and the suffering; for prisoners, refugees and those in danger; that they may be relieved and protected
Hear us, good Lord

From all blindness of heart; from pride, vanity and hypocrisy; from envy, hatred and malice; and from all uncharitableness
Good Lord, deliver us

From disordered and sinful affections, and from the deceits of the world, the flesh and the devil
Good Lord, deliver us

That it may please you to give us true repentance; to forgive us all our sins; and to fill us with the grace of the Holy Spirit to amend our lives according to your holy word
Hear us, good Lord

That we may so serve you in this life, that finally we lose not the life eternal
Hear us, good Lord

65 *Archbishop* Almighty God, you have promised to hear those who pray in the name of your Son. Grant that what we have asked in faith we may obtain according to your will; through Jesus Christ our Lord.
Amen

THE CHARGE

66 The Archbishop addresses the Bishop-elect

Jesus, who is Prophet, Priest and King, has called you to share in his work of sanctifying and shepherding his people, and of speaking in God's name.

My brother, you are to teach and interpret the truth as it is in Christ Jesus, to further the unity of the Church, to banish error, to proclaim the demands of justice and to lead God's people in their mission to the world. You will not do this on your own, for as a bishop among your fellow bishops you will represent the diocese to the wider Church and the wider Church to the diocese.

In a life of prayer you will seek God's blessing in all you do; you will baptize and confirm; you will preside at the Eucharist, lead your people in worship, and intercede for those committed to your charge. Those who are weak will be your special concern.

You will endeavour with a shepherd's love to exercise, with wisdom and mercy, the authority and oversight entrusted you by Christ our King. It is your responsibility and your joy to ordain deacons and priests and to send forth other ministers. You will guide and encourage those who share your ministry of building up the people of God.

No one is sufficient for these things. May the God who makes us able ministers of the new covenant equip you with his grace and give you his blessing and joy.

THE QUESTIONS

67 The Archbishop asks the Bishop-elect

Do you accept this call to be a bishop, believing it to be the will of our Lord Jesus Christ?

Answer **I do**

Archbishop Will you as shepherd and leader of his people faithfully fulfil this trust and obey our Lord Jesus Christ in your ministry?

Answer **With God's help, I will**

Archbishop Do you believe the faith of our Lord Jesus Christ as taught in the holy Scriptures, held by the undivided Church and declared in the catholic creeds?

Answer   **I do**

Archbishop Will you devote yourself to prayer, to reading the holy Scriptures, and to such studies as may deepen your faith and increase your love for God?

Answer   **With God's help, I will**

Archbishop Will you teach and proclaim the gospel of Christ and declare its meaning to the world?

Answer   **With God's help, I will**

Archbishop Will you accept the discipline of this church and faithfully exercise authority within it?

Answer   **With God's help, I will**

Archbishop Will you be faithful in ordaining and commissioning those whom you believe God has called, and will you constantly guide, support and encourage them in their ministries?

Answer   **With God's help, I will**

Archbishop Will you strive to fashion your own life and that of your household according to the way of Christ?

Answer   **With God's help, I will**

Archbishop Will you for Christ's sake be gentle and merciful to all, and defend those who have no helper?

Answer   **With God's help, I will**

Archbishop Almighty God who gives you the will to do all these things, grant you grace and power to perform them, that he may complete the good work he has begun in you, through Jesus Christ our Lord.

People   **Amen**

THE ORDINATION

68   The Archbishop calls the people to prayer, and silence is kept.

69   The hymn *Veni Creator* is sung

Come, Holy Ghost, our souls inspire,
and lighten with celestial fire;
Thou the anointing Spirit art,
Who dost thy sevenfold gifts impart.

Thy blessèd unction from above
Is comfort, life, and fire of love;
Enable with perpetual light
The dullness of our blinded sight.

Anoint and cheer our soilèd face
With the abundance of thy grace;
Keep far our foes, give peace at home;
Where thou art guide no ill can come.

Teach us to know the Father, Son,
And thee, of Both, to be but One;
That through the ages all along
This may be our endless song,

    Praise to thy eternal merit,
    Father, Son and Holy Spirit.   Amen

70   The Archbishop stands together with the bishops who assist him. The Bishop-elect kneels before the Archbishop, who stretches out his hands and says

We praise and glorify you, almighty Father, because you have formed throughout the world a holy people for your own possession, a royal priesthood, a universal Church.

We praise and glorify you because you have given us your only Son Jesus Christ to be the Apostle and High Priest of our faith, and the Shepherd of our souls.

We praise and glorify you that by his death he has overcome death; and that, having ascended into heaven, he has given his gifts abundantly to your people, making some, apostles; some, prophets; some, evangelists; some, pastors and teachers; to equip them for the work of ministry and to build up his Body.

And now we give you thanks that you have called this your servant, whom we consecrate in your name, to share this ministry entrusted to your Church.

Send down the Holy Spirit upon him for the office and work of a bishop in your Church.

Almighty Father, fill him with the grace and power which you gave to your apostles, that he may lead those committed to his charge in proclaiming the gospel of salvation. Through him increase your Church, renew its ministry, and unite its members in a holy fellowship of truth and love. Enable him as a true shepherd to feed and govern your flock; make him wise as a teacher, and steadfast as a guardian of its faith and sacraments. Guide and direct him in presiding at the worship of your people. Give him humility, that he may use his authority to heal, not to hurt; to build up, not to destroy. Defend him from all evil, that as a ruler over your household and an ambassador for Christ he may stand before you blameless, and finally, with all your servants, enter your eternal joy.

Accept our prayers, most merciful Father, through your Son Jesus Christ our Lord, to whom, with you and your Holy Spirit, belong glory and honour, worship and praise, now and for ever.

71   The people respond in a loud voice

Amen

72   The Archbishop and the bishops assisting lay their hands on the head
of the Bishop-elect, and the Archbishop says

N, receive the Holy Spirit for the office and work of a
bishop in the Church of God, now committed to you
by the laying on of our hands; in the name of the
Father, and of the Son, and of the Holy Spirit. Amen.
Remember to stir up the grace of God which is within
you, for God has not given us a spirit of fear, but of
power and of love and of a sound mind.

73   The new bishop is now vested according to the order of bishops.

THE GIVING OF THE BIBLE

74   The Archbishop presents the new bishop with the Bible, saying

Receive the holy Scriptures. Guard the faith of the
Church, and feed by word and sacrament the flock of
Christ committed to your charge.

THE GIVING OF CROSS, RING AND STAFF

75   The Archbishop gives the new bishop the pectoral cross, saying

Receive this cross; remember that he whom you serve
reconciled us by his own blood.

76   The Archbishop gives him the ring, saying

Take this ring; be merciful in your exercise of authority, and be faithful to the bride of Christ.

77   The Archbishop may give him the mitre, saying

Receive this mitre, and in the strength of the Holy
Spirit lay hold on the crown of everlasting life.

78   The Archbishop presents him with a pastoral staff, saying

Take this staff and watch over the flock of Christ.

79   The collation and the enthronement of a diocesan bishop may follow; a bishop suffragan may receive his commission.

80   A fanfare may sound and the people may express their joy by clapping or in some other manner.

THE PEACE

81   The Archbishop says

Hear the words of the risen Christ: as the Father has sent me, even so I send you.

82   **The peace of the Lord be with you always**
Peace be with you

83   The Peace is given according to local custom.

84   The Archbishop continues the Eucharist from the Presentation of Gifts, using this Proper Preface

And now we give you thanks because within the royal priesthood of your Church you ordain ministers to proclaim the word of God, to care for your people, to equip them for the work of ministry and to celebrate the sacraments of the new covenant.

85 This prayer may precede the Blessing

God our Father,
shepherd and guide of all your faithful people:
look with favour on *N* your servant
whom you have chosen to be a pastor over your
    Church;
and grant that by word and example
    he may lead the people committed to his charge
and with them come to your eternal kingdom;
through Jesus Christ our Lord.
Amen

86 The newly-consecrated Bishop gives the Blessing

Almighty God stir up in you the gifts of his grace and
sustain each one of you in your own ministry; and the
blessing of God Almighty, the Father, the Son, and the
Holy Spirit, be among you, and remain with you
always.
Amen

87 The Archbishop dismisses the people

Go in peace to love and serve the Lord
In the name of Christ.   Amen

THE PSALMS

A NOTE ON CHANTING

The psalms and canticles are pointed for singing to Anglican chants. In good chanting the rhythm and sense of the words are of paramount importance and should be similar to good deliberate speaking, with a natural flexible flow, free from monotony and exaggeration.

| in the text corresponds with a bar line in the chant.

· between two words or syllables shows the division of notes within the bar.

* shows where a breath should be taken. A shorter break, or 'mental comma', made without taking a breath, is indicated by an extra space between words. Breath is to be taken at the end of lines except when the pointing clearly forbids it, or when ‿ is used to indicate a carry-over to the following line.

† indicates the use of the second half of a double chant.

Verses between square brackets may be omitted.

A double space between verses indicates a change of mood in the psalm.

The following notes, for congregations and choirs alike, may assist towards good chanting:

From time to time it is good practice to read aloud together in a deliberate manner to establish the natural flow of the phrases. Then some of the singers should chant softly while the others continue to read.

The recitation portion in each verse (before the first bar line) should not be hurried. Particular care should be taken not to distort the two syllables before the first bar line.

A final unstressed syllable of a verse should be sung lightly.

Prepositions and conjunctions should generally be sung lightly.

Single syllable words vary in length and importance, unimportant ones should be sung lightly. Long words should be given due spaciousness and rhythm. In good chanting the words always sound fluent and natural.

PSALM 1

1 Blessèd is the man who has not walked ⌣
    in the counsel ǀ of the · unǀgodly:
  nor followed the way of sinners
    nor taken his ǀ seat aǀmongst the ǀ scornful.

2 But his delight is in the ǀ law · of the ǀ Lord:
  and on that law will he ǀ ponder ǀ day and ǀ night.

3 He is like a tree planted beside ǀ streams of ǀ water:
  that yields its ǀ fruit in ǀ due ǀ season.

4 Its leaves also ǀ shall not ǀ wither:
  and look   whatǀever · he ǀ does · it shall ǀ prosper.

5 As for the ungodly * it is not ǀ so with ǀ them:
  they are like the ǀ chaff · which the ǀ wind ǀ scatters.

6 Therefore the ungodly shall not stand ǀ up · at the ǀ judgment:
  nor sinners in the congreǀgation ǀ of the ǀ righteous.

†7 For the Lord cares for the ǀ way · of the ǀ righteous:
  but the ǀ way of · the unǀgodly · shall ǀ perish.

PSALM 2

1 Why are the ǀ nations · in ǀ tumult:
  and why do the peoples ǀ cherish · a ǀ vain ǀ dream?

2 The kings of the earth rise up
    and the rulers conǀspire toǀgether:
  against the Lord and aǀgainst · his anǀointed ǀ saying,

†3 'Let us break their ǀ bonds aǀsunder:
  let us throw ǀ off their ǀ chains ǀ from us.'

4 He that dwells in heaven shall ǀ laugh them · to ǀ scorn:
  the Lord will ǀ hold them ǀ in deǀrision.

5 Then will he speak to them in his wrath
    and terrify them ǀ in his ǀ fury:
  'I the Lord have set up my king on ǀ Zion · my ǀ holy ǀ hill.'

6 I will announce the Lord's decree
    that which I he has I spoken:
    'You are my son   this I day have I be|gotten you.

7 'Ask of me   and I will give you the nations for I
    your in|heritance:
    the uttermost parts of the I earth for I
    your pos|session.

†8 'You shall break them with a I rod of I iron:
    and shatter them in I pieces · like a I potter's I vessel.'

9 Now therefore be I wise O I kings:
    be advised   you that are I judges I of the I earth.

10 Serve the Lord with awe
    and govern yourselves in I fear and I trembling:
    lest he be angry and you I perish I in your I course.

†11 For his wrath is I quickly I kindled:
    blessèd are those that I turn to I him for I refuge.

PSALM 3

1 Lord how numerous I are my I enemies:
    many they I are that I rise a|gainst me.

2 Many there are that I talk of me · and I say:
    'There is no I help for · him I in his I God.'

3 But you Lord are about me I as a I shield:
    you are my glory   and the I lifter I up · of my I head.

4 I cry to the Lord with a I loud I voice:
    and he answers me I from his I holy I hill.

5 I lay myself I down and I sleep:
    I wake again be|cause the I Lord sus|tains me.

6 Therefore I will not be afraid _
    of the multitudes I of the I nations:
    who have set themselves a|gainst me · on I every I
    side.

7 Arise Lord   and deliver me I O my I God:
    for you will strike all my enemies upon the cheek
    you will I break the I teeth of · the un|godly.

8 Deliverance be⏐longs · to the ⏐ Lord:
  O let your ⏐ blessing · be up⏐on your ⏐ people.

PSALM 4

1 Answer me when I call O ⏐ God of · my ⏐
    righteousness:
  when I was hard-pressed you set me free
    be gracious to me ⏐ now and ⏐ hear my ⏐ prayer.

2 Sons of men   how long will you turn my ⏐ glory ·
    to my ⏐ shame:
  how long will you love what is worthless
    and ⏐ seek ⏐ after ⏐ lies?

3 Know that the Lord has shown me his ⏐ wonder·ful ⏐
    kindness:
  when I call to the ⏐ Lord ⏐ he will ⏐ hear me.

4 Tremble and ⏐ do no ⏐ sin:
  commune with your own heart up⏐on your ⏐ bed ·
    and be ⏐ still.

5 Offer the sacrifices ⏐ that are ⏐ right:
  and ⏐ put your ⏐ trust · in the ⏐ Lord.

6 There are many who say   'Who will ⏐ show us · any ⏐
    good?:
  the light of your countenance O ⏐ Lord has ⏐ gone ⏐
    from us.'

7 Yet you have given my ⏐ heart more ⏐ gladness:
  than they have when their corn ⏐ wine and ⏐
    oil in⏐crease.

8 In peace I will lie ⏐ down and ⏐ sleep:
  for you alone Lord ⏐ make me ⏐ dwell in ⏐ safety.

PSALM 5

1 Hear my words O Lord   give ⏐ heed · to my ⏐ groaning:
  listen to my cry   you that are my ⏐ king ⏐ and my ⏐
    God.

2 In the morning when I pray to you
    surely you will ⏐ hear my ⏐ voice:
  at daybreak I lay my prayers be⏐fore you · and ⏐ look ⏐
    up.

3 For you are not a God who takes | pleasure · in |
    wickedness:
    nor can any | evil | dwell with | you.

4 The boastful cannot | stand in · your | sight:
    you hate all | those that | work | mischief.

5 Those who speak | lies · you des|troy:
    you abhor the treacherous O Lord
    and | those · that are | stained with | blood.

6 But because of your great goodness ⌣
    I will | come into · your | house:
    I will bow down toward your holy |
    temple · in | awe and | fear of you.

7 Lead me O Lord in your righteousness
    for my enemies | lie in | wait:
    make | straight your | way be|fore me.

8 For there is no | truth · in their | mouth:
    and within they are | eaten | up by | malice.

9 Their throat is an | open | sepulchre:
    and their tongue speaks | smooth and | flatter·ing |
    words.

10 Destroy them O God * let them fall by their |
    own con|triving:
    cast them out for their many offences
    for | they have · re|belled a|gainst you.

11 But let all who put their trust in | you re|joice:
    let them | shout with | joy for | ever.

12 Be the defender of those who | love your | name:
    let them ex|ult be|cause of | you.

†13 For you will bless O Lord the | man · that is | righteous:
    you will cover him with your | favour | as · with a |
    shield.

PSALM 6

1 O Lord rebuke me not in your | indig|nation:
nor chasten me | in your | fierce dis|pleasure.

2 Have mercy upon me O Lord for | I am | weak:
O Lord heal me for my | very | bones · are a|fraid.

3 My soul also is | greatly | troubled:
and you Lord how | long will | you de|lay?

4 Turn again O Lord and de|liver · my | soul:
O save me | for your | mercy's | sake.

5 For in death | no man · re|members you:
and who can | give you | thanks · from the | grave?

6 I am wearied | with my | groaning:
every night I drown my bed with weeping
and | water · my | couch · with my | tears.

†7 My eyes waste a|way for | sorrow:
they grow dim be|cause of | all my | enemies.

8 Away from me all | you that · do | evil:
for the Lord has | heard the | voice · of my | weeping.

9 The Lord has heard my | suppli|cation:
the | Lord · will re|ceive my | prayer.

†10 All my enemies shall be put to shame and | greatly ·
dis|mayed:
they shall turn back and be con|founded | in a |
moment.

PSALM 7

1 O Lord my God   to you have I | come for | shelter:
save me from all who pursue me * O | save | and
de|liver me,

2 Lest like lions they | tear my | throat:
lest they carry me | off and | none can | save me.

3 O Lord my God   if I have | done · such a | thing:
if there is any | wicked·ness | on my | hands,

4 If I have repaid with evil him that | was my | friend:
or plundered my | enemy · with|out just | cause,

†5 Then let the enemy pursue me and I over|take me:
    let him trample my life to the ground
      and lay my I honour I in the I dust.

6 Arise O I Lord · in your I anger:
    rise up in I wrath a|gainst my I adversaries.

7 Awake my God * you that or|dain I justice:
    and let the assembly of the I peoples I
      gather · a|bout you;

8 Take your seat I high a|bove them:
    and sit in judgment O I Lord I over · the I nations.

9 Judge for me O Lord   according I to my I righteousness:
    and I as · my in|tegrity · re|quires.

10 Let the wickedness of the ungodly cease
      but es|tablish · the I righteous:
    for you try the very hearts and minds of I men ‿
      O I righteous I God.

11 God is my I shield I over me:
    he pre|serves the I true of I heart.

12 God is a I righteous I judge:
    and God condemns I evil I every I day.

13 If a man does not turn he I whets his I sword:
    he bends his I bow and I makes it I ready;

†14 He prepares the I instruments · of I death:
    and makes his I arrows I darts of I fire.

15 See how the ungodly con|ceives I mischief:
    how he swells with wickedness I and gives I birth to I
    lies.

16 He digs a pit and I hollows · it I out:
    but falls himself into the I trap · he had I made for I
    others.

17 His mischief rebounds upon his I own I head:
    and his violence comes I down · on his I own I pate.

18 I will thank the I Lord · for his I justice:
    I will sing I praises · to the I Lord Most I High.

PSALM 8

1 O | Lord our | Governor:
    how glorious is your | name in | all the | earth!

2 Your majesty above the heavens is | yet re|counted:
    by the | mouths of | babes and | sucklings.

†3 You have founded a strong defence ⌣
     a|gainst your | adversaries:
    to quell the | ene·my | and · the a|venger.

4 When I consider your heavens the | work of · your |
     fingers:
    the moon and the stars which | you have | set in |
     order,

5 What is man   that you should be | mindful | of him:
    or the son of | man that | you should | care for him?

6 Yet you have made him little | less · than a | god:
    and have | crowned him · with | glory · and | honour.

7 You have made him the | master · of your | handiwork:
    and have put all things in sub|jection · be|neath his |
     feet,

8 All | sheep and | oxen:
    and all the | creatures | of the | field,

9 The birds of the air and the | fish · of the | sea:
    and everything that moves ⌣
     in the pathways | of the | great | waters.

†10 O | Lord our | Governor:
    how glorious is your | name in | all the | earth!

PSALM 9

1 I will give you thanks O Lord with my | whole | heart:
    I will tell of all the | wonders | you have | done.

2 I will re|joice · and be | glad in you:
    I will make my songs to your | name | O Most | High.

3 For my enemies are | driven | back:
    they stumble and | perish | at your | presence.

4 You have maintained my I cause · and my I right:
   you sat enIthroned · as a I righteous I judge.

5 You rebuked the heathen nations
         you brought the I wicked · to deIstruction:
      you blotted out their I name for I ever · and I ever.

6 The strongholds of the enemy are made a perpetual I
         desoIlation:
      you plucked up their cities _
      and I even · their I memory · has I perished.

7 The Lord confounds them * but the Lord enIdures for I
         ever:
      he has I set up · his I throne for I judgment.

8 He shall judge the I world with I righteousness:
      and deal true I justice I to the I peoples.

9 The Lord is a strong tower to I him that · is opIpressed:
      he is a tower of I strength in I time of I need.

10 All who heed your name will I trust in I you:
      for you have never forIsaken I those that I seek you.

11 O sing praises to the Lord who I dwells in I Zion:
      tell among the peoples what I great things I he has I
         done.

12 For he that avenges blood has reImembered · the I poor:
      he has I not forIgotten · their I cry.

13 The Lord has been merciful toward me
         he saw what I I suffered · from my I foes:
      he raised me up aIgain · from the I gates of I death,

14 That I might tell all your praises in the I gates of I Zion:
      that I might reIjoice in I your deIliverance.

15 The nations have sunk into the pit they I dug for I
         others:
      in the very snare they I laid · is their I foot I taken;

16 The Lord has declared himself and upIheld the I right:
      the wicked are trapped in the I work · of their I own I
         hands.

17 The wicked shall be given ǀ over · to ǀ death:
　　and all the nations ǀ that forǀget ǀ God.

18 For the needy shall not always ǀ be forǀgotten:
　　nor shall the hope of the ǀ poor ǀ perish · for ǀ ever.

19 Arise Lord　let not ǀ man preǀvail:
　　let the ǀ nations · be ǀ judged beǀfore you.

20 Put them in ǀ fear O ǀ Lord:
　　and let the nations ǀ know · that they ǀ are but ǀ men.

PSALM 10

1 Why do you stand far ǀ off O ǀ Lord:
　　why do you hide your ǀ face in ǀ time of ǀ need?

2 The ungodly in their pride ǀ persecute · the ǀ poor:
　　let them be caught in the ǀ schemes they ǀ have
　　deǀvised.

3 For the ungodly man boasts of his ǀ heart's deǀsire:
　　he grasps at profit　he ǀ spurns ·
　　and blasǀphemes the ǀ Lord.

4 He says in his arrogance ǀ 'God will · not aǀvenge':
　　'There is no ǀ God' is ǀ all his ǀ thought.

5 He is settled in ǀ all his ǀ ways:
　　your statutes O Lord are far above him ǀ ＿
　　and he ǀ does not ǀ see.

6 He snorts defiance at his enemies
　　he says in his heart 'I shall ǀ never · be ǀ shaken:
　　I shall walk seǀcure from ǀ any · man's ǀ curse.'

7 His mouth is full of opǀpression · and deǀceit:
　　mischief and ǀ wickedness · lie ǀ under · his ǀ tongue.

8 He skulks aǀbout · in the ǀ villages:
　　and ǀ secret·ly ǀ murders · the ǀ innocent.

9 His eyes watch ǀ out · for the ǀ helpless:
　　he lurks conǀcealed · like a ǀ lion · in a ǀ thicket.

10 He lies in wait to ǀ seize up·on the ǀ poor:
　　he lays hold on the poor man and ǀ drags him ǀ off ·
　　in his ǀ net.

11 The upright are crushed and I humbled · beIfoIre him:
    and the helpless I fall inIto his I power.

12 He says in his heart I 'God · has forIgotten:
    he has covered his I face and I sees I nothing.'

13 Arise O Lord God   lift I up your I hand:
    forIget · not the I poor for I ever.

14 Why should the wicked man I spurn I God:
    why should he say in his heart I 'He will I not
      aIvenge'?

15 Surely you see the I trouble · and the I sorrow:
    you look on   and will take it I into · your I own I
      hands.

16 The helpless commits himIself to I you:
    for you are the I helper I of the I fatherless.

†17 Break the I power of · the unIgodly:
    search out his wickedness I till · it is I found no I more.

18 The Lord is king for I ever · and I ever:
    the heathen have I perished I from his I land.

19 You have heard the longing of the I meek O I Lord:
    you turned your I ear · to their I hearts' deIsire,

†20 To help the poor and fatherless I to their I right:
    that men may no more be I terri·fied I from their I
      land.

PSALM 11

1 In the Lord I have I found my I refuge:
    how then can you say to me I
      'Flee · like a I bird · to the I mountains;

2 'Look how the wicked bend their bows
    and notch the arrow upIon the I string:
    to shoot from the I darkness · at the I true of I heart;

3 'If the foundations I are desItroyed:
    what I can the I just man I do?'

4 The Lord is in his holy place
  the Lord is en|throned in | heaven:
  his eyes search out
  his glance | tries the | children · of | men.

5 He tries the | righteous · and the | wicked:
  and him that delights in | violence · his | soul ab|hors.

6 He will rain down coals of fire and brimstone ⌣
  up|on the | wicked:
  a scorching wind shall | be their | cup to | drink.

†7 For the Lord is righteous and loves | righteous | acts:
  the | upright · shall | see his | face.

PSALM 12

1 Help Lord   for there is not one | godly · man | left:
  the faithful have vanished from a|mong the |
    children · of | men.

2 Everyone tells | lies · to his | neighbour:
  they flatter with their lips ⌣
  but | speak · from a | double | heart.

3 If only the Lord would cut off all | flatter·ing | lips:
  and the | tongue that | speaks so | proudly!

4 They say   'By our tongues we | shall pre|vail:
  our lips are our servants   who is | lord | over | us?'

5 Because of the oppression of the poor
  because of the | groaning · of the | needy:
  'I will arise' says the Lord * 'and set them in safety ⌣
  from | those that | snarl | after them.'

6 The words of the Lord are pure
  as silver re|fined · in a | crucible:
  as gold that is seven times | puri·fied | in the | fire.

7 You will surely | guard us · O | Lord:
  and shield us for ever from this | evil | gener|ation,

8 Though the ungodly strut on | every | side:
  though the vilest of men have | master·y |
    of man|kind.

PSALM 13

1 How long O Lord will you so ǀ utterly · forǀget me:
　　how long will you ǀ hide your ǀ face ǀ from me?

2 How long must I suffer anguish in my soul
　　　and be so grieved in my heart ǀ day and ǀ night:
　　how long shall my ǀ ene·my ǀ triumph ǀ over me?

3 Look upon me O Lord my ǀ God and ǀ answer me:
　　lighten my ǀ eyes · lest I ǀ sleep in ǀ death;

4 Lest my enemy say　'I have preǀvailed aǀgainst him':
　　lest my foes exǀult ǀ at my ǀ overthrow.

5 Yet I put my trust in your unǀfailing ǀ love:
　　O let my heart reǀjoice in ǀ your salǀvation.

6 And I will make my ǀ song · to the ǀ Lord:
　　because he ǀ deals so ǀ bounti·fully ǀ with me.

PSALM 14

1 The fool has said in his heart 'There ǀ is no ǀ God':
　　they have all become vile and abominable in their ‿
　　　doings　there ǀ is not ǀ one that · does ǀ good.

2 The Lord looked down from heaven upon the ǀ
　　　children · of ǀ men:
　　to see if there were any who would act ǀ wisely ·
　　　and ǀ seek · after ǀ God.

†3 But they have all turned out of the way
　　　they have all alike beǀcome corǀrupt:
　　there is none that does ǀ good ǀ no not ǀ one.

4 Are all the evildoers devoid of ǀ underǀstanding:
　　who eat up my people as men eat bread ‿
　　　and ǀ do not ǀ pray · to the ǀ Lord?

5 They shall be ǀ struck with ǀ terror:
　　for God is with the ǀ compa·ny ǀ of the ǀ righteous.

6 Though they frustrate the poor man ǀ in his ǀ hopes:
　　surely the ǀ Lord ǀ is his ǀ refuge.

7 O that deliverance for Israel might come ⏐ forth from ⏐
  Zion:
  when the Lord turns again the fortunes of his people
   then shall Jacob re⏐joice and ⏐ Israel · be ⏐ glad.

PSALM 15

1 Lord who may a⏐bide in · your ⏐ tabernacle:
  or who may dwell up⏐on your ⏐ holy ⏐ hill?

2 He that leads an uncorrupt life
   and does the ⏐ thing · which is ⏐ right:
  who speaks the truth from his heart
   and has not ⏐ slandered ⏐ with his ⏐ tongue;

3 He that has done no evil ⏐ to his ⏐ fellow:
  nor vented a⏐buse a⏐gainst his ⏐ neighbour;

4 In whose eyes the worthless ⏐ have no ⏐ honour:
  but he makes much of ⏐ those that ⏐ fear the ⏐ Lord;

5 He that has ⏐ sworn · to his ⏐ neighbour:
  and will ⏐ not go ⏐ back · on his ⏐ oath;

6 He that has not put his ⏐ money · to ⏐ usury:
  nor taken a ⏐ bribe a⏐gainst the ⏐ innocent.

†7 He that ⏐ does these ⏐ things:
  shall ⏐ never · be ⏐ over⏐thrown.

PSALM 16

1 Preserve ⏐ me O ⏐ God:
  for in ⏐ you · have I ⏐ taken ⏐ refuge.

2 I have said to the Lord ⏐ You are ⏐ my lord:
  and all my ⏐ good de⏐pends on ⏐ you.

3 As for those who are held ⏐ holy · on the ⏐ earth:
  the other ⏐ gods · in whom ⏐ men de⏐light,

4 Though the idols are many that ⏐ men run ⏐ after:
  their offerings of blood I will not offer
   nor take their ⏐ name up⏐on my ⏐ lips.

5 The Lord is my appointed portion ⏐ and my ⏐ cup:
  you ⏐ hold my ⏐ lot · in your ⏐ hands.

6 The share that has fallen to me is in | pleasant | places:
   and a fair | land is | my pos|session.

7 I will bless the Lord who has | given · me | counsel:
   at night also | he · has in|structed · my | heart.

8 I have set the Lord | always · be|fore me:
   he is at my right | hand · and I | shall not | fall.

†9 Therefore my heart is glad and my | spirit · re|joices:
   my flesh | also · shall | rest se|cure.

10 For you will not give me over to the | power of | death:
   nor suffer your | faithful one · to | see the | Pit.

11 You will show me the | path of | life:
   in your presence is the fulness of joy * and from __
   your right hand flow de|lights for | ever|more.

PSALM 17

1 Hear my just cause O Lord give | heed to · my | cry:
   listen to my prayer that | comes from · no | lying |
   lips.

2 Let judgment for me come | forth from · your | presence:
   and let your | eyes dis|cern the | right.

3 Though you search my heart   and visit me | in the |
   night-time:
   though you try me by fire   you will | find no |
   wicked·ness | in me.

4 My mouth does not transgress like the | mouth of |
   others:
   for I have | kept the | word of · your | lips.

†5 My steps have held firm in the way of | your
   com|mands:
   and my feet have not | stumbled | from your | paths.

6 I call upon you O God for you will | surely | answer:
   incline your ear to | me and | hear my | words.

7 Show me the wonders of your steadfast love
   O saviour of those who come to | you for | refuge:

    who by your right hand deliver them ‿
      from | those that · rise | up a|gainst them.

8 Keep me as the | apple · of your | eye:
   hide me under the | shadow | of your | wings,

9 From the onslaught | of the | wicked:
   from my enemies that en|circle me · to | take my |
   life.

10 They have closed their | hearts to | pity:
    and their | mouths speak | proud | things.

11 They advance upon me * they surround me on | every |
    side:
    watching how they may | bring me | to the | ground,

†12 Like a lion that is | greedy · for its | prey:
    like a lion's whelp | lurking · in | hidden | places.

13 Arise O Lord * stand in their way and | cast them |
    down:
    deliver me from the | wicked | by your | sword.

[14 Slay them by your hand O Lord
    slay them so that they | perish · from the | earth:
    de|stroy them · from a|mong the | living.]

15 But as for your cherished ones   let their bellies be ‿
    filled and let their | sons be | satisfied:
    let them pass on their | wealth | to their | children.

(†)16 And I also shall see your face   because my | cause is |
    just:
    when I awake and see you as you | are I | shall be |
    satisfied.

PSALM 18

1 I love you O | Lord my | strength:
   O Lord my crag my | fortress · and | my de|liverer,

2 My God   the rock to which I | come for | refuge:
   my shield my mighty saviour | and my | high
   de|fence.

†3 I called to the Lord with I loud · lamenItation:
and I was I rescued I from my I enemies.

4 The waves of I death enIcompassed me:
and the floods of I chaos I overIwhelmed me;

5 The cords of the grave I tightened · aIbout me:
and the snares of I death lay I in my I path.

6 In my anguish I I called · to the I Lord:
I cried for I help I to my I God.

7 From his temple he I heard my I voice:
and my cry came I even I to his I ears.

8 The earth heaved and quaked
the foundations of the I hills were I shaken:
they I trembled · beIcause · he was I angry.

9 Smoke went I out · from his I nostrils:
and a consuming I fire I from his I mouth.

10 He parted the heavens and I came I down:
and there was I darkness I under · his I feet.

11 He rode upon the I cherubim · and I flew:
he came swooping upIon the I wings · of the I wind.

12 He made the I darkness · his I covering:
and his canopy was thick I cloud and I water·y I
darkness.

13 Out of his clouds   from the I brightness · beIfore him:
broke I hailstones · and I coals of I fire.

14 The Lord I thundered · in the I heavens:
the Most I High I uttered · his I voice.

15 He let loose his arrows
he scattered them on I every I side:
he hurled down I lightnings · with the I roar · of the I
thunderbolt.

16 The springs of the I sea · were unIcovered:
and the foundIations · of the I world laid I bare,

17 At your reIbuke O I Lord:
at the blast of the I breath of I your disIpleasure.

18 He reached down from on | high and | took me:
   he drew me | out of · the | great | waters.

19 He delivered me from my | strongest | enemy:
   from my |foes · that were | mightier · than | I.

20 They confronted me in the | day of · my cal|amity:
   but the | Lord was | my up|holder.

21 He brought me out into a | place of | liberty:
   and rescued me be|cause · I de|lighted · his | heart.

22 The Lord rewarded me for my | righteous | dealing:
   he recompensed me according to the | cleanness |
      of my | hands,

23 Because I had kept to the | ways · of the | Lord:
   and had not turned from my | God to | do | evil.

24 For I had an eye to | all his | laws:
   and did not | put · his com|mandments | from me.

25 I was also | blameless · be|fore him:
   and I kept my|self from | wrong|doing.

†26 Therefore the Lord re|warded · my | innocence:
   because my hands were | unde|filed · in his | sight.

27 With the faithful you | show your·self | faithful:
   with the | blameless · you | show your·self | blameless;

28 With the | pure · you are | pure:
   but with the | crookèd · you | show yourself ·
      per|verse.

29 For you will save a | humble | people:
   but you bring down the | high looks | of the | proud.

30 You light my lamp O | Lord my | God:
   you make my | darkness | to be | bright.

†31 For with your help I can charge a | troop of | men:
   with the help of my God I can | leap a | city | wall.

32 The way of our God is perfect
      the word of the Lord has been | tried · in the | fire:
   he is a shield to | all that | trust in | him.

623

33 For who is ǀ God · but the ǀ Lord:
  or who is our ǀ rock ǀ but our ǀ God?

34 It is God that ǀ girded me · with ǀ strength:
  that ǀ made my ǀ way ǀ perfect.

35 He made my feet like the ǀ feet · of a ǀ hind:
  and set me sureǀfooted · upǀon the ǀmountains.

36 He taught my ǀ hands to ǀ fight:
  and my arms to ǀ aim an ǀ arrow · of ǀ bronze.

37 You gave me the shield of ǀ your salǀvation:
  your right hand upheld me
    and your swift reǀsponse has ǀ made me ǀ great.

38 You lengthened my ǀ stride beǀneath me:
  and my ǀ ankles ǀ did not ǀ slip.

39 I pursued my enemies and ǀ overǀtook them:
  nor did I turn again ǀ till · I had ǀ made an ǀ
    end of them.

40 I smote them till they could ǀ rise no ǀ more:
  and they ǀ fell beǀneath my ǀ feet.

41 You girded me with ǀ strength · for the ǀ battle:
  you threw ǀ down my ǀ adver·saries ǀ under me.

42 You caused my enemies to ǀ show their ǀ backs:
  and I deǀstroyed ǀ those that ǀ hated me.

43 They cried for help   but there was ǀ none to ǀ save
    them:
  they cried to the ǀ Lord · but he ǀ would not ǀ answer.

44 I pounded them fine as dust beǀfore the ǀ wind:
  I trod them under ǀ like the ǀ mire · of the ǀ streets.

45 You delivered me from the strife of the peoples
    you made me the ǀ head · of the ǀ nations:
  a people that I had not ǀ known beǀcame my ǀ
    servants.

46 As soon as they heard me ǀ they oǀbeyed me:
  and aliens ǀ humbled · themǀselves beǀfore me.

47 The strength of the aliens ǀ withered · aǀway:
  they came ǀ falter·ing ǀ from their ǀ strongholds.

48 The Lord lives ‖ and blessèd ‖ be my ‖ rock:
    exalted be the ‖ God of ‖ my sal‖vation,

49 The God who sees to it that ‖ I am · a‖venged:
    who sub‖dues the ‖ peoples ‖ under me.

50 You set me free from my enemies
    you put me out of ‖ reach of · my at‖tackers:
    you de‖livered me · from ‖ vio·lent ‖ men.

51 For this will I give you thanks among the ‖ nations · O ‖ Lord:
    and sing ‖ praises ‖ to your ‖ name,

†52 To him that gives great triumphs ‖ to his ‖ king:
    that deals so faithfully with his anointed
    with David and ‖ with his ‖ seed for ‖ ever.

PSALM 19

1 The heavens declare the ‖ glory · of ‖ God:
    and the ‖ firmament · pro‖claims his ‖ handiwork;

2 One day ‖ tells it · to an‖other:
    and night to ‖ night com‖muni·cates ‖ knowledge.

3 There is no ‖ speech or ‖ language:
    nor ‖ are their ‖ voices ‖ heard;

4 Yet their sound has gone out through ‖ all the ‖ world:
    and their ‖ words · to the ‖ ends · of the ‖ earth.

5 There he has pitched a ‖ tent · for the ‖ sun:
    which comes out as a bridegroom from his chamber
    and rejoices like a ‖ strong · man to ‖ run his ‖ course.

6 Its rising is at one end of the heavens
    and its circuit to their ‖ farthest ‖ bound:
    and nothing is ‖ hidden ‖ from its ‖ heat.

7 The law of the Lord is perfect re‖viving · the ‖ soul:
    the command of the Lord is true ‖ _
    and makes ‖ wise the ‖ simple.

8 The precepts of the Lord are right _
    and re‖joice the ‖ heart:

the commandment of the Lord is pure I ⌣
  and gives I light · to the I eyes.

9 The fear of the Lord is clean and enIdures for I ever:
  the judgments of the Lord are unchanging ⌣
    and I righteous I every I one.

10 More to be desired are they than gold
      even I much fine I gold:
    sweeter also than honey
      than the I honey · that I drips · from the I comb.

11 Moreover by them is your I servant I taught:
  and in keeping them I there is I great reIward.

12 Who can know his own unIwitting I sins?:
  O cleanse me I from my I secret I faults.

13 Keep your servant also from presumptuous sins
      lest they get the I master·y I over me:
    so I shall be clean and I innocent · of I great ofIfence.

14 May the words of my mouth and the meditation of my
      heart   be acceptable I in your I sight:
    O Lord my I strength and I my reIdeemer.

PSALM 20

1 May the Lord hear you in the I day of I trouble:
  the God of Jacob I lift you I up to I safety.

2 May he send you his I help · from the I sanctuary:
  and be your I strong supIport from I Zion.

3 May he remember I all your I offerings:
  and accept with I favour · your I burnt I sacrifices,

4 Grant you your I heart's deIsire:
  and fulIfil I all your I purposes.

†5 May we also rejoice in your victory
      and triumph in the I name of · our I God:
    the Lord perIform all I your peItitions.

6 Now I know that the Lord will I save · his aInointed:
    that he will answer him from his holy heaven
      with the victorious I strength · of his I right I hand.

7 Some put their trust in chariots and | some in | horses:
    but we will trust in the | name · of the | Lord our |
      God.

8 They are brought | down and | fallen:
    but we are made | strong and | stand | upright.

9 O Lord | save the | king:
    and hear us | when we | call up|on you.

PSALM 21

1 The king shall rejoice in your | strength O | Lord:
    he shall ex|ult in | your sal|vation.

2 You have given him his | heart's de|sire:
    you have not de|nied him · the re|quest · of his | lips.

3 For you came to meet him with the | blessings ·
      of suc|cess:
    and placed a crown of | gold up|on his | head.

4 He asked you for | life · and you | gave it him:
    length of | days for | ever · and | ever.

5 Great is his glory because of | your sal|vation:
    you have | clothed him · with | honour · and | majesty.

6 You have given him ever|lasting · fe|licity:
    and made him | glad · with the | joy of · your |
      presence.

†7 For the king puts his | trust · in the | Lord:
    and through the tender mercy of the Most High | ⌣
    he shall | never · be | moved.

8 Your hand shall light up|on your | enemies:
    and your right hand shall | find out | all who |
      hate you.

9 You will make them like a blazing furnace ⌣
    in the | day of · your | coming:
    the Lord will overwhelm them in his wrath ⌣
    and | fire | shall con|sume them.

10 You will root out their offspring | from the | earth:
    and their seed from a|mong the | children · of | men;

11 Because they have stirred up I evil · algainst you:
and plotted mischief I which they I cannot ·
perlform.

12 Therefore will you set your I shoulder · tolward them:
and draw the string of the I bow to I strike at · their I
faces.

13 Arise O Lord in your I great I strength:
and we will I sing and I praise your I power.

PSALM 22

1 My God my God   why have I you forlsaken me:
why are you so far from helping me
and from the I words I of my I groaning?

2 My God I cry to you by day   but you I do not I answer:
and by night I also · I I take no I rest.

3 But you conltinue I holy:
you that I are the I praise of I Israel.

4 In you our I fathers I trusted:
they I trusted · and I you dellivered them;

5 To you they cried and I they were I saved:
they put their trust in you I and were I
not conlfounded.

6 But as for me   I am a worm and I no I man:
the scorn of I men · and delspised · by the I people.

7 All those that see me I laugh me · to I scorn:
they shoot out their lips at me and I wag their I heads I
saying,

8 'He trusted in the Lord   I let him · delliver him:
let him delliver him · if I he dellights in him.'

9 But you are he that took me I out of · the I womb:
that brought me to lie at I peace · on my I mother's I
breast.

10 On you have I been cast I since my I birth:
you are my God I even · from my I mother's I womb.

11 O go not from me   for trouble is I hard at I hand:
and I there is I none to I help.

12 Many I oxen · surIround me:
      fat bulls of Bashan close me I in on I every I side.

13 They gape I wide their I mouths at me:
      like I lions · that I roar and I rend.

14 I am poured out like water
         and all my bones are I out of I joint:
      my heart within my I breast · is like I melting I wax.

15 My mouth is dried I up · like a I potsherd:
      and my I tongue I clings · to my I gums.

16 My hands and my I feet are I withered:
      and you I lay me · in the I dust of I death.

17 For many dogs are I come aIbout me:
      and a band of evilIdoers I hem me I in.

18 I can count I all my I bones:
      they stand I staring · and I gazing · upIon me.

19 They part my I garments · aImong them:
      and cast I lots I for my I clothing.

20 O Lord do not I stand far I off:
      you are my helper   I hasten I to my I aid.

21 Deliver my I body · from the I sword:
      my I life · from the I power · of the I dogs;

22 O save me from the I lion's I mouth:
      and my afflicted soul from the I horns · of the I wild I
         oxen.

23 I will tell of your I name · to my I brethren:
      in the midst of the congreIgation I will I I praise you.

24 O praise the Lord all I you that I fear him:
      hold him in honour O seed of Jacob
         and let the seed of I Israel I stand in I awe of him.

†25 For he has not despised nor abhorred ⌣
         the poor man I in his I misery:
      nor did he hide his face from him
         but I heard him I when he I cried.

26 From you springs my praise in the I great ·
         congreIgation:
      I will pay my vows in the I sight of I all that I fear you;

27 The meek shall eat of the sacrifice | and be | satisfied:
   and those who seek the Lord shall praise him
      may their | hearts re|joice for | ever!

28 Let all the ends of the earth remember ⌣
      and | turn · to the | Lord:
   and let all the families of the | nations | worship ·
      be|fore him.

29 For the kingdom | is the | Lord's:
   and he shall be | ruler | over · the | nations.

30 How can those who sleep in the earth | do him | homage:
   or those that descend to the | dust bow | down
      be|fore him?

31 But he has saved my | life · for him|self:
   and | my pos|terity · shall | serve him.

†32 This shall be told of my Lord to a future | gener|ation:
   and his righteousness declared ⌣
      to a people yet un|born   that | he has | done it.

PSALM 23

1 The Lord | is my | shepherd:
   therefore | can I | lack | nothing.

2 He will make me lie down in | green | pastures:
   and | lead me · be|side still | waters.

3 He will re|fresh my | soul:
   and guide me in right pathways | for his | name's |
      sake.

4 Though I walk through the valley of the shadow of ⌣
      death   I will | fear no | evil:
   for you are with me
      your | rod · and your | staff | comfort me.

5 You spread a table before me
      in the face of | those who | trouble me:
   you have anointed my head with oil | and my | cup ·
      will be | full.

6 Surely your goodness and loving-kindness ⌣
      will follow me * all the | days · of my | life:
   and I shall dwell in the | house · of the | Lord for |
      ever.

PSALM 24

1 The earth is the Lord's and | all · that is | in it:
   the compass of the | world and | those who | dwell
   therein.

2 For he has founded it up|on the | seas:
   and es|tablished it · up|on the | waters.

3 Who shall ascend the | hill · of the | Lord:
   or who shall | stand · in his | holy | place?

4 He that has clean hands and a | pure | heart:
   who has not set his soul upon idols
   nor | sworn his | oath · to a | lie.

5 He shall receive | blessing · from the | Lord:
   and recompense from the | God of | his sal|vation.

6 Of such a kind as this are | those who | seek him:
   those who seek your | face O | God of | Jacob.

7 Lift up your heads O you gates
   and be lifted up you ever|lasting | doors:
   and the King of | glory | shall come | in.

8 Who is the | King of | glory?:
   the Lord strong and mighty * the | Lord | mighty · in |
   battle.

9 Lift up your heads O you gates
   and be lifted up you ever|lasting | doors:
   and the King of | glory | shall come | in.

10 Who is the | King of | glory?:
   the Lord of hosts | he · is the | King of | glory.

PSALM 25

1 In you O Lord my God have I | put my | hope:
   in you have I trusted   let me not be ashamed
   nor let my | ene·mies | triumph | over me.

2 Let none who wait for you be | put to | shame:
   but let those that break faith _
   be con|founded · and | gain | nothing.

3 Show me your | ways O | Lord:
   and | teach me | your | paths.

4 Lead me in the ways of your I truth and I teach me:
　　for you are the I God of I my salIvation.

5 In you have I hoped I all the · day I long:
　　beIcause of · your I goodness · O I Lord.

6 Call to mind your compassion and your I loving-
　　　IkindIness:
　　for I they are I from of I old.

7 Remember not the sins of my youth nor I
　　　my transIgressions:
　　but according I to your I mercy I think on me.

8 Good and upright I is the I Lord:
　　therefore will he direct I sinners I in the I way.

†9 The meek he will guide in the I path of I justice:
　　and I teach the I humble · his I ways.

10 All the paths of the Lord are I faithful · and I true:
　　for those who keep his I covenant · and I his
　　　comImandments.

11 For your name's I sake O I Lord:
　　be merciful to my I sin　though I it is I great.

12 Who is he that I fears the I Lord?:
　　him will the Lord direct in the I way that I he should I
　　　choose.

13 His soul shall I dwell at I ease:
　　and his I children · shall inIherit · the I land.

14 The confidences of God belong to I those that I fear him:
　　and his covenant shall I give them I underIstanding.

15 My eyes are ever I looking · to the I Lord:
　　for he will bring my I feet I out of · the I net.

16 Turn your face toward me I and be I gracious:
　　for I I am · aIlone · and in I misery.

17 O free my I heart from I pain:
　　and bring me I out of I my disItress.

18 Give heed to my afIfliction · and adIversity:
　　and forIgive me I all my I sins.

19 Consider my enemies how I many · they I are:
and they bear a I vio·lent I hate aIgainst me.

20 O keep my I life · and deIliver me:
put me not to shame　for I I come to I you for I refuge.

21 Let innocence and integrity I be my I guard:
for in I you I have I I hoped.

†22 O God deIliver I Israel:
out of I all his I tribuIlation.

PSALM 26

1 Give judgment for me O Lord
for I have walked in I my inItegrity:
I have trusted in the I Lord and I not I wavered.

2 Put me to the test O I Lord and I prove me:
try my I mind I and my I heart.

3 For your steadfast love has been ever beIfore my I eyes:
and I I have I walked in · your I truth.

4 I have not I sat · with deIceivers:
nor conIsorted I with the I hypocrites;

5 I hate the asIsembly · of the I wicked:
I will not I sit I with the · unIgodly.

6 I wash my hands in I innocence · O I Lord:
that I may I go aIbout your I altar,

†7 And lift up the I voice of I thanksgiving:
to tell of I all your I marvel·lous I works.

8 Lord I love the house of your I habitIation:
and the I place · where your I glory I dwells.

9 Do not sweep me aIway with I sinners:
nor my I life with I men of I blood,

10 In whose hand is aIbominIation:
and their right I hand is I full of I bribes.

11 As for me　I walk in I my inItegrity:
O ransom me I and be I favourable · toIward me.

†12 My foot stands on an I even I path:
I will bless the I Lord · in the I great · congreIgation.

PSALM 27

1 The Lord is my light and my salvation
    whom then I shall I I fear?:
  the Lord is the stronghold of my life
    of whom I shall I I be aIfraid?

2 When the wicked   even my enemies and my foes
    come upon me I to deIvour me:
  they shall I stumble I and I fall.

3 If an army encamp against me
    my heart shall I not · be aIfraid:
  and if war should rise aIgainst me I yet · will I I trust.

4 One thing I have asked from the Lord which I I
    will reIquire:
  that I may dwell in the house of the Lord I ⏜
    all the I days · of my I life,

†5 To see the fair I beauty · of the I Lord:
  and to I seek his I will · in his I temple.

6 For he will hide me under his shelter in the I day of I
    trouble:
  and conceal me in the shadow of his tent
    and set me I high upIon a I rock.

7 And now he will lift I up my I head:
  above my I ene·mies I round aIbout me.

†8 And I will offer sacrifices in his sanctuary with I
    exulItation:
  I will sing   I will sing I praises I to the I Lord.

9 O Lord hear my I voice · when I I cry:
  have I mercy · upIon me · and I answer me.

10 My heart has said of you I 'Seek his I face':
  your I face Lord I I will I seek.

11 Do not I hide your I face from me:
  or thrust your I servant · aIside · in disIpleasure;

12 For you have I been my I helper:
  do not cast me away or forsake me O I God of I
    my salIvation.

†13 Though my father and my | mother · for|sake me:
    the |Lord will | take me | up.

14 Teach me your | way O | Lord:
    and lead me in an even path | for they | lie in | wait for
       me.

15 Do not give me over to the | will of · my | enemies:
    for false witnesses have risen against me
       and | those who | breathe out | violence.

16 But I believe that I shall surely see the |
       goodness · of the | Lord:
    in the | land | of the | living.

17 O wait for the Lord   stand firm and he will |
       strengthen · your | heart:
    and | wait I | say · for the | Lord.

PSALM 28

1 To you will I cry O Lord my Rock
    be not | deaf · to my | prayer:
    lest if you turn away silent
       I become like those that go | down | to the | grave.

2 Hear the voice of my supplication ‿
    when I cry to | you for | help:
    when I lift up my hands ‿
       towards the | holi·est | place of · your | sanctuary.

3 Do not snatch me away with the ungodly
    with the | evil|doers:
    who speak peace to their neighbours
       but nourish | malice | in their | hearts.

4 Repay them ac|cording · to their | deeds:
    and according to the | wickedness · of |
       their en|deavours;

5 Requite them for the | work · of their | hands:
    and | give them | their de|serts.

6 For they pay no heed to the Lord's acts
    nor to the operation | of his | hands:
    therefore shall he break them | down · and not |
       build them | up.

7 Let the Lord's | name be | praised:
   for he has heard the | voice · of my | suppli|cation.

8 The Lord is my strength and my shield
      in him my heart trusts and | I am | helped:
   therefore my heart dances for joy
      and in my | song | will I | praise him.

9 The Lord is the | strength · of his | people:
   and a sure refuge for | his an|ointed | king.

10 O save your people * and give your | blessing · to your |
      own:
   be their shepherd and | bear them | up for | ever.

PSALM 29

1 Ascribe to the Lord you | sons of | heaven:
   ascribe to the | Lord | glory · and | might.

2 Ascribe to the Lord the honour | due · to his | name:
   O worship the Lord in the | beauty | of his | holiness.

3 The voice of the Lord is up|on the | waters:
   the God of glory thunders   the Lord up|on the |
      great | waters.

4 The voice of the Lord is mighty in | oper|ation:
   the voice of the | Lord · is a | glori·ous | voice.

5 The voice of the Lord | breaks the | cedar-trees:
   the Lord breaks in | pieces · the | cedars · of | Lebanon.

6 He makes them | skip · like a | calf:
   Lebanon and Sirion | like a | young wild | ox.

7 The voice of the Lord di|vides the | lightning-flash:
   the voice of the Lord whirls the sands of the desert
      the Lord | whirls the | desert · of | Kadesh.

8 The voice of the Lord rends the terebinth trees
      and strips | bare the | forests:
   in his | temple | all cry | 'Glory'.

9 The Lord sits enthroned a|bove the | water-flood:
   the Lord sits en|throned · as a | king for | ever.

10 The Lord will give | strength · to his | people:
   the Lord will give to his | people · the | blessing · of |
      peace.

PSALM 30

1 I will exalt you O Lord
   for you have drawn me ǀ up · from the ǀ depths:
  and have not suffered my ǀ foes to ǀ triumph ǀ
   over me.

2 O Lord my ǀ God I ǀ cried to you:
  and ǀ you have ǀ made me ǀ whole.

†3 You brought me back O Lord from the ǀ land of ǀ silence:
   you saved my life ⌣
   from among ǀ those that · go ǀ down · to the ǀ Pit.

4 Sing praises to the Lord all ǀ you his ǀ faithful ones:
  and give ǀ thanks · to his ǀ holy ǀ name.

5 For if in his anger is havoc
   in his good ǀ favour · is ǀ life:
  heaviness may endure for a night
   but ǀ joy comes ǀ in the ǀ morning.

6 In my prosperity I said   'I shall ǀ never · be ǀ moved:
   your goodness O Lord has ǀ set me · on so ǀ firm a ǀ
   hill.'

7 Then you ǀ hid your ǀ face from me:
  and ǀ I was ǀ greatly · disǀmayed.

8 I cried to ǀ you O ǀ God:
  and made my petition ǀ humbly ǀ to my ǀ Lord.

9 'What profit is there in my blood
   if I go ǀ down · to the ǀ Pit:
  can the dust give you thanks ǀ ⌣
   or deǀclare your ǀ faithfulness?

†10 'Hear O ǀ Lord · and be ǀ merciful:
  O ǀ Lord ǀ be my ǀ helper.'

11 You have turned my lamentation ǀ into ǀ dancing:
  you have put off my sackcloth and ǀ girded ǀ me with ǀ
  joy,

12 That my heart may sing your praise and ǀ never · be ǀ
  silent:
  O Lord my God   I will ǀ give you ǀ thanks for ǀ ever.

PSALM 31

1 To you Lord have I I come for I shelter:
    let me I never · be I put to I shame.

2 •O deliver me I in your I righteousness:
    incline your ear to me I and be I swift to I save me.

3 Be for me a rock of refuge   a fortress I to deIfend me:
    for you are my I high rock I and my I stronghold.

4 Lead me and guide me for your I name's I sake:
    bring me out of the net that they have secretly _
        laid for me * for I you I are my I strength.

5 Into your hands I comImit my I spirit:
    you will redeem me I O Lord I God of I truth.

6 I hate those that I clutch vain I idols:
    but my I trust is I in the I Lord.

7 I will rejoice and be glad in your I loving-Ikindness:
    for you have looked on my distress
        and I known me I in adIversity.

8 You have not given me over to the I power · of the I
        enemy:
    you have set my feet where I I may I walk at I liberty.

9 Have mercy upon me O Lord   for I I am · in I trouble:
    my eye wastes away for grief
        my throat also I and my I inward I parts.

10 For my life wears out in sorrow _
        and my I years with I sighing:
    my strength fails me in my affliction
        and my I bones I are conIsumed.

11 I am become the scorn of I all my I enemies:
    and my neighbours I wag their I heads · in deIrision.

12 I am a thing of I horror · to my I friends:
    and those that see me in the I street I shrink I from me.

13 I am forgotten like a dead man I out of I mind:
    I have beIcome · like a I broken I vessel.

14 For I hear the I whispering · of I many:
    and I fear · is on I every I side;

15 While they plot to|gether · a|gainst me:
　　and scheme to | take a|way my | life.

16 But in you Lord have I | put my | trust:
　　I have said　| 'You |are my | God.'

17 All my days are | in your | hand:
　　O deliver me from the power of my | enemies ·
　　　and | from my | persecutors.

18 Make your face to shine up|on your | servant:
　　and save me | for your | mercy's | sake.

19 O Lord let me not be confounded ⌣
　　　for I have | called up|on you:
　　but let the wicked be put to shame
　　　and brought to | silence | in the | grave.

20 Let the lying | lips be | dumb:
　　that in pride and contempt ⌣
　　　speak such | insolence · a|gainst the | just.

21 O how plentiful is your goodness
　　　stored up for | those that | fear you:
　　and prepared in the sight of men
　　　for all who | come to | you for | refuge.

22 You will hide them in the cover of your presence ⌣
　　　from the | plots of | men:
　　you will shelter them in your refuge | ⌣
　　　from the | strife of | tongues.

23 Blessèd be the | Lord our | God:
　　for he has wonderfully shown me his steadfast love
　　　when I was | as a | city · be|sieged.

24 When I was afraid I | said in · my | haste:
　　'I am | cut off | from your | sight.'

25 But you heard the voice of my | supplic|ation:
　　when I | cried to | you for | help.

26 Love the Lord all | you his | faithful ones:
　　for the Lord guards the true
　　　but | fully · re|quites the | proud.

+27 Be strong　and let your | heart take | courage:
　　all | you that | hope · in the | Lord.

PSALM 32

1 Blessèd is he whose I sin · is for|given:
      whose in|iquity · is I put a|way.

2 Blessèd is the man to whom the Lord im|putes no I
          blame:
      and in whose I spirit · there I is no I guile.

3 For whilst I I held my I tongue:
      my bones wasted a|way · with my I daily ·
          com|plaining.

4 Your hand was heavy upon me I day and I night:
      and my moisture was dried I up · like a I drought in I
          summer.

5 Then I ack|nowledged · my I sin to you:
      and my in|iquity · I I did not I hide;

6 I said   'I will confess my trans|gressions · to the I Lord':
      and so you forgave the I wicked·ness I of my I sin.

7 For this cause shall everyone that is faithful _
          make his prayer to you * in the I day of I trouble:
      and in the time of the great water-floods I _
          they shall I not come I near him.

8 You are a place to hide me in
          you will pre|serve me · from I trouble:
      you will surround me with de|liverance · on I every I
          side.

9 'I will instruct you
          and direct you in the way that I you should I go:
      I will fasten my eye up|on you · and I give you I
          counsel.

10 'Be not like horse or mule that have no I under|standing:
      whose forward course must be I curbed with I bit and I
          bridle.'

11 Great tribulations remain I for the · un|godly:
      but whoever puts his trust in the Lord
          mercy em|braces him · on I every I side.

12 Rejoice in the Lord you righteous I and be I glad:
      and shout for joy all I you · that are I true of I heart.

PSALM 33

1 Rejoice in the | Lord you | righteous:
  for it be|fits the | just to | praise him.

2 Give the Lord thanks up|on the | harp:
  and sing his praise to the | lute of | ten | strings.

3 O sing him a | new | song:
  make sweetest | melody · with | shouts of | praise.

4 For the word of the | Lord is | true:
  and | all his | works are | faithful.

5 He loves | righteousness · and | justice:
  the earth is filled with the loving-|kindness | of the |
  Lord.

6 By the word of the Lord were the | heavens | made:
  and their numberless | stars · by the | breath of · his |
  mouth.

7 He gathered the waters of the sea as | in a | water-skin:
  and laid up the | deep | in his | treasuries.

8 Let the whole earth | fear the | Lord:
  and let all the inhabitants of the | world | stand in |
  awe of him.

9 For he spoke and | it was | done:
  he commanded | and it | stood | fast.

10 The Lord frustrates the | counsels · of the | nations:
   he brings to nothing the de|vices | of the | peoples.

11 But the counsels of the Lord shall en|dure for | ever:
   the purposes of his heart from gener|ation · to |
   gener|ation.

12 Blessèd is that nation whose | God · is the | Lord:
   the people he chose to | be his | own pos|session.

13 The Lord looks down from heaven
       and surveys all the | children · of | men:
   he considers from his dwelling-place ⌣
       all the in|habit·ants | of the | earth;

14 He who fashioned the | hearts of · them | all:
   and compre|hends all | that they | do.

15 A king is not saved by a ǀ mighty ǀ army:
     nor is a warrior deǀlivered · by ǀ much ǀ strength;

16 A horse is a vain hope to ǀ save a ǀ man:
     nor can he rescue ǀ any · by his ǀ great ǀ power.

17 But the eye of the Lord is on ǀ those that ǀ fear him:
     on those that trust in ǀ his unǀfailing ǀ love,

18 To deǀliver them · from ǀ death:
     and to ǀ feed them · in the ǀ time of ǀ dearth.

19 We have waited eagerly ǀ for the ǀ Lord:
     for ǀ he is · our ǀ help · and our ǀ shield.

20 Surely our hearts shall reǀjoice in ǀ him:
     for we have ǀ trusted · in his ǀ holy ǀ name.

†21 Let your merciful kindness be upǀon us · O ǀ Lord:
     even as our ǀ hope ǀ is in ǀ you.

PSALM 34

1 I will bless the ǀ Lord conǀtinually:
     his praise shall be ǀ always ǀ in my ǀ mouth.

2 Let my soul ǀ boast · of the ǀ Lord:
     the humble shall ǀ hear it ǀ and reǀjoice.

3 O praise the ǀ Lord with ǀ me:
     let us exǀalt his ǀ name toǀgether.

4 For I sought the Lord's ǀ help · and he ǀ answered:
     and he ǀ freed me · from ǀ all my ǀ fears.

5 Look towards him and be ǀ bright with ǀ joy:
     your ǀ faces · shall ǀ not · be aǀshamed.

6 Here is a wretch who cried and the ǀ Lord ǀ heard him:
     and ǀ saved him · from ǀ all his ǀ troubles.

7 The angel of the Lord encamps round ǀ those who ǀ
        fear him:
     and deǀlivers · them ǀ in their ǀ need.

8 O taste and see that the ǀ Lord is ǀ good:
     happy the ǀ man who ǀ hides in ǀ him!

9 Fear the Lord all I you his I holy ones:
   for those who I fear him I never I lack.

10 Lions may suffer I want · and go I hungry:
   but those who seek the I Lord lack I nothing I good.

11 Come my children   I listen · to I me:
   and I will I teach you · the I fear · of the I Lord.

12 Which of you I relish·es I life:
   wants I time · to enIjoy good I things?

13 Keep your I tongue from I evil:
   and your I lips from I telling I lies.

14 Turn from evil and I do I good:
   seek I peace I and purIsue it.

15 The eyes of God are I on the I righteous:
   and his I ears toIwards their I cry.

16 The Lord sets his face against I wrongIdoers:
   to root out their I memo·ry I from the I earth.

17 The righteous cry   the I Lord I hears it:
   and I frees them · from I all · their afIflictions.

18 The Lord is close to those who are I broken-Ihearted:
   and the I crushed in I spirit · he I saves.

19 The trials of the I righteous · are I many:
   but our God deIlivers · him I from them I all.

20 He guards I all his I bones:
   so I that not I one is I broken.

21 Evil will I slay the I wicked:
   and those who hate the I righteous · will I be
   deIstroyed.

22 The Lord ransoms the I lives · of his I servants:
   and none who hide in I him will I be deIstroyed.

PSALM 35

1 Contend O Lord with those who conItend with I me:
   fight against I those that I fight aIgainst me.

2 Take up | shield and | buckler:
  and a|rise a|rise to | help me.

3 Draw the spear
      and bar the way against | those · that pur|sue me:
  say to me | 'I am | your de|liverer.'

4 Let those that seek my life ⌣
      be put to | shame · and dis|graced:
  let those that plot my destruction ⌣
      be | turned | back · and con|founded.

5 Let them be like chaff be|fore the | wind:
  with the | angel · of the | Lord | driving them;

6 Let their way be | dark and | slippery:
  with the | angel · of the | Lord pur|suing.

7 For without cause ⌣
      they have secretly | spread a | net for me:
  without cause they have | dug a | pit · to en|trap me.

8 Let sudden dis|aster | strike them:
  let the net that they have hidden catch them
      let them | fall to | their de|struction.

9 Then shall my soul be | joyful · in the | Lord:
  and I will re|joice in | his de|liverance.

10 All my bones shall say | 'Lord · who is | like you?:
      for you deliver the poor man from him that is too ⌣
      strong for him * the poor and needy from |
      him that | would de|spoil them.'

11 Malicious witnesses rise | up a|gainst me:
  I am questioned about things of | which I | know |
      nothing.

12 They repay me | evil · for | good:
  I am as | one be|reaved of · his | children.

13 Yet when they were sick I | put on | sackcloth:
  I af|flicted · my|self with | fasting.

14 And if my prayer returned unanswered | to my | bosom:
  I went about mourning
      as though for a | brother | or a · com|panion;

15 I was bowed I down with I grief:
  as I though · for my I own I mother.

16 But when I stumbled   they rejoiced and gathered ⌣
    together * they gathered to⏐gether · a⏐gainst me:
  as though they were strangers I never knew
    they I tore at · me I without I ceasing.

†17 When I I slipped they I mocked me:
  and I gnashed · at me I with their I teeth.

18 Lord how long will I you look I on?:
  take me from the evil they intend
    take me I from a⏐midst the I lions.

19 And I will give you thanks in the I great · congre⏐gation:
  I will I praise you · in the I throng · of the I people.

20 Let not those that wrongfully are my enemies I ⌣
    triumph I over me:
  let not those that hate me without cause I ⌣
    mock me I with their I eyes.

21 For they speak words that do not I make for I peace:
  they invent lies against those that are I quiet I in the I
    land.

22 They stretch their mouths to I jeer at me · and I say:
  'Aha aha!   We have I seen I all that · we I wish!'

23 And you also have seen O Lord   I do not · be I silent:
  O God I go not I far I from me.

24 Bestir yourself   awake to I do me I right:
  to plead my I cause O I Lord my I God.

25 Judge me O Lord my God   according I to your I
    righteousness:
  and let them I not re⏐joice I over me.

26 Let them not say in their hearts   'We I have our I wish':
  let them not I say   'We I have de⏐stroyed him.'

27 Let those that rejoice at my hurt ⌣
    be disgraced and confounded I alto⏐gether:
  let those that lord it over me ⌣
    be I clothed in I shame · and dis⏐honour.

28 But let those that long for my vindication ⌣
　　　shout for | joy · and re|joice:
　　let them say always that the Lord is great
　　　who takes such de|light · in his | servant's | good.

29 And my tongue shall | speak of · your | righteousness:
　　and of your | praise | all the · day | long.

PSALM 36

1 The transgressor speaks ⌣
　　　from the wickedness in his | own | heart:
　　there is no fear of | God be|fore his | eyes.

2 For he flatters himself in his | own | sight:
　　he hates his in|iquity · to be | found | out.

3 The words of his mouth are wickedness | and de|ceit:
　　he has ceased to act | wisely · and | do | good.

4 He plots mischief as he lies up|on his | bed:
　　he has set himself on a path that is not good
　　　he | does not | spurn | evil.

5 Your unfailing kindness O Lord is | in the | heavens:
　　and your faithfulness | reaches | to the | clouds.

6 Your righteousness is like the | strong | mountains:
　　and your justice as the great deep
　　　you O Lord | save both | man and | beast.

7 How precious O God is your en|during | kindness:
　　the children of men shall take refuge ⌣
　　　under the | shadow | of your | wings.

8 They shall be satisfied ⌣
　　　with the good things | of your | house:
　　and you will give them drink ⌣
　　　from the | river · of | your de|lights.

9 For with you is the | well of | life:
　　and in your | light shall | we see | light.

10 O continue your merciful kindness ⌣
　　　toward | those who | know you:
　　and your righteous dealing ⌣
　　　to | those · that are | true of | heart.

11 Let not the foot of the | proud · come a|gainst me:
nor the hand of the un|godly | drive · me a|way.

12 There are they fallen | those who · do | evil:
they are thrust down and | shall not | rise a|gain.

PSALM 37

1 Do not | vie · with the | wicked:
or | envy | those that · do | wrong;

2 For they will soon | wither · like the | grass:
and fade a|way · like the | green | leaf.

3 Trust in the | Lord and · do | good:
and you shall dwell in the land _
and | feed in | safe | pastures.

4 Let the Lord be | your de|light:
and he will | grant you · your | heart's de|sire.

5 Commit your | way · to the | Lord:
trust | him and | he will | act.

6 He will make your righteousness _
shine as | clear · as the | light:
and your | inno·cence | as the | noonday.

7 Be still before the Lord * and wait | patient·ly | for him:
do not be vexed when a man prospers
when he puts his | evil | purposes · to | work.

8 Let go of anger and a|bandon | wrath:
let not envy | move you · to | do | evil.

9 For the wicked shall be | cut | down:
but those who wait for the | Lord · shall pos|sess the |
land.

10 In a little while the ungodly shall | be no | more:
you will look for him in his place _
but | he will | not be | found.

†11 But the meek shall pos|sess the | land:
and en|joy · the a|bundance · of | peace.

12 The ungodly man plots a|gainst the | righteous:
and | gnashes · at him | with his | teeth.

13 But the Lord shall I laugh him · to I scorn:
　　for he sees that the I day · for his I overthrow · is I
　　near.

14 The ungodly have drawn the sword and I strung the I
　　bow:
　　to strike down the poor and needy
　　　to slaughter I those that I walk in I innocence.

15 Their swords shall pierce their I own I hearts:
　　and their I bows I shall be I broken.

16 Though the righteous man I has · but a I little:
　　it is better than the great I wealth of I the unIgodly.

17 For the strong arm of the ungodly I shall be I broken:
　　but the I Lord upIholds the I righteous.

18 The Lord cares for the I lives · of the I innocent:
　　and their heritage I shall be I theirs for I ever.

19 They shall not be put to shame in the I evil I days:
　　but in time of famine I they shall I eat their I fill.

†20 As for the ungodly they shall perish
　　　they are the enemies I of the I Lord:
　　like fuel in a furnace they shall I vanish · aIway in I
　　smoke.

21 The ungodly man borrows but does I not reIpay:
　　but the I righteous · is I gracious · and I gives.

22 Those who are blessed by God shall posIsess the I land:
　　but those whom he has I cursed · shall be I cut I down.

23 If a man's steps are I guided · by the I Lord:
　　and I he deIlights in · his I way,

24 Though he stumble he shall I not fall I headlong:
　　for the Lord I holds him I by the I hand.

25 I have been young and I now am I old:
　　but I never saw the righteous man forsaken
　　　or his I children I begging · their I bread.

26 He is ever I gracious · and I lends:
　　and his I children I shall be I blessed.

27 Turn from evil and | do | good:
and you shall | dwell · in the | land for | ever.

28 For the | Lord loves | justice:
he will | not for|sake his | faithful ones.

29 But the unjust shall be de|stroyed for | ever:
and the children of the un|godly · shall be | cut |
down.

30 The just shall pos|sess the | land:
and they shall | dwell in | it for | ever.

31 The mouth of the righteous man | utters | wisdom:
and his | tongue speaks | what is | right.

32 The law of his God is | in his | heart:
and his | footsteps | will not | slip.

33 The ungodly man watches | out · for the | righteous:
and | seeks oc|casion · to | slay him.

34 But the Lord will not abandon him | to his | power:
nor let him be con|demned when | he is | judged.

†35 Wait for the Lord and | hold to · his | way:
and he will raise you up to possess the land
to see the un|godly · when | they are · de|stroyed.

36 I have seen the ungodly in | terri·fying | power:
spreading himself | like a · lux|uri·ant | tree;

37 I passed by again and | he was | gone:
I searched for him | but · he could | not be | found.

38 Observe the blameless man and con|sider · the | upright:
for the man of | peace shall | have pos|terity.

39 But transgressors shall be de|stroyed · alto|gether:
and the posterity of the | wicked · shall be | cut |
down.

40 Deliverance for the righteous shall | come · from the |
Lord:
he is their | strength in | time of | trouble.

41 The Lord will help them | and de|liver them:
he will save them from the ungodly and deliver them
because they | come to | him for | refuge.

PSALM 38

1 O Lord rebuke me not I in your I anger:
    nor chasten me I in your I fierce dis|pleasure.

2 For your arrows have been I aimed a|gainst me:
    and your hand has come I down I heavy · up|on me.

3 There is no health in my flesh ⏜
        because of your I indig|nation:
    nor soundness in my bones by I reason I of my I sin.

4 The tide of my iniquities has gone I over · my I head:
    their weight is a burden too I heavy · for I me to I bear.

5 My wounds I stink and I fester:
    be|cause I of my I foolishness.

6 I am bowed down and I brought so I low:
    that I go I mourning I all the · day I long.

7 For my loins are filled with a I burning I pain:
    and there is no sound I part in I all my I body.

8 I am numbed and I stricken · to the I ground:
    I cry aloud in the I yearning I of my I heart.

9 O Lord   all I long for I is be|fore you:
    and my deep sighing I is not I hidden I from you.

10 My heart is in tumult   my I strength I fails me:
    and even the I light of · my I eyes has I gone from me.

11 My friends and my companions hold aloof from I
        my af|fliction:
    and my I kinsmen I stand far I off.

12 Those who seek my I life I strike at me:
    and those that desire my hurt spread evil tales
        and murmur I slanders I all the I day.

13 But I am like a deaf man and I hear I nothing:
    like one that is dumb who I does not I open · his I
        mouth.

14 So I have become as one who I cannot I hear:
    in whose I mouth · there is I no re|tort.

15 For in you Lord have I ǀ put my ǀ trust:
    and you will ǀ answer me · O ǀ Lord my ǀ God.

16 For I prayed 'Let them never exǀult ǀ over me:
    those who turn arrogant ǀ when my ǀ foot ǀ slips.'

17 Truly I am ǀ ready · to ǀ fall:
    and my ǀ pain is ǀ with me · conǀtinually.

18 But I acǀknowledge · my ǀ wickedness:
    and I am filled with ǀ sorrow ǀ at my ǀ sin.

19 Those that are my enemies without cause are ǀ great in ǀ
    number:
    and those who hate me ǀ wrongfulǀly are ǀ many.

20 Those also who repay evil for good ǀ are aǀgainst me:
    because I ǀ seek ǀ after ǀ good.

†21 Forsake me not O Lord
    go not far ǀ from me · my ǀ God:
    hasten to my ǀ help O ǀ Lord · my salǀvation.

PSALM 39

1 I said 'I will keep watch over my ways ‿
    lest I ǀ sin · with my ǀ tongue:
    I will keep a guard on my mouth ‿
    while the ǀ wicked · are ǀ in my ǀ sight.'

2 I held my tongue and ǀ said ǀ nothing:
    I kept ǀ silent · but ǀ found no ǀ comfort.

3 My pain was increased my heart grew ǀ
    hot withǀin me:
    while I mused the fire blazed and I ǀ spoke ǀ with my ǀ
    tongue;

4 'Lord let me ǀ know my ǀ end:
    and the ǀ number ǀ of my ǀ days,

†5 'That I may know how ǀ short my ǀ time is:
    for you have made my days but a handsbreadth
    and my whole ǀ span · is as ǀ nothing · beǀfore you.'

6 Surely every man though he stand secure ǀ is but ǀ
    breath:
    man ǀ lives · as a ǀ passing ǀ shadow.

7 The riches he heaps are but a | puff of | wind:
    and he cannot | tell | who will | gather them.

8 And now Lord | what is · my | hope?:
    truly my | hope | is in | you.

9 O deliver me from | all · my trans|gressions:
    do not | make me · the | butt of | fools.

10 I was dumb I did not | open · my | mouth:
    for surely | it was | your | doing.

11 Take away your | plague | from me:
    I am brought to an | end · by the | blows · of your | hand.

12 When with rebukes you chastise a | man for | sin:
    you cause his fair looks to dissolve in putrefaction
    surely | every · man | is but | breath.

13 Hear my prayer O Lord and give | ear to · my | cry:
    be not | silent | at my | tears.

14 For I am but a | stranger · with | you:
    a passing guest as | all my | fathers | were.

15 Turn your eye from me that I may | smile a|gain:
    before I go | hence and | am no | more.

PSALM 40

1 I waited patiently | for the | Lord:
    and he in|clined to me · and | heard my | cry.

2 He brought me up from the pit of roaring waters
    out of the | mire and | clay:
    and set my feet upon a | rock · and made | firm my | foothold.

3 And he has put a new | song · in my | mouth:
    even a song of | thanks·giving | to our | God.

4 Many shall | see it · and | fear:
    and shall | put their | trust · in the | Lord.

5 Blessèd is the man who has made the | Lord his | hope:
    who has not turned to the proud
    or to those who | wander | in de|ceit.

6 O Lord my God
   great are the wonderful things which you have ⌣
   done   and your thoughts which I are tolwards us:
   there is none to I be comlpared with I you;

†7 Were I to delclare them · and I speak of them:
   they are more than I am I able I to exlpress.

8 Sacrifice and offering you do I not delsire:
   but my I ears · you have I marked · for olbedience;

9 Burnt-offering and sin-offering you have I not relquired:
   then I said I I   Lo I I come.

10 In the scroll of the book it is written of me ⌣
   that I should I do your I will:
   O my God I long to do it * your I law dellights my I
   heart.

11 I have declared your righteousness ⌣
   in the I great · congrelgation:
   I have not restrained my lips O I Lord ⌣
   and I that you I know.

12 I have not hidden your righteousness I in my I heart:
   I have spoken of your faithfulness I and of I
   your sallvation.

13 I have not kept back your loving-kindness I and your I
   truth:
   from the I great I congrelgation.

14 O Lord do not withhold your I mercy I from me:
   let your loving-kindness and your I truth I ever ·
   prelserve me.

15 For innumerable troubles have I come uplon me:
   my sins have overtaken me I and I I cannot I see.

16 They are more in number than the I hairs · of my I head:
   therelfore my I heart I fails me.

17 Be pleased O I Lord · to delliver me:
   O I Lord make I haste to I help me.

18 Let those who seek my life to I take it · alway:
   be put to shame and conlfounded I altolgether.

19 Let them be turned back and disgraced who ǀ wish me ǀ
      evil:
    let them be aghast for shame who ǀ
      say to me ·   'Aǀha aǀha!'

20 Let all who seek you be joyful and ǀ
      glad beǀcause of you:
    let those who love your salvation say ǀ always ·
      'The ǀ Lord is ǀ great.'

21 As for me I am ǀ poor and ǀ needy:
    but the ǀ Lord will ǀ care ǀ for me.

†22 You are my helper and ǀ my deǀliverer:
    make no long deǀlay O ǀ Lord my ǀ God.

PSALM 41

1 Blessèd is he that considers the ǀ poor and ǀ helpless:
    the Lord will deliver him ǀ in the ǀ day of ǀ trouble.

2 The Lord will guard him and preserve his life
      he shall be counted ǀ happy · in the ǀ land:
    you will not give him ǀ over · to the ǀ will · of his ǀ
      enemies.

†3 And if he lies sick on his bed the ǀ Lord · will susǀtain
      him:
    if illness lays him ǀ low · you will ǀ overǀthrow it.

4 I said 'O Lord be ǀ merciful · toǀward me:
    heal me for ǀ I have ǀ sinned aǀgainst you.'

5 My enemies speak evil ǀ of me ǀ saying:
    'When will he die and his ǀ name ǀ perish · for ǀ
      ever?'

6 And if one should come to see me   he mouths ǀ
      empty ǀ words:
    while his heart gathers mischief
      and ǀ when he · goes ǀ out he ǀ vents it.

7 All those that hate me whisper toǀgether · aǀgainst me:
    they deǀvise ǀ plots aǀgainst me.

8 They say   'A deadly ǀ thing has · got ǀ hold of him:
    he will not get up aǀgain from ǀ where he ǀ lies.'

9 Even my bosom friend in | whom I | trusted:
   who shared my bread   has | lifted · his |
      heel a|gainst me.

10 But you O Lord be gracious and | raise me | up:
   and I will repay them | what they | have de|served.

11 By this will I | know that · you | favour me:
   that my enemy | shall not | triumph | over me.

12 Because of my innocence you | hold me | fast:
   you have set me be|fore your | face for | ever.

13 Blessèd be the Lord the | God of | Israel:
   from everlasting to everlasting * | Amen | A–|men.

PSALM 42

1 As a deer longs for the | running | brooks:
   so longs my | soul for | you O | God.

2 My soul is thirsty for God * thirsty for the | living | God:
   when shall I | come and | see his | face?

3 My tears have been my food | day and | night:
   while they ask me all day long | 'Where now |
      is your | God?'

4 As I pour out my soul by myself I re|member | this:
   how I went to the house of the Mighty One | _
      into · the | temple · of | God,

†5 To the shouts and | songs of · thanks|giving:
   a multitude | keeping | high | festival.

6 *Why are you so full of | heaviness · my | soul:*
   and | why · so un|quiet · with|in me?

7 *O put your | trust in | God:*
   for I will praise him yet
      who is my de|liver·er | and my | God.

8 My soul is | heavy · with|in me:
   therefore I will remember you from the land of
      Jordan
      from Mizar a|mong the | hills of | Hermon.

9 Deep calls to deep in the | roar of · your | waters:
    all your waves and | breakers | have gone | over me.

10 Surely the Lord will grant his loving mercy | in the |
    day-time:
    and in the night his song will be with me
    a | prayer · to the | God · of my | life.

11 I will say to God my rock   'Why have |
    you for|gotten me:
    why must I go like a mourner be|cause the | enemy ·
    op|presses me?'

†12 Like a sword through my bones my | enemies · have |
    mocked me:
    while they ask me all day long | 'Where now |
    is your | God?'

13 *Why are you so full of | heaviness · my | soul:*
    and | why · so un|quiet · with|in me?

14 *O put your | trust in | God:*
    for I will praise him yet
    who is my de|liver·er | and my | God.

PSALM 43

1 Give judgment for me O God
    take up my cause against an un|godly | people:
    deliver me from de|ceitful · and | wicked | men.

2 For you are God my refuge   why have you | turned · me
    a|way:
    why must I go like a mourner _
    be|cause the | enemy · op|presses me?

3 O send out your light and your truth and | let them | lead
    me:
    let them guide me to your holy | hill and | to your |
    dwelling.

4 Then I shall go to the altar of God
    to God my joy and | my de|light:
    and to the harp I shall sing your | praises · O |
    God my | God.

5 *Why are you so full of | heaviness · my | soul:*
  and | why · so un|quiet · with|in me?

6 *O put your | trust in | God:*
  for I will praise him yet
  who is my de|liver·er | and my | God.

PSALM 44

1 We have heard with our ears O God ⌣
   our | fathers · have | told us:
   what things you did in their | time · in the | days of |
   old;

2 How by your own hand you drove out the nations ⌣
   and | planted · us | in:
   how you crushed the peoples
   but caused | us to | root and | grow.

3 For it was not by their swords ⌣
   that our fathers took pos|session · of the | land:
   nor did their own | arm | get them · the | victory,

4 But your right hand   your arm ⌣
   and the | light of · your | countenance:
   be|cause · you de|lighted · in | them.

5 You are my | king · and my | God:
   who or|dained | victory · for | Jacob.

6 By your power we struck our | ene·mies | through:
   in your name we trod down | those that |
   rose a|gainst us.

7 For I did not | trust · in my | bow:
   nor | could my | sword | save me;

8 But it was you that delivered us | from our | enemies:
   and put our | adver·saries | to con|fusion.

†9 In God we made our boast | all the · day | long:
   we gave | thanks to · your | name with·out | ceasing.

10 But now you have cast us off and | brought us · to |
    shame:
    you | go not | out · with our | armies.

11 You have caused us to show our I backs · to the I enemy:
   so that our foes I plunder I us at I will.

12 You have given us like I sheep · to be I butchered:
   you have I scattered us · aImong the I nations.

13 You have sold your I people · for I nothing:
   and I made a I profit·less I bargain.

14 You have made us a laughing-stock I to our I
      neighbours:
   mocked and held in deIrision · by I those aIbout us.

15 You have made us a byword aImong the I nations:
   so that the peoples I toss their I heads in I scorn.

16 My disgrace is before me I all the I day:
   and I shame has I covered · my I face,

17 At the voice of the slanderer I and reIviler:
   at the sight of the I ene·my I and aIvenger.

18 All this has come upon us   though we have I not
      forIgotten you:
   we have I not beItrayed your I covenant.

19 Our hearts have I not turned I back:
   nor have our steps I strayed I from your I paths.

20 And yet you have crushed us in the I haunt of I jackals:
   and covered us I with the I shadow · of I death.

21 If we had forgotten the I name of · our I God:
   or stretched out our hands in I prayer to · some I
      strange I god,

22 Would not God I search it I out?:
   for he knows the very I secrets I of the I heart.

23 But for your sake are we killed I all the · day I long:
   we are I counted · as I sheep · for the I slaughter.

24 Rouse yourself O Lord   I why · do you I sleep?:
   awake   do not I cast us I off for I ever.

25 Why do you I hide your I face:
   and forget our I misery · and I our afIfliction?

26 Our souls are I bowed · to the I dust:
   our I bellies I cleave · to the I ground.

27 Arise O | Lord to | help us:
    and redeem us | for your | mercy's | sake.

PSALM 45

1 My heart is astir with fine phrases
    I make my | song · for a | king:
    my tongue is the | pen · of a | ready | writer.

2 You are the fairest of the sons of men
    grace | flows · from your | lips:
    therefore has God | blessed you · for | ever · and | ever.

3 Gird your sword upon your thigh O | mighty | warrior:
    in glory and majesty tread | down your | foes and | triumph!

4 Ride on in the | cause of | truth:
    and | for the | sake of | justice.

5 Your right hand shall teach a | terrible · in|struction:
    peoples shall fall beneath you * your arrows shall be ⌣
    sharp in the | hearts · of the | king's | enemies.

6 Your throne is the throne of God   it en|dures for | ever:
    and the sceptre of your | kingdom · is a | righteous | sceptre.

7 You have loved righteousness and | hated | evil:
    therefore God your God * has anointed you ⌣
    with the oil of | gladness · a|bove your | fellows.

8 All your garments are fragrant ⌣
    with myrrh | aloes · and | cassia:
    music from ivory | pala·ces | makes you | glad.

†9 Kings' daughters are among your | noble | women:
    the queen is at your right | hand in | gold of | Ophir.

10 Hear O daughter   consider and in|cline your | ear:
    forget your own | people · and your | father's | house.

11 The king de|sires your | beauty:
    he is your lord | therefore · bow | down be|fore him.

†12 The richest among the people O | daughter · of | Tyre:
　　　 shall en|treat your | favour · with | gifts.

13 The king's daughter is all | glorious · with|in:
　　 her clothing is em|broidered | cloth of | gold.

14 In robes of many colours she is led to | you O | king:
　　 and after her the | virgins | that are | with her.

†15 They are led with | gladness · and re|joicing:
　　　 they enter the | palace | of the | king.

16 In place of your fathers | you shall · have | sons:
　　 and make them princes | over | all the | land.

17 And I will make known your name to every |
　　　 gener|ation:
　　 therefore the peoples shall | give you | praise for |
　　　 ever.

PSALM 46

1 God is our | refuge · and | strength:
　 a very | present | help in | trouble.

2 Therefore we will not fear though the | earth be | moved:
　 and though the mountains are | shaken · in the |
　　　 midst · of the | sea;

†3 Though the waters | rage and | foam:
　　 and though the mountains quake at the |
　　　 rising | of the | sea.

4 There is a river whose streams make glad the | city · of |
　　　 God:
　 the holy dwelling-place | of the | Most | High.

5 God is in the midst of her
　　　 therefore she shall | not be | moved:
　 God will | help her · and at | break of | day.

6 The nations make uproar and the | kingdoms · are |
　　　 shaken:
　 but God has lifted his | voice · and the | earth shall |
　　　 tremble.

7 *The Lord of | hosts is | with us:*
  the God of | Jacob | is our | stronghold.

8 Come then and see what the | Lord has | done:
  what destruction he has | brought up|on the | earth.

9 He makes wars to cease in | all the | world:
  he breaks the bow and shatters the spear
    and burns the | chari·ots | in the | fire.

10 'Be still and know that | I am | God:
   I will be exalted among the nations
     I will be ex|alted · up|on the | earth.'

11 *The Lord of | hosts is | with us:*
   the God of | Jacob | is our | stronghold.

PSALM 47

1 O clap your hands | all you | peoples:
  and cry aloud to | God with | shouts of | joy.

2 For the Lord Most High | is to · be | feared:
  he is a great | King · over | all the | earth.

3 He cast down | peoples | under us:
  and the | nations · be|neath our | feet.

4 He chose us a land for | our pos|session:
  that was the pride of | Jacob | whom he | loved.

5 God has gone up with the | sound · of re|joicing:
  and the | Lord · to the | blast · of the | horn.

6 O sing praises sing | praises · to | God:
  O sing praises sing | praises | to our | King.

7 For God is the King of | all the | earth:
  O | praise him · in a | well-wrought | psalm.

8 God has become the | King · of the | nations:
  he has taken his seat up|on his | holy | throne.

9 The princes of the peoples are | gathered · to|gether:
  with the | people · of the | God of | Abraham.

10 For the mighty ones of the earth ⌣
      are become the ǀ servants · of ǀ God:
  and ǀ he is ǀ greatly · exǀalted.

PSALM 48

1 Great is the Lord and ǀ greatly · to be ǀ praised:
  in the ǀ city ǀ of our ǀ God.

2 High and beautiful is his ǀ holy ǀ hill:
  it is the ǀ joy of ǀ all the ǀ earth.

†3 On Mount Zion where godhead truly dwells
      stands the city of the ǀ Great ǀ King:
  God is well known in her palaces ǀ as a ǀ sure deǀfence.

4 For the kings of the ǀ earth asǀsembled:
  they gathered toǀgether · and ǀ came ǀ on;

5 They saw   they were ǀ struck ǀ dumb:
  they were aǀstonished · and ǀ fled in ǀ terror.

6 Trembling took ǀ hold on them · and ǀ anguish:
  as on a ǀ woman ǀ in her ǀ travail;

7 Like the breath of the ǀ east ǀ wind:
  that ǀ shatters · the ǀ ships of ǀ Tarshish.

8 As we have heard so have we seen ⌣
      in the city of the ǀ Lord of ǀ hosts:
  in the city of our God ⌣
      which ǀ God · has esǀtablished · for ǀ ever.

9 We have called to mind your loving-ǀkindness · O ǀ God:
  in the ǀ midst of ǀ your ǀ temple.

10 As your name is great O God so also ǀ is your ǀ praise:
  even to the ǀ ends ǀ of the ǀ earth.

11 Your right hand is full of victory
      let Zion's ǀ hill reǀjoice:
  let the daughters of Judah be ǀ glad ⌣
      beǀcause of · your ǀ judgments.

12 Walk about Zion go round about her ⌣
  and ǀ count · all her ǀ towers:

consider well her ramparts ⎸ pass ⎸ through her ⎸ palaces;

13 That you may tell those who come after that ⎸ such is ⎸ God:
 our God for ever and ever * and ⎸ he will ⎸ guide us ·
 e⎸ternally.

PSALM 49

1 O hear this ⎸ all you ⎸ peoples:
 give ear all you in⎸habit·ants ⎸ of the ⎸ world,

2 All children of men and ⎸ sons of ⎸ Adam:
 both ⎸ rich and ⎸ poor a⎸like.

3 For my mouth shall ⎸ speak ⎸ wisdom:
 and the thoughts of my heart ＿
 shall be ⎸ full of ⎸ under⎸standing.

4 I will incline my ⎸ ear · to a ⎸ riddle:
 and unfold the mystery to the ⎸ sounds ⎸ of the ⎸ harp.

5 Why should I fear in the ⎸ evil ⎸ days:
 when the wickedness of ⎸ my de⎸ceivers · sur⎸rounds
 me,

6 Though they trust to their ⎸ great ⎸ wealth:
 and boast of the a⎸bundance ⎸ of their ⎸ riches?

7 No man may ⎸ ransom · his ⎸ brother:
 or give ⎸ God a ⎸ price ⎸ for him,

8 So that he may ⎸ live for ⎸ ever:
 and ⎸ never ⎸ see the ⎸ grave;

9 For to ransom men's ⎸ lives · is so ⎸ costly:
 that he must a⎸bandon ⎸ it for ⎸ ever.

10 For we see that ⎸ wise men ⎸ die:
 and perish with the foolish and the ignorant ⎸
 leaving · their ⎸ wealth to ⎸ others.

†11 The tomb is their home for ever
 their dwelling-place throughout ⎸ all · gener⎸ations:
 though they called estates ⎸ after · their ⎸ own ⎸ names.

12 A rich man without I underIstanding:
    is I like the I beasts that I perish.

13 This is the I lot · of the I foolish:
    the end of those who are I pleased · with their I own I
        words.

14 They are driven like sheep into the grave ⌣
        and I death · is their I shepherd:
    they slip down I easi·ly I into · the I tomb.

15 Their bright forms shall wear aIway · in the I grave:
    and I lose their I former I glory.

†16 But God will I ransom · my I life:
    he will take me I from the I power · of the I grave.

17 Do not fear when a I man grows I rich:
    when the I wealth · of his I household · inIcreases,

18 For he will take nothing aIway · when he I dies:
    nor will his I wealth go I down I after him.

19 Though he counts himself happy I while he I lives:
    and praises you I also I when you I prosper,

20 He will go to the company I of his I fathers:
    who will I never I see the I light.

†21 A rich man without I underIstanding:
    is I like the I beasts that I perish.

PSALM 50

1 The Lord our God the I Mighty One · has I spoken:
    and summoned the earth * from the rising of ⌣
        the sun to its I setting I in the I west.

2 From Zion I perfect · in I beauty:
    God has I shone I out in I glory.

3 Our God is coming   he will I not keep I silent:
    before him is devouring fire
        and I tempest I whirls aIbout him.

4 He calls to the I heavens · aIbove:
    and to the earth so I he may I judge his I people.

5 'Gather to ǀ me my ǀ faithful ones:
  those who by sacrifice ǀ made a ǀ coven·ant ǀ with me.'

6 The heavens shall proǀclaim his ǀ righteousness:
  for ǀ God himǀself is ǀ judge.

7 'Listen my people and ǀ I will ǀ speak:
  O Israel I am God your God   and ǀ I will ǀ give my ǀ
  testimony.

8 'It is not for your sacrifices that ǀ I reǀprove you:
  for your burnt-ǀofferings · are ǀ always · beǀfore me.

9 'I will take no ǀ bull · from your ǀ farms:
  or ǀ he-goat ǀ from your ǀ pens.

10 'For all the beasts of the forest beǀlong to ǀ me:
  and so do the ǀ cattle · upǀon the ǀ mountains.

11 'I know all the ǀ birds · of the ǀ air:
  and the grasshoppers of the ǀ field are ǀ in my ǀ sight.

12 'If I were hungry I ǀ would not ǀ tell you:
  for the whole world is ǀ mine and ǀ all · that is ǀ in it.

13 'Do I eat the ǀ flesh of ǀ bulls:
  or ǀ drink the ǀ blood of ǀ goats?

14 'Offer to God a sacrifice of ǀ thanksǀgiving:
  and pay your ǀ vows · to the ǀ Most ǀ High.

†15 'Call upon me in the ǀ day of ǀ trouble:
  I will bring you out   and ǀ you shall ǀ glori·fy ǀ me.'

16 But God ǀ says · to the ǀ wicked:
  'What have you to do with reciting my laws
  or taking my ǀ coven·ant ǀ on your ǀ lips,

17 'Seeing you ǀ loathe ǀ discipline:
  and have ǀ tossed my ǀ words beǀhind you?

18 'When you saw a thief you ǀ went aǀlong with him:
  and you ǀ threw in · your ǀ lot · with adǀulterers.

19 'You have loosed your ǀ mouth in ǀ evil:
  and your ǀ tongue strings ǀ lies toǀgether.

20 'You sit and speak aǀgainst your ǀ brother:
  and slander your ǀ own ǀ mother's ǀ son.

21 'These things you have done   and I I held my I tongue:
   and you thought I was just such anIother I
      as yourIself.

22 'But I I will conIvict you:
   and set before your I eyes what I you have I done.

23 'O consider this   you who forIget I God:
   lest I tear you in pieces   and I there be I no one · to I
      save you.

†24 'He honours me who brings sacrifice of I thanksIgiving:
   and to him who keeps to my way ⌣
      I will I show the · salIvation · of I God.'

PSALM 51

1 Have mercy on me O God in your enIduring I goodness:
   according to the fulness of your compassion I ⌣
      blot out I my ofIfences.

2 Wash me thoroughly I from my I wickedness:
   and I cleanse me I from my I sin.

3 For I acknowledge I my reIbellion:
   and my I sin is I ever · beIfore me.

4 Against you only have I sinned
      and done what is evil I in your I eyes:
   so you will be just in your sentence
      and I blameless I in your I judging.

5 Surely in wickedness I was I brought to I birth:
   and in I sin my I mother · conIceived me.

6 You that desire truth in the I inward I parts:
   O teach me wisdom in the secret I places I of the I
      heart.

7 Purge me with hyssop and I I shall be I clean:
   wash me and I I shall be I whiter · than I snow.

8 Make me hear of I joy and I gladness:
   let the bones which I you have I broken · reIjoice.

9 Hide your I face · from my I sins:
   and I blot out I all · my inIiquities.

10 Create in me a clean ⏐ heart O ⏐ God:
    and re⏐new a · right ⏐ spirit · with⏐in me.

11 Do not cast me ⏐ out · from your ⏐ presence:
    do not take your ⏐ holy ⏐ spirit ⏐ from me.

12 O give me the gladness of your ⏐ help a⏐gain:
    and sup⏐port me · with a ⏐ willing ⏐ spirit.

†13 Then will I teach trans⏐gressors · your ⏐ ways:
    and sinners shall ⏐ turn to ⏐ you a⏐gain.

14 O Lord God of my salvation   de⏐liver me · from ⏐
    bloodshed:
    and my ⏐ tongue shall ⏐ sing of · your ⏐ righteousness.

15 O Lord ⏐ open · my ⏐ lips:
    and my ⏐ mouth · shall pro⏐claim your ⏐ praise.

16 You take no pleasure in sacrifice or ⏐ I would ⏐ give it:
    burnt-⏐offerings · you ⏐ do not ⏐ want.

17 The sacrifice of God is a ⏐ broken ⏐ spirit:
    a broken and contrite heart O God ⏐ you will ⏐
    not de⏐spise.

18 In your graciousness do ⏐ good to ⏐ Zion:
    re⏐build the ⏐ walls · of Je⏐rusalem.

19 Then will you delight in right sacrifices
    in burnt-offerings ⏐ and ob⏐lations:
    then will they offer young ⏐ bulls up⏐on your ⏐ altar.

PSALM 52

1 Why O man of power do you boast ⏐ all the · day ⏐ long:
    of mischief done to ⏐ him · that is ⏐ faithful · to ⏐ God?

2 You contrive de⏐stroying ⏐ slanders:
    your tongue is like a sharpened ⏐
    razor·   it ⏐ cuts de⏐ceitfully.

3 You have loved evil ⏐ and not ⏐ good:
    to tell lies ⏐ rather · than to ⏐ speak the ⏐ truth.

4 You love all words that ⏐ may do ⏐ hurt:
    and ⏐ every · de⏐ceit · of the ⏐ tongue.

5 But God will de|stroy you | utterly:
    he will snatch you away and pluck you out of your ⌣
      dwelling
      he will up|root you · from the | land · of the | living.

6 The righteous shall | see it · and | fear:
    they shall | laugh you · to | scorn and | say,

†7 'Behold   this is the man ⌣
      who did not take | God · for his | strength:
    but trusted in the abundance of his riches
      and | found his | strength in | slander.'

8 As for me   I am like a green olive tree in the | house of |
      God:
    I will trust in the goodness of | God for | ever · and |
      ever.

9 I will always give you thanks * for this was | your |
      doing:
    I will glorify your name before the faithful
      for | it is | good to | praise you.

PSALM 53

1 The fool has said in his heart   'There | is no | God':
    they have all become vile and abominable in their ⌣
      wickedness * there | is not | one that · does | good.

2 God looked down from heaven upon the | children · of |
      men:
    to see if there were any who would act | wisely ·
      and | seek · after | God.

3 But they have all turned aside
      they have all alike be|come cor|rupt:
    there is none that does | good | no not | one.

4 Are all the evildoers devoid of | under|standing:
    who eat up my people as men eat bread
      and | do not | pray to | God?

5 They shall be | struck with | terror:
    for God will scatter the | bones | of the · un|godly.

6 They shall be I put to · conIfusion:
because I God I has reIjected them.

†7 O that deliverance for Israel might come I forth from I
Zion:
when the Lord turns again the fortunes of his people
then shall Jacob reIjoice and I Israel · be I glad.

PSALM 54

1 Save me O God by the I power of · your I name:
and I vindicate · me I by your I might.

2 Hear my I prayer O I God:
and I listen · to the I words of · my I mouth.

3 For the insolent have I risen · aIgainst me:
ruthless men who have not set God beIfore them I ⌣
seek my I life.

4 But surely I God is · my I helper:
the Lord is the upIholder I of my I life.

5 Let evil recoil on those that I would wayIlay me:
O deIstroy them I in your I faithfulness!

6 Then will I offer you sacrifice with a I willing I heart:
I will praise your name O I Lord for I it is I good.

†7 For you will deliver me from I every I trouble:
my eyes shall see the I downfall I of my I enemies.

PSALM 55

1 Hear my I prayer O I God:
and do not hide yourIself from I my peItition.

2 Give heed to I me and I answer me:
I am I restless · in I my comIplaining.

3 I am in turmoil at the I voice · of the I enemy:
at the I onslaught I of the I wicked.

4 For they bring down disIaster · upIon me:
they persecute I me with I bitter I fury.

5 My heart I writhes withIin me:
and the terrors of I death have I fallen · upIon me.

6 Fear and trembling I come upΙon me:
 and I horror I overIwhelms me.

7 And I said   'O for the I wings · of a I dove:
 that I might fly aIway and I find I rest.

8 'Then I would I flee far I off:
 and make my I lodging I in the I wilderness.

9 'I would hasten to I find me · a I refuge:
 out I of the I blast of I slander,

10 'Out of the tempest of their I calumny · O I Lord:
 and I far · from their I double I tongues.'

11 For I have seen violence and I strife · in the I city:
 day and night they go I round it · upΙon its I walls.

12 Evil and wickedness I are withIin it:
 iniquity is within it * oppression and fraud do I
 not deΙpart · from its I streets.

13 It was not an enemy that reviled me
  or I I might have I borne it:
 it was not my foe that dealt so insolently with me
  or I might have I hidden · myΙself I from him;

14 But it was you   a I man · like myΙself:
 my companion I and · my famΙiliar I friend.

†15 Together we enΙjoyed sweet I fellowship:
 in the I house I of our I God.

[16 Let them pass aIway · in conΙfusion:
 let death I carry · them I to desΙtruction;

17 Let them go down aIlive to I Sheol:
 for evil is aImong them I in their I dwellings.]

18 But I will I call to I God:
 and the I Lord my I God will I save me.

19 At evening at morning I and at I noon-day:
 I comΙplain and I groan aIloud.

20 And he will I hear my I voice:
 and I ransom · my I soul in I peace,

21 From those that bear ǀ down upǀon me:
　　for ǀ there are ǀ many · aǀgainst me.

22 God will hear and ǀ bring them ǀ low:
　　he that ǀ is enǀthroned for ǀ ever.

23 For they do not ǀ keep their ǀ word:
　　and they ǀ have no ǀ fear of ǀ God.

24 They lay violent hands ‿
　　　　on those that ǀ are at ǀ peace with them:
　　they ǀ break ǀ solemn ǀ covenants.

25 Their mouths are smooth as butter
　　　　but war is ǀ in their ǀ hearts:
　　their words are softer than oil
　　　　yet ǀ they are ǀ drawn ǀ swords.

26 Cast your burden on the Lord and ǀ
　　　　he · will susǀtain you:
　　he will never suffer the ǀ righteous ǀ man to ǀ stumble.

27 But as for them　you will bring them ǀ down O ǀ God:
　　even ǀ to the ǀ depths · of the ǀ Pit.

†28 Bloodthirsty and deceitful men ‿
　　　　shall not live out ǀ half their ǀ days:
　　but ǀ I will ǀ trust in ǀ you.

PSALM 56

1 Be merciful to me O God　for men are ǀ treading · me ǀ
　　　　down:
　　all day long my ǀ adver·sary ǀ presses · upǀon me.

2 My enemies tread me down ǀ all the ǀ day:
　　for there are many that ǀ arrogant·ly ǀ
　　　　fight aǀgainst me.

3 In the ǀ hour of ǀ fear:
　　I will ǀ put my ǀ trust in ǀ you.

4 In God whose word I praise * in God I ǀ trust and ǀ
　　　　fear not:
　　what can ǀ flesh ǀ do to ǀ me?

5 All day long they afflict me ǀ with their ǀ words:
　　and every thought is ǀ how to ǀ do me ǀ evil.

6 They stir up hatred I and con‖ceal themselves:
    they watch my steps   while they I lie in I
        wait for · my I life.

7 Let there be I no es‖cape for them:
    bring down the I peoples · in your I wrath O I God.

8 You have counted my anxious tossings
    put my I tears · in your I bottle:
    are not these things I noted I in your I book?

9 In the day that I call to you   my enemies shall I turn I
        back:
    this I I know   for I God is I with me.

10 In God whose word I praise * in God I I trust and I
        fear not:
    what can I man I do to I me?

11 To you O God must I per‖form my I vows:
    I will pay the thank-‖offer·ing I that is I due.

12 For you will deliver my soul from death ‿
        and my I feet from I falling:
    that I may walk before I God · in the I light · of the I
        living.

PSALM 57

1 Be merciful to me O I God be I merciful:
    for I I come to I you for I shelter;

2 And in the shadow of your wings will I I take I refuge:
    until these I troubles · are I over-‖past.

3 I will call to I God Most I High:
    to the God who will ful‖fil his I purpose I for me.

4 He will send from I heaven · and I save me:
    he will send forth his faithfulness and his ‿
        loving-kindness
    and rebuke I those · that would I trample · me I down.

5 For I lie amidst I raven·ing I lions:
    men whose teeth are spears and arrows
        and their I tongue a I sharpened I sword.

6 *Be exalted O God a⏐bove the ⏐ heavens:*
   and let your glory be ⏐ over ⏐ all the ⏐ earth.

7 They have set a net for my feet   and I am ⏐ brought ⏐
      low:
   they have dug a pit before me
      but shall ⏐ fall · into ⏐ it them⏐selves.

8 My heart is fixed O God my ⏐ heart is ⏐ fixed:
   I will ⏐ sing and ⏐ make ⏐ melody.

9 Awake my soul   awake ⏐ lute and ⏐ harp:
   for ⏐ I · will a⏐waken · the ⏐ morning.

10 I will give you thanks O Lord a⏐mong the ⏐ peoples:
   I will sing your ⏐ praise a⏐mong the ⏐ nations.

11 For the greatness of your mercy ⏐ reaches · to the ⏐
      heavens:
   and your ⏐ faithful·ness ⏐ to the ⏐ clouds.

12 *Be exalted O God a⏐bove the ⏐ heavens:*
   and let your glory be ⏐ over ⏐ all the ⏐ earth.

PSALM 58

[1 Do you indeed decree what is ⏐ just O ⏐ rulers:
   do you with uprightness ⏐ judge the ⏐ children · of ⏐
      men?

2 No   you work in the land with ⏐ evil ⏐ heart:
   you look on the violence ⏐ that your ⏐ hands have ⏐
      wrought.

3 The wicked are estranged ⏐ even · from the ⏐ womb:
   they are liars that go a⏐stray ⏐ from their ⏐ birth.

4 They are venomous with the ⏐ venom · of ⏐ serpents:
   like the deaf ⏐ asp that ⏐ stops its ⏐ ears,

†5 And will not heed the ⏐ voice · of the ⏐ charmers:
   though the ⏐ binder · of ⏐ spells be ⏐ skilful.

6 Break their teeth O ⏐ God · in their ⏐ mouths:
   shatter the jaws of the ⏐ young ⏐ lions · O ⏐ Lord.

7 Let them dissolve and drain a⏐way like ⏐ water:
   let them be trodden down   ⏐ let them ⏐ wither · like ⏐
      grass,

8 Like a woman's miscarriage that melts and ǀ passes ·
    aǀway:
    like an abortive birth that ǀ has not ǀ seen the ǀ sun.

9 Before they know it   let them be cut ǀ down like ǀ
        thorns:
    like brambles which a ǀ man sweeps ǀ angrily · aǀside.

10 The righteous shall rejoice when he ǀ sees the ǀ
        vengeance:
    he will wash his feet in the ǀ blood of ǀ the unǀgodly.

11 And men will say   'There is reǀward · for the ǀ
        righteous:
    there is indeed a ǀ God who ǀ judges · on ǀ earth.']

PSALM 59

1 Deliver me from my ǀ enemies · O ǀ God:
    lift me to safety from ǀ those that ǀ rise aǀgainst me;

2 O deliver me from the ǀ evilǀdoers:
    and ǀ save me · from ǀ blood·thirsty ǀ men.

3 For they lie in ǀ wait · for my ǀ life:
    savage men ǀ stir up ǀ violence · aǀgainst me.

4 Not for my sin or my transgression O Lord
        not for any ǀ evil · I have ǀ done:
    do they run and take ǀ up poǀsition · aǀgainst me.

5 Arise to ǀ meet me · and ǀ see:
    you that are Lord of ǀ hosts and ǀ God of ǀ Israel.

6 Awake to punish ǀ all the ǀ nations:
    have no mercy on those that so ǀ treacherous·ly ǀ do ǀ
        wrong.

7 They return every evening   they ǀ howl like ǀ dogs:
    they ǀ prowl aǀround the ǀ city.

8 Look how their ǀ mouths ǀ slaver:
    swords strike from their lips
        for they ǀ say ǀ 'Who will ǀ hear it?'

9 But you O Lord will ǀ laugh them · to ǀ scorn:
    you will deǀride ǀ all the ǀ nations.

10 I will look to I you · O my I strength:
for I God is · my I strong I tower.

11 My God in his steadfastness will I come to I meet me:
God will show me the I downfall I of my I enemies.

12 Slay them not O Lord   lest my I people · forIget:
but make them stagger by your I power and I
bring them I down.

13 Give them over to punishment * for the sin of their _
mouths for the I words of · their I lips:
let them be I taken I in their I pride.

14 For the curses and lies that they have uttered
O consume them I in your I wrath:
consume them I till they I are no I more;

†15 That men may know that God I rules · over I Jacob:
even to the I ends I of the I earth.

16 They return every evening   they I howl like I dogs:
they I prowl aIround the I city.

17 They roam here and there I looking · for I food:
and I growl · if they I are not I filled.

18 But I will I sing of · your I might:
I will sing aloud each I morning I of your I goodness.

19 For you have been my I strong I tower:
and a sure refuge in the I day of I my disItress.

†20 I will sing your praises I O my I strength:
for I God is · my I strong I tower.

PSALM 60

1 O God you have cast us I off and I broken us:
you were enraged against us   I O reIstore us ·
aIgain!

2 You have caused the land to quake   you have I rent it I
open:
heal the rifts for the I earth I quivers · and I breaks.

3 You have steeped your people in a I bitter I draught:
you have given them a I wine to I make them I
stagger.

4 You have caused those that fear you to | take | flight:
  so that they | run | from the | bow.

†5 O save us by your right | hand and | answer us:
  that those whom you | love may | be de|livered.

6 God has said in his | holy | place:
  'I will exult and divide Shechem
    I will parcel | out the | valley · of | Succoth.

7 'Gilead is mine and Ma|nasseh · is | mine:
  Ephraim is my helmet and | Judah · my |
    rod · of com|mand.

†8 'Moab is my wash-bowl   over Edom will I | cast my |
    shoe:
  against Philistia | will I | shout in | triumph.'

9 Who will lead me into the | forti·fied | city:
  who will | bring me | into | Edom?

10 Have you not cast us | off O | God?:
  you | go not | out · with our | armies.

11 Give us your help a|gainst the | enemy:
  for | vain · is the | help of | man.

12 By the power of our God we | shall do | valiantly:
  for it is he that will | tread | down our | enemies.

PSALM 61

1 Hear my loud | crying · O | God:
  and give | heed | to my | prayer.

2 From the ends of the earth I call to you ⌣
    when my | heart | faints:
  O set me on the | rock · that is | higher · than | I.

3 For you have | been my | refuge:
  and my strong | tower a|gainst the | enemy.

4 I will dwell in your | tent for | ever:
  and find shelter in the | cover·ing | of your | wings.

5 For you have heard my ǀ vows O ǀ God:
   you have granted the desire of ǀ those that ǀ fear your ǀ
      name.

6 You will give the ǀ king long ǀ life:
   and his years shall endure through ǀ many ǀ
      generǀations.

7 He shall dwell before ǀ God for ǀ ever:
   loving-kindness and ǀ truth shall ǀ be his ǀ guard.

8 So will I ever sing praises ǀ to your ǀ name:
   while I ǀ daily · perǀform my ǀ vows.

PSALM 62

1 My soul waits in ǀ silence · for ǀ God:
   for from ǀ him comes ǀ my salǀvation.

2 He only is my rock and ǀ my salǀvation:
   my strong tower   so that ǀ I shall ǀ never · be ǀ moved.

3 How long will you all plot against a ǀ
         man · to deǀstroy him:
   as though he were a leaning ǀ fence · or a ǀ buckling ǀ
      wall?

4 Their design is to thrust him from his height
         and their deǀlight · is in ǀ lies:
   they bless with their ǀ lips but ǀ inwardly · they ǀ curse.

5 Nevertheless my soul   wait in ǀ silence · for ǀ God:
   for from ǀ him ǀ comes my ǀ hope.

6 He only is my rock and ǀ my salǀvation:
   my strong tower   so that ǀ I shall ǀ not be ǀ moved.

7 In God is my deliverance ǀ and my ǀ glory:
   God is my strong ǀ rock ǀ and my ǀ shelter.

8 Trust in him at all times ǀ O my ǀ people:
   pour out your hearts before him   for ǀ God ǀ is our ǀ
      refuge.

9 The children of men are but breath
         the children of ǀ men · are a ǀ lie:
   place them in the scales and they fly upward
         they ǀ are as ǀ light as ǀ air.

10 Put no trust in extortion
    do not grow ı worthless · by ı robbery:
    if riches increase ı set not · your ı heart upıon them.

11 God has spoken once   twice have I ı heard him ı say:
    that ı power beılongs to ı God,

12 That to the Lord belongs a ı constant ı goodness:
    for you reward a man acıcording ı to his ı works.

PSALM 63

1 O God ı you are · my ı God:
    eagerly ı will I ı seek ı you.

2 My soul thirsts for you   my ı flesh ı longs for you:
    as a dry and thirsty ı land · where no ı water ı is.

3 So it was when I beheld you ı in the ı sanctuary:
    and ı saw your ı power · and your ı glory.

4 For your unchanging goodness is ı better · than ı life:
    thereıfore my ı lips shall ı praise you.

5 And so I will bless you as ı long as · I ı live:
    and in your name will I ı lift my ı hands on ı high.

6 My longing shall be satisfied ＿
    as with ı marrow · and ı fatness:
    my mouth shall ı praise you · with exıultant ı lips.

7 When I remember you upıon my ı bed:
    when I meditate upıon you · in the ı night ı watches,

8 How you have ı been my ı helper:
    then I sing for joy in the ı shadow ı of your ı wings,

†9 Then my ı soul ı clings to you:
    and ı your right ı hand upıholds me.

10 Those that seek my life are ı marked · for deıstruction:
    they shall go down to the deep ı places ı of the ı earth.

11 They shall be deılivered · to the ı sword:
    they shall ı be a ı portion · for ı jackals.

†12 The king will rejoice in God
    and all who take oaths on his ı name shall ı glory:
    but the mouths of ı liars ı shall be ı stopped.

PSALM 64

1 Hear my voice O God in I my comIplaining:
   preserve my I life from I fear · of the I enemy.

2 Hide me from the conspiracy I of the I wicked:
   from the I throng of I evilIdoers,

3 Who sharpen their I tongues like I swords:
   who string the bow   who take I arrows · of I bitter I
   words,

4 To shoot from hiding at the I blameless I man:
   to strike at him I sudden·ly I and unIseen.

5 They are confirmed in an I evil I purpose:
   they confide it to one another while they lay the ⌣
   snares   I saying I 'Who will I see them?'

6 They hatch mischief   they hide a well-conIsidered I
   plan:
   for the mind and heart of I man is I very I deep.

7 But God will shoot at them with his I swift I arrows:
   they shall be I sudden·ly I struck I through.

8 The Lord will bring them down ⌣
   for what their I tongues have I spoken:
   and all that see it shall I toss their I heads in I scorn.

9 Then I all men · shall I fear:
   and tell what the Lord has I done and I ponder · his I
   works.

10 The righteous man shall rejoice in the Lord
   and find in I him his I refuge:
   and all the I upright · in I heart · shall exIult.

PSALM 65

1 You are to be praised O I God in I Zion:
   to you shall vows be paid I   you that I answer I
   prayer.

2 To you shall all flesh come to conIfess their I sins:
   when our misdeeds prevail against us I ⌣
   you will I purge · them aIway.

†3 Blessèd is the man whom you choose
    and take to yourself to dwell with|in your | courts:
  we shall be filled with the good things ⌣
    of your house | of your | holy | temple.

4 You will answer us in your righteousness ⌣
    with terrible deeds O | God our | saviour:
  you that are the hope of all the ends of the earth ⌣
    and | of the | distant | seas;

5 Who by your strength made | fast the | mountains:
  you | that are | girded · with | power;

6 Who stilled the raging of the seas ⌣
    the | roaring · of the | waves:
  and the | tumult | of the | peoples.

7 Those who dwell at the ends of the earth ⌣
    are a|fraid at · your | wonders:
  the dawn and the | even·ing | sing your | praises.

8 You tend the | earth and | water it:
  you | make it | rich and | fertile.

9 The river of God is | full of | water:
  and so providing for the earth ⌣
    you pro|vide | grain for | men.

10 You drench its furrows   you level the | ridges ·
    be|tween:
  you soften it with showers and | bless its | early |
    growth.

11 You crown the | year · with your | goodness:
  and the tracks where you have | passed | drip with |
    fatness.

12 The pastures of the | wilderness · run | over:
  and the | hills are | girded· with | joy.

13 The meadows are | clothed with | sheep:
  and the valleys stand so thick with corn ⌣
    they | shout for | joy and | sing.

PSALM 66

1 O shout with joy to God I all the I earth:
 sing to the honour of his name
 and give him I glory I as his I praise.

2 Say to God 'How fearful I are your I works:
 because of your great might ⌣
 your I enemies · shall I cower · belfore you.'

3 All the I earth shall I worship you:
 and sing to you and sing I praises I to your I name.

4 Come then and see what I God has I done:
 how terrible are his I dealings · with the I
 children · of I men.

5 He turned the sea into dry land
 they crossed the I river · on I foot:
 then I were we I joyful · belcause of him.

6 By his power he rules for ever
 his eyes keep I watch · on the I nations:
 and rebels shall I never I rise algainst him.

7 O bless our I God you I peoples:
 and cause his I praises I to relsound,

8 Who has held our I souls in I life:
 who has not I suffered · our I feet to I slip.

9 For you have I proved us · O I God:
 you have I tried us · as I silver · is I tried.

10 You brought us I into · the I net:
 you laid sharp I torment I on our I loins.

†11 You let men ride over our heads
 we went through I fire and I water:
 but you brought us out I into · a I place of I liberty.

12 I will come into your house with I burnt-Iofferings:
 and I I will I pay you · my I vows,

13 The vows that I opened · my I lips:
 that my mouth uttered I when I I was in I trouble.

14 I will offer you burnt-offerings of fattened beasts
    with the sweet I smoke of I rams:
    I will sacrifice a I bull · and the I flesh of I goats.

15 Come then and hear   all I you that · fear I God:
    and I will I tell what I he has I done for me.

16 I called to him I with my I mouth:
    and his I praise was I on my I tongue.

17 If I had cherished wickedness I in my I heart:
    the I Lord would I not have I heard me.

18 But I God has I heard me:
    he has I heeded · the I voice of · my I prayer.

19 Praise I be to I God:
    who has not turned back my prayer
    or his I steadfast I love I from me.

PSALM 67

1 Let God be gracious to I us and I bless us:
    and make his I face I shine up|on us,

2 That your ways may be I known on I earth:
    your liberating I power · a|mong all I nations.

3 Let the peoples I praise you · O I God:
    let I all the I peoples I praise you.

4 Let the nations be I glad and I sing:
    for you judge the peoples with integrity
    and govern the I nations · up|on I earth.

5 Let the peoples I praise you · O I God:
    let I all the I peoples I praise you.

6 Then the earth will I yield its I fruitfulness:
    and I God our I God will I bless us.

†7 God I shall I bless us:
    and all the I ends · of the I earth will I fear him.

PSALM 68

1 God shall arise   and his enemies I shall be I scattered:
  those that hate him shall I flee belfore his I face.

2 As smoke is dispersed   so shall I they · be dislpersed:
  as wax melts before a fire * so shall the wicked I perish
    · at the I presence · of I God.

3 But the righteous shall be glad and exlult be·fore I God:
  they I shall reljoice with I gladness.

4 O sing to God   sing praises I to his I name:
  glorify him that rode through the deserts * him _
    whose name is the Lord I and exlult belfore him.

5 He is the father of the fatherless
    he upholds the I cause · of the I widow:
  God I in his I holy I dwelling place.

6 He gives the desolate a home to dwell in
    and brings the prisoners out I into · prosIperity:
  but rebels must I dwell · in a I barren I land.

7 O God   when you went out belfore your I people:
  when you I marched I through the I wilderness,

8 The earth shook   the heavens I poured down I water:
  before the God of Sinai   before I God the I God of I
    Israel.

9 You showered down a generous I rain O I God:
  you prepared the land of your posIsession · when I
    it was I weary.

10 And there your I people I settled:
  in the place that your goodness O God _
    had made I ready I for the I poor.

11 The Lord spoke the word * and great was the _
    company of those that I carried · the I tidings:
  'Kings with their armies are I fleeing · are I fleeing ·
    alway.

12 'Even the women at home may I share · in the I spoil:
  and will you sit I idly · almong the I sheepfolds?

13 'There are images of doves ⏜
    whose wings are ǀ covered · with ǀ silver:
and their ǀ pinions · with ǀ shining ǀ gold.'

14 When the Almighty ǀ scattered ǀ kings:
    they were like snow ǀ falling · upǀon Mount ǀ
    Zalmon.

15 The mountain of Bashan is a ǀ mighty ǀ mountain:
    the mountain of Bashan is a ǀ mountain · of ǀ many ǀ
    peaks.

16 O mountains of many peaks   why ǀ look so ǀ
    enviously:
at the mountain where God is pleased to dwell
    where the ǀ Lord · will reǀmain for ǀ ever?

17 The chariots of God are twice ten thousand ⏜
    and ǀ thousands up·on ǀ thousands:
the Lord came from Sinai ǀ into · his ǀ holy ǀ place.

18 When you ascended the heights you led the enemy ⏜
    captive * you received ǀ tribute · from ǀ men:
but rebels shall not ǀ dwell · in the ǀ presence · of ǀ
    God.

19 Blessèd be the Lord day by day
    who bears us ǀ as his ǀ burden:
he is the ǀ God of ǀ our deǀliverance.

20 God is to us a ǀ God who ǀ saves:
    by God the Lord do ǀ we esǀcape ǀ death.

[21 But God shall smite the ǀ heads · of his ǀ enemies:
    the hairy scalp of ǀ those that ǀ walk · in their ǀ sins.

22 The Lord said 'I will bring them ǀ back from ǀ Bashan:
    I will bring them aǀgain · from the ǀ deep ǀ sea';

[†]23 That you may dip your ǀ feet in ǀ blood:
    and the tongues of your ǀ dogs ·
    in the ǀ blood of · your ǀ enemies.]

24 Your procession is ǀ seen O ǀ God:
    the procession of my ǀ God and ǀ King · in the ǀ
    sanctuary.

25 The singers go before   the mu|sicians · come | after:
 and around them the maidens | beating | on the |
  timbrels.

26 In their choirs they | bless | God:
 those that are sprung from the fount of | Israel | ＿
  bless the | Lord.

27 There is the little tribe of | Benja·min | leading them:
 the throng of the princes of Judah   the princes of |
  Zebulun · and the | princes · of | Naphtali.

28 Give the command my God * in accordance |
   with your | power:
 that godlike | power where|by you | act for us.

29 Give the command from your temple | at Je|rusalem:
 and | kings shall | bring you | tribute.

30 Rebuke the beast of the reeds
   the herd of bulls amidst the | brutish | peoples:
 tread down those that are greedy for silver
   scatter the | peoples · that | relish | war.

31 Let them bring | bronze from | Egypt:
 let the hands of the Nubians | carry · it | swiftly · to |
  God.

32 Sing to God you | kingdoms · of the | earth:
 O sing | praises | to the | Lord,

33 To him that rides upon the highest heavens
   that were | from · the be|ginning:
 who utters his voice which | is a | mighty | voice.

34 Ascribe power to God   whose majesty is | over |
   Israel:
 and his | might is | in the | clouds.

35 Terrible is God who comes from his | holy | place:
 the God of Israel who gives   power and strength ＿
  to his people * | Blessèd | be | God.

PSALM 69

1 Save ǀ me O ǀ God:
>   for the waters have come up ǀ even ǀ to my ǀ throat.

2 I sink in the deep mire ǀ where no ǀ footing is:
>   I have come into deep waters ǀ and the ǀ
>   flood sweeps ǀ over me.

3 I am weary with crying out   my ǀ throat is ǀ parched:
>   my eyes fail with ǀ watching · so ǀ long · for my ǀ God.

4 Those that hate me without cause
>   are more in number than the ǀ hairs · of my ǀ head:
>   those that would destroy me are many
>   they oppose me wrongfully
>   for I must restore ǀ things · that I ǀ never ǀ took.

5 O God you ǀ know my ǀ foolishness:
>   and my ǀ sins · are not ǀ hidden ǀ from you.

6 Let not those who wait for you be shamed ‿
>   because of me   O Lord ǀ God of ǀ hosts:
>   let not those who seek you be disgraced on ǀ ‿
>   my account · O ǀ God of ǀ Israel.

7 For your sake have I ǀ suffered · reǀproach:
>   and ǀ shame has ǀ covered · my ǀ face.

8 I have become a stranger ǀ to my ǀ brothers:
>   an alien ǀ to my · own ǀ mother's ǀ sons.

9 Zeal for your house has ǀ eaten · me ǀ up:
>   and the taunts of those who taunt ǀ you have ǀ
>   fallen · on ǀ me.

10 I afflicted myǀself with ǀ fasting:
>   and that was ǀ turned to ǀ my reǀproach.

11 I made ǀ sackcloth · my ǀ clothing:
>   and I beǀcame a ǀ byword ǀ to them.

12 Those who sit in the gate ǀ talk of ǀ me:
>   and the ǀ drunkards · make ǀ songs aǀbout me.

13 But to you Lord I ǀ make my ǀ prayer:
>   at ǀ an acǀcepta·ble ǀ time.

14 Answer me O God in your a|bundant | goodness:
   and | with your | sure de|liverance.

15 Bring me out of the mire   so that I | may not | sink:
   let me be delivered from my enemies ⌣
      and | from the | deep | waters.

16 Let not the flood overwhelm me
      or the depths | swallow · me | up:
   let not the | Pit · shut its | mouth up|on me.

17 Hear me O Lord   as your loving-|kindness · is | good:
   turn to me   as | your com|passion · is | great.

18 Do not hide your | face · from your | servant:
   for I am in trouble | O be | swift to | answer me!

19 Draw near to me | and re|deem me:
   O | ransom me · be|cause of · my | enemies!

20 You know | all their | taunts:
   my adversaries are | all | in your | sight.

21 Insults have | broken · my | heart:
   my shame and dis|grace are | past | healing.

22 I looked for someone to have pity on me
      but | there was | no man:
   for some to | comfort me · but | found | none.

†23 They gave me | poison · for | food:
   and when I was thirsty they | gave me | vinegar · to | drink.

[24 Let their table be|come a | snare:
   and their sacri|fici·al | feasts a | trap.

25 Let their eyes be darkened   so that they | cannot | see:
   and make their | loins | shake con|tinually.

26 Pour out your | wrath up|on them:
   and let your fierce | anger | over|take them.

27 Let their | camp be | desolate:
   and let | no man | dwell · in their | tents.

28 For they persecute him whom | you have | stricken:
   and multiply the pain of | him whom | you have | wounded.

29 Let them have punishment up|on | punishment:
    let them | not re|ceive · your for|giveness.

†30 Let them be blotted out of the | book · of the | living:
    let them not be written | down a|mong the |
        righteous.]

31 As for me I am | poor · and in | misery:
    O God let your de|liver·ance | lift me | up.

32 And I will praise the name of | God · in a | song:
    and | glori·fy | him with | thanksgiving.

33 And that will please the Lord | more · than an | ox:
    more than a bull with | horns and | cloven | hoof.

34 Consider this you that are | meek ·   and re|joice:
    seek God and | let your | heart be | glad.

35 For the Lord | listens · to the | poor:
    he does not despise his | servants | in cap|tivity.

36 Let the heavens and the | earth | praise him:
    the | seas and | all that | moves in them.

37 For God will | save | Zion:
    he will re|build the | cities · of | Judah.

38 His people shall live there and possess it
    the seed of his servants | shall in|herit it:
    and those who | love his | name shall | dwell in it.

PSALM 70

1 O God be | pleased · to de|liver me:
    O | Lord make | haste to | help me.

2 Let them be put to shame and confounded who |
        seek my | life:
    let them be turned back and dis|graced who |
        wish me | evil.

3 Let them turn a|way for | shame:
    who | say to me · 'A|ha a|ha!'

4 Let all who seek you be joyful and |
        glad be|cause of you:
    let those who love your salvation say |
        always | 'God is | great.'

5 As for me I am I poor and I needy:
   O I God be I swift to I save me.

6 You are my helper and I my deǀliverer:
   O I Lord make I no deǀlay.

PSALM 71

1 To you Lord have I I come for I shelter:
   let me I never · be I put to I shame.

2 In your righteousness rescue I and deǀliver me:
   incline your I ear to I me and I save me.

3 Be for me a rock of refuge * a fortress I to deǀfend me:
   for you are my high I rock I and my I stronghold.

4 Rescue me O my God from the I hand · of the I wicked:
   from the grasp of the I piti·less I and unǀjust.

5 For you Lord I are my I hope:
   you are my confidence O I God · from my I youth I
   upward.

6 On you have I I leaned · since my I birth:
   you are he that brought me out of my mother's womb
   and my I praise · is of I you conǀtinually.

7 I have become as a fearful I warning · to I many:
   but I you are · my I strength · and my I refuge.

8 My mouth shall be I filled · with your I praises:
   I shall sing of your I glory I all the · day I long.

9 Cast me not away in the I time of · old I age:
   nor forsake me I when my I strength I fails.

10 For my enemies I speak aǀgainst me:
   and those that watch for my life ‿
   conǀspire toǀgether I saying,

†11 'God I has forǀsaken him:
   pursue him   take him   for I there is I none to I save
   him.'

12 Be not far I from me · O I God:
   my I God make I haste to I help me.

13 Let my adversaries be confounded and ı put to ı shame:
    let those who seek my hurt ‿
        be ı covered · with ı scorn · and disıgrace.

14 As for me   I will wait in ı hope conıtinually:
    and I will ı praise you ı more and ı more.

15 My mouth shall speak of your righteousness ı all the ı
        day:
    and tell of your salvation ı though it · exıceeds my ı
        telling.

16 I will begin with the mighty acts of the ı Lord my ı God:
    and declare your righteous ı dealing   ı yours aılone.

17 O God you have taught me from my ı youth ı upward:
    and to this day I proıclaim your ı marvel·lous ı works.

18 Forsake me not O God in my old age   when I am ı
        grey-ıheaded:
    till I have shown the strength of your arm ‿
        to future generations * and your ı might to ı
            those that · come ı after.

19 Your righteousness O God ı reaches · to the ı heavens:
    great are the things that you have done
        O ı God ı who is ı like you?

20 You have burdened me with many and bitter troubles
        O ı turn · and reınew me:
    and raise me up aıgain · from the ı depths · of the ı
        earth.

21 Bless me beyond my ı former ı greatness:
    O ı turn to me · aıgain and ı comfort me.

22 Then will I praise you upon the lute ‿
        for your faithfulness ı O my ı God:
    and sing your praises to the harp O ı Holy ı One of ı
        Israel.

23 My lips shall reıjoice in · my ı singing:
    and my soul ı also · for ı you have ı ransomed me.

†24 My tongue shall speak of your righteous dealing ı
        all the · day ı long:
    for they shall be put to shame and disgraced ‿
        that ı seek to ı do me ı evil.

PSALM 72

1 Give the king your | judgment · O | God:
　and your righteousness to the | son | of a | king.

2 That he may judge your | people | rightly:
　and the | poor · of the | land with | equity.

3 Let the mountains be laden with peace ⌣
　　be|cause of · his | righteousness:
　and the hills also with pros|peri·ty | for his | people.

4 May he give justice to the poor a|mong the | people:
　and rescue the children of the | needy ·
　　and | crush · the op|pressor.

5 May he live while the | sun en|dures:
　and while the moon gives light through|out all |
　　gener|ations.

6 May he come down like rain upon the | new-mown |
　　fields:
　and as | showers · that | water · the | earth.

7 In his time shall | righteous·ness | flourish:
　and abundance of peace till the | moon shall | be no |
　　more.

8 His dominion shall stretch from | sea to | sea:
　from the Great | River · to the | ends · of the | earth.

9 His adversaries shall bow | down be|fore him:
　and his | enemies · shall | lick the | dust.

10 The kings of Tarshish and of the isles shall |
　　bring | tribute:
　the kings of Sheba and | Seba · shall | offer | gifts.

†11 All kings shall fall | down be|fore him:
　and all | nations | do him | service.

12 He will deliver the needy | when they | cry:
　and the | poor man · that | has no | helper.

13 He will pity the helpless | and the | needy:
　and | save the | lives · of the | poor.

†14 He will redeem them from op|pression · and | violence:
   and their blood shall be | precious | in his | sight.

15 Long may he live   and be given of the | gold of | Sheba:
   may prayer be made for him continually
      and men | bless him | every | day.

16 Let there be abundance of | wheat · in the | land:
   let it | flourish · on the | tops · of the | mountains;

†17 Let its ears grow fat like the | grain of | Lebanon:
   and its sheaves | thicken · like the | grass · of the |
      field.

18 Let his name | live for | ever:
   and en|dure as | long · as the | sun.

19 Let all peoples use his | name in | blessing:
   and all | nations | call him | blessèd.

20 Blessèd be the Lord God the | God of | Israel:
   who a|lone does | great | wonders.

21 Blessèd be his glorious | name for | ever:
   and let the whole earth be filled with his glory |
      Amen | A–|men.

PSALM 73

1 God is indeed | good to | Israel:
   to | those whose | hearts are | pure.

2 Nevertheless my feet were | almost | gone:
   my | steps had | well-nigh | slipped.

3 For I was filled with envy | at the | boastful:
   when I saw the un|godly · had | such tran|quillity.

4 For they | suffer · no | pain:
   and their | bodies · are | hale and | fat.

5 They come to no mis|fortune · like | other folk:
   nor | are they | plagued like | other men.

6 Therefore they put on | pride · as a | necklace:
  and clothe themselves in | vio·lence | as · in a |
    garment.

7 Their eyes shine from | folds of | fatness:
  and they have | all that | heart could | wish.

8 Their talk is | malice · and | mockery:
  and they hand down | slanders | from on | high.

9 Their mouths blas|pheme a·gainst | heaven:
  and their tongues go | to and | fro on | earth.

10 Therefore my | people | turn to them:
   and | find in | them no | fault.

11 They say | 'How can · God | know:
   is there under|standing · in the | Most | High?'

12 Behold | these are · the un|godly:
   yet they | prosper · and in|crease in | riches.

13 Was it for nothing then that I | cleansed my | heart:
   and | washed my | hands in | innocence?

14 Have I been stricken all day | long in | vain:
   and re|buked | every | morning?

†15 If I had said | 'I will · speak | thus':
   I should have betrayed the | fami·ly | of your |
     children.

16 Then I thought to under|stand | this:
   but it | was too | hard | for me,

17 Till I went into the | sanctuary · of | God:
   and then I under|stood · what their | end will | be.

18 For you set them in | slipper·y | places:
   and cause them to | fall · from their | treacher·ous |
     footholds.

19 How suddenly they are | laid | waste:
   they come to an | end   they | perish · in | terror.

†20 As with a dream when | one a|wakes:
   so when you rouse yourself O Lord | ‿
     you will · de|spise their | image.

21 When my | heart was | soured:
   and I was | wounded | to the | core,

22 I was but I brutish · and I ignorant:
    no I better · than a I beast beIfore you.

23 Nevertheless I am I always I with you:
    for you hold me I by my I right I hand.

24 You will guide me I with your I counsel:
    and afterwards I you will I lead me · to I glory.

25 Whom have I in I heaven · but I you?:
    and there is no one upon earth ⌣
        that I deIsire · in comIparison · with I you.

26 Though my flesh and my I heart I fail me:
    you O I God · are my I portion · for I ever.

27 Behold those who forIsake you · shall I perish:
    and all who whore after other I gods you I
        will deIstroy.

28 But it is good for me to draw I near to I God:
    I have made the Lord God my refuge
        and I will tell of I all that I you have I done.

PSALM 74

1 O Lord our God   why cast us I off so I utterly:
    why does your anger burn aIgainst the I
        sheep of · your I pasture?

2 Remember your congregation * whom you took ⌣
        to yourIself of I old:
    the people that you redeemed to be your own ⌣
        possession
            and Mount I Zion · where I you have I dwelt.

3 Rouse yourself and go to the I utter I ruins:
    to all the harm that the I enemy · has I done · in the I
        sanctuary.

4 Your adversaries have made uproar ⌣
        in the place appointed I for your I praise:
    they have set I up their I standards · inI triumph.

5 They have destroyed on I every I side:
    like those who take axes I up · to a I thicket · of I trees.

6 All the carved woodwork they have I broken I down:
  and I smashed it · with I hammers · and I hatchets.

7 They have set I fire to · your I sanctuary:
  and defiled to the ground the I dwelling-· place I
      of your I name.

8 They have said in their hearts 'Let us make I havoc I
      of them':
  they have burned down ⌣
      all the holy I places · of I God · in the I land.

9 We see no signs * there is not one I prophet I left:
  there is none who knows how I long these I
      things shall I be.

10 How long shall the adversary I taunt you · O I God:
   shall the enemy blasIpheme your I name for I ever?

†11 Why do you hold I back your I hand:
   why do you keep your I right hand I in your I bosom?

12 Yet God is my I king · from of I old:
   who wrought deIliverance · upIon the I earth.

13 You divided the I sea · by your I might:
   you shattered the heads of the I dragons I in the I
       waters.

14 You crushed the I heads · of LeIviathan:
   and gave him as food to the I creatures · of the I
       desert I waste.

15 You cleft open I spring and I fountain:
   you dried up the I everIflowing I waters.

16 The day is yours * and so also I is the I night:
   you have esItablished · the I moon · and the I sun.

17 You set all the boundaries I of the I earth:
   you creIated I winter · and I summer.

18 Remember O Lord the I taunts · of the I enemy:
   how a mindless I people · have blasIphemed your I
       name.

19 Do not give to the wild beasts the ǀ soul that ǀ
        praises you:
    do not forget for ever the ǀ life of ǀ your afǀflicted.

20 Look on all that ǀ you have ǀ made:
    for it is full of darkness
        and ǀ violence · inǀhabits · the ǀ earth.

21 Let not the oppressed and reviled turn aǀway reǀjected:
    but let the poor and ǀ needy ǀ praise your ǀ name.

22 Arise O God * plead your ǀ own ǀ cause:
    remember how a mindless people ǀ taunt you ǀ all day
        ǀ long.

23 Do not forget the ǀ clamour · of your ǀ adversaries:
    or how the shouting of your ǀ
        enemies · asǀcends conǀtinually.

PSALM 75

1 We give you thanks O God we ǀ give you ǀ thanks:
    we call upon your name
        and tell of all the ǀ wonders ǀ you have ǀ done.

2 'I will surely apǀpoint a ǀ time:
    when I the ǀ Lord will ǀ judge with ǀ equity.

3 'Though the earth shake and ǀ all who ǀ dwell in it:
    it is ǀ I · that have ǀ founded · its ǀ pillars.

4 'I will say to the boasters ǀ "Boast no ǀ more":
    and to the wicked ǀ "Do not ǀ flaunt your ǀ horns;

†5 '"Do not flaunt your ǀ horns so ǀ high:
    or speak so ǀ proud and ǀ stiff-ǀnecked."'

6 For there is none from the east or ǀ from the ǀ west:
    or from the wilderness ǀ who can ǀ raise ǀ up;

7 But it is God who ǀ is the ǀ judge:
    who puts down ǀ one · and exǀalts anǀother.

8 For there is a cup in the ǀ Lord's ǀ hand:
    and the wine ǀ foams · and is ǀ richly ǀ mixed;

9 He gives it in turn to each of the ǀ wicked · of the ǀ earth:
    they drink it and ǀ drain it ǀ to the ǀ dregs.

10 But I will sing praises to the ∣ God of ∣ Jacob:
    I will ∣ glorify · his ∣ name for ∣ ever.

11 All the horns of the ∣ wicked · I will ∣ break:
    but the horns of the ∣ righteous · shall be ∣ lifted ∣ high.

PSALM 76

1 In Judah ∣ God is ∣ known:
    his ∣ name is ∣ great in ∣ Israel.

2 At Salem ∣ is his ∣ tabernacle:
    and his ∣ dwelling ∣ is in ∣ Zion.

3 There he broke in pieces the flashing ∣ arrows · of the ∣ bow:
    the shield the ∣ sword · and the ∣ weapons · of ∣ battle.

4 Radiant in ∣ light are ∣ you:
    greater in majesty ∣ than · the e∣ternal ∣ hills.

5 The valiant were dumbfounded   they ∣ sleep their ∣ sleep:
    and all the men of ∣ war have ∣ lost their ∣ strength.

6 At the blast of your voice O ∣ God of ∣ Jacob:
    both horse and ∣ chariot · were ∣ cast a∣sleep.

7 Terrible are ∣ you Lord ∣ God:
    and who may stand be∣fore you · when ∣ you are ∣ angry?

8 You caused your sentence to be ∣ heard from ∣ heaven:
    the earth ∣ feared ∣ and was ∣ still,

9 When God a∣rose to ∣ judgment:
    to ∣ save · all the ∣ meek · of the ∣ earth.

10 For you crushed the ∣ wrath of ∣ man:
    you bridled the ∣ remnant ∣ of the ∣ wrathful.

11 O make vows to the Lord your ∣ God and ∣ keep them:
    let all around him bring gifts _
      to him that is ∣ worthy ∣ to be ∣ feared.

12 For he cuts down the ∣ fury · of ∣ princes:
    and he is terrible to the ∣ kings ∣ of the ∣ earth.

PSALM 77

1 I call to my God   I cry I out tolward him:
    I call to my God   and I surely I he will I answer.

2 In the day of my distress I seek the Lord
        I stretch out my hands to I him by I night:
    my soul is poured out without ceasing
        it relfuses I all I comfort.

3 I think upon God and I groan alloud:
    I I muse · and my I spirit I faints.

4 You hold my I eyelids I open:
    I am so I dazed · that I I cannot I flee.

5 I consider the I times · that are I past:
    I remember the I years of I long algo.

6 At night I am I grieved · to the I heart:
    I ponder I and my I spirit · makes I search;

7 'Will the Lord cast us I off for I ever:
    will he I show us · his I favour · no I more?

8 'Is his mercy clean I gone for I ever:
    and his promise come to an I end for I all ·
        generlations?

9 'Has God forIgotten · to be I gracious:
    has he shut up his I pity I in disIpleasure?'

10 And I say * 'Has the right hand of the Most High I
        lost its I strength:
    has the I arm · of the I Lord I changed?'

11 I will declare the mighty I acts · of the I Lord:
    I will call to I mind your I wonders · of I old.

12 I will think on all that I you have I done:
    and I meditate · uplon your I works.

13 Your way O I God is I holy:
    who is so I great a I god as I our God?

14 You are the God that I works I wonders:
    you made known your I power almong the I nations;

15 By your mighty arm you reIdeemed your I people:

the | children · of | Jacob · and | Joseph.

16 The waters saw you O God
    the waters saw you and | were a|fraid:
the | depths | also · were | troubled.

17 The clouds poured out water   the | heavens | spoke:
and your | arrows | darted | forth.

18 The voice of your thunder was | heard · in the |
    whirlwind:
your lightnings lit the world
    the | earth | shuddered · and | quaked.

19 Your way was in the sea * your path in the | great |
    waters:
and your | footsteps | were not | seen.

20 You led your | people · like | sheep:
by the | hand of | Moses · and | Aaron.

PSALM 78

1 Give heed to my teaching | O my | people:
incline your | ears · to the | words of · my | mouth;

2 For I will open my | mouth · in a | parable:
and expound the | mysteries · of | former | times.

3 What we have | heard and | known:
what | our fore|fathers · have | told us,

4 We will not hide from their children
    but declare to a generation | yet to | come:
the praiseworthy acts of the Lord
    his | mighty · and | wonderful | works.

5 He established a law in Jacob
    and made a de|cree in | Israel:
which he commanded our fore|fathers · to |
    teach their | children,

6 That future generations might know
    and the children | yet un|born:
that they in turn might | teach it | to their | sons;

7 So that they might put their | confidence · in | God:
and not forget his | works but |
    keep · his com|mandments,

8 And not be as their forefathers
    a stubborn and re|bellious · gener|ation:
  a generation that did not set their heart aright
    whose spirit I was not I faithful · to I God.

9 The children of Ephraim I armed · with the I bow:
    turned I back · in the I day of I battle.

10 They did not keep God's covenant
    they refused to I walk in · his I law:
  they forgot what he had done
    and the I wonders I he had I shown them.

11 For he did marvellous things ‿
    in the I sight of · their I fathers:
  in the land of Egypt I in the I country · of I Zoan.

12 He divided the sea and I let them · pass I through:
    he made the I waters · stand I up · in a I heap.

13 In the daytime he I led them · with a I cloud:
    and all night I long · with the I light of I fire.

14 He cleft I rocks · in the I wilderness:
    and gave them drink in abundance I ‿
      as from I springs of I water.

†15 He brought streams I out of · the I rock:
    and caused the waters to I flow I down like I rivers.

16 But for all this they sinned yet I more a|gainst him:
    and rebelled against the Most I High I in the I desert.

17 They wilfully put I God · to the I test:
    and de|manded I food · for their I appetite.

18 They spoke against I God and I said:
    'Can God prepare a I table I in the I wilderness?

19 'He indeed struck the rock * so that the waters gushed ‿
    and the I streams · over|flowed:
  but can he also give bread
    or provide I meat I for his I people?'

20 When the Lord heard it he was angry
    and a fire was kindled a|gainst I Jacob:
  his wrath I blazed a|gainst I Israel.

21 For they put no | trust in | God:
  nor would they be|lieve his | power to | save.

†22 Then he commanded the | clouds a|bove:
  and | opened · the | doors of | heaven.

23 He rained down manna for | them to | eat:
  and | gave them · the | grain of | heaven.

24 So men ate the | bread of | angels:
  and he | sent them | food · in a|bundance.

25 He stirred up the south east | wind · in the | heavens:
  and | guided · it | by his | power.

26 He rained down meat upon them | thick as | dust:
  and winged | birds · like the | sands · of the | sea.

27 He made them fall into the | midst of · their | camp:
  and | all a|bout their | tents.

28 So they ate and were | well-|filled:
  for he had | given · them | what · they de|sired.

29 But before they had | satisfied · their | craving:
  while the | food was | still in · their | mouths,

30 The anger of God | blazed · up a|gainst them:
  and he slew their strongest men
    and laid | low the | youth of | Israel.

31 But for all this they | sinned yet | more:
  and | put no | faith · in his | wonders.

32 So he ended their | days · like a | breath:
  and their | years with | sudden | terror.

33 When he struck them down | then they | sought him:
  they turned and | sought | eagerly · for | God.

34 They remembered that | God · was their | rock:
  that God Most | High was | their re|deemer.

35 But they lied to him | with their | mouths:
  and dis|sembled | with their | tongues;

36 For their hearts were not | fixed up|on him:
  nor | were they | true to · his | covenant.

37 Yet he being merciful
  forgave their iniquity and did | not de|stroy them:
 many times he turned his anger aside
  and would not | wholly · a|rouse his | fury.

38 He remembered that they | were but | flesh:
 like a wind that passes | and does | not re|turn.

39 How often they rebelled against him | in the|
  wilderness:
 and | grieved him | in the | desert!

40 Again and again they put | God · to the | test:
 and provoked the | Holy | One of | Israel.

41 They did not re|member · his | power:
 or the day when he re|deemed them | from the |
  enemy;

42 How he wrought his | signs in | Egypt:
 his | wonders · in the | country · of | Zoan.

43 For he turned their | rivers · into | blood:
 so that they | could not | drink · from the | streams.

44 He sent swarms of | flies · that de|voured them:
 and | frogs that | laid them | waste.

45 He gave their | crops · to the | locust:
 and the fruits of their | labour | to the | grasshopper.

46 He struck down their | vines with | hailstones:
 and their | syco·more | trees with | frost.

47 He gave up their | cattle · to the | hail:
 and their | flocks · to the | flash · of the | lightning.

48 He loosed on them the fierceness of his anger
  his fury his indignation | and dis|tress:
 and these were his | messen·gers | of de|struction.

49 He opened a | path · for his | fury:
 he would not spare them from death
  but gave | up their | lives · to the | pestilence.

50 He struck down the | firstborn · of | Egypt:
 the firstfruits of their manhood | ⌣
  in the | dwellings · of | Ham.

51 As for his own people   he led them ⎪ out like ⎪ sheep:
　　and guided them in the ⎪ wilder·ness ⎪ like a ⎪ flock.

52 He led them in safety   and they were ⎪ not a⎪fraid:
　　but the ⎪ sea ⎪ covered · their ⎪ enemies.

53 He brought them to his ⎪ holy ⎪ land:
　　to the mountains that his ⎪ own right ⎪ hand had ⎪
　　　won.

54 He drove out the nations before them
　　　and apportioned their lands ⎪ as a · pos⎪session:
　　and settled the tribes of ⎪ Israel ⎪ in their ⎪ tents.

55 But they rebelled against God Most High ⌣
　　　and ⎪ put him · to the ⎪ test:
　　they would ⎪ not o⎪bey · his com⎪mandments.

56 They turned back and dealt treacherously ⎪ ⌣
　　　like their ⎪ fathers:
　　they turned aside ⎪ slack · as an ⎪ unstrung ⎪ bow.

57 They provoked him to anger with their ⎪ heathen ⎪
　　　shrines:
　　and moved him to jealousy ⎪ with their ⎪ carved ⎪
　　　images.

58 God heard and was angry * he utterly re⎪jected ⎪ Israel:
　　he forsook the tabernacle at Shiloh
　　　the ⎪ tent · where he ⎪ dwelt a·mong ⎪ men.

59 He gave the ark of his might ⎪ into · cap⎪tivity:
　　and his glory ⎪ into · the ⎪ hands · of the ⎪ enemy.

60 He delivered his ⎪ people · to the ⎪ sword:
　　and was enraged a⎪gainst his ⎪ own pos⎪session.

61 Fire de⎪voured the · young ⎪ men:
　　there was ⎪ no one · to be⎪wail the ⎪ maidens;

62 Their priests ⎪ fell · by the ⎪ sword:
　　and there was ⎪ none to ⎪ mourn · for the ⎪ widows.

63 Then the Lord awoke like a ⎪ man · out of ⎪ sleep:
　　like a warrior that had been ⎪ over⎪come with ⎪ wine.

64 He struck the backs of his enemies I as they I fled:
and I put them · to perIpetu·al I shame.

65 He rejected the I family · of I Joseph:
he reIfused the I tribe of I Ephraim.

66 But he chose the I tribe of I Judah:
and the hill of I Zion I which he I loved.

67 He built his sanctuary like the I heights of I heaven:
like the earth which I he had I founded · for I ever.

68 He chose I David · his I servant:
and I took him I from the I sheepfolds;

69 He brought him from I following · the I ewes:
to be the shepherd of his people Jacob
and of I Israel · his I own posIsession.

70 So he tended them with I upright I heart:
and I guided them · with I skilful I hand.

PSALM 79

1 O God the heathen have I come in·to your I land:
they have defiled your holy temple
they have made JeIrusalem · a I heap of I stones.

2 They have given the dead bodies of your servants ⌣
as food to the I birds · of the I air:
and the flesh of your faithful ones ⌣
to the wild I beasts I of the I earth.

3 Their blood they have spilt like water ⌣
on every I side · of JeIrusalem:
and I there is I none to I bury them.

4 We have become a mockery I to our I neighbours:
the scorn and I laughing-stock · of I those aIbout us.

5 How long O Lord shall your anger be I so exItreme:
will your jealous I fury I burn like I fire?

6 Pour out your wrath on the nations that I do not I know
you:
on the kingdoms that have not I called upIon your I
name.

7 For they have de|voured | Jacob:
  and made his | dwelling-place · a | deso|lation.

8 Do not remember against us the sin of | former | times:
  but let your compassion hasten to meet us
    for we are | brought | very | low.

†9 Help us O God our saviour for the | honour · of your | name:
  O deliver us and expiate our | sins · for your | name's | sake.

10 Why should the heathen say | 'Where is · their | God?':
  O let vengeance for the blood of your servants that ⌣
    is shed
      be shown upon the | nations | in our | sight.

11 Let the sorrowful sighing of the prisoners | come be|fore
    you:
  and as your power is great   reprieve |
    those con|demned to | die.

12 For the taunts with which our neighbours ⌣
    have taunted | you O | Lord:
  repay them seven times | over | into · their | bosoms.

13 So we that are your people and the sheep of your
    pasture shall give you | thanks for | ever:
  we will declare your praise in | every | gener|ation.

PSALM 80

1 Hear O Shepherd of Israel
    you that led | Joseph · like a | flock:
  you that are enthroned upon the cherubim | ⌣
    shine | out in | glory;

2 Before Ephraim Benjamin | and Man|asseh:
  stir up your | power and | come to | save us.

†3 *Restore us again O | Lord of | hosts:*
  show us the light of your countenance | ⌣
    and we | shall be | saved.

4 O Lord | God of | hosts:
  how long will you be | angry · at your | people's |
    prayer?

 5 You have fed them with the ⏐ bread of ⏐ tears:
    and given them tears to ⏐ drink in ⏐ good ⏐ measure.

 6 You have made us the victim ⏐ of our ⏐ neighbours:
    and our ⏐ ene·mies ⏐ laugh us · to ⏐ scorn.

 7 *Restore us again O ⏐ Lord of ⏐ hosts:*
    show us the light of your countenance ⏐ ⏑
      and we ⏐ shall be ⏐ saved.

 8 You brought a ⏐ vine · out of ⏐ Egypt:
    you drove out the ⏐ nations · and ⏐ planted · it ⏐ in.

 9 You cleared the ⏐ ground be⏐fore it:
    and it struck ⏐ root and ⏐ filled the ⏐ land.

10 The hills were ⏐ covered · with its ⏐ shadow:
    and its boughs were like the ⏐ boughs · of the ⏐ great ⏐
    cedars.

11 It stretched out its ⏐ branches · to the ⏐ sea:
    and its tender ⏐ shoots · to the ⏐ Great ⏐ River.

12 Why then have you broken ⏐ down its ⏐ walls:
    so that every passer-⏐by can ⏐ pluck its ⏐ fruit?

13 The wild boar out of the woods ⏐ roots it ⏐ up:
    and the locusts from the ⏐ wild ⏐ places · de⏐vour it.

14 Turn to us again O ⏐ Lord of ⏐ hosts:
    look ⏐ down from ⏐ heaven · and ⏐ see.

15 Bestow your care up⏐on this ⏐ vine:
    the stock which your ⏐ own right ⏐ hand has ⏐ planted.

16 As for those that burn it with fire and ⏐ cut it ⏐ down:
    let them perish at the re⏐buke ⏐ of your ⏐ countenance.

17 Let your power rest on the man at your ⏐ right ⏐ hand:
    on that son of man whom you ⏐ made so ⏐ strong ·
    for your⏐self.

18 And so we shall ⏐ not turn ⏐ back from you:
    give us life   and we will ⏐ call up⏐on your ⏐ name.

19 *Restore us again O ⏐ Lord of ⏐ hosts:*
    show us the light of your countenance ⏐ ⏑
      and we ⏐ shall be ⏐ saved.

PSALM 81

1 O sing joyfully to ǀ God our ǀ strength:
     shout in ǀ triumph · to the ǀ God of ǀ Jacob.

2 Make music and ǀ beat up·on the ǀ drum:
     sound the ǀ lute and · the melǀodi·ous ǀ harp.

3 Blow the ram's horn at the ǀ new ǀ moon:
     and at the full moon ǀ of our ǀ day of ǀ festival.

4 For this was a ǀ statute · for ǀ Israel:
     a comǀmandment · of the ǀ God of ǀ Jacob,

†5 Which he laid on Joseph as a ǀ solemn ǀ charge:
     when he came ǀ out of · the ǀ land of ǀ Egypt.

6 I heard a voice that I had not ǀ known ǀ saying:
     'I eased your shoulders of the burden
        and your ǀ hands were ǀ freed · from the ǀ load.

7 'You called to me in trouble ǀ and I ǀ rescued you:
     I answered you from the secret place of my thunder
        I put you to the ǀ test · at the ǀ waters · ofǀ Meribah.

8 'Listen my people and ǀ I · will adǀmonish you:
     O Israel if ǀ only ǀ you would ǀ hear me.

9 'There shall be no strange ǀ god aǀmong you:
     nor shall you bow ǀ down · to an ǀ ali·en ǀ god.

†10 'I am the Lord your God
        who brought you up from the ǀ land of ǀ Egypt:
     open wide your ǀ mouth and ǀ I will ǀ fill it.

11 'But my people would not ǀ listen · to my ǀ voice:
     and ǀ Israel ǀ would have ǀ none of me.

12 'So I left them to the stubbornness ǀ of their ǀ hearts:
     to walk acǀcording · to their ǀ own deǀsigns.

13 'If only my ǀ people · would ǀ listen:
     if Israel ǀ would but ǀ walk in · my ǀ ways,

14 'I would soon put ǀ down their ǀ enemies:
     and turn my ǀ hand aǀgainst their ǀ adversaries.

15 'Those that hate the Lord would ǀ cringe beǀfore him:
     and their ǀ punishment · would ǀ last for ǀ ever.

16 'But Israel I would feed with the ǀ finest ǀ wheat:
   and satisfy you with ǀ honey ǀ from the ǀ rocks.'

PSALM 82

1 God has stood up in the ǀ council · of ǀ heaven:
   in the midst of the ǀ gods ǀ he gives ǀ judgment.

2 'How long will you ǀ judge unǀjustly:
   and ǀ favour · the ǀ cause · of the ǀ wicked?

3 'Judge for the ǀ poor and ǀ fatherless:
   vindicate the afǀflicted ǀ and opǀpressed.

4 'Rescue the ǀ poor and ǀ needy:
   and ǀ save them · from the ǀ hands · of the ǀ wicked.

5 'They do not know   they do not understand
      they walk aǀbout in ǀ darkness:
   all the foundǀations · of the ǀ earth are ǀ shaken.

6 'Therefore I say ǀ "Though · you are ǀ gods:
   and all of you ǀ sons · of the ǀ Most ǀ High,

7 '"Nevertheless you shall ǀ die like ǀ man:
   and ǀ fall like ǀ one of · the ǀ princes."'

8 Arise O God and ǀ judge the ǀ earth:
   for you shall take all ǀ nations · as ǀ your posǀsession.

PSALM 83

1 Hold not your ǀ peace O ǀ God:
   O God be not ǀ silent ǀ or unǀmoved.

2 See how your ǀ enemies · make ǀ uproar:
   how those that hate you have ǀ lifted ǀ up their ǀ heads.

3 For they lay shrewd plots aǀgainst your ǀ people:
   they scheme against ǀ those whom ǀ you have ǀ
   cherished.

4 'Come' they say 'let us destroy them
      that they may no ǀ longer · be a ǀ nation:
   that the very name of Israel may ǀ be reǀmembered · no ǀ
   more.'

5 With one mind they con|spire to|gether:
   they | make al|liance · a|gainst you,

6 The tribes of Edom | and the | Ishmaelites:
   the people of | Moab | and the | Hagarites,

7 Gebal and | Ammon · and | Amalek:
   Philistia | and · the in|habitants · of | Tyre;

8 Asshur | also · is | joined with them:
   and lends a friendly | arm · to the | children · of | Lot.

9 Do to them as you | did to | Midian:
   as to Sisera and Jabin | at the | river · of | Kishon,

10 Who were de|stroyed at | Endor:
   and be|came like | dung · for the | earth.

11 Make their leaders as | Oreb · and | Zeeb:
   and all their princes like | Zebah | and Zal|munna,

12 Who said 'Let us | take pos|session:
   let us | seize the | pastures · of | God.'

13 Make them like | thistledown · my | God:
   or like chaff | blown be|fore the | wind.

14 As fire con|suming · a | thicket:
   or as flame that | sets the | hillsides · a|blaze,

15 Pursue them | with your | tempest:
   and | terrify · them | with your | storm-wind.

16 Cover their faces with | shame O | Lord:
   that | they may | seek your | name.

17 Let them be disgraced and dis|mayed for | ever:
   let them | be con|founded · and | perish,

18 That they may know that you whose | name · is the | Lord:
   are alone the Most | High · over | all the | earth.

PSALM 84

1 How lovely I is your I dwelling-place:
      O I Lord I God of I hosts!

2 My soul has a desire and longing ⌣
        to enter the I courts · of the I Lord:
      my heart and my flesh re|joice · in the I living I God.

3 The sparrow has found her a home   and the swallow ⌣
        a nest where she may I lay her I young:
      even your altar   O Lord of I hosts my I
        King · and my I God.

4 Blessèd are those who I dwell in · your I house:
      they will I always · be I praising I you.

5 Blessèd is the man whose I strength · is in I you:
      in whose I heart · are the I highways · to I Zion;

6 Who going through the valley of dryness
        finds there a spring from I which to I drink:
      till the autumn I rain shall I clothe it · with I blessings.

†7 They go from I strength to I strength:
      they appear every one of them ⌣
        before the I God of I gods in I Zion.

8 O Lord God of hosts I hear my I prayer:
      give I ear O I God of I Jacob.

9 Behold O God I him who · reigns I over us:
      and look upon the I face of I your a|nointed.

10 One day in your courts is I better · than a I thousand:
      I would rather stand at the threshold of the house ⌣
        of my God
           than I dwell · in the I tents of · un|godliness.

11 For the Lord God is a rampart and a shield
        the Lord gives I favour · and I honour:
      and no good thing will he withhold ⌣
        from I those who I walk in I innocence.

†12 O Lord I God of I hosts:
      blessèd is the man who I puts his I trust in I you.

PSALM 85

1 O Lord you were gracious ⏐ to your ⏐ land:
    you re⏐stored the ⏐ fortunes · of ⏐ Jacob.

2 You forgave the iniquity ⏐ of your ⏐ people:
    and ⏐ covered ⏐ all their ⏐ sin.

3 You put aside ⏐ all your ⏐ wrath:
    and turned away from your ⏐ fierce ⏐ indig⏐nation.

4 Return to us again O ⏐ God our ⏐ saviour:
    and ⏐ let your ⏐ anger ⏐ cease from us.

5 Will you be displeased with ⏐ us for ⏐ ever:
    will you stretch out your wrath ⏎
        from one gener⏐ation ⏐ to an⏐other?

6 Will you not give us ⏐ life a⏐gain:
    that your ⏐ people ⏐ may re⏐joice in you?

†7 Show us your ⏐ mercy · O ⏐ Lord:
    and ⏐ grant us ⏐ your sal⏐vation.

8 I will hear what the Lord ⏐ God will ⏐ speak:
    for he will speak peace to his people * to his ⏎
        faithful ones whose ⏐ hearts are ⏐ turned to ⏐ him.

9 Truly his salvation is near to ⏐ those that ⏐ fear him:
    and his ⏐ glory · shall ⏐ dwell · in our ⏐ land.

10 Mercy and truth are ⏐ met to⏐gether:
    righteousness and ⏐ peace have ⏐ kissed each ⏐ other;

11 Truth shall flourish ⏐ out of · the ⏐ earth:
    and righteousness ⏐ shall look ⏐ down from ⏐ heaven.

12 The Lord will also give us ⏐ all · that is ⏐ good:
    and our ⏐ land shall ⏐ yield its ⏐ plenty.

13 For righteousness shall ⏐ go be⏐fore him:
    and tread the ⏐ path be⏐fore his ⏐ feet.

PSALM 86

1 Incline your ear to me O I God and I answer me:
    for I I am I poor · and in I misery.

2 Preserve my life for I I am I faithful:
    my God save your servant who I puts his I trust in I you.

3 Be merciful to I me O I Lord:
    for I I call to · you I all the · day I long.

4 O make glad the I soul of · your I servant:
    for I put my I hope in I you O I Lord.

5 For you Lord are I good · and for|giving:
    of great and continuing kindness ‿
        to I all who I call up|on you.

6 Hear my I prayer O I Lord:
    and give heed to the I voice · of my I suppli|cation.

†7 In the day of my trouble I I call up|on you:
    for I you will I surely I answer.

8 Among the gods there is none like I you O I Lord:
    nor are there I any I deeds like I yours.

9 All the nations you have made ‿
        shall come and I worship · be|fore you:
    O Lord they shall I glori|fy your I name.

10 For you are great and do I marvel·lous I things:
    and I you a|lone are I God.

11 Show me your way O Lord   and I will I walk in · your|
        truth:
    let my heart de|light to I fear your I name.

12 I will praise you O Lord my God with I all my I heart:
    and I will I glorify · your I name for I ever.

13 For great is your abiding I love to|ward me:
    and you have delivered my life ‿
        from the I lowest I depths · of the I grave.

14 Insolent men O God have I risen · a|gainst me:
    a band of ruthless men seek my life
        they have not set I God be|fore their I eyes.

15 But you Lord are a God | gracious · and com|passionate:
  slow to anger | full of | goodness · and | truth.

16 Turn to me and be merciful
      give your | strength · to your | servant:
   and | save the | son of · your | handmaid.

17 Show me some token | of your | goodness:
      that those who hate me may see it and be ashamed
      because you Lord are my | helper | and my |
      comforter.

PSALM 87

1 He has founded it upon a | holy | hill:
   and the Lord loves the gates of Zion ‿
      more than | all the | dwellings · of | Jacob.

2 Glorious things shall be | spoken · of | you:
   O Zion | city | of our | God.

3 I might speak of my kinsmen in Egypt | or in | Babylon:
   in Philistia Tyre or Nubia | where | each was | born.

4 But of Zion it | shall be | said:
      many were born in her
      he that is Most | High | has es|tablished her.

5 When the Lord draws up the record | of the | nations:
   he shall take note where | every | man was | born.

6 And the singers and the | dancers · to|gether:
   shall | make their | song · to your | name.

PSALM 88

1 O Lord my God   I call for | help by | day:
   and by night also I | cry | out be|fore you.

2 Let my prayer come | into · your | presence:
   and turn your | ear · to my | loud | crying.

†3 For my soul is | filled with | trouble:
   and my life has come | even · to the | brink · of the |
   grave.

713

4 I am reckoned among those that go | down · to the | Pit:
　　I am a | man that | has no | help.

5 I lie among the dead
　　　　like the slain that | sleep · in the | grave:
　　whom you remember no more
　　　　who are cut | off | from your | power.

6 You have laid me in the | lowest | Pit:
　　in darkness and | in the | water·y | depths.

7 Your wrath lies | heavy · up|on me:
　　and all your | waves are | brought a|gainst me.

8 You have put my | friends far | from me:
　　and made me to | be ab|horred | by them.

9 I am so fast in prison I | cannot · get | free:
　　my eyes fail be|cause of | my af|fliction.

10 Lord I call to you | every | day:
　　I stretch | out my | hands to|ward you.

11 Will you work | wonders · for the | dead:
　　or will the shades rise | up a|gain to | praise you?

12 Shall your love be de|clared · in the | grave:
　　or your faithfulness | in the | place · of de|struction?

13 Will your wonders be made | known · in the | dark:
　　or your righteousness ⏜
　　　　in the land where | all things | are for|gotten?

14 But to you Lord | will I | cry:
　　early in the morning my | prayer shall |
　　　　come be|fore you.

15 O Lord why have | you re|jected me:
　　why do you | hide your | face | from me?

16 I have been afflicted and wearied from my | youth |
　　　　upward:
　　I am tossed high and | low　　I | cease to | be.

17 Your fierce anger has | over|whelmed me:
　　and your | terrors · have | put me · to | silence.

18 They surround me like a flood | all the · day | long:
　　they close up|on me · from | every | side.

19 Friend and acquaintance you have put ǀ far ǀ from me:
and kept my comǀpanions ǀ from my ǀ sight.

PSALM 89

1 Lord I will sing for ever of your ǀ loving-ǀkindnesses:
my mouth shall proclaim your faithfulness ⌣
throughǀout all ǀ generǀations.

2 I have said of your loving-kindness ⌣
that it is ǀ built for ǀ ever:
you have established your ǀ faithful·ness ǀ in the ǀ
heavens.

3 The Lord said   'I have made a covenant ǀ with my ǀ
chosen:
I have sworn an ǀ oath · to my ǀ servant ǀ David.

4 'I will establish your ǀ line for ǀ ever:
and build up your ǀ throne for ǀ all · generǀations.'

5 Let the heavens praise your ǀ wonders · O ǀ Lord:
and let your faithfulness be sung ⌣
in the asǀsembly ǀ of the ǀ holy ones.

6 For who amidst the clouds can be comǀpared · to the ǀ
Lord:
or who is like the Lord aǀmong the ǀ sons of ǀ heaven?

7 A God to be feared in the council ǀ of the ǀ holy ones:
great and terrible above ǀ all that ǀ are aǀround him.

8 O Lord God of hosts   ǀ who is ǀ like you?
your power and your ǀ faithfulness · are ǀ
all aǀbout you.

9 You rule the ǀ raging · of the ǀ sea:
when its ǀ waves ǀ surge   you ǀ still them.

10 You crushed Rahab ǀ like a ǀ carcase:
you scattered your enemies ǀ by your ǀ mighty ǀ
arm.

11 The heavens are yours * so also ǀ is the ǀ earth:
you founded the ǀ world and ǀ all · that is ǀ in it.

12 You created the ǀ north · and the ǀ south:
    Tabor and Mount ǀ Hermon · shall ǀ
        sing of · your ǀ name.

13 Mighty ǀ is your ǀ arm:
    strong is your hand * and your right ǀ hand is ǀ
        lifted ǀ high.

14 Righteousness and justice are the foundation ǀ
        of your ǀ throne:
    loving-kindness and ǀ faithfulness · atǀtend your ǀ
        presence.

15 Happy the people who know the triǀumphal ǀ shout:
    who walk O ǀ Lord · in the ǀ light of · your ǀ
        countenance.

16 They rejoice all the day long beǀcause of · your ǀ name:
    because of your ǀ righteousness · they ǀ are exǀalted.

17 For you are their glory ǀ and their ǀ strength:
    and our heads are upǀlifted ǀ by your ǀ favour.

18 Our king beǀlongs · to the ǀ Lord:
    he that rules over us to the ǀ Holy ǀ One of ǀ Israel.

19 You spoke ǀ once · in a ǀ vision:
    and ǀ said ǀ to your ǀ faithful one,

20 'I have set a youth aǀbove a ǀ warrior:
    I have exalted a ǀ young man ǀ out of · the ǀ people.

21 'I have found my ǀ servant ǀ David:
    and anointed him ǀ with my ǀ holy ǀ oil.

22 'My hand ǀ shall upǀhold him:
    and my ǀ arm ǀ shall ǀ strengthen him.

23 'No enemy ǀ shall deǀceive him:
    no ǀ evil ǀ man shall ǀ hurt him.

24 'I will crush his ǀ adversaries · beǀfore him:
    and ǀ strike down ǀ those that ǀ hate him.

25 'My faithfulness and loving-kindness ǀ shall be ǀ
        with him:
    and through my name his ǀ head · shall be ǀ lifted ǀ
        high.

26 'I will set the hand of his dominion ⏜
    upon the ǀ Western ǀ Sea:
  and his right hand shall stretch ⏜
    to the ǀ streams of ǀ Meso·poǀtamia.

27 'He will call to me   ǀ "You · are my ǀ Father:
  my God and the ǀ Rock of ǀ my salǀvation."

28 'I will make him my ǀ first-born ǀ son:
  and highest aǀmong the ǀ kings · of the ǀ earth.

29 'I will ever maintain my loving-ǀkindness ·
    toǀward him:
  and my covenant ǀ with him · shall ǀ stand ǀ firm.

30 'I will establish his ǀ line for ǀ ever:
  and his ǀ throne · like the ǀ days of ǀ heaven.

31 'If his children forǀsake my ǀ law:
  and ǀ will not ǀ walk in · my ǀ judgments;

32 'If they proǀfane my ǀ statutes:
  and ǀ do not ǀ keep · my comǀmandments,

33 'Then I will punish their reǀbellion · with the ǀ rod:
  and ǀ their inǀiquity · with ǀ blows.

34 'But I will not cause my loving-ǀkindness · to ǀ
    cease from him:
  nor will ǀ I beǀtray my ǀ faithfulness.

35 'I will not proǀfane my ǀ covenant:
  or alter ǀ what has ǀ passed from · my ǀ lips.

36 'Once and for all I have ǀ sworn · by my ǀ holiness:
  I will ǀ not prove ǀ false to ǀ David.

37 'His posterity shall enǀdure for ǀ ever:
  and his throne be ǀ as the ǀ sun beǀfore me;

38 'Like the moon that is esǀtablished · for ǀ ever:
  and stands in the ǀ heavens · for ǀ everǀmore.'

39 Yet you have been enraged aǀgainst · your anǀointed:
  you have abǀhorred him ǀ and reǀjected him.

40 You have spurned the covenant ǀ with your ǀ servant:
  and deǀfiled his ǀ crown · to the ǀ dust.

41 You have broken down ǀ all his ǀ walls:
  and ǀ made his ǀ strongholds ǀ desolate.

42 All that pass ǀ by ǀ plunder him:
  he has beǀcome the ǀ scorn of · his ǀ neighbours.

43 You have exalted the right hand ǀ of his ǀ adversaries:
  and ǀ gladdened ǀ all his ǀ enemies.

44 His bright sword you have ǀ turned ǀ backward:
  you have not enǀabled him · to ǀ stand · in the ǀ
    battle.

45 You have brought his ǀ lustre · to an ǀ end:
  you have ǀ cast his ǀ throne · to the ǀ ground.

46 You have cut short the ǀ days of · his ǀ youth:
  and ǀ clothed him ǀ with disǀhonour.

47 How long O Lord will you hide yourǀself so ǀ utterly:
  how long shall your ǀ fury ǀ·burn like ǀ fire?

48 Remember how I draw to my eǀternal ǀ end:
  have you created ǀ all manǀkind for ǀ nothing?

49 Where is the man who can live and ǀ not see ǀ death:
  who can deliver his ǀ life · from the ǀ power · of the ǀ
    grave?

50 Where O Lord are your loving-ǀkindnesses · of ǀ old:
  which you have vowed to ǀ David ǀ in your ǀ
    faithfulness?

51 Remember O Lord how your servant ǀ is reǀviled:
  how I bear in my bosom the ǀ onslaught ǀ of the ǀ
    peoples;

52 Remember how your ǀ ene·mies ǀ taunt:
  how they mock the ǀ footsteps · of ǀ your anǀointed.

†53 Blessèd be the ǀ Lord for ǀ ever:
  Aǀmen and ǀ A—ǀmen.

PSALM 90

1 Lord you have I been our I refuge:
   from one generIation I to anIother.

2 Before the mountains were born
   or the earth and the world were I brought to I be:
   from eternity to etIerni·ty I you are I God.

3 You turn manI back · into I dust:
   saying 'Return to I dust you I sons of I Adam.'

4 For a thousand years in your sight ⌣
   are like I yester·day I passing:
   or I like one I watch · of the I night.

5 You cut them I short · like a I dream:
   like the fresh I grass I of the I morning;

6 In the morning it is I green and I flourishes:
   at evening it is I withered · and I dried I up.

7 And we are conIsumed · by your I anger:
   because of your indigInation · we I cease to I be.

8 You have brought our inIiquities · beIfore you:
   and our secret I sins · to the I light of · your I
   countenance.

9 Our days decline beIneath your I wrath:
   and our years I pass aIway · like a I sigh.

10 The days of our life are three score years and ten
   or if we have I strength   four I score:
   the pride of our labours is but toil and sorrow
   for it passes quickly aIway and I we are I gone.

11 Who can know the I power of · your I wrath:
   who can know your indigInation · like I those that I
   fear you?

12 Teach us so to I number · our I days:
   that we may apIply our I hearts to I wisdom.

13 Relent O Lord * how long will I you be I angry?:
   take I pity I on your I servants.

'14 O satisfy us early ǀ with your ǀ mercy:
    that all our days we ǀ may reǀjoice and ǀ sing.

15 Give us joy for all the days you ǀ have afǀflicted us:
    for the ǀ years · we have ǀ suffered · adǀversity.

16 Show your ǀ servants · your ǀ work:
    and let their ǀ children ǀ see your ǀ glory.

†17 May the gracious favour of the Lord our ǀ
        God · be upǀon us:
    prosper the work of our hands
        O ǀ prosper · the ǀ work · of our ǀ hands!

PSALM 91

1 He who dwells in the shelter of the ǀ Most ǀ High:
    who abides under the ǀ shadow ǀ of the · Alǀmighty,

2 He will say to the Lord
        'You are my refuge ǀ and my ǀ stronghold:
    my ǀ God in ǀ whom I ǀ trust.'

3 For he will deliver you from the ǀ snare · of the ǀ hunter:
    and ǀ from the · deǀstroying ǀ curse.

4 He will cover you with his wings
        and you will be safe ǀ under · his ǀ feathers:
    his faithfulness will ǀ be your ǀ shield · and deǀfence.

5 You shall not be afraid of any ǀ terror · by ǀ night:
    or of the ǀ arrow · that ǀ flies by ǀ day,

6 Of the pestilence that walks aǀbout in ǀ darkness:
    or the ǀ plague · that deǀstroys at ǀ noonday.

7 A thousand may fall beside you
        and ten thousand at your ǀ right ǀ hand:
    but ǀ you it ǀ shall not ǀ touch;

8 Your own ǀ eyes shall ǀ see:
    and look on the reǀward ǀ of the · unǀgodly.

9 The Lord himǀself · is your ǀ refuge:
    you have ǀ made the · Most ǀ High your ǀ stronghold.

10 Therefore no ǀ harm · will beǀfall you:
    nor will any ǀ scourge come ǀ near your ǀ tent.

11 For he will com|mand his | angels:
    to | keep you · in | all your | ways.

12 They will bear you | up · in their | hands:
    lest you dash your | foot a|gainst a | stone.

13 You will tread on the | lion · and the | adder:
    the young lion and the serpent ⌣
      you will | trample | under | foot.

14 'He has set his love upon me
    and therefore I | will de|liver him:
    I will lift him out of danger be|cause · he has |
      known my | name.

15 'When he calls upon me | I will | answer him:
    I will be with him in trouble
    I will | rescue him · and | bring him · to | honour.

16 'With long | life · I will | satisfy him:
    and | fill him · with | my sal|vation.'

PSALM 92

1 How good to give | thanks · to the | Lord:
    to sing praises to your | name | O Most | High,

2 To declare your | love · in the | morning:
    and at | night to | sing of · your | faithfulness,

†3 Upon the lute   upon the lute of | ten | strings:
    and to the | melo·dy | of the | lyre.

4 For in all you have done O Lord you have | made me |
      glad:
    I will sing for joy be|cause of · the | works · of your |
      hands.

5 Lord how glorious | are your | works:
    your | thoughts are | very | deep.

6 The brutish do | not con|sider:
    and the | fool · cannot | under|stand

7 That though the wicked | sprout like | grass:
    and | all wrong|doers | flourish,

8 They flourish to be de|stroyed · for | ever:
   but you Lord are ex|alted · for | ever|more.

9 For behold   your enemies O Lord ⌣
      your | enemies · shall | perish:
   and all the workers of | wicked·ness | shall be |
      scattered.

10 You have lifted up my head
      like the horns of the | wild | oxen:
    I am an|ointed · with | fresh | oil;

11 My eyes have looked | down · on my | enemies:
    and my ears have heard the ruin ⌣
      of | those who · rose | up a|gainst me.

12 The righteous shall | flourish · like the | palm tree:
    they shall spread a|broad · like a | cedar · in | Lebanon;

13 For they are planted in the | house · of the | Lord:
    and flourish in the | courts of | our | God.

14 In old age they shall be | full of | sap:
    they shall be | sturdy · and | laden · with | branches;

15 And they will say that the | Lord is | just:
    the Lord my Rock in | whom is | no un|righteousness.

PSALM 93

1 The Lord is King * and has put on | robes of | glory:
   the Lord has put on his glory
      he has | girded · him|self with | strength.

2 He has made the | world so | firm:
   that it | cannot | be | moved.

3 Your throne is es|tablished · from of | old:
   you | are from | ever|lasting.

4 The floods have lifted up O Lord
      the floods have lifted | up their | voice:
    the | floods lift | up their | pounding.

5 But mightier than the sound of many waters
      than the mighty waters or the | breakers · of the |
         sea:
    the | Lord on | high is | mighty.

6 Your decrees are I very I sure:
   and holiness O Lord aIdorns your I house for I ever.

PSALM 94

1 O Lord God to whom I vengeance · beIlongs:
   O God to whom vengeance beIlongs shine I out in I
   glory.

2 Arise I judge · of the I earth:
   and requite the I proud as I they deIserve.

3 Lord how I long · shall the I wicked:
   how I long · shall the I wicked I triumph?

4 How long shall all evildoers I pour out I words:
   how I long · shall they I boast and I flaunt themselves?

5 They crush your I people · O I Lord:
   they opIpress your I own posIsession.

6 They murder the I widow · and the I alien:
   they I put the I fatherless · to I death.

7 And they say 'The I Lord · does not I see:
   nor does the I God of I Jacob · conIsider it.'

8 Consider this   you senseless aImong the I people:
   fools I when · will you I underIstand?

9 He who planted the ear   does I he not I hear:
   he who formed the I eye   does I he not I see?

10 He who disciplines the nations will I he not I punish:
   has the I teacher · of manIkind no I knowledge?

†11 The Lord knows the I thoughts of I man:
   he I knows · that they I are mere I breath.

12 Blessèd is the man whom you I discipline · O I Lord:
   and I teach I from your I law,

13 Giving him rest from I days of I misery:
   till a I pit is I dug · for the I wicked.

14 The Lord will not cast I off his I people:
   nor I will he · forIsake his I own.

Psalm 95

15 For justice shall return to the | righteous | man:
   and with him to | all the | true of | heart.

16 Who will stand up for me a|gainst the | wicked:
   who will take my part a|gainst the | evil|doers?

17 If the Lord had not | been my | helper:
   I would soon have | dwelt · in the | land of | silence.

18 But when I said   'My | foot has | slipped':
   your | mercy · O | Lord was | holding me.

19 In all the | doubts · of my | heart:
   your consol|lations · de|lighted · my | soul.

20 Will you be any friend to the | court of | wickedness:
   that contrives | evil · by | means of | law?

21 They band together against the | life · of the | righteous:
   and con|demn | inno·cent | blood.

22 But the | Lord · is my | stronghold:
   my | God · is my | rock · and my | refuge.

23 Let him requite them for their wickedness
   and silence them | for their | evil:
   the | Lord our | God shall | silence them.

PSALM 95

1 O come let us sing | out · to the | Lord:
   let us shout in triumph to the | rock of | our sal|vation.

2 Let us come before his | face with | thanksgiving:
   and cry | out to · him | joyfully · in | psalms.

3 For the Lord is a | great | God:
   and a great | king a·bove | all | gods.

4 In his hand are the | depths · of the | earth:
   and the peaks of the | mountains · are | his | also.

†5 The sea is his and | he | made it:
   his hands | moulded | dry | land.

6 Come let us worship and | bow | down:
   and kneel be|fore the | Lord our | maker.

724

7 For he is the ǀ Lord our ǀ God:
  we are his ǀ people · and the ǀ sheep of · his ǀ pasture.

8 Today if only you would hear his voice
    'Do not harden your ǀ hearts · as at ǀ Meribah:
  as on that day at ǀ Massah ǀ in the ǀ wilderness;

9 'When your ǀ fathers ǀ tested me:
  put me to proof though ǀ they had ǀ seen my ǀ works.

10 'Forty years long I loathed that generǀation · and ǀ said:
    "It is a people who err in their hearts
      for they ǀ do not ǀ know my ǀ ways";

11 'Of whom I ǀ swore · in my ǀ wrath:
    "They ǀ shall not ǀ enter · my ǀ rest." ' '

PSALM 96

1 O sing to the Lord a ǀ new ǀ song:
  sing to the ǀ Lord ǀ all the ǀ earth.

2 Sing to the Lord and bless his ǀ holy ǀ name:
  proclaim the good news of his salǀvation · from ǀ
      day to ǀ day.

3 Declare his glory aǀmong the ǀ nations:
  and his ǀ wonders · aǀmong all ǀ peoples.

4 For great is the Lord and ǀ greatly · to be ǀ praised:
  he is more to be ǀ feared than ǀ all ǀ gods.

5 As for all the gods of the nations ǀ they are · mere ǀ idols:
  it is the ǀ Lord who ǀ made the ǀ heavens.

6 Majesty and ǀ glory · are beǀfore him:
  beauty and ǀ power are ǀ in his ǀ sanctuary.

7 Render to the Lord you families ǀ of the ǀ nations:
  render to the ǀ Lord ǀ glory · and ǀ might.

8 Render to the Lord the honour ǀ due · to his ǀ name:
  bring offerings and ǀ come inǀto his ǀ courts.

9 O worship the Lord in the beauty ǀ of his ǀ holiness:
  let the whole earth ǀ stand in ǀ awe of ǀ him.

10 Say among the nations that the I Lord is I king:
    he has made the world so firm that it can never be _
      moved * and he shall I judge the I peoples · with I
      equity.

11 Let the heavens rejoice   and let the I earth be I glad:
    let the sea I roar and I all that I fills it;

12 Let the fields rejoice and I every·thing I in them:
    then shall all the trees of the wood _
      shout with I joy be|fore the I Lord;

†13 For he comes   he comes to I judge the I earth:
    he shall judge the world with righteousness
      and the I peoples I with his I truth.

PSALM 97

1 The Lord is king   let the I earth re|joice:
    let the I multitude · of I islands · be I glad.

2 Clouds and darkness are I round a|bout him:
    righteousness and justice are the found|ation I of his I
      throne.

3 Fire I goes be|fore him:
    and burns up his I enemies · on I every I side.

4 His lightnings I light the I world:
    the I earth I sees it · and I quakes.

5 The mountains melt like wax be|fore his I face:
    from before the face of the I Lord of I all the I earth.

6 The heavens have pro|claimed his I righteousness:
    and all I peoples · have I seen his I glory.

7 They are ashamed * all those who serve idols _
      and glory in I mere I nothings:
    all I gods bow I down be|fore him.

8 Zion heard and was glad * and the daughters of I Judah ·
      re|joiced:
    be|cause of · your I judgments · O I God.

9 For you Lord are most high over I all the I earth:
    you are exalted I far a·bove I all I gods.

10 The Lord loves I those that · hate I evil:
    the Lord guards the life of the faithful
        and delivers them from the I hand of I the unIgodly.

11 Light I dawns · for the I righteous:
    and I joy · for the I true of I heart.

12 Rejoice in the I Lord you I righteous:
    and give I thanks · to his I holy I name.

PSALM 98

1 O sing to the Lord a I new I song:
    for he has I done I marvel·lous I things;

2 His right hand and his I holy I arm:
    they have I got I him the I victory.

3 The Lord has made I known · his salIvation:
    he has revealed his just deIliverance · in the I sight of ·
        the I nations.

4 He has remembered his mercy and faithfulness ⌣
        towards the I house of I Israel:
    and all the ends of the earth ⌣
        have seen the salIvation I of our I God.

5 Shout with joy to the Lord I all the I earth:
    break into I singing · and I make I melody.

6 Make melody to the Lord upIon the I harp:
    upon the harp and I with the I sounds of I praise.

7 With trumpets I and with I horns:
    cry out in triumph beIfore the I Lord the I king.

8 Let the sea roar and I all that I fills it:
    the good earth and I those who I live upIon it.

9 Let the rivers I clap their I hands:
    and let the mountains ring out toIgether · beIfore the I
        Lord;

10 For he comes to I judge the I earth:
    he shall judge the world with righteousness
        and the I peoples I with I equity.

PSALM 99

1 The Lord is king   let the | nations | tremble:
  he is enthroned upon the cherubim | let the |
      earth | quake.

2 The Lord is | great in | Zion:
  he is | high a|bove all | nations.

3 Let them praise your great and | terri·ble | name:
  for | holy | is the | Lord.

4 The Mighty One is king and | loves | justice:
  you have established equity * you have dealt | _
      righteousness · and | justice · in | Jacob.

†5 *O exalt the | Lord our | God:*
  and bow down before his | footstool · for | he is | holy.

6 Moses and Aaron among his priests
      and Samuel among those who call up|on his | name:
  they called to the | Lord | and he | answered.

7 He spoke to them from the | pillar · of | cloud:
  they kept to his teachings | and the | law · that he |
      gave them.

8 You answered them O | Lord our | God:
  you were a forgiving God to them
      and | pardoned · their | wrong|doing.

9 *O exalt the | Lord our | God:*
  and bow down towards his holy hill
      for the | Lord our | God is | holy.

PSALM 100

1 O shout to the Lord in triumph | all the | earth:
  serve the Lord with gladness
      and come before his | face with | songs of | joy.

2 Know that the Lord | he is | God:
  it is he who has made us and we are his
      we are his | people · and the | sheep of · his |
      pasture.

3 Come into his gates with thanksgiving
      and into his | courts with | praise:
  give thanks to him and | bless his | holy | name.

4 For the Lord is good * his loving mercy ∣ is for ∣ ever:
   his faithfulness through∣out all ∣ gener∣ations.

PSALM 101

1 My song shall be of ∣ steadfastness · and ∣ justice:
   to ∣ you Lord ∣ will I ∣ sing.

2 I will be wise in the ∣ way of ∣ innocence:
   O ∣ when ∣ will you ∣ come to me?

3 I will walk with∣in my ∣ house:
   in∣ puri∣ty of ∣ heart.

4 I will set nothing evil be∣fore my ∣ eyes:
   I hate the sin of backsliders   it shall ∣ get no ∣ hold ∣
   on me.

†5 Crookedness of heart shall de∣part ∣ from me:
   I will ∣ know ∣ nothing · of ∣ wickedness.

6 The man who secretly slanders his neighbour I ∣
   will de∣stroy:
   the proud look and the arrogant ∣ heart · I will ∣
   not en∣dure.

7 My eyes shall look to the faithful in the land
   and they shall ∣ make their ∣ home with me:
   one who walks in the way of innocence ∣ _
   he shall ∣ minis·ter ∣ to me.

8 No man who practises deceit shall ∣ live in · my ∣ house:
   no one who utters ∣ lies shall ∣ stand in · my ∣ sight.

9 Morning by morning I will destroy _
   all the ∣ wicked · of the ∣ land:
   and cut off all evildoers from the ∣ city ∣ of the ∣ Lord.

PSALM 102

1 O Lord ∣ hear my ∣ prayer:
   and ∣ let my ∣ cry ∣ come to you.

2 Do not hide your face from me in the ∣ day of · my ∣
   trouble:
   turn your ear to me
   and when I ∣ call be ∣ swift to ∣ answer.

3 For my days pass a|way like | smoke:
    and my bones | burn as | in a | furnace.

4 My heart is scorched and | withered · like | grass:
    and I for|get to | eat my | bread.

5 I am weary with the | sound of · my | groaning:
    my | bones stick | fast to · my | skin.

6 I have become like an | owl · in the | wilderness:
    like a | screech-owl · a|mong the | ruins.

7 I keep watch   and | flit · to and | fro:
    like a | sparrow · up|on a | housetop.

8 My enemies taunt me | all day | long:
    and those who | rave at me · make | oaths a|gainst me.

9 Surely I have eaten | ashes · for | bread:
    and | mingled · my | drink with | tears,

10 Because of your wrath and | indig|nation:
    for you have taken me | up and | tossed · me a|side.

†11 My days de|cline · like a | shadow:
    and I | wither · a|way like | grass.

12 But you Lord are en|throned for | ever:
    and your name shall be known through|out all | gener|ations.

13 You will arise and have | mercy up·on | Zion:
    for it is time to pity her   the ap|pointed | time has | come.

14 Your servants love | even · her | stones:
    and her | dust moves | them to | pity.

15 Then shall the nations fear your | name O | Lord:
    and all the | kings · of the | earth your | glory,

16 When the Lord has | built up | Zion:
    when he | shows him|self · in his | glory,

17 When he turns to the | prayer · of the | destitute:
    and does not de|spise their | suppli|cation.

†18 Let this be written down for | those who · come | after:
    and a people yet un|born will | praise the | Lord.

19 For the Lord has looked down from the ǀ height · of his ǀ
    holiness:
    from heaven he has ǀ looked upǀon the ǀ earth,

20 To hear the ǀ groaning · of the ǀ prisoner:
    to deliver ǀ those conǀdemned to ǀ die;

21 That they may proclaim the name of the ǀ Lord in ǀ Zion:
    and his ǀ praises ǀ in Jeǀrusalem,

22 When the nations are ǀ gathered · toǀgether:
    and the ǀ kingdoms · to ǀ serve the ǀ Lord.

23 He has broken my strength beǀfore my ǀ time:
    he has ǀ cut ǀ short my ǀ days.

24 Do not take me away O God in the ǀ midst of · my ǀ life:
    you whose years exǀtend through ǀ all · generǀations.

25 In the beginning you laid the foundǀations · of the ǀ
    earth:
    and the ǀ heavens · are the ǀ work of · your ǀ hands.

26 They shall perish   but ǀ you · will enǀdure:
    they shall all grow old like a garment * like clothes ⌣
    you will change them and ǀ they shall ǀ pass aǀway.

27 But you are the ǀ same for ǀ ever:
    and your ǀ years will ǀ never ǀ fail.

28 The children of your servants shall ǀ rest seǀcure:
    and their seed shall be esǀtablished ǀ in your ǀ sight.

PSALM 103

1 Praise the Lord ǀ O my ǀ soul:
    and all that is within me ǀ praise his ǀ holy ǀ name.

2 Praise the Lord ǀ O my ǀ soul:
    and forǀget not ǀ all his ǀ benefits,

3 Who forgives ǀ all your ǀ sin:
    and ǀ heals ǀ all · your inǀfirmities,

4 Who redeems your ǀ life · from the ǀ Pit:
    and crowns you with ǀ mercy ǀ and comǀpassion;

†5 Who satisfies your being with | good | things:
    so that your | youth · is re|newed · like an | eagle's.

  6 The Lord | works | righteousness:
    and justice for | all who | are op|pressed.

  7 He made known his | ways to | Moses:
    and his | works · to the | children · of | Israel.

  8 The Lord is full of com|passion · and | mercy:
    slow to anger | and of | great | goodness.

  9 He will not | always · be | chiding:
    nor will he | keep his | anger · for | ever.

10 He has not dealt with us ac|cording · to our | sins:
    nor rewarded us ac|cording | to our | wickedness.

11 For as the heavens are high a|bove the | earth:
    so great is his | mercy · over | those that | fear him;

12 As far as the east is | from the | west:
    so far has he | set our | sins | from us.

13 As a father is tender to|wards his | children:
    so is the Lord | tender · to | those that | fear him.

†14 For he knows of | what · we are | made:
    he re|members · that we | are but | dust.

15 The days of man are | but as | grass:
    he flourishes | like a | flower · of the | field;

16 When the wind goes over it | it is | gone:
    and its | place will | know it · no | more.

17 But the merciful goodness of the Lord * endures for _
    ever and ever toward | those that | fear him:
    and his righteousness up|on their | children's |
    children;

18 Upon those who | keep his | covenant:
    and re|member · his com|mandments · to | do them.

19 The Lord has established his | throne in | heaven:
    and his | kingdom | rules · over | all.

20 Praise the Lord all you his angels   you that ex|cel in |
    strength:

you that fulfil his word
   and obey the | voice of | his com|mandment.

21 Praise the Lord all | you his | hosts:
   his | servants · who | do his | will.

22 Praise the Lord all his works
   in all places of | his do|minion:
   praise the | Lord | O my | soul!

PSALM 104

1 Bless the Lord | O my | soul:
   O Lord my | God how | great you | are!

2 Clothed with | majesty · and | honour:
   wrapped in | light as | in a | garment.

3 You have stretched out the | heavens · like a | tent-cloth:
   and laid the beams of your | dwelling · up|on their |
   waters;

4 You make the | clouds your | chariot:
   and | ride up · on the | wings · of the | wind;

5 You make the | winds your | messengers:
   and | flames of | fire your | ministers;

6 You have set the earth on | its found|ations:
   so | that it · shall | never · be | moved.

7 The deep covered it | as · with a | mantle:
   the waters | stood a|bove the | hills.

8 At your re|buke they | fled:
   at the voice of your | thunder · they | hurried · a|way;

9 They went up to the mountains
   they went | down · by the | valleys:
   to the place which | you · had ap|pointed | for them.

10 You fixed a limit which they | may not | pass:
   they shall not return a|gain to | cover · the | earth.

11 You send springs | into · the | gullies:
   which | run be|tween the | hills;

12 They give drink to every | beast · of the | field:
   and the wild | asses | quench their | thirst.

13 Beside them the birds of the air ǀ build their ǀ nests:
 and ǀ sing aǀmong the ǀ branches.

14 You water the mountains from your ǀ dwelling · on ǀ
  high:
 and the earth is ǀ filled · by the ǀ fruits of · your ǀ work.

15 You cause the grass to ǀ grow · for the ǀ cattle:
 and all green things for the ǀ servants ǀ of manǀkind.

16 You bring food ǀ out of · the ǀ earth:
 and wine that makes ǀ glad the ǀ heart of ǀ man,

17 Oil to give him a ǀ shining ǀ countenance:
 and ǀ bread to ǀ strengthen · his ǀ heart.

18 The trees of the Lord are ǀ well-ǀwatered:
 the cedars of ǀ Lebanon · that ǀ he has ǀ planted,

19 Where the birds ǀ build their ǀ nests:
 and the stork ǀ makes her ǀ home · in the ǀ pine-tops.

20 The high hills are a refuge for the ǀ wild ǀ goats:
 and the crags a ǀ cover ǀ for the ǀ conies.

21 You created the moon to ǀ mark the ǀ seasons:
 and the sun ǀ knows the ǀ hour · of its ǀ setting.

22 You make darkness ǀ and it · is ǀ night:
 in which all the beasts of the ǀ forest ǀ move by ǀ
  stealth.

23 The lions ǀ roar · for their ǀ prey:
 seekǀing their ǀ food from ǀ God.

24 When the sun rises ǀ they reǀtire:
 and ǀ lay them·selves ǀ down · in their ǀ dens.

†25 Man goes ǀ out · to his ǀ work:
 and to his ǀ labour · unǀtil the ǀ evening.

26 Lord how various ǀ are your ǀ works:
 in wisdom you have made them all
  and the ǀ earth is ǀ full of · your ǀ creatures.

27 There is the wide imǀmeasur·able ǀ sea:
 there move living things without ǀ number ǀ
  great and ǀ small;

28 There go the ships | to and | fro:
    and there is that Leviathan
        whom you | formed to | sport · in the | deep.

29 These all | look to | you:
    to give them their | food in | due | season.

30 When you give it to | them they | gather it:
    when you open your hand they are | satisfied · with |
        good | things.

31 When you hide your | face · they are | troubled:
    when you take away their breath ⌣
        they | die · and re|turn · to their | dust.

†32 When you send forth your spirit they | are cre|ated:
    and you re|new the | face · of the | earth.

33 May the glory of the Lord en|dure for | ever:
    may the | Lord re|joice · in his | works.

34 If he look upon the | earth · it shall | tremble:
    if he but touch the | mountains | they shall | smoke.

35 I will sing to the Lord as | long as · I | live:
    I will praise my | God · while I | have · any | being.

36 May my meditation be | pleasing | to him:
    for my | joy shall | be · in the | Lord.

†37 May sinners perish from the earth
    let the wicked | be no | more:
    bless the Lord O my soul
    O | praise | – the | Lord.

PSALM 105

1 O give thanks to the Lord   and call up|on his | name:
    tell among the | peoples · what | things · he has |
        done.

2 Sing to him O | sing | praises:
    and be telling of | all his | marvel·lous | works.

3 Exult in his | holy | name:
    and let those that seek the | Lord be | joyful · in | heart.

4 Seek the | Lord · and his | strength:
O | seek his | face con|tinually.

5 Call to mind what wonders | he has | done:
his marvellous acts   and the | judgments | of his |
mouth,

6 O seed of | Abraham · his | servant:
O | children · of | Jacob · his | chosen one.

7 For he is the | Lord our | God:
and his judgments | are in | all the | earth.

8 He has remembered his | covenant · for | ever:
the word that he ordained for a | thousand |
gener|ations,

9 The covenant that he | made with | Abraham:
the | oath · that he | swore to | Isaac,

10 And confirmed it to | Jacob · as a | statute:
to Israel as an | ever|lasting | covenant,

11 Saying   'I will give you the | land of | Canaan:
to be the | portion · of | your in|heritance',

12 And that when they | were but | few:
little in number   and | ali·ens | in the | land.

13 They wandered from | nation · to | nation:
from one people and | kingdom | to an|other.

14 He suffered no man to | do them | wrong:
but re|proved · even | kings for · their | sake,

†15 Saying 'Touch not | my an|ointed:
and | do my | prophets · no | harm.'

16 Then he called down a | famine · on the | land:
and destroyed the | bread that | was their | stay.

17 But he had sent a | man a|head of them:
Joseph | who was | sold · into | slavery,

18 Whose feet they | fastened · with | fetters:
and thrust his | neck in·to a | hoop of | iron.

19 Till the time that his | words proved | true:
he was | tested · by the | Lord's com|mand.

20 Then the king I sent and I loosed him:
   the ruler of I nations I set him I free;

21 He made him master I of his I household:
   and ruler I over I all · his posIsessions,

†22 To rebuke his I officers · at I will:
   and to I teach his I counsel·lors I wisdom.

23 Then Israel I came · into I Egypt:
   and Jacob I dwelt · in the I land of I Ham.

24 There the Lord made his I people I fruitful:
   too I numer·ous I for their I enemies,

25 Whose hearts he turned to I hate his I people:
   and to deal deIceitful·ly I with his I servants.

26 Then he sent I Moses · his I servant:
   and I Aaron · whom I he had I chosen.

27 Through them he I manifested · his I signs:
   and his I wonders · in the I land of I Ham.

28 He sent darkness I and it · was I dark:
   yet they would I not oIbey · his comImands.

29 He turned their I waters · into I blood:
   and I slew the I fish thereIin.

30 Their country I swarmed with I frogs:
   even the inner I chambers I of their I kings.

31 He spoke the word   and there came great I swarms of I
      flies:
   and I gnats with·in I all their I borders.

32 He sent them I storms of I hail:
   and darts of I fire I into · their I land.

33 He struck their I vines · and their I fig-trees:
   and shattered the I trees withIin their I borders.

34 He commanded   and there I came I grasshoppers:
   and young I locusts · withIout I number.

35 They ate up every green thing I in the I land:
   and deIvoured the I fruit · of the I soil.

36 He smote all the first-born I in their I land:
 the I firstfruits · of I all their I manhood.

37 He brought Israel out with silver I and with I gold:
 and not one among their I tribes was I seen to I
 stumble.

38 Egypt was I glad · at their I going:
 for dread of I Israel · had I fallen · up|on them.

39 He spread out a I cloud · for a I covering:
 and I fire to I lighten · the I night.

40 The people asked and he I brought them I quails:
 and satisfied them I with the I bread from I heaven.

41 He opened a rock so that the I waters I gushed:
 and ran in the parched I land I like a I river.

42 For he had remembered his I holy I word:
 that he gave to I Abra|ham his I servant.

43 So he led out his I people · with re|joicing:
 his I chosen ones · with I shouts of I joy;

44 He gave them the I land · of the I nations:
 and they took possession of the I fruit _
 of I other · men's I toil,

†45 So that they might I keep his I statutes:
 and faithfully obey his laws
 O I praise I – the I Lord.

PSALM 106

1 Praise the Lord
 O give thanks to the Lord for I he is I good:
 and his I mercy · en|dures for I ever.

2 Who can express the mighty I acts · of the I Lord:
 or I fully I voice his I praise?

3 Blessèd are those who act ac|cording · to I justice:
 who at I all times I do the I right.

4 Remember me O Lord
 when you visit your people I with your I favour:

and come to me ∣ also · with ∣ your sal∣vation,

†5 That I may see the prosperity ∣ of your ∣ chosen:
    that I may rejoice with the rejoicing of your people
    and exult with ∣ those who ∣ are your ∣ own.

6 We have sinned ∣ like our ∣ fathers:
    we have acted per∣versely · and ∣ done ∣ wrong.

7 Our fathers when they ∣ were in ∣ Egypt:
    took no ∣ heed ∣ of your ∣ wonders;

8 They did not remember ⏜
    the multitude of your ∣ loving-∣kindnesses:
    but they re∣belled · at the ∣ Red ∣ Sea.

9 Nevertheless he saved them for his ∣ name's ∣ sake:
    that he ∣ might make ∣ known his ∣ power.

10 He commanded the Red Sea and it ∣ dried ∣ up:
    and he led them through the ∣ deep as ∣ through a ∣
    desert.

11 He delivered them from the ∣ hand · of their ∣ adversary:
    and redeemed them ∣ from the ∣ power · of the ∣
    enemy.

12 The waters closed over ∣ their op∣pressors:
    so that not ∣ one was ∣ left a∣live.

13 Then they be∣lieved his ∣ words:
    and ∣ sang him ∣ songs of ∣ praise.

14 But in a little while they forgot what ∣ he had ∣ done:
    and would ∣ wait · for his ∣ counsel · no ∣ more.

15 Greed took hold of them ∣ in the ∣ desert:
    and they put ∣ God · to the ∣ test · in the ∣ wilderness.

16 So he gave them that which ∣ they de∣sired:
    but sent a ∣ wasting ∣ sickness · a∣mong them.

17 Then they grew envious of Moses ∣ in the ∣ camp:
    and of Aaron the ∣ holy · one ∣ of the ∣ Lord;

18 Whereupon the earth opened and ∣ swallowed · up ∣
    Dathan:
    it closed over the ∣ compan·y ∣ of A∣biram;

19 Fire flared out a⏐gainst their ⏐ number:
   and ⏐ flame de⏐voured · the un⏐godly.

20 At Horeb they ⏐ made themselves · a ⏐ calf:
   and bowed down in ⏐ worship ⏐ to an ⏐ image.

21 And so they exchanged the ⏐ glory · of ⏐ God:
   for the likeness of an ⏐ ox that ⏐ eats ⏐ hay.

22 They forgot God who ⏐ was their ⏐ saviour:
   that had done such ⏐ great ⏐ things in ⏐ Egypt,

23 Who had worked his wonders in the ⏐ land of ⏐ Ham:
   and his terrible ⏐ deeds · at the ⏐ Red ⏐ Sea.

†24 Therefore he ⏐ thought · to de⏐stroy them:
   had not Moses his servant stood before him in the ‿
      breach * to turn a⏐way his ⏐
      wrath · from de⏐stroying them.

25 Then they despised the ⏐ pleasant ⏐ land:
   and ⏐ put no ⏐ faith · in his ⏐ promise,

26 But murmured ⏐ in their ⏐ tents:
   and would not o⏐bey the ⏐ voice · of the ⏐ Lord.

27 So he lifted his hand to swear an ⏐ oath a⏐gainst them:
   that he would ⏐ strike them ⏐ down · in the ⏐
      wilderness,

28 And cast out their children a⏐mong the ⏐ nations:
   and ⏐ scatter them · through ⏐ all the ⏐ lands.

29 Then they joined themselves to the ⏐ Baal · of ⏐ Peor:
   and ate things sacrificed to ⏐ gods that ⏐ have no ⏐ life.

30 They provoked him to anger with their ⏐ wanton ⏐ deeds:
   and ⏐ plague broke ⏐ out a⏐mong them.

31 Then stood up Phinehas and ⏐ inter⏐posed:
   and ⏐ so the ⏐ plague was ⏐ ended;

32 And that was counted to ⏐ him for ⏐ righteousness:
   throughout all gener⏐ations · for ⏐ ever⏐more.

33 They angered God also at the ⏐ waters · of ⏐ Meribah:
   so that Moses ⏐ suffered · for ⏐ their mis⏐deeds;

34 For they had em|bittered · his | spirit:
and he spoke | rashly | with his | lips.

35 They did not de|stroy the | peoples:
as the Lord had com|manded | them to | do,

36 But they mingled themselves | with the | heathen:
and | learned to | follow · their | ways.

37 They worshipped | foreign | idols:
and | these be|came their | snare,

38 So that they | sacrificed · their | sons:
and their | own | daughters · to | demons.

39 They shed | inno·cent | blood:
even the blood of their | own | sons and | daughters,

40 Whom they offered to the | idols · of | Canaan:
and the | land · was de|filed with | blood.

41 They made themselves | foul · by their | acts:
and with wanton deeds | whored · after | strange | gods.

42 Then was the wrath of the Lord kindled a|gainst his | people:
and he | loathed his | own pos|session;

43 He gave them into the | hands · of the | nations:
and their | adver·saries | ruled | over them.

44 Their enemies be|came · their op|pressors:
and they were brought into sub|jection · be|neath their | power.

45 Many a | time he | saved them:
but they rebelled against him to follow their own designs * and were brought | down | by their | wickedness.

46 Nevertheless he looked on | their dis|tress:
when he | heard their | loud | crying.

47 He remembered his | coven·ant | with them:
and relented   according to the a|bundance · of his | loving-|kindness.

48 And he caused them I to be I pitied:
    even by I those that I held them I captive.

49 Save us O Lord our God
    and gather us from aImong the I nations:
    that we may give thanks to your holy name
    and I make our I boast · in your I praises.

50 Blessèd be the Lord the God of Israel
    from everlasting to I everIlasting:
    and let all the people say Amen I
    Praise I – the I Lord.

PSALM 107

1 O give thanks to the Lord for I he is I good:
    for his loving I mercy I is for I ever.

2 Let the Lord's reIdeemed I say so:
    whom he has redeemed from the I hand I of the I enemy,

†3 And gathered in from every land
    from the east and I from the I west:
    from the I north and I from the I south.

4 Some went astray in the wilderness and I in the I desert:
    and found no I path to · an inIhabit·ed I city;

5 They were I hungry · and I thirsty:
    and their I heart I fainted · withIin them.

6 Then they cried to the Lord in I their disItress:
    and he I took them I out of · their I trouble.

7 He led them by the I right I path:
    till they I came to · an inIhabit·ed I city.

8 *Let them thank the I Lord · for his I goodness:*
    and for the wonders that he I does · for the I children · of I men;

9 *For he I satisfies · the I thirsty:*
    and fills the I hungry · with I good I things.

10 Some sat in darkness and in | deadly | shadow:
   bound | fast · in af|fliction · and | iron,

11 Because they had rebelled against the | words of | God:
   and scorned the purposes | of the | Most | High.

12 So he bowed down their | hearts · with af|fliction:
   they tripped | headlong · with | none to | help them.

13 Then they cried to the Lord in | their dis|tress:
   and he | took them | out of · their | trouble.

†14 He brought them out from darkness and | deadly |
      shadow:
   and | broke their | chains in | two.

15 *Let them thank the | Lord · for his | goodness:*
   and for the wonders that he | does · for the | children · of |
      men;

16 *For he shatters the | doors of | bronze:*
   and | cleaves the | bars of | iron.

17 Fools were far | gone · in trans|gression:
   and be|cause of · their | sins · were af|flicted.

18 They sickened at | any | food:
   and had | come · to the | gates of | death.

19 Then they cried to the Lord in | their dis|tress:
   and he | took them | out of · their | trouble.

20 He sent his | word and | healed them:
   and | saved their | life · from the | Pit.

21 *Let them thank the | Lord · for his | goodness:*
   and for the wonders that he | does · for the | children · of |
      men;

22 *Let them offer sacrifices of | thanks|giving:*
   and tell what he has | done with | shouts of | joy.

23 Those who go down to the | sea in | ships:
   and follow their | trade on | great | waters,

24 These men have seen the | works of | God:
   and his | wonders | in the | deep.

25 For he spoke and I raised the I storm-wind:
    and it lifted I high the I waves · of the I sea.

26 They go up to the sky   and down aIgain · to the I
        depths:
    their courage melts aIway · in the I face · of disIaster.

27 They reel and stagger like I drunken I men:
    and are I at their I wits' I end.

28 Then they cried to the Lord in I their disItress:
    and he I took them I out of · their I trouble.

29 He calmed the I storm · to a I silence:
    and the I waves · of the I sea were I stilled.

30 Then they were glad beIcause · they were I quiet:
    and he I brought them · to the I haven · they I
        longed for.

31 *Let them thank the I Lord · for his I goodness:*
    and for the wonders that he I does · for the I children · of I
        men;

32 *Let them exalt him in the asIsembly · of the I people:*
    and I praise him · in the I council · of I elders.

33 He turns the I rivers · into I desert:
    and springs of I water · into I thirsty I ground.

34 He makes of a fruitful land a I salty I waste:
    beIcause · its inIhabitants · are I evil.

35 He turns the wilderness into a I pool of I water:
    and parched I ground · into I flowing I springs.

36 And there he I settles · the I hungry:
    and they I build a I city · to I live in.

37 They sow fields and I plant I vineyards:
    which I give them I fruitful I harvest.

38 He blesses them   and they I multi·ply I greatly:
    he does not I let their I cattle · dimIinish.

39 But he pours conItempt up·on I princes:
    and makes them I stray · in the I pathless I desert;

40 They are weakened and I brought I low:

through ǀ stress of · adǀversity · and ǀ sorrow.

41 But he lifts the ǀ poor · out of ǀ misery:
and increases their ǀ families · like ǀ flocks of ǀ sheep.

42 The upright shall ǀ see it · and reǀjoice:
and all ǀ wickedness · shall ǀ shut its ǀ mouth.

†43 Whoever is wise   let him obǀserve these ǀ things:
and consider the loving-ǀkindness ǀ of the ǀ Lord.

PSALM 108

1 My heart is fixed O God my ǀ heart is ǀ fixed:
I will ǀ sing and ǀ make ǀ melody.

2 Awake my soul   awake ǀ lute and ǀ harp:
for ǀ I · will aǀwaken · the ǀ morning.

3 I will give you thanks O Lord aǀmong the ǀ peoples:
I will sing your ǀ praise aǀmong the ǀ nations.

4 For the greatness of your mercy ǀ reaches · to the ǀ
heavens:
and your ǀ faithful·ness ǀ to the ǀ clouds.

5 Be exalted O God aǀbove the ǀ heavens:
and let your glory be ǀ over ǀ all the ǀ earth;

6 That those whom you love may ǀ be deǀlivered:
O save us by ǀ your right ǀ hand and ǀ answer me.

7 God has said in his ǀ holy ǀ place:
'I will exult and divide Shechem
I will parcel ǀ out the ǀ valley · of ǀ Succoth.

8 'Gilead is mine and Manǀasseh · is ǀ mine:
Ephraim is my helmet and ǀ Judah · my ǀ rod ·
of comǀmand.

†9 'Moab is my wash-bowl   over Edom will I ǀ cast my ǀ
shoe:
against Philistia ǀ will I ǀ shout in ǀ triumph.'

10 Who will lead me into the ǀ forti·fied ǀ city:
who will ǀ bring me ǀ into ǀ Edom?

11 Have you not cast us I off O I God?:
    you I go not I out · with our I armies.

12 Give us your help a‌Igainst the I enemy:
    for I vain · is the I help of I man.

13 By the power of our God we I shall do I valiantly:
    for it is he that I will tread I down our I enemies.

PSALM 109

1 O God of my praise do I not be I silent:
   for evil and deceitful I mouths are I
       opened · a‌Igainst me.

2 They speak of me with I lying I tongues:
   they surround me with words of hatred
       they fight a‌Igainst me · with‌Iout I cause.

3 In return for my friendship I they op‌Ipose me:
   and I that for · no I fault of I mine.

4 They repay me I evil · for I good:
   and I hatred · for I my af‌Ifection.

[5 Appoint an evil man to I stand a‌Igainst him:
   and let an adversary I be at · his I right I hand.

6 When he is judged   let him be I found I guilty:
   let his prayer for I help be I counted · as I sin.

7 Let his I days be I few:
   and let another I take what I he has I hoarded.

8 Let his children be I made I fatherless:
   and his I wife be‌Icome a I widow.

9 Let his children be I vagabonds · and I beggars:
   let them seek alms I far · from their I own I homes.

10 Let the usurer exact I all · that he I has:
    and let strangers I plunder · the I fruit · of his I toil.

11 Let no man be I loyal · to I him:
    and let no one have I pity · on his I father·less I
        children.

12 Let his line be‌Icome ex‌Itinct:
    in one generation let their I name be I blotted I out.

13 Let the sins of his fathers be re│membered · by the │
    Lord:
    and his mother's iniquity │ not be │ wiped a│way.

14 Let their sins be constantly be│fore the │ Lord:
    may he root out their │ memo·ry │ from the │ earth.

15 For he was a man that did not remember to │ show │
    loyalty:
    but he persecuted the humble the poor and the ‿
    crushed in spirit
    and │ sought to │ put them · to │ death.

16 He loved to curse * let curses │ fall on │ him:
    he took no pleasure in blessing
    so let │ it be │ far from │ him.

17 He clothed himself in cursing │ like a │ garment:
    so let it seep like water into his body
    and like │ oil │ into · his │ bones.

18 Let it be as the clothes he │ wraps a│bout him:
    or like the │ girdle · that he │ wears each │ day.

[†]19 This is the Lord's recompense to │
    those · that op│pose him:
    to │ those that · speak │ evil · a│gainst me.]

20 Act for me O Lord my God for your │ name's │ sake:
    and deliver me   as your │ steadfast │ love is │ good.

21 For I am │ poor and │ needy:
    and my │ heart │ writhes with│in me.

22 I fade like a │ lengthen·ing │ shadow:
    I am │ shaken │ off · like a │ locust.

23 My knees are │ weak from │ fasting:
    my │ flesh grows │ lean and │ shrunken.

†24 I have become the │ scorn of · my │ enemies:
    and when they see me they │ toss their │
    heads · in de│rision.

25 Help me O │ Lord my │ God:
    and save me │ for your │ mercy's │ sake,

26 That men may know it was I your I hand:
    that I you O I Lord have I done it.

27 Though they curse yet I give me · your I blessing:
    and those that come against me will be put to shame
    and your I servant I shall reI joice.

28 Let those that oppose me be I covered · with disI grace:
    let them I wear their I shame · as a I garment.

29 And I will give the Lord great I thanks · with my I
    mouth:
    and I praise him · in the I midst · of a I multitude.

30 For the Lord will stand at the right I hand · of the I poor:
    to save him from I those that I would conI demn him.

PSALM 110

1 The Lord I said to I my lord:
    'Sit at my right hand
    until I I make your I enemies · your I footstool.'

2 The Lord commits to you the sceptre I of your I power:
    reign from I Zion · in the I midst of · your I enemies.

3 Noble are you * from the day of your birth upon the I
    holy I hill:
    radiant are you even from the womb
    in the I morning I dew of · your I youth.

4 The Lord has sworn and will I not turn I back:
    'You are a priest for ever * after the I order I
    of MelI chizedek.'

5 The king shall stand at your right I hand O I Lord:
    and shatter I kings · in the I day of · his I wrath.

6 Glorious in majesty * he shall judge aI mong the I
    nations:
    and shatter heads I over · a I wide I land.

†7 He shall slake his thirst from the brook beI side the I way:
    therefore shall I he lift I up his I head.

PSALM 111

1 O praise the Lord
        I will praise the Lord with my ⁞ whole ⁞ heart:
    in the company of the upright
        and a⁞mong the ⁞ congre⁞gation.

2 The works of the ⁞ Lord are ⁞ great:
        and studied by ⁞ all who ⁞ take de⁞light in them.

3 His deeds are ma⁞jestic · and ⁞ glorious:
        and his ⁞ righteous·ness ⁞ stands for ⁞ ever.

4 His marvellous acts have won him a name to ⁞
        be re⁞membered:
    the ⁞ Lord is ⁞ gracious · and ⁞ merciful.

5 He gives food to ⁞ those that ⁞ fear him:
        he re⁞members · his ⁞ covenant · for ⁞ ever.

6 He showed his people the ⁞ power · of his ⁞ acts:
        in giving them the ⁞ herit·age ⁞ of the ⁞ heathen.

7 The works of his hands are ⁞ faithful · and ⁞ just:
        and ⁞ all · his com⁞mandments · are ⁞ sure;

8 They stand firm for ⁞ ever · and ⁞ ever:
        they are done in ⁞ faithful·ness ⁞ and in ⁞ truth.

9 He sent redemption to his people
        he ordained his ⁞ covenant · for ⁞ ever:
    holy is his name and ⁞ worthy ⁞ to be ⁞ feared.

10 The fear of the Lord is the beginning of wisdom
        and of good understanding are those that ⁞ keep ·
        his com⁞mandments:
    his ⁞ praise · shall en⁞dure for ⁞ ever.

PSALM 112

1 O praise the Lord
        Blessèd is the man who ⁞ fears the ⁞ Lord:
    and greatly de⁞lights in ⁞ his com⁞mandments.

2 His children shall be ⁞ mighty · in the ⁞ land:
        a race of upright ⁞ men who ⁞ will be ⁞ blessed.

3 Riches and plenty shall be ⁞ in his ⁞ house:
        and his ⁞ righteous·ness ⁞ stands for ⁞ ever.

4 Light arises in darkness I for the I upright:
    gracious and merciful I is the I righteous I man.

5 It goes well with the man who acts I generously · and I
      lends:
    who I guides · his afIfairs with I justice.

6 Surely he shall I never · be I moved:
    the righteous shall be held in I everIlasting ·
      reImembrance.

7 He will not I fear bad I tidings:
    his heart is steadfast   I trusting I in the I Lord.

8 His heart is confident and I will not I fear:
    he will see the I downfall I of his I enemies.

9 He gives I freely · to the I poor:
    his righteousness stands for ever
    his I head is · upIlifted · in I glory.

10 The wicked man shall see it I and be I angry:
    he shall gnash his teeth and consume away
    and the I hope · of the I wicked · shall I fail.

PSALM 113

1 Praise the Lord
      O sing praises you that I are his I servants:
    O I praise the I name · of the I Lord.

2 Let the name of the I Lord be I blessed:
    from this time I forward I and for I ever.

3 From the rising of the sun to its I going I down:
    let the I name · of the I Lord be I praised.

4 The Lord is exalted over I all the I nations:
    and his I glory · is aIbove the I heavens.

5 Who can be likened to the I Lord our I God:
    in I heaven · or upIon the I earth,

6 Who has his I dwelling · so I high:
    yet condescends to I look on I things beIneath?

7 He raises the I lowly · from theI dust:
    and lifts the I poor from I out of · the I dungheap;

8 He gives them a place aˡmong the ˡ princes:
  even among the ˡ princes ˡ of his ˡ people.

†9 He causes the barren woman to ˡ keep ˡ house:
  and makes her a joyful mother of children ˡ
    Praise ˡ – the ˡ Lord.

PSALM 114

1 When Israel came ˡ out of ˡ Egypt:
  and the house of Jacob from among a ˡ people · of an ˡ
    alien ˡ tongue,

2 Judah beˡcame his ˡ sanctuary:
  and ˡ Israel ˡ his doˡminion.

3 The sea saw ˡ that and ˡ fled:
  Jorˡdan was ˡ driven ˡ back.

4 The mountains ˡ skipped like ˡ rams:
  and the little ˡ hills like ˡ young ˡ sheep.

5 What ailed you O ˡ sea · that you ˡ fled:
  O Jordan that ˡ you were ˡ driven ˡ back?

6 You mountains that you ˡ skipped like ˡ rams:
  and you little ˡ hills like ˡ young ˡ sheep?

7 Tremble O earth at the ˡ presence · of the ˡ Lord:
  at the ˡ presence · of the ˡ God of ˡ Jacob,

8 Who turned the rock into a ˡ pool of ˡ water:
  and the flint-stone ˡ into · a ˡ welling ˡ spring.

PSALM 115

1 Not to us O Lord not to us
    but to your name ˡ give the ˡ glory:
  for the sake of your faithfulness ˡ and your ˡ loving-
    ˡkindness.

2 Why should the heathen say ˡ 'Where is · their ˡ God?':
  our God is in heaven   he ˡ does whatˡever · he ˡ wills.

3 As for their idols   they are ˡ silver · and ˡ gold:
  the ˡ work · of a ˡ man's ˡ hand.

4 They have ˡ mouths but ˡ speak not:
  they have ˡ eyes · but they ˡ cannot ˡ see.

5 They have ears yet I hear I nothing:
    they have I noses · but I cannot I smell.

6 Hands they have but handle nothing
      feet but they I do not I walk:
    they I make no I sound · with their I throats.

†7 Those who make them I shall be I like them:
    so shall I everyone · that I trusts in I them.

8 O Israel I trust · in the I Lord:
    he is your I help I and your I shield.

9 O house of Aaron I trust · in the I Lord:
    he is your I help I and your I shield.

10 You that fear the Lord I trust · in the I Lord:
    he is your I help I and your I shield.

11 The Lord has remembered us and I he will I bless us:
    he will bless the house of Israel
      he will I bless the I house of I Aaron.

12 He will bless all those that I fear the I Lord:
    both I high and I low to I gether.

13 May the Lord in I crease you I greatly:
    you I and your I children I after you.

14 The blessing of the I Lord · be up I on you:
    he that I made I heaven · and I earth.

15 As for the heavens I they · are the I Lord's:
    but the earth he has I given · to the I children · of I
    men.

16 The dead do not I praise the I Lord:
    nor do I any · that go I down to I silence.

17 But we will I bless the I Lord:
    both now and for evermore
      O I praise I – the I Lord.

PSALM 116

1 I love the Lord because he I heard my I voice:
  the I voice of · my I suppliIcation;

2 Because he inIclined his I ear to me:
  in the I day I that I I called to him.

3 The cords of death encompassed me
      the snares of the I grave took I hold on me:
  I I was in I anguish · and I sorrow.

4 Then I called upon the I name · of the I Lord:
  'O I Lord · I beIseech you · deIliver me!'

5 Gracious and righteous I is the I Lord:
  full of comIpassion I is our I God.

6 The Lord preIserves the I simple:
  when I I was · brought I low he I saved me.

7 Return O my I soul · to your I rest:
  for the I Lord I has reIwarded you.

8 For you O Lord have delivered my I soul from I death:
  my eyes from I tears · and my I feet from I falling.

†9 I will walk beIfore the I Lord:
  in the I land I of the I living.

10 I believed that I would perish   I was I brought · very I
      low:
  I said in my haste I 'All I men are I liars.'

11 How shall I reIpay the I Lord:
  for I all his I bene·fits I to me?

12 I will take up the I cup of · salIvation:
  and I call up·on the I name · of the I Lord.

13 I will pay my I vows · to the I Lord:
  in the I presence · of I all his I people.

14 Grievous in the I sight · of the I Lord:
  is the I death I of his I faithful ones.

15 O Lord I am your servant
      your servant and the I son of · your I handmaid:
  you I have unIloosed my I bonds.

16 I will offer you a sacrifice of | thanks|giving:
 and | call up·on the | name · of the | Lord.

17 I will pay my | vows · to the | Lord:
 in the | presence · of | all his | people,

†18 In the courts of the | house · of the | Lord:
 even in your midst O Jerusalem |
  Praise | – the | Lord.

PSALM 117

1 O praise the Lord | all you | nations:
 O | praise him | all you | peoples.

2 For great is his loving-|kindness · to|ward us:
 and the faithfulness of the Lord endures for ever |
  Praise | – the | Lord.

PSALM 118

1 O give thanks to the Lord for | he is | good:
 his | mercy · en|dures for | ever.

2 Let Israel | now pro|claim:
 that his | mercy · en|dures for | ever.

3 Let the house of | Aaron · pro|claim:
 that his | mercy · en|dures for | ever.

4 Let those who fear the | Lord pro|claim:
 that his | mercy · en|dures for | ever.

5 In my danger I | called · to the | Lord:
 he | answered · and | set me | free.

6 The Lord is on my side   I | shall not | fear:
 what can | man | do to | me?

7 The Lord is at my side | as my | helper:
 I shall see the | downfall | of my | enemies.

8 It is better to take refuge | in the | Lord:
 than to | put your | trust in | man;

†9 It is better to take refuge | in the | Lord:
 than to | put your | trust in | princes.

10 All the | nations · sur|rounded me:
    but in the name of the | Lord I | drove them | back.

11 They surrounded   they surrounded me on | every |
    side:
    but in the name of the | Lord I | drove them | back.

12 They swarmed about me like bees
    they blazed like fire a|mong the | thorns:
    in the name of the | Lord I | drove them | back.

13 I was pressed so hard that I | almost | fell:
    but the | Lord | was my | helper.

†14 The Lord is my | strength · and my | song:
    and has be|come | my sal|vation.

15 The sounds of | joy · and de|liverance:
    are | in the | tents · of the | righteous.

16 The right hand of the Lord does | mighty | things:
    the right hand of the | Lord | raises | up.

17 I shall not | die but | live:
    and pro|claim the | works · of the | Lord.

18 The Lord has | disciplined · me | hard:
    but he has not | given · me | over · to | death.

19 Open me the | gates of | righteousness:
    and I will enter and give | thanks | to the | Lord.

20 This is the | gate · of the | Lord:
    the | righteous | shall | enter it.

21 I will praise you | for you | answered me:
    and have be|come | my sal|vation.

22 The stone that the | builders · re|jected:
    has be|come the | head · of the | corner.

23 This is the | Lord's | doing:
    and it is | marvel·lous | in our | eyes.

24 This is the day that the | Lord has | made:
    let us re|joice | and be | glad in it.

25 O Lord | save us · we | pray:
    O Lord | send | us pros|perity.

26 Blessèd is he who comes in the ǀ name · of the ǀ Lord:
   from the ǀ house · of the ǀ Lord we ǀ bless you.

27 The Lord is God   and he has ǀ given · us ǀ light:
   guide the festal throng up to the ǀ horns ǀ of the ǀ altar.

28 You are my God and ǀ I will ǀ praise you:
   you are my ǀ God I ǀ will exǀalt you.

†29 O give thanks to the Lord for ǀ he is ǀ good:
   and his ǀ mercy · enǀdures for ǀ ever.

PSALM 119

1

1 Blessèd are those whose ǀ way is ǀ blameless:
   who ǀ walk · in the ǀ law · of the ǀ Lord.

2 Blessèd are those who ǀ keep · his comǀmands:
   and seek him ǀ with their ǀ whole ǀ heart;

3 Those who ǀ do no ǀ wrong:
   but ǀ walk · in the ǀ ways of · our ǀ God.

4 For you Lord ǀ have comǀmanded us:
   to perseǀvere in ǀ all your ǀ precepts.

5 If only my ǀ ways · were unǀerring:
   towards the ǀ keeping ǀ of your ǀ statutes!

6 Then I should ǀ not · be aǀshamed:
   when I ǀ looked on ǀ all · your comǀmandments.

7 I will praise you with sinǀcerity · of ǀ heart:
   as I ǀ learn your ǀ righteous ǀ judgments.

8 I will ǀ keep your ǀ statutes:
   O forǀsake me ǀ not ǀ utterly.

2

9 How shall a young man's ǀ path be ǀ pure:
   unǀless he ǀ keep to · your ǀ word?

10 I have sought you with my ǀ whole ǀ heart:
   let me not ǀ stray from ǀ your comǀmandments.

11 I have treasured your ǀ words · in my ǀ heart:
   that I ǀ might not ǀ sin aǀgainst you.

12 Blessèd are | you Lord | God:
   O | teach me | your | statutes.

13 With my lips I | have been | telling:
   all the | judgments | of your | mouth;

14 And I find more joy in the way of | your com|mands:
   than in | all | manner · of | riches.

15 I will meditate | on your | precepts:
   and give | heed | to your | ways;

16 For my delight is wholly | in your | statutes:
   and I will | not for|get your | word.

3

17 O be bountiful to your servant that | I may | live:
   in o|bedi·ence | to your | word.

18 Take away the | veil · from my | eyes:
   that I may see the | wonders | of your | law.

19 I am but a | stranger · on the | earth:
   do not | hide · your com|mandments | from me.

20 My soul is con|sumed with | longing:
   for your | judgments | day and | night.

21 You have re|buked the | proud:
   and cursed are those who | stray from |
      your com|mandments;

22 Turn away from me their re|proach and | scorn:
   for | I have | kept · your com|mands.

23 Though princes sit and plot to|gether · a|gainst me:
   your servant shall | medi·tate | on your | statutes:

24 For your commands are | my de|light:
   and they are | counsellors · in | my de|fence.

4

25 I am humbled | to the | dust:
   O give me life ac|cording | to your | word.

26 If I ex|amine · my | ways:
   surely you will answer me * O | teach me | your |
      statutes!

27 Make me to understand the I way of · your I precepts:
    and I shall meditate I on your I marvel·lous I works.

28 My soul pines aIway for I sorrow:
    O raise me up acIcording I to your I word.

29 Keep me far from the I way of · deIception:
    and I grant me · the I grace of · your I law.

30 I have chosen the I way of I truth:
    and have I set your I judgments · beIfore me.

31 I hold fast to I your comImands:
    O Lord let me I never I be conIfounded.

32 Let me run the way of I your comImandments:
    for I you will I liberate · my I heart.

5

33 Teach me O Lord the I way of · your I statutes:
    and I will I honour · it I to the I end.

34 Give me understanding   that I may I keep your I law:
    that I may keep it I with my I whole I heart.

35 Guide me in the path of I your comImandments:
    for thereIin is I my deIlight.

36 Incline my heart to I your comImands:
    and I not to I selfish I gain.

37 Turn away my eyes from I looking · on I vanities:
    as I walk in your I way I give me I life.

38 Make good your promise I to your I servant:
    the promise that enIdures for I all who I fear you.

39 Turn aside the I taunts · that I I dread:
    for your I judgments · are I very I good.

40 Lord I I long for · your I precepts:
    in your I righteous·ness I give me I life.

6

41 Let your loving mercy come to I me O I Lord:
    and your salvation acIcording I to your I word.

42 Then I shall have an answer for I
   those · who reIproach me:
  for I I trust I in your I word.

43 Do not take the word of truth utterly I out of · my I
   mouth:
  for in your I judgments I is my I hope.

44 Let me keep your I law conItinually:
  O I let me I keep it · for I ever.

45 And so I shall I walk at I liberty:
  beIcause · I have I sought your I precepts.

46 I shall speak of your comImands be·fore I kings:
  and shall I not be I put to I shame.

47 My delight shall be in I your comImandments:
  which I I have I greatly I loved;

48 I shall worship you with I outstretched I hands:
  and I shall I medi·tate I on your I statutes.

7

49 Remember your I word · to your I servant:
  on I which · you have I built my I hope.

50 This has been my comfort in I my afIfliction:
  for your I word has I brought me I life.

51 Though the proud have I laughed me · to I scorn:
  I have not I turned aIside from · your I law;

52 But I called to mind O Lord your I judgments · of I old:
  and in I them · I have I found · consolIation.

53 I am seized with indignation I at the I wicked:
  for I they have · forIsaken · your I law.

54 But your statutes have beIcome my I songs:
  in the I house I of my I pilgrimage.

55 I think on your name O I Lord · in the I night:
  and I I obIserve your I law;

56 This has I been · my reIward:
  beIcause · I have I kept your I precepts.

8

57 The Lord ǀ is my ǀ portion:
    I have ǀ promised · to ǀ keep your ǀ words.

58 I have sought your favour with my ǀ whole ǀ heart:
    O be gracious to me acǀcording ǀ to your ǀ word.

59 I have taken ǀ stock of · my ǀ ways:
    and have turned back my ǀ feet to ǀ your comǀmands.

60 I made haste and did ǀ not deǀlay:
    to ǀ keep ǀ your comǀmandments.

61 The snares of the ǀ wicked · enǀcompassed me:
    but I did ǀ not forǀget your ǀ law;

62 At midnight I rise to ǀ give you ǀ thanks:
    for the ǀ righteous·ness ǀ of your ǀ judgments.

63 I am a friend to ǀ all who ǀ fear you:
    to ǀ those who ǀ keep your ǀ precepts.

64 The earth O Lord is full of your ǀ loving ǀ mercy:
    O ǀ teach me ǀ your ǀ statutes.

9

65 Lord you have done ǀ good to · your ǀ servant:
    in acǀcordance ǀ with your ǀ word.

66 O teach me right ǀ judgment · and ǀ knowledge:
    for I ǀ trust in ǀ your comǀmandments.

67 Before I was afflicted I ǀ went aǀstray:
    but ǀ now I ǀ keep your ǀ word.

68 You are good and you ǀ do ǀ good:
    O ǀ teach me ǀ your ǀ statutes.

69 The proud have ǀ smeared me · with ǀ lies:
    but I will keep your precepts ǀ with my ǀ whole ǀ heart.

70 Their hearts are ǀ gross like ǀ fat:
    but my deǀlight is ǀ in your ǀ law.

71 It is good for me that ǀ I was · afǀflicted:
    so ǀ I might ǀ learn your ǀ statutes.

72 The law of your mouth is ǀ dearer · to ǀ me:
   than a ǀ wealth of ǀ gold and ǀ silver.

10

73 Your hands have ǀ made me · and ǀ fashioned me:
   O give me understanding ⏝
      that ǀ I may ǀ learn · your comǀmandments.

74 Those who fear you shall see me ǀ and reǀjoice:
   for my ǀ hope is ǀ in your ǀ word.

75 I know Lord that your ǀ judgments · are ǀ right:
   and that in ǀ faithfulness · you ǀ have afǀflicted me.

76 Let your merciful kindness ǀ be my ǀ comfort:
   according to your ǀ promise ǀ to your ǀ servant.

77 O let your mercy come to me that ǀ I may ǀ live:
   for your ǀ law is ǀ my deǀlight.

78 Let the proud be shamed
      who steal my ǀ rights · through their ǀ lies:
   but I will ǀ medi·tate ǀ on your ǀ precepts.

79 Let those who fear you ǀ turn to ǀ me:
   and ǀ they shall ǀ know · your comǀmands.

80 O let my heart be ǀ sound in · your ǀ statutes:
   that I may ǀ never · be ǀ put to ǀ shame.

11

81 My soul languishes for ǀ your salǀvation:
   but my ǀ hope is ǀ in your ǀ word;

82 My eyes fail with ǀ watching · for your ǀ promise:
   saying 'O ǀ when ǀ will you ǀ comfort me?'

83 I am parched as a wineskin ǀ in the ǀ smoke:
   yet I do ǀ not forǀget your ǀ statutes.

84 How many are the ǀ days of · your ǀ servant:
   and ǀ when · will you ǀ judge my ǀ persecutors?

85 The proud have dug ǀ pitfalls ǀ for me:
   in deǀfiance ǀ of your ǀ law.

86 All your com|mandments · are | true:
    but they persecute me with lies * O | come | to my |
      help!

87 They have almost made an end of me | on the | earth:
    but I have | not for|saken · your | precepts.

88 In your merciful goodness | give me | life:
    that I may keep the com|mands | of your | mouth.

12

89 Lord your | word · is for | ever:
    it stands | firm | in the | heavens.

90 Your faithfulness abides from one gener|ation ·
      to an|other:
    firm as the | earth which | you have | made.

91 As for your judgments   they stand | fast this | day:
    for | all things | are your | servants.

92 If your law had not been | my de|light:
    I would have | perished · in | my af|fliction.

93 I will never for|get your | precepts:
    for by | them · you have | given · me | life.

94 I am | yours   O | save me:
    for | I have | sought your | precepts.

95 The wicked have lain in wait for me | to de|stroy me:
    but I | think on | your com|mands.

96 I have seen that all perfection | comes · to an | end:
    only your com|mandment | has no | bounds.

13

97 Lord how I | love your | law:
    it is my medi|tation | all the · day | long.

98 Your commandments have made me wiser | than my |
      enemies:
    for they re|main with | me for | ever.

99 I have more understanding than | all my | teachers:
    for I | study | your com|mands.

100 I am wiser | than the | agèd:
    be|cause · I have | kept your | precepts.

101 I have held back my feet from every | evil | path:
    that | I might | keep your | word;

102 I have not turned a|side from · your | judgments:
    for | you your|self are · my | teacher.

103 How sweet are your | words · to my | tongue:
    sweeter than | honey | to my | mouth.

104 Through your precepts I get | under|standing:
    therefore I | hate all | lying | ways.

14

105 Your word is a lantern | to my | feet:
    and a | light | to my | path.

106 I have vowed and | sworn an | oath:
    to | keep your | righteous | judgments.

107 I have been afflicted be|yond | measure:
    Lord give me life ac|cording | to your | word.

108 Accept O Lord the freewill offerings | of my | mouth:
    and | teach me | your | judgments.

109 I take my life in my | hands con|tinually:
    yet I do | not for|get your | law.

110 The wicked have | laid a | snare for me:
    but I | have not | strayed from · your | precepts.

111 Your commands are my in|heritance · for | ever:
    they | are the | joy of · my | heart.

112 I have set my heart to ful|fil your | statutes:
    always | even | to the | end.

15

113 I loathe those who are | double-|minded:
    but your | law | do I | love.

114 You are my shelter | and my | shield:
    and in your | word | is my | hope.

115 Away from me all I you that · do I evil:
    I will keep the comImandments I of my I God.

116 Be my stay according to your word that I I may I live:
    and do not disapIpoint me I in my I hope.

117 Hold me up and I I shall be I safe:
    and I will ever deIlight I in your I statutes.

118 You scorn all those who I swerve from · your I statutes:
    for their I calumnies · aIgainst me · are I lies;

119 All the ungodly of the earth you I count as I dross:
    therefore I I love I your comImands.

120 My flesh I shrinks for I fear of you:
    and I am aIfraid I of your I judgments.

16

121 I have done what is I just and I right:
    O do not give me I over · to I my opIpressors.

122 Stand surety for your I servant's I good:
    let I not the I proud opIpress me.

123 My eyes fail with watching for I your salIvation:
    for the fulfilment I of your I righteous I word.

124 O deal with your servant according to your I loving I
      mercy:
    and I teach me I your I statutes.

125 I am your servant   O give me I underIstanding:
    that I I may I know · your comImands.

126 It is time for the I Lord to I act:
    for they I vio·late I your I law.

127 Therefore I I love · your comImandments:
    more than gold   I more · than the I finest I gold;

128 Therefore I straighten my paths by I all your I precepts:
    and I I hate all I lying I ways.

17

129 Wonderful are I your comImands:
    and I therefore · my I soul I keeps them.

130 The unfolding of your I word gives I light:
　　it gives underIstanding I to the I simple.

131 I open my mouth and draw I in my I breath:
　　for I I yearn for I your comImandments.

132 O turn to me and be I merci·ful I to me:
　　as is your way with I those who I love your I name.

133 Order my steps according I to your I word:
　　that no evil I may get I master·y I over me.

134 Deliver me from I man's opIpression:
　　that I I may I keep your I precepts.

135 Make your face shine upIon your I servant:
　　and I teach me I your I statutes.

136 My eyes gush out with I streams of I water:
　　because they I pay no I heed to · your I law.

18

137 Righteous are I you Lord I God:
　　and I just are I your I judgments;

138 The commands that I you · have comImanded:
　　are exIceeding·ly I righteous · and I true.

139 Zeal and indignation have I choked my I mouth:
　　because my enemies I have forIgotten · your I words.

140 Your word has been I tried · in the I fire:
　　and I therefore · your I servant I loves it.

141 I am small and of I no acIcount:
　　but I have I not forIgotten · your I precepts.

142 Your righteousness is an everIlasting I righteousness:
　　and your I law I is the I truth.

143 Trouble and anguish have I taken I hold on me:
　　but your comImandments · are I my deIlight.

144 The righteousness of your commands is I everIlasting:
　　O give me underIstanding · and I I shall I live.

19

145 I call with my I whole I heart:
    hear me O Lord   I I will I keep your I statutes.

146 I cry out to I you O I save me:
    and I I will I heed · your comImands.

147 Before the morning light I I rise · and I I call:
    for in your I word I is my I hope.

148 Before the night watch my I eyes I wake:
    that I may I meditate · upIon your I words.

149 Hear my voice O Lord in your I loving I mercy:
    and according to your I judgments I give me I life.

150 They draw near to me who malIicious·ly I persecute me:
    but I they are I far from · your I law.

151 You Lord are I close at I hand:
    and I all · your comImandments · are I true.

152 I have known long since from I your comImands:
    that you have I founded I them for I ever.

20

153 Consider my affliction I and deIliver me:
    for I do I not forIget your I law.

154 Plead my cause and I set me I free:
    O give me life acIcording I to your I word.

155 Salvation is I far · from the I wicked:
    for they I do not I seek your I statutes.

156 Numberless O Lord are your I tender I mercies:
    according to your I judgments I give me I life.

157 Many there are that persecute I me and I trouble me:
    but I have not I swerved from I your comImands.

158 I am cut to the heart when I I see the I faithless:
    for they I do not I keep your I word.

159 Consider O Lord how I I love your I precepts:
    and in your I mercy I give me I life.

160 The sum of your I word is I truth:
    and all your righteous I judgments I stand for I ever.

21

161 Princes have persecuted me withıout a ı cause:
  but my heart ı stands in ı awe of · your ı word.

162 I am as ı glad of · your ı word:
  as ı one who ı finds rich ı spoil.

163 Lies I ı hate · and abıhor:
  but your ı law ı do I ı love.

164 Seven times a ı day I ı praise you:
  beıcause of · your ı righteous ı judgments.

165 Great is the peace of those who ı love your ı law:
  and ı nothing · shall ı make them ı stumble.

166 Lord I have waited for ı your salıvation:
  and I have ı done ı your comımandments.

167 My soul has heeded ı your comımands:
  and I ı love them · beıyond ı measure.

168 I have kept your precepts ı and comımands:
  for all my ı ways are ı open · beıfore you.

22

169 Let my cry ı come to you · O ı Lord:
  O give me understanding acıcording ı to your ı word;

170 Let my supplication ı come beıfore you:
  and deliver me acıcording ı to your ı promise.

171 My lips shall pour ı forth your ı praise:
  beıcause you ı teach me · your ı statutes;

172 My tongue shall ı sing of · your ı word:
  for ı all · your comımandments · are ı righteousness.

173 Let your hand be ı swift to ı help me:
  for ı I have ı chosen · your ı precepts.

174 Lord I have longed for ı your salıvation:
  and your ı law is ı my deılight.

175 O let my soul live that ı I may ı praise you:
  and let your ı judgments ı be my ı help.

176 I have gone astray like a ı sheep · that is ı lost:
  O seek your servant
    for I do ı not forıget · your comımandments.

PSALM 120

1 I call to the I Lord · in my I trouble:
   that I he may I answer I me.

2 O Lord deliver me from I lying I lips:
   and I from the I treacher·ous I tongue.

3 What will he do to you * and what more will he do ⌣
          to you O I treacher·ous I tongue?:
   you are sharp as the arrows of a warrior
          that are I tempered · in I coals of I juniper.

4 Alas for me * I am like a I stranger · in I Meshech:
   like one who dwells aImidst the I tents of I Kedar.

5 My soul has I been too I long:
   among I those · who are I enemies · to I peace.

6 I am for peace   but I when I I speak of it:
   they I make them·selves I ready · for I war.

PSALM 121

1 I lift up my I eyes · to the I hills:
   but I where · shall I I find I help?

2 My help I comes · from the I Lord:
   who has I made I heaven · and I earth.

3 He will not suffer your I foot to I stumble:
   and he who watches I over · you I will not I sleep.

4 Be sure he who has I charge of I Israel:
   will I neither I slumber · nor I sleep.

5 The Lord himIself is · your I keeper:
   the Lord is your defence upIon your I right I hand;

6 The sun shall not I strike you · by I day:
   nor I shall the I moon by I night.

7 The Lord will defend you from I all I evil:
   it is I he · who will I guard your I life.

8 The Lord will defend your going out and your I coming I
          in:
   from this time I forward · for I everImore.

PSALM 122

1 I was glad when they I said to I me:
   'Let us I go · to the I house · of the I Lord.'

2 And now our I feet are I standing:
   withIin your I gates · O JeIrusalem;

†3 Jerusalem which is I built · as a I city:
   where the I pilgrims I gather · in I unity.

4 There the tribes go up   the I tribes · of the I Lord:
   as he commanded Israel
      to give I thanks · to the I name · of the I Lord.

5 There are set I thrones of I judgment:
   the I thrones · of the I house of I David.

6 O pray for the I peace · of JeIrusalem:
   may I those who I love you I prosper.

7 Peace be withIin your I walls:
   and prosIperi·ty I in your I palaces.

8 For the sake of my brothers I and comIpanions:
   I will I pray that I peace be I with you.

9 For the sake of the house of the I Lord our I God:
   I will I seek I for your I good.

PSALM 123

1 To you I lift I up my I eyes:
   you who are enIthroned I in the I heavens.

2 As the eyes of servants look to the I hand of · their I
   master:
   or as the eyes of a maid toIward the I hand of · her I
   mistress,

†3 So our eyes look to the I Lord our I God:
   unItil he I show us · his I mercy.

4 Have mercy upon us O Lord have I mercy · upIon us:
   for we have I had our I fill · of deIrision.

5 Our souls overflow with the mockery of I those at I ease:
   and with the I contempt I of the I proud.

PSALM 124

1 If the Lord had not been on our side
    now may I Israel I say:
  if the Lord had not been on our side ⌣
    when I men rose I up aIgainst us,

2 Then they would have I swallowed us · aIlive:
  when their I anger · was I kindled · aIgainst us.

3 Then the waters would have overwhelmed us
    and the I torrent · gone I over us:
  the raging waters I would have I gone clean I over us.

4 But praised I be the I Lord:
  who has not given us as a I prey I to their I teeth.

5 We have escaped like a bird from the I snare · of the I
    fowler:
  the snare is I broken · and I we have · gone I free.

6 Our help is in the I name · of the I Lord:
  who has I made I heaven · and I earth.

PSALM 125

1 Those who put their trust in the Lord ⌣
    shall I be as · Mount I Zion:
  which cannot be I shaken · but enIdures for I ever.

2 As the mountains stand about Jerusalem
    so stands the Lord aIbout his I people:
  from this time I forward · for I everImore.

3 For the sceptre of wickedness shall have no sway
    over the land apportioned I to the I righteous:
  lest the righteous I set their I hands to · do I evil.

4 Do good O Lord to I those · who are I good:
  to I those · that are I upright · in I heart.

†5 As for those who turn aside to crooked ways
    let the Lord lead them away with the I evilIdoers:
  and in I Israel I let there · be I peace.

PSALM 126

1 When the Lord turned again the ǀ fortunes · of ǀ Zion:
 then were we like ǀ men reǀstored to ǀ life.

2 Then was our mouth ǀ filled with ǀ laughter:
 and ǀ our ǀ tongue with ǀ singing.

3 Then said they aǀmong the ǀ heathen:
 'The Lord has ǀ done great ǀ things for ǀ them.'

4 Truly the Lord has done great ǀ things for ǀ us:
 and ǀ therefore ǀ we reǀjoiced.

5 Turn again our ǀ fortunes · O ǀ Lord:
 as the streams reǀturn · to the ǀ dry ǀ south.

6 Those that ǀ sow in ǀ tears:
 shall ǀ reap with ǀ songs of ǀ joy.

†7 He who goes out weeping ǀ bearing · the ǀ seed:
 shall come again in gladness ǀ ‿
 bringing · his ǀ sheaves ǀ with him.

PSALM 127

1 Unless the Lord ǀ builds the ǀ house:
 their labour ǀ is but ǀ lost that ǀ build it.

2 Unless the Lord ǀ keeps the ǀ city:
 the ǀ watchmen ǀ watch in ǀ vain.

3 It is in vain that you rise up early and go so late to rest
 eating the ǀ bread of ǀ toil:
 for the Lord bestows honour ǀ and on ǀ those ·
 whom he ǀ loves.

4 Behold children are a heritage ǀ from the ǀ Lord:
 and the ǀ fruit · of the ǀ womb is · his ǀ gift.

5 Like arrows in the ǀ hand · of a ǀ warrior:
 are the ǀ sons · of a ǀ man's ǀ youth.

6 Happy the man who has his ǀ quiver ǀ full of them:
 he will not be put to shame
 when he confronts his ǀ enem·ies ǀ at the ǀ gate.

PSALM 128

1 Blessèd is everyone who I fears the I Lord:
   and walks in the I confine I of his I ways.

2 You will eat the I fruit of · your I labours:
   happy shall you I be and I all · shall go I well with you.

3 Your wife with I in your I house:
   shall I be · as a I fruitful I vine;

4 Your children a I round your I table:
   like the fresh I shoots I of the I olive.

5 Behold thus shall the I man be I blessed:
   who I lives · in the I fear · of the I Lord.

6 May the Lord so I bless you · from I Zion:
   that you see Jerusalem in prosperity I ⌣
     all the I days of · your I life.

†7 May you see your I children's I children:
   and in I Israel I let there · be I peace.

PSALM 129

1 Many a time from my youth upward have they I
     fought a I gainst me:
   now I may I Israel I say,

2 Many a time from my youth upward have they I
     fought a I gainst me:
   but I they have I not pre I vailed.

3 They have scored my back as I with a I ploughshare:
   they have I opened I long I furrows.

4 But the I Lord is I righteous:
   and he has cut me I free · from the I thongs · of the I
     wicked.

5 They shall be confounded and I turned I backward:
   all I those who I hate I Zion.

6 They shall be as the grass that grows up I on the I
     housetops:
   which withers before it I comes to I any I good,

7 With which no reaper may I fill his I hand:
   nor the I binder · of I sheaves his I bosom.

8 And none who pass by shall say to them
    'The blessing of the I Lord · be upıon you:
    we I bless you · in the I name · of the I Lord.'

PSALM 130

1 Out of the depths have I called to I you O I Lord:
    Lord I hear I my I voice;

2 O let your ears conIsider I well:
    the I voice · of my I suppliIcation.

3 If you Lord should note what I we do I wrong:
    who I then O I Lord could I stand?

4 But there is forIgiveness · with I you:
    so that I you I shall be I feared.

5 I wait for the Lord * my I soul I waits for him:
    and I in his I word · is my I hope.

6 My soul I looks · for the I Lord:
    more than watchmen for the morning
        more I say than I watchmen I for the I morning.

7 O Israel trust in the Lord * for with the I Lord ·
    there is I mercy:
    and with I him is I ample · reIdemption.

8 He will reIdeem I Israel:
    from the I multi·tude I of his I sins.

PSALM 131

1 O Lord my I heart is · not I proud:
    nor I are my I eyes I haughty.

2 I do not busy myself in I great I matters:
    or in I things too I wonder·ful I for me.

3 But I have calmed and quieted my soul
    like a weaned child upon its I mother's I breast:
    like a child on its mother's breast I is my I
    soul withIin me.

4 O Israel I trust · in the I Lord:
    from this time I forward I and for I ever.

PSALM 132

1 Lord remember David and | all his | trouble:
    how he swore an oath to the Lord
        and vowed to the | Mighty | One of | Jacob;

2 'I will not enter the | shelter · of my | house:
    nor climb into the | comfort | of my | bed;

3 'I will not give | sleep to · my | eyes:
    or | slumber | to my | eyelids,

4 'Till I find out a place for the | ark · of the | Lord:
    a dwelling for the | Mighty | One of | Jacob.'

5 Lo we | heard of it · at | Ephrathah:
    we | found it · in the | fields of | Ja-ar.

6 Let us go to the | place of · his | dwelling:
    let us fall upon our | knees be|fore his | footstool.

7 Arise O Lord | into · your | resting-place:
    you | and the | ark of · your | might.

8 Let your priests be | clothed with | righteousness:
    and let your | faithful · ones | shout for | joy.

†9 For the sake of | David · your | servant:
    do not turn away the | face of | your an|ointed.

10 The Lord has | sworn to | David:
    an | oath · which he | will not | break;

11 'One who is the | fruit of · your | body:
    I will | set up|on your | throne.

12 'If your children will keep my covenant
        and the com|mands · which I | teach them:
    their children also shall sit up|on your | throne for |
        ever.'

13 For the Lord has chosen | Zion · for him|self:
    he has de|sired it · for his | habi|tation.

14 'This shall be my | resting-place · for | ever:
    here will I dwell   for | my de|light · is in | her.

15 'I will bless her pro|visions · with a|bundance:

I will I satisfy · her I poor with I bread.

16 'I will clothe her I priests with · salIvation:
and her I faithful ones · shall I shout for I joy.

17 'There will I make a horn to sprout ⏝
for the I family · of I David:
I have prepared a I lamp for I my anIointed.

†18 'As for his enemies   I will I cover them · with I shame:
but upon his I head · shall his I crown be I bright.'

PSALM 133

1 Behold how good and how I lovely · it I is:
when brothers I live toIgether · in I unity.

2 It is fragrant as oil upon the head
that runs down I over · the I beard:
fragrant as oil upon the beard of Aaron
that ran down over the I collar I of his I robe.

3 It is like a I dew of I Hermon:
like the dew that falls upIon the I hill of I Zion.

4 For there the Lord has comImanded · his I blessing:
which is I life for I everImore.

PSALM 134

1 Come bless the Lord   all you I servants · of the I Lord:
you that by night I stand · in the I house of · our I God.

2 Lift up your hands toward the holy place ⏝
and I bless the I Lord:
may the Lord bless you from Zion
the I Lord who · made I heaven · and I earth.

PSALM 135

1 Praise the Lord
praise the I name · of the I Lord:
praise him you I servants I of the I Lord,

2 Who stand in the I house · of the I Lord:
in the I courts · of the I house of · our I God.

3 Praise the Lord for the ǀ Lord is ǀ gracious:
  sing praises to his ǀ name for ǀ it is ǀ good.

4 For the Lord has chosen Jacob ǀ for himǀself:
  and Israel ǀ as his ǀ own posǀsession.

5 I know that the ǀ Lord is ǀ great:
  and that our ǀ Lord · is aǀbove all ǀ gods.

6 He does whatever he wills * in heaven and upǀon the ǀ
    earth:
  in the seas and ǀ in the ǀ great ǀ depths.

7 He brings up clouds from the ǀ ends · of the ǀ earth:
  he makes lightning for the rain
    and brings the ǀ wind ǀ out of · his ǀ storehouses.

8 He struck down the ǀ firstborn · of ǀ Egypt:
  both ǀ man and ǀ beast aǀlike.

9 He sent signs and wonders into your ǀ midst O ǀ Egypt:
  against Pharaoh and aǀgainst ǀ all his ǀ servants.

10 He struck down ǀ great ǀ nations:
  and ǀ slew ǀ mighty ǀ kings,

11 Sihon king of the Amorites   and Og the ǀ king of ǀ
    Bashan:
  and ǀ all the ǀ princes · of ǀ Canaan.

12 He made over their ǀ land · as a ǀ heritage:
  a ǀ heritage · for ǀ Israel · his ǀ people.

13 O Lord your name shall enǀdure for ǀ ever:
  so shall your renown throughǀout all ǀ generǀations.

14 For the Lord will ǀ vindicate · his ǀ people:
  he will take ǀ pity ǀ on his ǀ servants.

15 As for the idols of the nations
    they are but ǀ silver · and ǀ gold:
  the ǀ work · of a ǀ man's ǀ hand.

16 They have ǀ mouths but ǀ speak not:
  they have ǀ eyes · but they ǀ cannot ǀ see.

17 They have ears yet ǀ hear ǀ nothing:
  there is no ǀ breath ǀ in their ǀ nostrils.

18 Those who make them I shall be I like them:
    so shall I every|one that I trusts in them.

19 Bless the Lord O I house of I Israel:
    bless the I Lord O I house of I Aaron.

20 Bless the Lord O I house of I Levi:
    you that I fear the · Lord I bless the I Lord.

†21 Blessèd be the I Lord from I Zion:
    he that dwells in Jerusalem I
        Praise I – the I Lord.

PSALM 136

1 O give thanks to the Lord for I he is I good:
    for his I mercy · en|dures for I ever.

2 O give thanks to the I God of I gods:
    for his I mercy · en|dures for I ever.

†3 O give thanks to the I Lord of I lords:
    for his I mercy · en|dures for I ever;

4 To him who alone does I great I wonders:
    for his I mercy · en|dures for I ever;

5 Who by wisdom I made the I heavens:
    for his I mercy · en|dures for I ever;

6 Who stretched out the earth up|on the I waters:
    for his I mercy · en|dures for I ever;

7 Who made the I great I lights:
    for his I mercy · en|dures for I ever,

8 The sun to I rule the I day:
    for his I mercy · en|dures for I ever,

9 The moon and the stars to I govern · the I night:
    for his I mercy · en|dures for I ever;

10 Who struck down Egypt I and its I firstborn:
    for his I mercy · en|dures for I ever;

11 Who brought out Israel I from a|mong them:
    for his I mercy · en|dures for I ever,

†12 With a strong hand and with | outstretched | arm:
    for his | mercy · en|dures for | ever;

13 Who divided the Red Sea into | two | parts:
    for his | mercy · en|dures for | ever,

14 And made Israel pass | through the | midst of it:
    for his | mercy · en|dures for | ever;

15 Who cast off Pharaoh and his host into the | Red | Sea:
    for his | mercy · en|dures for | ever;

16 Who led his people | through the | wilderness:
    for his | mercy · en|dures for | ever;

17 Who struck down | great | kings:
    for his | mercy · en|dures for | ever;

18 Who slew | mighty | kings:
    for his | mercy · en|dures for | ever,

19 Sihon | king · of the | Amorites:
    for his | mercy · en|dures for | ever,

20 And Og the | king of | Bashan:
    for his | mercy · en|dures for | ever;

21 Who made over their | land · as a | heritage:
    for his | mercy · en|dures for | ever,

22 As a heritage for | Israel · his | servant:
    for his | mercy · en|dures for | ever;

23 Who remembered us in our hu|mili|ation:
    for his | mercy · en|dures for | ever,

24 And delivered us | from our | enemies:
    for his | mercy · en|dures for | ever;

25 Who gives food to | all that | lives:
    for his | mercy · en|dures for | ever.

26 O give thanks to the | God of | heaven:
    for his | mercy · en|dures for | ever.

PSALM 137

1 By the waters of Babylon we sat I down and I wept:
  when I we reImembered I Zion.

2 As for our harps we I hung them I up:
  upon the I trees · that are I in that I land.

3 For there those who led us away captive ⌣
    reIquired of us · a I song:
    and those who had despoiled us demanded mirth
    saying 'Sing us I one of · the I songs of I Zion.'

*4 How can we sing the Lord's I song · in a I strange I land?

5 If I forget you I O JeIrusalem:
  let my right I hand forIget its I mastery.

6 Let my tongue cling to the I roof of · my I mouth:
    if I do not remember you
    if I do not prefer Jerusalem aIbove my I chief I joy.

[7 Remember O Lord against the Edomites ⌣
    the I day · of JeIrusalem:
    how they said 'Down with it   down with it I
    raze it · to I its foundIations.'

8 O daughter of Babylon   I you that · lay I waste:
    happy shall he be who serves I you as I you have ·
    served I us;

†9 Happy shall he be who I takes your I little ones:
    and I dashes them · aIgainst the I stones.]

* sung to the last four bars of the chant.

PSALM 138

1 I will give you thanks O Lord with my I whole I heart:
  even before the I gods · will I I sing your I praises.

2 I will bow down toward your holy temple
    and give I thanks to · your I name:
    because of your faithfulness and your loving-kindness
    for you have made your name and your I
    word suIpreme · over I all things.

3 At a time when I called to you you | gave me | answer:
   and put new | strength with|in my | soul.

4 All the kings of the earth shall | praise you · O | Lord:
   for they have | heard the | words of · your | mouth;

5 And they shall sing of the | ways · of the | Lord:
   that the | glory · of the | Lord is | great.

6 For though the Lord is exalted   he looks up|on the |
      lowly:
   but he | humbles · the | proud · from a|far.

7 Though I walk in the midst of danger
         yet will you pre|serve my | life:
   you will stretch out your hand __
      against the fury of my enemies
         and | your right | hand shall | save me.

8 The Lord will complete his | purpose | for me:
   your loving-kindness O Lord endures for ever
      do not forsake the | work · of your | own | hands.

PSALM 139

1 O Lord you have searched me | out and | known me:
   you know when I sit or when I stand
      you comprehend my | thoughts | long be|fore.

2 You discern my path   and the places | where I | rest:
   you are ac|quainted · with | all my | ways.

3 For there is not a | word · on my | tongue:
   but you Lord | know it | alto|gether.

4 You have encompassed me be|hind · and be|fore:
   and have | laid your | hand up|on me.

†5 Such knowledge is too | wonder·ful | for me:
   so | high · that I | cannot · en|dure it.

6 Where shall I | go · from your | spirit:
   or where shall I | flee | from your | presence?

7 If I ascend into heaven | you are | there:
   if I make my bed in the grave | you are | there | also.

8 If I spread out my wings to|wards the | morning:
   or dwell in the | utter·most | parts · of the | sea,

9 Even there your I hand shall I lead me:
and I your right I hand shall I hold me.

10 If I say   'Surely the I darkness · will I cover me:
and the I night I will enIclose me',

11 The darkness is no darkness with you
but the night is as I clear · as the I day:
the darkness and the I light are I both aIlike.

12 For you have created my I inward I parts:
you knit me together I in my I mother's I womb.

13 I will praise you for I you are · to be I feared:
fearful are your I acts and I wonderful · your I works.

14 You knew my soul * and my bones were not I hidden I
from you:
when I was formed in secret
and I woven · in the I depths · of the I earth.

15 Your eyes saw my limbs when they were I
yet imIperfect:
and in your book were I all my I members I written;

†16 Day by I day · they were I fashioned:
and not I one was I late in I growing.

17 How deep are your thoughts to I me O I God:
and how I great I is the I sum of them!

18 Were I to count them
they are more in number I than the I sand:
were I to come to the I end · I would I still be I
with you.

19 If only you would slay the I wicked · O I God:
if only the men of I blood · would deIpart I from me!

20 For they affront you I by their I evil:
and your enemies exIalt themIselves aIgainst you.

21 Do I not hate them O Lord that I I hate I you:
do I not loathe I those · who reIbel aIgainst you?

22 I hate them with a I perfect I hatred:
they I have beIcome my I enemies.

23 Search me out O God and | know my | heart:
　　put me to the | proof and | know my | thoughts.

24 Look well lest there be any way of | wicked·ness |
　　　in me:
　　and lead me in the | way · that is | ever|lasting.

PSALM 140

1 Deliver me O Lord from | evil | men:
　　and pre|serve me · from | vio·lent | men,

2 Who devise mischief | in their | hearts:
　　who stir up | enmi·ty | day by | day.

3 They have sharpened their | tongues · like a |
　　　serpent's:
　　and the venom of | asps is | under · their | lips.

4 Keep me O Lord from the | power · of the | wicked:
　　preserve me from violent men
　　　who think to | thrust me | from my | course.

5 The arrogant have laid a snare for me
　　　and rogues have | stretched the | net:
　　they have set | traps a|long my | way.

6 But I have said to the Lord | 'You are · my | God':
　　hear O | Lord the | voice of · my | pleading.

7 O Lord my God and my | sure | stronghold:
　　you have covered my | head · in the | day of | battle.

8 Do not fulfil O Lord the de|sire · of the | wicked:
　　nor further the | evil · that he | has de|vised.

[9 Let not those that beset me | lift their | heads:
　　but let the mischief that is | on their | lips | bury
　　　them.

10 Let hot burning coals be | poured up|on them:
　　let them be plunged into that miry pit ⌣
　　　from | which · they shall | never · a|rise.

[†]11 Let no man of evil tongue find | footing · in the | land:
　　the evil　　the violent man　　let him be |
　　　hunted | to the | end.]

12 I know that the Lord will work justice ∣ for ·
     the op∣pressed:
    and right ∣ judgments ∣ for the ∣ poor.

13 Surely the righteous shall have cause to ∣ praise your ∣
     name:
    and the ∣ just shall ∣ dwell in · your ∣ sight.

PSALM 141

1 O Lord I call to you   make ∣ haste to ∣ help me:
    and ∣ hear my ∣ voice · when I ∣ cry.

2 Let my prayer be as ∣ incense · be∣fore you:
    and the lifting up of my ∣ hands · as the ∣ evening ∣
     sacrifice.

3 Set a guard O ∣ Lord · on my ∣ mouth:
    and ∣ keep the ∣ door · of my ∣ lips.

4 Let not my heart incline to evil speech
     to join in wickedness with ∣ wrong∣doers:
    let me not taste the ∣ pleasures ∣ of their ∣ table.

5 But let the righteous ∣ man chas∣tise me:
    and the ∣ faithful ∣ man re∣buke me.

6 Let not the oil of the wicked an∣oint my ∣ head:
    for I pray to you ∣ still a∣gainst their ∣ wickedness.

[7 They shall be cast down ‿
     by that Mighty One who ∣ is their ∣ judge:
    and how pleasing shall my ∣ words be ∣ to them ∣ then!

8 As when a farmer ∣ breaks the ∣ ground:
    so shall their bones lie ∣ scattered · at the ∣ mouth of ∣
     Sheol.]

9 But my eyes look to you O ∣ Lord my ∣ God:
    to you I come for refuge   ∣ do not · pour ∣ out my ∣
     life.

10 Keep me from the snare that ∣ they have ∣ laid for me:
    and from the ∣ traps · of the ∣ evil∣doers.

†11 Let the wicked fall together into their ∣ own ∣ nets:
    whilst ∣ I pass ∣ safely ∣ by.

PSALM 142

1 I call to the Lord with a I loud I voice:
  with loud I voice · I enItreat his I favour.

2 I pour out my comIplaint beIfore him:
  and I tell him I all my I trouble.

3 When my spirit is faint within me you I know my I path:
  in the way where I walk I ＿
    they have I hidden · a I snare for me.

4 I look to my right I hand and I see:
  but I no I man will I know me;

5 All esIcape is I gone:
  and I there is I no one · who I cares for me.

6 I call to you O Lord I say I 'You are · my I refuge:
  you are my I portion · in the I land · of the I living.'

7 Heed my loud crying for I am I brought · very I low:
  O save me from my persecutors I ＿
    for they I are too I strong for me.

8 Bring me I out of · the I prison-house:
  that I I may I praise your I name.

†9 When you have given me I my reIward:
  then will the I righteous I gather · aIbout me.

PSALM 143

1 Hear my I prayer O I Lord:
  in your faithfulness consider my petition
    and in your I righteous·ness I give me I answer.

2 Bring not your servant I into I judgment:
  for in your sight can I no man I living · be I justified.

3 For the enemy has pursued me
    he has crushed my I life · to the I ground:
  he has made me dwell in darkness ＿
    like I those for I ever I dead.

4 Therefore my I spirit · grows I faint:
  and my I heart · is apIpalled withIin me.

5 I remember the days of old
    I think on all that I you have I done:

I con|sider · the | works of · your | hands.

6 I stretch out my | hands to|ward you:
   my soul yearns for you | like a | thirsty | land.

7 Be swift to hear me O Lord   for my | spirit | fails:
   hide not your face from me
      lest I be like | those who · go | down · to the | Pit.

8 O let me hear of your merciful kindness in the morning
      for my | trust · is in | you:
   show me the way that I should go
      for | you | are my | hope.

9 Deliver me from my | enemies · O | Lord:
   for I | run to | you for | shelter.

10 Teach me to do your will   for | you are · my | God:
    let your kindly spirit | lead me · in an | even | path.

11 For your name's sake O Lord pre|serve my | life:
    and for the sake of your righteousness | bring me |
       out of | trouble.

12 In your merciful goodness slay my enemies
       and destroy all those that | come a|gainst me:
    for | truly · I | am your | servant.

PSALM 144

1 Blessèd be the | Lord my | Rock:
   who teaches my hands to | war · and my | fingers · to |
      fight;

2 My strength and my stronghold
       my fortress and | my de|liverer:
   my shield to whom I come for refuge
      who sub|dues the | peoples | under me.

3 Lord what is man   that you should be |
       mindful | of him:
   or the son of man |that you | should con|sider him?

4 Man is but a |breath of | wind:
   his days are like a | shadow · that | passes · a|way.

5 Part the heavens O Lord and | come | down:
   touch the | mountains · and | they shall | smoke.

6 Dart forth your lightnings
  and scatter them on ǀ every ǀ side:
 let loose your ǀ arrows · with the ǀ roar · of the ǀ
  thunderbolt.

7 Reach down your hand from on high
  rescue me and pluck me out of the ǀ great ǀ waters:
 out of the ǀ hands ǀ of the ǀ aliens,

8 Whose ǀ mouths speak ǀ perjury:
 and their right hand ǀ is a · right ǀ hand of ǀ falsehood.

9 I will sing you a new ǀ song O ǀ God:
 on the ten-stringed ǀ lute · will I ǀ sing your ǀ praises.

10 You have given ǀ victory · to ǀ kings:
 and deǀliverance · to ǀ David · your ǀ servant.

11 O save me from the ǀ peril · of the ǀ sword:
 pluck me out of the ǀ hands ǀ of the ǀ aliens,

12 Whose ǀ mouths speak ǀ perjury:
 and their right hand ǀ is a · right ǀ hand of ǀ falsehood.

13 Our sons in their youth shall be like ǀ sturdy ǀ plants:
 and our daughters as the ǀ carved ǀ corners · of ǀ
  palaces.

14 Our barns shall be full and give food of ǀ every ǀ kind:
 the sheep shall lamb in our fields ⌣
  in ǀ thousands · and ǀ tens of ǀ thousands.

15 Our cattle shall be heavy with calf
  there shall be no miscarriage or unǀtimely ǀ birth:
 and no loud ǀ crying ǀ in our ǀ streets.

16 Happy the people whose lot is ǀ such as ǀ this:
 happy that people who ǀ have the ǀ Lord for · their ǀ
  God!

PSALM 145

1 I will exalt you O ǀ God my ǀ king:
 I will bless your ǀ name for ǀ ever · and ǀ ever.

2 Every ǀ day · will I ǀ bless you:
 and praise your ǀ name for ǀ ever · and ǀ ever.

3 Great is the Lord * and wonderfully | worthy · to be | praised:
   his greatness is | past | searching | out.

4 One generation shall praise your | works · to an|other:
   and de|clare your | mighty | acts.

5 As for me * I will be talking ⌣
   of the glorious splendour | of your | majesty:
   I will tell the | story · of your | marvel·lous | works.

6 Men shall recount the power of your | terri·ble | deeds:
   and | I will · pro|claim your | greatness.

+7 Their lips shall flow with the remembrance ⌣
   of your a|bundant | goodness:
   they shall | shout for | joy at · your | righteousness.

8 The Lord is | gracious · and com|passionate:
   slow to anger | and of | great | goodness.

9 The Lord is | loving · to | every man:
   and his mercy is | over | all his | works.

10 All creation | praises you · O | Lord:
   and your faithful | servants | bless your | name.

11 They speak of the glory | of your | kingdom:
   and | tell of · your | great | might,

+12 That all mankind may know your | mighty | acts:
   and the glorious | splendour | of your | kingdom.

13 Your kingdom is an ever|lasting | kingdom:
   and your dominion en|dures through | all ·
   gener|ations.

14 The Lord upholds all | those who | stumble:
   and raises up | those · that are | bowed | down.

15 The eyes of all look to | you in | hope:
   and you give them their | food in | due | season;

16 You open | wide your | hand:
   and fill all things | living · with your | bounte·ous |
   gift.

17 The Lord is just in | all his | ways:
   and | faithful · in | all his | dealings.

18 The Lord is near to all who I call up|on him:
     to all who I call up|on him · in I truth.

19 He will fulfil the desire of I those that I fear him:
     he will I hear their I cry and I save them.

20 The Lord preserves all I those that I love him:
     but the wicked I he will I utterly · de|stroy.

†21 My mouth shall speak the I praises · of the I Lord:
     and let all flesh bless his holy I name for I
          ever · and I ever.

PSALM 146

1 Praise the Lord
     praise the Lord I O my I soul:
     while I I live · I will I praise the I Lord;

2 While I I have · any I being:
     I will sing I praises I to my I God.

3 Put not your I trust in I princes:
     nor in the sons of I men who I cannot I save.

4 For when their breath goes from them
     they return a|gain · to the I earth:
     and on that day I all their I thoughts I perish.

5 Blessèd is the man whose help is the I God of I Jacob:
     whose hope is I in the I Lord his I God,

6 The God who made I heaven · and I earth:
     the sea and I all I that is I in them,

†7 Who keeps I faith for I ever:
     who deals justice to I those that I are op|pressed.

8 The Lord gives I food · to the I hungry:
     and I sets the I captives I free.

9 The Lord gives I sight · to the I blind:
     the Lord lifts up I those · that are I bowed I down.

10 The Lord I loves the I righteous:
     the Lord cares for the I stranger I in the I land.

11 He upholds the I widow · and the I fatherless:
     as for the way of the wicked he I turns it I upside I
          down.

†12 The Lord shall be | king for | ever:
　　　your God O Zion shall reign through all generations |
　　　　　Praise | – the | Lord.

PSALM 147

1　O praise the Lord
　　　for it is good to sing praises | to our | God:
　　and to | praise him · is | joyful · and | right.

2　The Lord is re|building · Je|rusalem:
　　　he is gathering together ‿
　　　　the | scattered | outcasts · of | Israel.

3　He heals the | broken · in | spirit:
　　and | binds | up their | wounds.

4　He counts the | number · of the | stars:
　　and | calls them | all by | name.

5　Great is our Lord and | great · is his | power:
　　there is no | measuring · his | under|standing.

6　The Lord re|stores the | humble:
　　but he brings down the | wicked | to the | dust.

7　O sing to the Lord a | song of | thanksgiving:
　　sing praises to our | God up|on the | harp.

8　He covers the heavens with cloud
　　　and prepares | rain · for the | earth:
　　and makes the grass to | sprout up|on the |
　　　mountains.

9　He gives the | cattle · their | food:
　　and feeds the young | ravens · that | call | to him.

10　He takes no pleasure in the | strength · of a | horse:
　　nor does he de|light in | any · man's | legs,

†11　But the Lord's delight is in | those that | fear him:
　　who | wait in | hope · for his | mercy.

12　Praise the | Lord · O Je|rusalem:
　　sing | praises · to your | God O | Zion.

13　For he has strengthened the | bars of · your | gates:
　　and | blessed your | children · with|in you.

14 He makes peace with|in your | borders:
   and satisfies you | with the | finest | wheat.

15 He sends his com|mand · to the | earth:
   and his | word runs | very | swiftly.

16 He gives | snow like | wool:
   and | scatters · the | hoar-frost · like | ashes.

17 He sprinkles his ice like | morsels · of | bread:
   and the waters | harden | at his | frost.

†18 He sends out his | word and | melts them:
   he blows with his | wind · and the | waters | flow.

19 He made his word | known to | Jacob:
   his | statutes · and | judgments · to | Israel.

20 He has not dealt so with any | other | nation:
   nor have they knowledge of his laws |
      Praise | – the | Lord.

PSALM 148

1 Praise the Lord
      praise the | Lord from | heaven:
   O | praise him | in the | heights.

2 Praise him | all his | angels:
   O | praise him | all his | host.

3 Praise him | sun and | moon:
   praise him | all you | stars of | light.

4 Praise him you | highest | heaven:
   and you waters that | are a|bove the | heavens.

5 Let them praise the | name · of the | Lord:
   for he com|manded · and | they were | made.

6 He established them for | ever · and | ever:
   he made an ordinance which | shall not | pass a|way.

7 O praise the | Lord · from the | earth:
   praise him you sea-|monsters · and | all | deeps;

8 Fire and hail | mist and | snow:
   and storm-wind ful|filling | his com|mand;

9 Mountains and I all I hills:
   fruiting I trees and I all I cedars;

10 Beasts of the wild and I all I cattle:
   creeping I things and I winged I birds;

11 Kings of the earth and I all I peoples:
   princes and all I rulers I of the I world;

12 Young I men and I maidens:
   old I men and I children · to|gether.

13 Let them praise the I name · of the I Lord:
   for I his · name a|lone · is ex|alted.

14 His glory is above I earth and I heaven:
   and he has lifted I high the I horn · of his I people.

†15 Therefore he is the praise of I all his I servants:
   of the children of Israel   a people that is near him I
      Praise I – the I Lord.

PSALM 149

1 O praise the Lord
      and sing to the Lord a I new I song:
   O praise him in the as|sembly I of the I faithful.

2 Let Israel rejoice in I him that I made him:
   let the children of Zion be I joyful I in their I king.

3 Let them praise him I in the I dance:
   let them sing his praise with I timbrel I and with I
      harp.

4 For the Lord takes de|light · in his I people:
   he adorns the I meek with I his sal|vation.

5 Let his faithful ones ex|ult · in his I glory:
   let them sing for I joy up|on their I beds.

6 Let the high praises of God be I in their I mouths:
   and a I two-edged I sword · in their I hands,

7 To execute vengeance I on the I nations:
   and I chastisement · up|on the I peoples,

8 To bind their I kings in I chains:
   and their I nobles · with I fetters · of I iron,

†9 To visit upon them the judgment that ⎸ is de⎸creed:
    such honour belongs to all his faithful servants ⎸
        Praise ⎸ – the ⎸ Lord.

PSALM 150

1 Praise the Lord
    O praise ⎸ God · in his ⎸ sanctuary:
    praise him in the ⎸ firma·ment ⎸ of his ⎸ power.

2 Praise him for his ⎸ mighty ⎸ acts:
    praise him according to ⎸ his a⎸bundant ⎸ goodness.

3 Praise him in the ⎸ blast · of the ⎸ ram's horn:
    praise him up⎸on the ⎸ lute and ⎸ harp.

4 Praise him with the ⎸ timbrel · and ⎸ dances:
    praise him up⎸on the ⎸ strings and ⎸ pipe.

5 Praise him on the ⎸ high-·sounding ⎸ cymbals:
    praise him up⎸on the ⎸ loud ⎸ cymbals.

6 Let everything that has breath ⎸ praise the ⎸ Lord:
    O ⎸ praise ⎸ – the ⎸ Lord!

ACKNOWLEDGEMENTS

Texts are reproduced with the permission of copyright owners as
follows:

The Psalms: A New Translation for Worship (The Liturgical Psalter) ©
English text 1976, 1977 David L Frost, John A Emerton, Andrew A
Macintosh, all rights reserved. © pointing 1976, 1977 and 1984 William
Collins Sons & Co Ltd.

Prayers and extracts, some of which have been adapted, from *A Book of
Common Prayer*, CPSA revised edition 1982 © the Provincial Trustees of
the Church of the Province of Southern Africa.

English translation by International Consultation on Common Texts:
Glory to the Father; Lord, have mercy; Sursum corda; Sanctus/
Benedictus; Our Father; Jesus, Lamb of God; Song of Zechariah; Song of
Mary; Song of Simeon; Apostles' Creed.

English translation originally prepared by International Consultation on
English Texts and revised in 1987 by the English Language Liturgical
Consultation: Nicene Creed (adapted); Lamb of God; Song of the
Church.

*Common Lectionary: The Lectionary Proposed by the Consultation on Common
Texts* © 1983, James M. Schellman for the Consultation on Common
Texts.

Eucharistic Prayer 4 (The Eucharistic Prayer of Hippolytus), as altered
and adapted with permission in *The Book of Alternative Services of the
Anglican Church of Canada*, copyright © 1985 by the General Synod of
the Anglican Church of Canada, from the English translation © 1983
International Committee on English in the Liturgy. All rights reserved.

The English translation of the Chrism Mass, the general intercessions
and responses for Good Friday, the texts for the blessing of the Easter
candle, the opening prayer, and the Easter Proclamation from the *Rite of
Holy Week* © 1970, International Committee on English in the Liturgy,
Inc. (ICEL); excerpts from the English translation of *Rite of Funerals*
© 1970, ICEL; excerpts from the English translation of *The Roman Missal*
© 1973, ICEL. Altered and adapted with permission. All rights
reserved.

Occasional Prayers and Thanksgivings 15, 21, 23, 24 adapted from *The
Book of Alternative Services of the Anglican Church of Canada*, copyright
© 1985 by the General Synod of the Anglican Church of Canada (based
on texts in the *Book of Common Prayer* of the Episcopal Church, USA).

Occasional Prayers and Thanksgivings 38, 39 adapted from *An Alternative Prayer Book 1984*, copyright © 1984 the General Synod of the Church of Ireland, published by Collins.

Canticles 6, 9, 15, 17, 19, Collects and other prayers reproduced from, or adapted from, *The Alternative Service Book 1980; Ministry to the Sick; Lent, Holy Week, Easter: Services and Prayers*; © 1980 The Central Board of Finance of the Church of England.

The prayer at 81 in Ministry to the Sick and Dying, from *The Spiritual Exercises of St Ignatius: A Literal Translation and A Contemporary Reading*, David L. Fleming SJ, Institute of Jesuit Sources, St Louis, Mo., USA 1978.

The Collect for the Venerable Bede by permission of the author, G.B. Timms.

Scripture quotations are taken from a variety of translations, notably *Revised Standard Version, New English Bible, New International Version*.